Barron's Regents Exams and Answers

United States History and Government

EUGENE V. RESNICK, B.A., M.A.
Social Studies Teacher, Midwood High School, Brooklyn, New York

JOHN McGEEHAN, B.A., M.A., J.D.
Consultant and Writer, New York State Education Department, Bureau of Social Studies Education, Educational Testing, and Curriculum Development

MORRIS GALL, J.D., Ph.D.
Former President, Association of Teachers of Social Studies in the City of New York

WILLIAM STREITWIESER, B.A., M.A.
Former Social Studies Teacher, Northport High School, Northport, New York

**Test-Taking Tips by
MARK WILLNER, M.A.**
Chairman of Social Studies Department, Midwood High School, Brooklyn, New York

BARRON'S

Barron's Educational Series, Inc.

All inquiries should be addressed to:
Barron's Educational Series, Inc.
250 Wireless Boulevard
Hauppauge, New York 11788
www.barronseduc.com

ISBN: 978-0-8120-3344-1
ISSN 1071-4847

PRINTED IN THE UNITED STATES OF AMERICA
9 8 7 6 5 4 3 2 1

Contents

What the Exam Is About   1

What Is the United States History and
Government Regents Examination Like?   2

How to Use This Book   3

Test-Taking Tips   3
Previous Regents Examinations and Answers   3
Self-Analysis Charts   4
Important Terms to Know   5

Test-Taking Tips   6

Taking the Regents Examination   6
General Helpful Tips   6
Specific Helpful Tips for the Short-Answer
    (Multiple-Choice) Questions   10
Specific Helpful Tips for the Essay Questions   24

Glossary of Terms   43

Regents Examinations, Answers, Self-Analysis Charts, and Regents Specification Grids 79

August 2008 81
June 2009 163
August 2009 249
June 2010 333
August 2010 417

What the Exam Is About

If you are reading this, you probably are a student at the end of the 11th grade preparing to take the Regents examination in Social Studies (or the parent of an 11th-grader). You probably already know that New York State requires you to take the United States History and Government Regents examination if you want to earn a Regents diploma. Almost every 11th-grade student in New York State will be taking the same examination at the same time you are.

United States History and Government is part of a sequence of social studies courses students are required to take from the 1st grade through the 12th grade. The purpose of social studies is to help you understand the events and developments that shape the nation and world you live in. In the 9th and 10th grades you studied cultures on continents other than North America because you should understand that we live in an interdependent world. In the 11th grade, you returned to a study of your own nation. Now that you are more mature and will be eligible to vote in a year or two, you should have a clear understanding of the nature of our Constitution and the workings of our government.

Students in the 11th-grade Social Studies course learn about the Constitutional foundations of American society before studying the history of the United States from after the Civil War to modern times. However, a unit on United States geography is to be added to the program of study.

WHAT IS THE UNITED STATES HISTORY AND GOVERNMENT REGENTS EXAMINATION LIKE?

If you took the Global Studies Regents examination last year, you already have some idea of what the exam is like. The United States History and Government Regents is divided into three parts. All parts have questions on the topics, themes, and skills covered in the 11th grade.

The exam is constructed as follows:

• 50 Multiple-Choice Questions	50 minutes	55 percent of grade
• One Thematic Essay	45 minutes	15 percent of grade
• 8 Document-Based Questions • One Document-Based Essay	60 minutes	30 percent of grade

Many students lose points because they neglect to answer some parts of questions or misread the questions. Be sure to review the following sections: "How to Use This Book" (pages 3–5) and "Test-Taking Tips" (beginning on page 6).

How to Use This Book

This book is designed to help you get the most out of your review for the Regents examination in United States History and Government.

TEST-TAKING TIPS

The first section, Test-Taking Tips, will help you become a *better* test taker. Be sure to read this valuable material carefully. The brief rules, many hints, and practice questions will increase your understanding and confidence in answering short-answer and essay questions. The sample answers will enable you to distinguish between a complete and well-written essay and a poor one.

Reread the Test-Taking Tips after taking two or more of the examinations, and feel your assurance grow.

PREVIOUS REGENTS EXAMINATIONS AND ANSWERS

The second section contains previous Regents examinations and answer analyses. The examinations will serve as a content review and as a study guide to indicate what is important. By answering the multiple-choice and essay questions, you will be able to discover your weak points. Then you will be able to remedy your deficiencies by studying carefully the answers provided. They are more than just model answers; additional facts and explanations have been included to further a more thorough understanding of the subjects on which the questions are based. Careful study of the answers will increase your skill in interpreting the questions and in applying the facts learned.

SELF-ANALYSIS CHARTS

The Self-Analysis Chart enables you to note the content areas tested in the exam and the number of questions in each content area. You can calculate your score in each of the content areas of a test to see in which content areas you show strengths or weakness.

Each chart has three columns:

1. Column 1 names each topic included in the exam.
2. Column 2 lists the number of each short-answer question on that topic asked in the given exam.
3. Column 3 shows the total point value of short answer questions on each topic. Since each correct answer is worth about $1^1/_7$ points, totals are shown to the nearest full point in each content category.

You can calculate the number of points you earned for each content category by multiplying the number of questions you got right by the point value for each question noted at the bottom of the Self-Evaluation Chart. You can calculate the percentage of questions you got right in each content category by dividing the number of points you earned by the total number of points for each category given in Column 3.

If you score lower than 75 percent on any topic, first review your class notes and textbook material; then review the model answers in the book AND the explanations of all choices for each question on that topic. Studying the explanations of the wrong choices will greatly enhance your understanding of the subject matter and alert you to possible errors. It also helps you review additional content.

SKILLS QUESTIONS

Please note that space has been provided in the Self-Analysis Charts for you to score and compare separately your achievement on the skills questions on each exam. The skills material includes interpretation of reading passages, cartoons, charts, diagrams, graphs, and maps.

SUMMARY

1. Read the first section, Test-Taking Tips.
2. Take the first examination under test conditions.
3. Answer as many essay questions as possible.
4. Mark Part I of the exam.
5. Complete the Self-Analysis Chart for that exam.
6. Record your weak spots.
7. Answer both the Part II and Part III question.
8. Study the answers to ALL the questions you could not answer, or answered inadequately.
9. Review your notes and text material on those topics before taking the next exam. Reread the Test-Taking Tips.

Repeat this procedure, exam by exam, and watch that mark soar.

IMPORTANT TERMS TO KNOW

The Glossary of Terms is designed to allow you to see which terms or concepts appeared most frequently on past tests. As you review the Glossary of Terms, you will notice one, two, or three asterisks (*) preceding some of the terms defined. While all the terms are important to know, those with asterisks should be considered most crucial. One asterisk (*) denotes a term that is frequently tested; two asterisks (**) denote a term that is **very** frequently tested; and three asterisks (***) denote a term that is **most** frequently tested.

Test-Taking Tips

TAKING THE REGENTS EXAMINATION

Although teachers and students alike find an "all or nothing" examination at the completion of the course distasteful, the Regents examination in United States History and Government in some ways, unfortunately, falls into this category. Without passing the Regents examination, the student cannot obtain a Regents diploma.

Although this brief section does not claim to provide a comprehensive study guide for taking a Regents examination, it does contain several tips to help you achieve a good grade on the U.S. History and Government Regents exam. They are divided into GENERAL HELPFUL TIPS and SPECIFIC HELPFUL TIPS.

GENERAL HELPFUL TIPS

TIP 1
Be confident and prepared.

SUGGESTIONS
- Review short-answer sections from previous tests.
- Use a clock or watch, and take previous exams at home under examination conditions, (i.e., don't have the radio or television on.)
- Get a review book. (The preferred book is Barron's *Let's Review: U.S. History and Government*.)

- Visit *www.barronseduc.com* for the latest information on the Regents exams.
- Talk over the answers to questions on these tests with someone else. Use Barron's web site to communicate with subject specialists.
- Finish all your homework assignments.
- Look over classroom exams that your teacher gave during the term.
- Take class notes carefully.
- Practice good study habits.
- Know that there are answers for every question.
- Be aware that the people who made up the Regents exam want you to pass.
- Remember that thousands of students over the last few years have taken and passed a U.S. History and Government Regents. You can pass too!
- On the night prior to the exam day lay out all the things you will need, such as clothing, pens, and admission cards.
- Go to bed early; eat wisely.
- Bring at least two pens to the exam room.
- Bring your favorite good luck charm/jewelry to the exam.
- Once you are in the exam room, arrange things, get comfortable, be relaxed, attend to personal needs (the bathroom).
- Keep your eyes on your own paper; do not let them wander over to anyone else's paper.
- Be polite in making any reasonable demands of the exam room proctor, such as changing your seat or having window shades raised or lowered.

TIP 2

Read test instructions and questions carefully.

SUGGESTIONS
- Be familiar with the test directions ahead of time.
- Decide upon the task(s) that you have to complete.
- Know how the test will be graded.
- Know which question or questions are worth the most points.

- Give only the information that is requested.
- Underline important words and phrases.
- Ask for assistance from the exam room proctor if you do not understand the directions.

TIP 3

Budget your test time in a balanced manner.

SUGGESTIONS

- Bring a watch or clock to the test.
- Know how much time is allowed.
- Arrive on time; leave your home earlier than usual.
- Prepare a time schedule and try to stick to it. (The suggested times for each section are 50 minutes for the 50 multiple-choice questions, 45 minutes for the one thematic essay, and 60 minutes for the document-based questions.)
- Answer the easier questions first.
- Devote more time to the harder questions and to those worth more credit.
- Don't get "hung up" on a question that is proving to be very difficult; go on to another question and return later to the difficult one.
- Ask the exam room proctor for permission to go to the lavatory, if necessary, or if only to "take a break" from sitting in the room.
- Plan to stay in the room for the entire three hours. If you finish early, read over your work—there may be some things that you omitted or that you may wish to add. You also may wish to refine your grammar, spelling, and penmanship.

TIP 4

Be "kind" to the exam grader/evaluator.

SUGGESTIONS
- Assume that you are the teacher grading/evaluating your test paper.
- Answer questions in an orderly sequence.
- Write legibly.
- Use proper grammar, spelling, and sentence structure.
- Write essay answers in ink.
- Proofread your answers prior to submitting your exam paper. Have you answered all the short-answer questions and the required number of essays?

TIP 5

Use your reasoning skills.

SUGGESTIONS
- Answer *all* questions.
- Relate (connect) the question to anything that you studied, wrote in your notebook, or heard your teacher say in class.
- Relate (connect) the question to any film you saw in class, any project you did, or to anything you may have learned from newspapers, magazines, or television.
- Decide whether your answers would be approved by your teacher.
- Look over the entire test to see whether one part of it can help you answer another part.
- Write down as many of the **sixteen key concepts** and the **thirteen enduring constitutional issues** that you remember from your U.S. History and Government classes. (Among the **concepts** are culture, diversity, empathy, and interdependence.) Try to remember the meanings of these terms. Use them in answering questions, where relevant.

TIP 6

Don't be afraid to guess.

SUGGESTIONS
- In general, go with your first answer choice.
- Eliminate obvious incorrect choices.
- If still unsure of an answer, make an educated guess.
- There is no penalty for guessing; therefore, answer ALL questions. An omitted answer gets no credit.

Let's now review the six GENERAL HELPFUL TIPS for short-answer questions:

SUMMARY OF TIPS
1. Be confident and prepared.
2. Read test instructions and questions carefully.
3. Budget your test time in a balanced manner.
4. Be "kind" to the exam grader/evaluator.
5. Use your reasoning skills.
6. Don't be afraid to guess.

SPECIFIC HELPFUL TIPS FOR THE SHORT-ANSWER (MULTIPLE-CHOICE) QUESTIONS

TIP 1

Answer the easy questions first.

The best reason for using this hint is that it can build up your confidence. It also enables you to use your time more efficiently. You should answer these questions first, while skipping over and circling the numbers of the more difficult questions. You can always return to these later during the exam. Easy questions usually contain short sentences and few words. The answer can often be arrived at quickly from the information presented.

EXAMPLE

The authors of the United States Constitution believed that the voice of the people should be heard frequently. Which part of the Government was instituted to respond most directly to the will of the people?

1 Senate
2 House of Representatives
3 Supreme Court
4 Presidency

(from an actual Regents exam)

The correct answer, choice 2, is obvious. It is the only choice describing a component—in fact, the only component—in the original Constitution that was chosen directly by *the will of the people*. Senators were initially chosen by state legislatures (choice 1). Supreme Court judges have always been appointed (choice 3), while the President (choice 4) is chosen via an indirect vote by the people and at times has not been reflective of *the will of the people*.

TIP 2

Consider what the questioner wants you to do, and underline key words.

Remember that the people who made up the Regents questions had specific tasks they want you to accomplish. These tasks can be understood if you read instructions carefully, underline key words, and put yourself "in their shoes." Try to figure out what they would want a student to do with a given question. Determine for yourself exactly what is being tested. Underlining helps you focus on the key ideas in the question.

EXAMPLE

At times, the United States Government has passed protective
tariffs to
1 encourage foreign trade
2 help the nation's manufacturers
3 reduce the cost of consumer goods
4 improve the quality of goods

(from an actual Regents exam)

By underlining *protective tariffs*, you are on your way to focusing on
the thrust of this question. You are being asked to identify something
done that was presumed to be beneficial to the United States economy
at specific times in history. The correct answer, choice 2, contains the
only beneficial impact that a protective tariff would have. Choices 1
and 3, although beneficial, describe consequences likely to occur with
the removal of tariffs. Choice 4 has little to do with whether or not tariffs
exist. Now, in the next question, underline the key words.

The Republican presidents of the 1920s generally followed
a foreign policy based on
1 collective security
2 brinkmanship
3 noninvolvement
4 militarism

(from an actual Regents exam)

The key words in the stem that needed to be underlined were
Republican and *1920s*. You would thus be led to conclude that the
only relevant choice would be 3, which describes the isolationist foreign policy of the United States in the post-World War I period. All
the presidents in the 1920s were Republicans and generally wanted to
reduce America's involvement with other nations.

TIP 3

Look for clues among choices, in the question as well as in other questions.

By reading questions and choices carefully, you may often find words and phrases that provide clues to an answer. This hint is important because it assists you in making links and connections between various questions.

EXAMPLES

Which events best support the image of the 1920s as a decade of nativist sentiment?
1 the passage of the National Origins Act and the rise of the Ku Klux Klan
2 the Scopes trial and the passage of women's suffrage
3 the Washington Naval Conference and the Kellogg-Briand Pact
4 the growth of the auto industry and the Teapot Dome affair
(from an actual Regents exam)

Choice 1 is correct. It is the only choice naming events that were connected to harsh feelings toward foreigners. That harshness was part of the thinking of Americans who had *nativist sentiments*.

Let's examine another attempt to find a clue.

In the Colonial Era, developments such as the New England town meetings and the establishment of the Virginia House of Burgesses represented
1 colonial attempts to build a strong national government
2 efforts by the British to strengthen their control over the colonies
3 steps in the growth of representative democracy
4 early social reform movements
(from an actual Regents exam)

Can you determine the right answer? Both developments were political in purpose, and both were examples of democracy. The only choice that relates to these features is 3.

TIP 4

Examine all possibilities.
Beware of tricky and tempting foils (decoys).

By remembering this tip you will be careful to survey all possible responses before making a selection. A given choice, or two, may initially appear to be the correct answer. This often happens when you are asked to make a generalization about a group of people or events.

EXAMPLE

A similarity between the Red Scare of the 1920s and McCarthyism in the 1950s was that during each period
1 thousands of American citizens were expelled from the United States
2 the Communist Party gained many members in the United States
3 many government employees were convicted of giving secrets to the Soviet Union
4 the civil liberties of American citizens were threatened
(from an actual Regents exam)

Choice 4 is correct; however, all the other choices certainly "sound" correct. Indeed, the other choices represent true decoys. Choices 1 and 2 are tempting, as they do have a connection with the color *Red* in *Red Scare*. Choice 1 is certainly something "scary," even though no such event ever occurred in American history.

TIP 5

Always select the more broad, encompassing choice.

This tip is most helpful when two or more choices are correct, but you conclude that one choice is broader (or more encompassing) than the other. Indeed, one choice may actually include the other or others.

EXAMPLES

"Up to our own day, American history is the history of the colonization of the Great West. The existence of an area of free land, . . . and the advance of American settlement westward explain American development."
This quotation of the 1890s suggests that the American frontier
1 should be preserved for free use by all the people
2 has mirrored European values and social patterns
3 will continue indefinitely as a region to be colonized
4 has had a positive effect on the growth of the United States

(from an actual Regents exam)

Choices 1, 2, and 3 have some validity, as they have been characteristic of varying attitudes toward the frontier. However, choice 4 is the best choice. It more fully and broadly answers the question. Examine the next question and see if you can figure out the answer.

Throughout United States history, the most important aim of the country's foreign policy has been
1 participation in international organizations
2 advancement of national self-interest
3 containment of communism
4 development of military alliances

(from an actual Regents exam)

Choices 1, 3, and 4 have all characterized U.S. foreign policy at varying times in our nation's history. However, each of these policies was put forth only when we decided it helped meet what we perceived to be our national self-interest at the time. Therefore, choice 2 is the best, all-encompassing answer for this question.

TIP 6

Use a process of elimination.

This tip provides a very good way of arriving at an answer. It is particularly useful when you face a difficult question and are unsure of the best response. Also, it increases your chances of coming up with the correct answer and (1) assists in discarding *unacceptable* choices, and (2) narrows the possible *acceptable* choices. (You may wish to physically cross out on the question page the choices that you decide are incorrect.)

EXAMPLE

How did the personal diplomacy conducted by President Franklin D. Roosevelt during World War II affect the presidency?

1 Subsequent presidents have refused to use this unsuccessful method.
2 The president's role in shaping United States foreign policy was strengthened.
3 The president's war powers as Commander in Chief were sharply reduced.
4 Congress increased its power over the executive branch.

(from an actual Regents exam)

In wartime, a president's ability to expand his powers as a result of his role as Commander in Chief is very great. This was certainly true of Franklin D. Roosevelt during World War II. Choice 3, therefore, is clearly wrong as it states an untrue situation. Choice 4 is wrong, as Congress during wartime will usually side with the president. Choice 1 can be eliminated, as it is simply untrue. Presidents since Roosevelt have sought to increase their diplomatic powers, well aware of his precedent-setting actions. Therefore, choice 2 is correct.

See if you can use a process of elimination to figure out the right answer in the question below.

Which statement is accurate about American culture during the Great Depression?
1 The Federal Government provided money to support the arts.
2 Most movies featured realistic themes and unhappy endings.
3 Rock-and-roll music became popular.
4 Interest in professional sports declined.

(from an actual Regents exam)

Did you pick choice 1? Good! Choice 2 can be eliminated, as it describes the opposite of what happened—most movie themes had happy themes, and sought to uplift peoples' spirits. The sadness of the times also spurred people to seek some enjoyment in entertainment forms such as sporting events (choice 4). Rock-and-roll music was not to become popular until the 1950s, many years after the Great Depression.

TIP 7

Detect differences among the choices presented.

You should be careful in picking out foils and decoys, something we mentioned in Tip #4. In a similar manner, this tip helps you in choosing among general and specific answers. This is especially important when you have reduced your selections to two choices.

EXAMPLE

In the 1920s, the depressed situation of United States agriculture was chiefly caused by
1 overregulation by government
2 mechanization and overproduction
3 inefficient production techniques
4 stock-market speculation

(from an actual Regents exam)

The four choices all sound like factors that would lead to economic crises but, upon closer examination, choices 1 and 3 can be ruled out as neither was characteristic of the United States in the 1920s. There was little regulation by government, as laissez-faire was a commonly held belief. Also, while production techniques were inefficient by today's standards, they were adequate in the 1920s as they resulted in a surplus of goods. Choices 2 and 4 were indeed factors leading to the Great Depression, yet stock-market speculation, choice 4, did not significantly affect *the depressed situation of United States agriculture*. Factors that did affect this situation are described in choice 2, the correct answer.

TIP 8

Don't choose an answer that is correct in itself but incorrect as it relates to the question.

It is crucial to keep this tip in mind when evaluating a question that has attractive choices. They will appear attractive because each has an element of truth; however, you must decide which one of these has the greatest relationship to the question itself. Let's look at a question we have seen elsewhere—Tip #**7**.

EXAMPLE

In the 1920s, the depressed situation of United States agriculture was chiefly caused by
1 overregulation by government
2 mechanization and overproduction
3 inefficient production techniques
4 stock-market speculation

(from an actual Regents exam)

As you know, the correct answer is choice 2. Yet, although choices 2 and 4 were factors leading to the Great Depression, it is only choice 2 that best relates to the question. (See the discussion for Tip #**7**.) Now, try the following question.

EXAMPLE

Which event of the early 1900s is evidence that Upton
Sinclair's novel, *The Jungle*, had an important impact on the
United States?
1 adoption of reforms in public education
2 passage of legislation limiting immigration
3 adoption of the 18th Amendment establishing Prohibition
4 passage of legislation requiring federal inspection of meat

(from an actual Regents exam)

Choice 4 is the correct answer, as it describes an event relating
directly to Upton Sinclair's novel. The other three choices describe
events that did occur in the first third of the twentieth century, but had
nothing to do with the novel.

TIP 9

Look for "giveaways" and "freebies."

There are times when a test question practically gives away the
answer. You can determine such rare moments by focusing on obvious
words, prefixes, grammatical construction, and other revealing tips.

EXAMPLE

Which New Deal program was chiefly designed to correct
abuses in the stock market?
1 Federal Emergency Relief Act
2 Civilian Conservation Corps
3 Works Progress Administration
4 Securities and Exchange Commission

(from an actual Regents exam)

Choice 4 stands out as the correct answer; *securities* is a word practically synonymous with *stock market*. The New Deal programs named in
choices 1, 2, and 3 had nothing to do with correcting *abuses in the stock
market*.

TIP 10

Think out the answer before looking at the possible choices.

This tip helps to stimulate memory recall. As you read a question, your "intellectual radar" may pick up something that will jog loose a key thought, concept, or fact in your mind.

EXAMPLE

> The Great Society of Lyndon Johnson is most similar to which other presidential program?
> 1 Warren Harding's Return to Normalcy
> 2 Franklin D. Roosevelt's New Deal
> 3 Ronald Reagan's New Federalism
> 4 George Bush's Thousand Points of Light
>
> (from an actual Regents exam)

As you were reading the question, you should have thought about some well-known president and his domestic program that aimed to improve our nation's standard of living. Choice 2 meets these criteria. Along with the Great Society program, the New Deal sought to have the federal government take an active role in promoting peoples' health and welfare. The programs identified in choices 1, 3, and 4 did not have this goal.

This tip is also useful when interpreting cartoons. As you look at a cartoon, try to guess its meaning prior to looking at the choices. Most cartoon interpretation questions will require you to decide on a title for the cartoon or to indicate the message of the cartoonist.

EXAMPLE

Which aspect of the United States Government is best illustrated by the cartoon?
1 system of checks and balances
2 veto power of the president
3 congressional committee system
4 civilian control of the military

(from an actual Regents exam)

The cartoon suggests something that the Senate can do and/or has already done. It also conveys a negative thought, to judge by the torn paper in a wastebasket labeled "rejections." The correct choice is 1. Choices 2, 3, and 4 do not deal with a specific power of the Senate, even though they do describe ways by which a governmental action can be restricted.

TIP 11

Make informed and educated guesses.

If you are not sure of an answer, don't be afraid to guess. Any answer is better than no answer—you have nothing to lose, as there is no penalty for guessing. Remember that the correct answer is there, somewhere, right on the exam page, waiting for you to find it. If you've eliminated one or more options, then your chances of picking the right answer increases from one out of four to one out of three, etc. A word of caution—guessing should be used only as a last resort. Do not go into the Regents exam room expecting to pass by guessing your way through the questions. There is no substitute for careful, diligent exam preparation long before the exam date itself.

EXAMPLE

Which New Deal reforms most directly targeted the basic problem of the victims of the Dust Bowl?
1 guaranteeing workers the right to organize and bargain collectively
2 regulating the sale of stocks and bonds
3 providing farmers low-cost loans and parity payments
4 raising individual and corporate income tax rates
                                                    (from an actual Regents exam)

Choice 3 is the correct answer. It contains the word *farmers*, a clear link to the phrase *Dust Bowl*. Even if you did not recognize this phrase right away, you could certainly eliminate choices 2 and 4; they do not refer to people (*victims*). While choice 1 does refer to people (*workers*), it does not name a group that would be associated with *dust*. Let's look at another question whose answer could be arrived at by making an informed and educated guess.

The widespread use of computers had led to a national concern over
1 increased pollution of the environment
2 guarding the right of privacy
3 protection of the right to petition
4 a decline in television viewing
                                                    (from an actual Regents exam)

At first reading, this question might appear strange because you might not expect to see a question about computers on a history exam. In addition, it is possible that your teacher did not cover the subject of computers in your social studies class. Nevertheless, even if these things were true and if you don't know how to use a computer, you can still guess at the answer. Careful rereading of the question would reveal that choices 3 and 4 are not really items causing *national concern*. Choices 1 and 2 do describe issues of such concern; however, using computers has little to do with causing pollution. Since they do have the capacity to store great amounts of information about people, abuse of this capacity could cause problems affecting the right to privacy—choice 2.

Let's now review the eleven SPECIFIC HELPFUL TIPS for short-answer questions:

SUMMARY OF TIPS

1. Answer the easy questions first.
2. Consider what the questioner wants you to do, and underline key words.
3. Look for clues among choices in the question, as well as in other questions.
4. Examine all possibilities. Beware of tricky and tempting foils (decoys).
5. Always select the more broad, encompassing choice.
6. Use a process of elimination.
7. Detect differences among the choices presented.
8. Don't choose an answer that is correct in itself but incorrect as it relates to the question.
9. Look for "giveaways" and "freebies."
10. Think out the answer before looking at the possible choices.
11. Make informed and educated guesses.

In addition to these SPECIFIC HELPFUL TIPS, here are five more bonus ones:

1. Read each question twice.
2. Generally, try to go with your first inclination.
3. Avoid looking for patterns.
4. Be aware that universals (i.e., *always, never, only*) should usually be disregarded as possible correct choices.
5. Bear in mind that sometimes the essays will provide answers to the short answers.

SPECIFIC HELPFUL TIPS FOR THE ESSAY QUESTIONS

TIP 1

Understand the essay format: thematic and document-based questions.

Part II of the Regents exam consists of one thematic essay for which there will be 45 minutes to write. The thematic essay will be worth 15 percent of the score. Write a well-organized essay that includes an introduction, several paragraphs that address the task, and a conclusion. Be aware of key terms in the question, for example, *show, discuss, compare.* The thematic essay does not ask only for a recollection of facts, but rather asks the student to focus on themes and to demonstrate critical thinking. Those scoring the essay will use the following Generic Scoring Rubric:

GENERIC SCORING RUBRIC
THEMATIC ESSAY

5

- Shows a thorough understanding of the theme
- Addresses all aspects of the task
- Shows an ability to analyze, evaluate, compare, and/or contrast issues and events
- Richly supports essay with relevant facts, examples, and details
- Writes a well-developed essay, consistently demonstrating a logical and clear plan of organization
- Includes a strong introduction and conclusion

4

- Shows a good understanding of the theme
- Addresses all aspects of the task
- Shows an ability to analyze, evaluate, compare, and/or contrast issues and events
- Includes relevant facts, examples, and details, but may not support all aspects of the task evenly
- Writes a well-developed essay, demonstrating a logical and clear plan of organization
- Includes a good introduction and conclusion

3

- Presents a satisfactory understanding of the theme
- Addresses most aspects of the task or addresses all aspects in a limited way
- Is able to analyze or evaluate issues and events, but not in any depth
- Writes a satisfactorily developed essay, demonstrating a general plan of organization
- Uses some facts, examples, and details
- Restates the theme in the introduction and concludes with a simple restatement of the theme

2

- Attempts to address the theme, but uses vague and/or inaccurate information
- Develops a faulty analysis or evaluation of theme
- Writes a poorly organized essay, lacking focus and using few facts, examples, and details
- Has vague or missing introduction and/or conclusion

1

- Shows limited understanding of the theme; omits concrete examples; details are weak or nonexistent
- Lacks an analysis or evalution of the issues and events beyond stating vague and/or inaccurate facts
- Attempts to complete the task, but essay demonstrates a major weakness in organization
- Uses little or no accurate or relevant facts, details, or examples
- Has no introduction or conclusion

0

- Fails to address the theme
- Is illegible
- Blank paper

Part III of the Regents exam consists of one document-based question for which there will be 60 minutes to write. The document-based essay will be worth 30 percent of the score. The document-based question will be divided into two parts; a Part A short-answer section (15 percent) and a Part B essay (15 percent). Following the questions, approximately eight short documents will be provided. Each Part A question will address a specific document. Answer the question using the document and the author's point of view and incorporate information about the time period from which the document has been selected. The Part B essay requires that student's state their position (thesis) in an introductory paragraph, then develop their argument in the body of the essay using information from most of the documents to support their position. Using outside information from the students' knowledge of the time period will enhance the essay. Students should include a brief conclusion restating their position. As with the multiple-choice section, budget your time. Those scoring the essay will use the following Generic Scoring Rubric:

GENERIC SCORING RUBRIC
DOCUMENT-BASED QUESTION

5

- Thoroughly addresses all aspects of the task by accurately analyzing and interpreting most of the documents
- Incorporates relevant outside information
- Richly supports essay with relevant facts, examples, and details
- Writes a well-developed essay, consistently demonstrating a logical and clear plan of organization
- Uses information from the documents in the body of the essay
- Includes a strong introduction and conclusion

4

- Addresses all aspects of the task by accurately analyzing and interpreting most of the documents
- Incorporates relevant outside information
- Includes relevant facts, examples, and details, but discussion may be more descriptive than analytical
- Writes a well-developed essay, demonstrating a logical and clear plan of organization
- Includes a good introduction and conclusion

3

- Addresses most aspects of the task or addresses all aspects in a limited way; uses some of the documents
- Incorporates limited or no relevant outside information
- Uses some facts, examples, and details, but discussion is more descriptive than analytical
- Writes a satisfactorily developed essay, demonstrating a general plan of organization

- States the theme in the introduction and concludes with a simple restatement of the theme or topic

2

- Attempts to address some aspects of the task, making limited use of the documents
- Presents no relevant outside information
- Uses few facts, examples, and details; discussion simply restates contents of the documents
- Writes a poorly organized essay, lacking focus
- Has vague or missing introduction and/or conclusion

1

- Shows limited understanding of the task with vague, unclear references to the documents
- Presents no relevant outside information
- Attempts to complete the task, but essay demonstrates a major weakness in organization
- Uses little or no accurate or relevant facts, details, or examples
- Has no introduction or conclusion

0

- Fails to address the task
- Is illegible
- Blank paper

TIP 2

Go over the thematic essay before writing any answers and draw initial impressions.

Write down some ideas that come to mind, while underlining key words and phrases. This tip is valuable as it helps you retain initial ideas and thoughts about the subject matter of the question. In addition, it could provide you with some outline notes that could ultimately be used for your answer.

TIP 3

Go over the document-based question and draw initial impressions.

Go over the Historical Context section and the Task sections of the document-based question. Write down any quick notes about the time period being addressed by the question. Once again, this could provide you with some outline notes that could ultimately be used for your answer.

TIP 4

Prepare a time schedule.

This tip enables you to organize your test-taking time and allows you to focus your attention on those essays that are easiest for you. Allow sufficient time for each essay part. If there are three parts to an essay, decide how much time to allocate for each part. Write as much as you know for each part. The more you write, using as many examples as possible to answer the question, the better your chances for obtaining maximum credit. However, make adjustments according to the number of parts and to the value of each one. If you allocate 30 minutes for a three-part essay in which each part has equal worth, and then devote 20 minutes to part *a*, you will probably get maximum credit for part *a* but very little credit for parts *b* and *c*. Apportion time and values accordingly.

TIP 5

Look for key words, both in the directions and in the question itself.

By understanding key words in the directions, you are on your way to answering the question in a proper manner. The key directive words for all Regents essay questions are listed in a set of general instructions on the exam itself, between the short-answer questions and the essay questions.

The key directive words in the instructions are *discuss*, *describe*, *explain*, and *evaluate*. They are defined and these definitions should be referred to as you answer the essay question.

Part II: Thematic Essay

Directions: Write a well-organized essay that includes an introduction, several paragraphs addressing the task below, and a conclusion.

Theme: Government—Power of the Judiciary

> Shortly after the formation of the new constitutional government, the Supreme Court established itself as an equal to the legislative and executive branches.

Task:

> From your study of the Supreme Court under the leadership of Chief Justice John Marshall, identify two cases that strengthened the power of the Supreme Court.
>
> For each case identified:
> - *Discuss* the facts of the case
> - *Describe* the court's decision
> - *Explain* how the decision strengthened the power of the Supreme Court and the federal government

You may use cases decided during the Marshall Court era. Some suggestions you might wish to consider are *Marbury v. Madison* (1803), *McCulloch v. Maryland* (1819), and *Gibbons v. Ogden* (1824).

You are *not* limited to these suggestions.

Guidelines: The key content words in the question are *judiciary, equal, strengthened, decision*. The focus of the thematic essay should be concentrating on how the Supreme Court strengthened itself with powers granted or assumed through the cases provided. It is critical that you limit your discussion after describing the facts and the decision to how the case strengthened the power of the Supreme Court.

TIP 6

Outline an answer before writing.

By following this tip, you will be able to begin organizing your essay answers in a definitive manner. You will also be able to put down important ideas quickly and clearly. Your outline can be structured in any format you wish—it will not be graded. It can be placed in your exam booklet.

EXAMPLE

An example of a simple, usable outline is given below. It is based on the Thematic Essay from a Regents exam.

Theme: Reform Movements in the United States

Reform movements are intended to improve different aspects of American life. Through the actions of individuals, organizations, or the government, the goals of these reform movements have been achieved, but with varying degrees of success.

Task:

Identify **two** reform movements that have had an impact on American life and for **each**
- *Discuss* **one** major goal of the movement
- *Describe* **one** action taken by an individual, an organization, or the government in an attempt to achieve this goal
- *Evaluate* the extent to which this goal was achieved

You may use any reform movement from your study of United States history. Some suggestions you might wish to consider include the abolitionist movement, women's suffrage movement, temperance movement, progressive movement, civil rights movement, women's rights movement, and environmental movement.

You are *not* limited to these suggestions.

I. Progressive Movement
> A. Major goal
>> Use the power of the government to address problems associated with the rise of industry in the United States, such as unsafe and unsanitary conditions.
> B. Action taken
>> In 1906, Upton Sinclair, one of several "muckrakers," wrote *The Jungle*, a novel that exposed the dangerous and unhealthy conditions in the meatpacking industry.
> C. Level of success
>> The Progressive Movement was successful in achieving its goal. In 1906 the federal government passed the Meat Inspection Act and the Pure Food and Drug Act.

II. Civil Rights Movement
> A. Major goal
>> Change policies in the United States that segregated African Americans from whites in public facilities, and that limited the ability of African Americans to vote.
> B. Action taken
>> In 1955, the Rev. Martin Luther King, Jr., led the African American community in Montgomery, Alabama, to boycott the bus system following the arrest of Rosa Parks for not giving up her seat to a white rider.

C. Level of success

The bus boycott was successful in pressuring the city of Montgomery to end its discriminatory policies in regard to bus ridership. By the mid 1960s, the movement was successful in pushing for major legislation in regard to civil rights, such as the Civil Rights Act (1964) and the Voting Rights Act (1965).

This outline is like a skeleton. A good essay will add "muscle, flesh, ligaments," etc., in complete sentences.

TIP 7

Make use of the question to compose your introductory sentence.

Directions: Write a well-organized essay that includes an introduction, several paragraphs addressing the task below, and a conclusion.

Theme: Separation of Powers

> The balance of the three branches of the federal government has, historically, been in a constant state of flux.

Task:

> From your study of the Reconstruction Period (1863–1876), identify two examples of the operation of checks and balances within the federal government.
>
> For each example identified:
> * *Discuss* a specific proposed action by the particular branch of government (executive, legislative, or judicial).
> * *Describe* the reaction to the action by another branch of government.
> * *Explain* the settlement or outcome of the debated issue.

You may use any examples from the Reconstruction Period. Some suggestions you might wish to consider are Lincoln's Proclamation of Amnesty and Reconstruction (December 1863) and Congress' Wade-Davis Bill (July 1864), President Johnson's plan of Reconstruction (May 1865) and the reaction of Congress with the passage of the Military Reconstruction Act (March 1867) and the passage by Congress of the Tenure in Office Act (March 1867), President Johnson's veto of the Act (1867), and the subsequent impeachment of President Johnson (1868).

You are *not* limited to these suggestions.

Guidelines: Once you have read the question and decided on the two examples of checks and balances, you can begin to write your answer with a topic sentence that "borrows" words from the question. Consider the following:

EXAMPLE

> The Reconstruction Period (1863–1876) provides a helpful time period in United States history to discuss examples of the system of checks and balances and how the system has contributed to the flexibility of government.

TIP 8

Be sure to include sufficient details and examples in your answer.

This tip is very important and will help you to do well on an answer by letting the grader know that *you know* your material. Following this tip will show that you have explained and given support to the main ideas you have expressed. You should use it after writing your topic sentence and any other introductory statements. For the general statements you make, along with the main ideas you express, you must present any necessary, requested supporting data. This could include events, names, dates, reason, results, or other facts. As you write your essay answers, make believe that the person who will grade them is *not* a social studies teacher. Therefore, it becomes your responsibility to state *all* necessary information in a clear, logical, and supportive manner. Below is an essay question and a sample, partial answer to each of three parts.

Directions: Write a well-organized essay that includes an introduction, several paragraphs addressing the task below, and a conclusion.

Theme: Government—Power of the Judiciary

> Shortly after the formation of the new constitutional government, the Supreme Court established itself as an equal to the legislative and executive branches.

Task:

> From your study of the Supreme Court under the leadership of Chief Justice John Marshall, identify two cases which strengthened the power of the Supreme Court.
>
> For each case identified:
> • *Discuss* the facts of the case
> • *Describe* the court's decision
> • *Explain* how the decision strengthened the power of the Supreme Court and the federal government

You are *not* limited to these suggestions.

Guidelines: You may use cases decided during the Marshall Court era. Some suggestions you might wish to consider are *Marbury v. Madison* (1803), *McCulloch v. Maryland* (1819), and *Gibbons v. Ogden* (1824).

EXAMPLE

> *Gibbons v. Ogden* (1824) involved competing steamboat companies navigating the waters of the Hudson River between New Jersey and New York. The fact that the Hudson River made the common boundary of New York and New Jersey, the issue became one involving interstate commerce, a power delegated in the Constitution to the Congress of the United States. The Supreme Court's decision clearly defined Congress' power to regulate interstate (and foreign) commerce.

TIP 9

Use connective and linking words in your answers.

The use of such words, also called transitional words, is important when writing your essay answers. These words make your answers clearer and more logical, while helping the reader to understand the development of your ideas. The words are also useful in providing supporting data for main ideas, as well as changing from one idea to another. Here is a list of words that are often used to make connections and linkages, along with the specific purposes they serve in constructing a meaningful essay answer.

Connective and Linking Words	Purpose
1. first, second, next, last	to show sequence and order
2. because, therefore, thus, consequently, ultimately	to show cause and effect
3. for example, in other words, indeed	to emphasize something, to clarify an idea
4. however, but, yet, on the other hand, instead, still, although	to show contrast or change
5. similarly, in like manner	to show no change
6. furthermore, moreover, in addition, also, another	to note added information
7. meanwhile, presently, previously, subsequently	to show time relationship
8. finally, in conclusion, to sum up	to present a summary, to tie things together

The above suggestions would be useful when doing any kind of expository writing, whether in social studies or any other subject. Try them out on your next U.S. History and Government classroom exam, as well as when practicing essay writing with previous Regents exam essay questions.

TIP 10

If you are short of time, give an answer in outline form.

A Regents exam is three hours long; however, for any number of reasons, you may find yourself running short of time. If this happens, you should briefly, but neatly, put your answer in an outline form. (*Some* answer is better than *no* answer.) You should do this *only* as an *emergency measure*—not something you planned to do initially. For that reason, be assured that this tip is not contradicting **#6**. The advice in that tip was simply a guideline for you, to help in putting forth the complete essay answer that would be graded. In regard to the advice in this tip, however, the outline *is* the answer; it is what will be graded. Consequently, you should devote much care to its construction. It should follow a specific, easy-to-read style, such as the Harvard outline standard. Roman numerals, followed by capital letters and Arabic numerals should be used. Sentences and phrases, as both topics and sub-topics, should be written in the same form and in the same tense. This is called *parallel construction*.

TIP 11

If you are uncertain about what to write, make an informed and educated guess.

If you are not sure of what to write down for an answer, don't be afraid to guess. This is the advice we gave you in Tip #11 for the short-answer questions. With the essays, as with the short answers, you have nothing to lose by making an educated guess; there is no penalty for guessing. Indeed, with the essays, you may even be able to get some extra credit—part credit is certainly better than no credit at all! You cannot afford to leave blank a fifteen-point question. Present whatever information you can give about an item.

A word of caution, however, as we said in Tip **#11** for short answers. Guessing should be used *only* as a last resort in answering a question. Do not go into the Regents exam room expecting to pass by guessing your way through the questions. There is no substitute for careful, diligent exam preparation long before the exam date itself.

Part III: Document-Based Essay

The following questions (Part A and Part B) are based on the accompanying documents (1–6). Some of these documents have been edited for the purpose of this exercise. The question is designed to test your ability to work with historical documents and to demonstrate knowledge of the subject matter being presented. As you analyze the documents, take into account both the source of the document and the author's point of view.

Directions: Write a well-organized essay that includes your analysis of the documents. You should include specific historical details and you may discuss documents not provided in the question.

Historical Context:
The Bill of Rights was added to the Constitution in 1791 to protect individual liberties against government abuse.

Part A

The documents below relate to issued concerning the Fourth, Fifth, Sixth, and Eighth Amendments. Examine each document carefully and then answer the questions that follow.

Document 1

I have little patience with people who take the Bill of Rights for granted. The Bill of Rights, contained in the first ten amendments to the Constitution, is every American's guarantee of freedom.

President Harry Truman, Memoirs, Vol. II (1955)

1 What did President Truman mean by the statement "the first ten
   amendments . . . is every American's guarantee of freedom"?

   _____

   _____

   _____

   _____

   _____

Note: Eight documents form this segment of the actual exam. A single
document is supplied as an example.

Part B

Essay Response:
Your essay should be well organized with an introductory paragraph
that states your position on the question. Develop your position in the
next paragraphs and then write a conclusion. In your essay, include
specific historical details and refer to the specific documents you ana-
lyzed in Part A. You may include additional information from your
knowledge of social studies.

EXAMPLE

> The Bill of Rights were added to the Constitution in 1791 to
> protect individual liberties against government abuse. Assess
> the validity of this statement with particular attention to the
> areas of search, interrogation, and prosecution.

Even if you are not familiar with President Truman and the specific
cases defining amendments in the areas of search, interrogation, and
prosecution, you would most likely be able to respond to the question
by describing protections in your own environment, perhaps the
school setting. Can your locker be searched by the school principal?
What steps have to be taken by the school before you can be suspended or expelled? You know more than you think!

TIP 12

Write a suitable summary statement.

A suitable summary statement shows that you have successfully developed your main ideas in your essay. In addition, composing your summary statement helps to conclude your essay in a logical manner. A summary statement can be a rephrasing of the major points asserted in the introduction to the essay. It can also present the conclusions of the essay, which contains an orderly development of ideas. Thus, the person grading your essay will be impressed with its ending.

EXAMPLE

Write a well-organized essay that includes an introduction, several paragraphs addressing the task below, and a conclusion.

Theme: Science and Technology

> Science and technology have brought about great changes in many areas of American life.

Task:

From your study of the twentieth century, choose three major scientific/technological developments:

For each administration identified:
- *Identify* the scientific/technological development.
- *Describe* the effects of the scientific/technological development on American life.
- *Discuss* the extent to which the development had a positive or a negative effect on American life.

You may use any major scientific/technological developments from your study of twentieth-century United States history. Some suggestions you may wish to consider are mass production of the automobile (1900–1930), invention of the airplane and eventual trans-Atlantic flight (1903–1927), television (1945–present), nuclear weapons (1945–present), and home use of the personal computer (1980–present).

You are *not* limited to these suggestions.

Guidelines: After selecting the examples you chose to use and presenting the required descriptions and discussions, finish with a summary statement that "returns" to the main point of the essay identified in the question. A suitable summary statement for this essay would be as follows:

EXAMPLE

> Science and technology have brought about great changes in many areas of American life. The effects of the development of nuclear weapons and missile defense systems have had a negative effect on American life in the sense that they have contributed to society living in a perpetual state of fear of the nuclear holocaust. On the other hand, the home use of the personal computer has brought much of the world's information into people's homes through the Internet, therefore having a positive effect on American life.

TIP 13

Edit and proofread your writing.

You should make use of this tip after writing each essay answer to be sure that you have checked the following: legible penmanship, organization of the answer, sufficient content, and proper grammar and spelling. A sloppy and poorly written answer is not going to make a good impression on the grader. If you cannot read your own handwriting, you cannot expect a grader to be able to read it.

Below are some guidelines that will assist you in editing your answers to essay questions. Did you:

1. write an introductory topic sentence that states what the essay is about?
2. compose factual and detailed sentences that support the main ideas?
3. express a complete thought in each sentence?
4. use suitable transitional and connective words? (See #**9**.)
5. indent the first word of each paragraph?
6. begin each sentence with a capital letter?
7. punctuate your sentences correctly?
8. spell all names and words correctly?
9. write legibly?
10. answer the question?
11. answer the question without extraneous and unwanted material?
12. write your answer in a clear manner, so that even a non-social studies teacher could understand it?

TIP 14

Refer to the sources, dates, and authors of the documents in the document-based question.

Let's now review the fourteen SPECIFIC HELPFUL TIPS for answering essay questions described above:

SUMMARY OF TIPS

1. Understand the essay format: thematic and document-based questions.
2. Go over the thematic essay before writing any answers and draw initial impressions.
3. Go over the document-based question and draw initial impressions.
4. Prepare a time schedule.
5. Look for key words, both in the directions and in the question itself.
6. Outline an answer before writing.

7. Make use of the question to compose your introductory sentence.
8. Be sure to include sufficient details and examples in your answer.
9. Use connective and linking words in your answers.
10. If you are short of time, give an answer in outline form.
11. If you are uncertain about what to write, make an informed and educated guess.
12. Write a suitable summary statement.
13. Edit and proofread your writing.
14. Refer to sources, dates, and authors of the documents in the document based-question.

In addition to these tips, here are five more bonus ones:

1. Read each question twice.
2. Include everything in an answer that you wish to say. Don't cross-reference answers. (Don't make reference in one essay answer to something in another answer.) It is very possible that no teacher will grade more than one of your three essays.
3. Select the essays easiest for you, and not those that you feel will impress the graders.
4. Do not abbreviate. Write *and*, not *&*. Write *United States*, not *U.S.* Write *twenty-five*, not *25*.
5. Write as much as you know that is relevant for the thematic essay. The more you write, the better your chances for obtaining maximum credit.

Glossary of Terms

* **Abolitionists** those who supported doing away with (abolishing) the institution of slavery.
* **abortion** the ending of a pregnancy before a live birth.
  acid rain rain, snow, or sleet containing nitric or sulphuric acid produced from the contamination of the atmosphere by smokestack and automobile emissions. It can damage plants and animals and erode stone and buildings.
* **acculturation** the modification of a people's **culture** through adaptation or borrowing from other cultures; the merging of cultures.
* **activism** belief in direct vigorous action.
  administration the management of government; the body of officials in the executive branch; the term of office of a **president**.
* **advocate** 1) to plead a case or support a particular issue; 2) one who pleads such a case or supports an issue.
* **affirmative action** public policy of incorporating women and racial and **ethnic** minorities into economic, political, and social institutions; usually applied through legislation or court orders.
* **affluent** wealthy, well-to-do.
* **aggression** unprovoked attack or act of violence.
** **agrarian** relating to agriculture or land.
* **airlift** supplying a city or region by airplane. In the Berlin Airlift of 1948–1949, the United States and allies flew food and other necessities into West Berlin because the Soviet Union had imposed a blockade on land routes.

  ° Denotes a term that has been frequently tested on past exams.
  °° Denotes a term that has been **very** frequently tested on past exams.
  °°° Denotes a term that has been **most** frequently tested on past exams.

** **ally**   a person, party, or country joined with another for a common purpose.

*** **amendment**   change or addition made in the **Constitution**; proposed by **Congress** or a national convention called by Congress and ratified by state legislatures or special state conventions.

amnesty   a general pardon for political offenses, generally to a large group of individuals.

anarchist   one who believes in the abolition of government or is opposed to organized government.

* **anarchy**   the absence of government; a state of disorder or chaos.

* **Antifederalists**   opponents of **ratification** of the **Constitution** in 1787 and 1788; opponents of the extension of federal power.

* **antitrust**   relating to the limitation or control of monopolies, trusts, or unfair business combinations.

apartheid   racial **segregation**, specifically in South Africa before 1991.

Appalachia   region of the Appalachian Mountains from Alabama to New York and western New England characterized in many parts by poverty and economic underdevelopment.

* **appeasement**   attempts to conciliate an aggressor by making concessions. The policy of appeasement toward Hitler in the 1930s ultimately failed to avoid war.

* **appoint**   to name to an office. A president's major appointments must be confirmed by the **Senate**.

apportionment   allotment of voting districts as required by law.

* **arbitration**   process of settling a dispute by referring it to a third party; both sides usually agree beforehand to abide by the arbitrator's decision.

armageddon   a vast, final, destructive conflict.

armistice   a truce preliminary to a peace treaty.

* **Articles of Confederation**   the charter of the first national government of the United States; in effect from 1781 until replaced by the **Constitution** in 1789.

assembly   a gathering or body of representatives, usually of a state or locality.

* **assimilation**   process of being absorbed into a group or culture.

Atlantic Charter   document issued in 1941 by President Franklin Roosevelt and Prime Minister Winston Churchill outlining the mutual wartime goals of England and the United States and their principles for assuring peace after the war.

backlash   strong negative reaction to a law or political event.

* **balance of power**   policy aimed at securing peace by maintaining approximate military equality among countries or **blocs**.

* **balanced budget**   plan for government taxes and spending in which expenses do not exceed income.

belligerent   a participant in a war.

bicameral legislature   law-making body made up of two houses or chambers.

** **big business**   group of large profit-making corporations.

* **Big Stick policy**   willingness to use military power to influence foreign affairs. It derives from Theodore Roosevelt's saying, "Walk softly, but carry a big stick."

** **Bill of Rights**   first ten amendments to the **Constitution**, adopted in 1791.

bipartisan   involving the cooperation of two political parties.

* **birth control**   artificial or natural means of avoiding pregnancy.

** **black codes**   a series of laws that sought to control and regulate the conduct of freed slaves during and after the **Reconstruction** period in the Southern states. Generally, they denied blacks their basic civil rights.

* **bloc**   a group of countries or voters.

Bolsheviks   radical socialists and communists under the leadership of Lenin and Trotsky who came to power following the Russian Revolution in 1917.

bonus   a government payment to war veterans usually based on length of service.

* **boom**   period of economic expansion.

Boston Massacre   incident in 1770 in which five colonists were killed in Boston when British soldiers fired on a crowd throwing rocks and snowballs; the soldiers were tried and acquitted of murder.

Boston Tea Party   incident in Boston, December 16, 1773, when colonists dressed as Indians forced their way aboard merchant ships in the harbor and threw overboard their cargoes of tea so that recently imposed British taxes on it could not be collected.

bourgeoisie economic and social class between the aristocracy or the very wealthy class and the working class (the **proletariat**); the commercial or professional class; the middle class.

** **boycott** method used by unions and other political groups to force concessions from management or opponents. To boycott is to join together in refusing to deal with or buy from a party in order to influence them to negotiate or make concessions.

brain trust experts without official positions who served as advisors to President Franklin Roosevelt.

brinkmanship pushing a dangerous situation to the limit before stopping.

* **brown power** phrase describing attempts by Hispanic Americans to use their growing numbers to improve their political and economic standing.

* **budget** financial plan for income and expenses.

* **budget deficit** the amount by which a government's expenses exceed its revenue or income.

bureaucracy administrative officials of government.

* **cabinet** the advisors to the **president** who also manage the principal executive departments of the U.S. government. The **cabinet** is not mentioned in the **Constitution**, but has grown and developed over time from custom and practice.

* **Camp David Accords** agreements reached in 1978 between President Sadat of Egypt and Prime Minister Begin of Israel, negotiated by President Carter at the presidential retreat in Camp David, Maryland. The accords evolved into a peace treaty between Israel and Egypt in 1979, providing for Egypt's official recognition of Israel and Israel's withdrawal from the Sinai Peninsula.

* **capital** (1) the seat or main location of a government; (2) money invested or used to return a profit.

* **capital gains tax** a tax on profits made from the sale of property or securities.

** **capital punishment** death sentence imposed by a court.

* **capitalism** economic system in which the means of production and distribution are privately owned and operated for profit.

Carpetbaggers Northerners who went to the South during the **Reconstruction** period to participate in and profit from its political reorganization.

caucus   a closed meeting of a political party.

censorship   preventing the publication of written material or the showing of a film, television program, or play because the government or a segment of society finds it objectionable.

* **census**   a counting of the inhabitants of a region.

* **Central Powers**   in World War I, Germany, Austro-Hungary, and their allies.

centralized   with power or authority concentrated in a central organization.

charter   written document establishing the rules under which an organization will operate; an organization's constitution.

** **checks and balances**   division of powers among the three branches of the federal government so that each branch may limit actions and power of the others. *See also* **separation of powers**.

chicanos   Americans of Mexican origin or descent.

** **citizen**   person entitled to the rights and protection provided by the state or nation.

civil   relating to the state, politics, or government.

** **civil disobedience**   refusal to obey a law in order to draw attention to its unfairness or undesirability.

* **civil liberties**   *see* **civil rights**.

*** **civil rights**   the liberties and privileges of citizens, especially those guaranteed in the **Bill of Rights**.

* **civil service**   system for filling government jobs through impartial and nonpolitical means, such as standardized exams. Begun by the federal government in the 1880s.

* **civilian**   a person who is not a member of the military or armed forces; pertaining to matters outside the military.

clandestine   secret; performed secretly.

* **clear and present danger**   standard established by the Supreme Court for determining when the right of free speech may be limited or denied—"when there is a clear and present danger that they will bring about the substantive evils that [the government] has a right to prevent."

* **coalition**   temporary alliance of groups or factions.

* **coinage**   money made of metal; sometimes called hard money.

* **cold war**   a conflict between nations short of actual military conflict; the political, diplomatic, economic, and strategic competi-

tion between the United States and the Soviet Union from 1946 until 1991.

** **collective bargaining** method by which workers negotiate as a group with their employer through their union representatives.

** **collective security** agreement among a group of nations to help each other maintain their safety and territory; usually by agreeing that an attack by a foreign power upon one nation will be considered an attack upon all.

** **colonialism** international policy based on control over dependent areas or colonies.

** **colony** a territory ruled or administered by a distant nation, usually for the benefit of the ruling nation.

* **commerce** the exchange or buying and selling of goods; business.

* **commerce among the states** business carried on across state lines, which **Congress** is given power to regulate by Article I, Section 8, of the **Constitution**.

* **committee** a group of people appointed or delegated for a particular purpose.

* **commodities** common economic goods that are bought and sold, such as agricultural products.

common law body of law formed over time by accumulation of precedents and prior decisions, as opposed to laws enacted by legislative bodies.

Common Sense a pamphlet by Thomas Paine that helped rally public support for the Revolutionary War.

commonwealth an organization of independent states; form of government of several states in the United States.

communiqué official bulletin, statement, or other communication.

*** **communism** political philosophy advocating collective ownership of property and the means of production and the abolition of the capitalist economic system.

compact theory of union doctrine held by many states' rights supporters that the **union** was a voluntary compact among the states and that states had the right to leave the union in the same manner they had chosen to enter it.

compromise a settlement in which each side makes concessions.

concession something yielded or given up, often in exchange for something else.

Confederate States   the eleven Southern states that seceded or officially withdrew from the Union in 1860 and 1861 to form an independent nation called the Confederate States of America. Their withdrawal was not recognized by the federal government or the remaining states. They were defeated in the Civil War and reabsorbed into the Union.

* **confirm**   to approve or agree with.

*****Congress**   the legislative branch of the federal government; composed of the **Senate** and the **House of Representatives**.

conscription   compulsory enrollment into the armed forces; forced military service; draft.

consensus   general agreement.

* **conservation**   careful management and protection, especially of natural resources.

conservative   reluctant or resistant to change; favoring traditional views and values; one belonging to a conservative party or political group.

constituents   the citizens represented by an elected public official; group of supporters.

*** **Constitution**   the basic charter of the United States government, effective since 1789; it was written by the **Constitutional Convention** in 1787, ratified by the states 1787–1788, and put into effect in 1789.

constitutionalism   belief that government is limited by legal and political restraints and accountable to the governed.

* **Constitutional Convention**   gathering of delegates from the thirteen states in 1787 in Philadelphia for the purpose of revising the **Articles of Confederation**; instead, they drafted an entirely new **Constitution** that was adopted in 1788 and put into effect in 1789.

Constitutional Republicanism   elected government limited by legally defined guidelines.

* **consumer**   the final buyer and user of a product.

* **consumerism**   protection of the interests and rights of consumers against false advertising or faulty or dangerous products.

** **containment**   policy adopted by the Western democracies after World War II to prevent the further expansion of communism and the Soviet Union.

* **Continental Congress**   (1) any of several assemblies of delegates from the American colonies before the Revolution to promote cooperation on various issues; (2) the national legislative body under the **Articles of Confederation** (1781–1788).

* **convention** a meeting of political delegates.

conventional traditional or ordinary; in military affairs, it refers to forces or measures other than nuclear weapons.

* **cooperative** a corporation owned collectively by members who share in the profits and benefits. **Cooperatives** were first developed by farmers in the late nineteenth century to avoid high prices charged by middlemen for grain storage, transportation, and farm supplies.

corollary a proposition that follows a previous one, which it modifies or enlarges, such as the **Roosevelt Corollary** to the **Monroe Doctrine**.

* **corporation** an organization legally empowered to act as one person, including the ability to borrow and lend money, make contracts, own property, and engage in business.

* **corruption** illegal or improper practices; abuses of authority, especially in connection with bribery or theft.

coup an overturning; a coup d'état is the overthrow of a government.

craft union labor union made up of workers with the same skill or craft, such as carpenters or electricians.

credibility grounds for being believed or trusted.

Crédit Mobilier railroad construction company that cheated on government contracts and bribed congressmen during the late 1860s.

* **creditor nation** a nation that exports more than it imports, so that it is owed money by other nations.

* **cultural pluralism** the acceptance and encouragement of multiple ethnic, religious, and racial groups within one society; respect for ethnic diversity.

** **culture** the beliefs, social forms, and accumulated knowledge of a group, race, or people.

* **currency** money in circulation, especially paper money.

* **Darwinism** (1) the theories of biologist Charles Darwin, who explained the evolution of species by natural selection; (2) social theories loosely based on Darwin's work and arguing that "the survival of the fittest" meant that government should not protect the weak from exploitation by the strong.

Dayton Accord   agreement to end the war in Bosnia negotiated by the presidents of Bosnia, Croatia, and Yugoslavia at Dayton, Ohio in November 1995 with the assistance of the United States; agreement that established two autonomous regions—a Serb republic and a Muslim-Croat federation—within the nation of Bosnia and Herzegovina and provided for a multinational **United Nations** force to supervise the agreement.

debasement   a reduction of value.

* **debtor nation**   a nation that imports more than it exports and so owes money to other nations.

* **Declaration of Independence**   document passed and signed by the **Continental Congress**, effective July 4, 1776, declaring the United States an independent and sovereign nation.

** **defense spending**   government spending for military armaments, equipment, and personnel.

degradation   a decline into a lower or worse condition.

* **delegate**   a representative chosen to act for a group or another person.

demilitarized zone   area where no military equipment or personnel may be deployed.

demobilize   to discharge from military service.

Democratic party   political party that evolved out of the **Democratic Republicans** around 1820.

Democratic Republicans   political party formed around 1800 by Jefferson, Madison, and others opposed to the **Federalists**.

demographic   relating to the statistical study of human populations.

** **depression**   an economic downturn, especially one characterized by high unemployment.

* **desegregation**   the ending of **segregation**, which is the separation of whites and blacks.

despot   a **sovereign** or authority without legal restraints; an absolute monarch; tyrant.

* **détente**   relaxation of strained relations or tensions.

* **diplomacy**   the practice of conducting relations between countries by negotiations rather than force.

** **direct election**   election in which votes are cast by the people themselves rather than by their representatives.

directive   order issued by a high authority calling for specific action.

* **disarmament**   giving up or reducing armed forces.

* **discrimination** partiality, **prejudice**, or distinctions in treatment; the denial of rights and advantages to minority groups.

disenfranchise to take away the right to vote.

dissenting opinion written statement by a member of a court disagreeing with the court's decision.

distribution of wealth statistical measure of how the property or wealth of a nation is divided among its population.

* **diversity** variety; being made up of unlike parts.

dollar diplomacy use of American political and military power abroad (usually in Latin America) to promote or advance the interests of American businesses.

* **domestic** having to do with the internal affairs of a country.

* **domino theory** belief in the 1950s and 1960s that the fall of one nation to communism would lead to the fall of neighboring nations.

** **due process of law** doctrine that government's power cannot be used against an individual except as prescribed by established law. Applied to the state governments by the Fourteenth Amendment.

* **ecological** concerning the relationship between living things and the environment.

** **economy** the total system for business, production, consumption, and investment in a country.

* **Eisenhower Doctrine** statement made in 1957 by President Eisenhower that the United States would provide military and economic aid—and direct military intervention, if necessary—to nations of the Middle East if they were threatened by communist aggression.

* **elastic clause** part of the **Constitution** (Article I, Section 8) that gives the federal government the right to make laws "necessary and proper" to carry out its specific powers and functions; it has sometimes been used to expand the powers of the federal government; also known as the "necessary and proper clause."

** **election** process of choosing officers by vote.

* **electoral college** means of electing a **president** and vice president established by the **Constitution** and subsequent amendments; voters in each state choose "electors" who later meet to elect the **president** and vice president. Electors were originally free to vote for any candidate they chose, but they are currently

pledged to vote for specific candidates. The number of electors from each state is equal to the number of **Representatives** and **Senators** from that state.

emancipation the act of setting free; freeing from restraint or, especially, slavery.

* **Emancipation Proclamation** issued by President Lincoln in 1863, it declared free the slaves in the Southern states in rebellion but did not affect slaves held in states loyal to the Union, such as Maryland, Kentucky, or Missouri.

* **embargo** prohibition on commerce with a nation or region, usually to apply pressure or force concessions.

* **emigrate** to leave one country or region to settle in another.

encroachment step-by-step interference with the rights or possessions of others.

endorsement approval or recommendation.

* **enjoin** to legally forbid or prohibit, usually by court order or **injunction**.

Enlightenment era during the seventeenth and eighteenth centuries when reason replaced religion as a guide to politics, philosophy, and government.

* **environmentalists** persons concerned about the quality of air, water, and land and the protection of natural resources, "green" space, and plant and animal species.

envoy a messenger or **representative**.

** **equal protection** principle that all people be treated the same under the law.

* **equality** condition of having the same rights, privileges, and advantages as all other citizens.

* **escalate** to increase the extent, level, or volume.

espionage the act or practice of spying.

* **ethnic** belonging to a particular group identified by nationality or national origin and **culture** or customs.

* **ethnocentric** believing that one's own ethnic group is superior to others.

evacuate to remove to a safer area.

* **evolution** change over time; an adjustment in the existing order.

*** **executive** person or office having administrative and managerial functions; in government, the branch responsible for carrying out the laws and for the conduct of national affairs—it includes the **president** and **cabinet** and the departments under their jurisdiction.

* **executive privilege** principle that an **executive** (such as the **president**) should not divulge certain sensitive or protected information.

* **expansionism** policy of adding to a country's territory, usually by seizing land from other nations.

exploitation wrongful or unethical use of someone or something for one's own benefit.

extraterritoriality right of a resident of a foreign country to be tried in the judicial system of his or her home country.

fascism political philosophy advocating **totalitarian** government power, intense **nationalism**, and military **expansionism**. Mussolini's Fascist party governed Italy from the 1920s through World War II.

* **Far East** the nations on the Pacific coast of Asia.

* **favorable balance of trade** exporting or selling more goods than are imported or bought.

*** **federal** relating to the central national government created by the **Constitution**.

Federal Housing Administration federal agency established in 1934 to insure mortgages and set construction standards.

Federal Reserve Note currency or paper money issued by the **Federal Reserve System** and representing a promissory obligation of the federal government. **Federal Reserve Notes** replaced the older gold and silver certificates, which were backed by or based upon specific reserves of gold and silver.

* **Federal Reserve System** federal agency created by Congress in 1913 to regulate the banking system. Federal Reserve banks in 12 districts supervise banking operations, lend money to banks, and issue currency; a Federal Reserve Commission sets and regulates interest rates.

** **federalism** system of government in which powers are divided between a central authority and local subdivisions.

* **Federalists** advocates of adopting the **Constitution** in 1787–1788 and of more powerful central government during the period 1789–1820. Many **Federalists** later joined the **Whig** party.

* **feminism** movement advocating equal rights and privileges for women, including economic, political, legal, and social status.

filibuster use of delaying tactics, such as unlimited debate in the Senate, to prevent action on a legislative proposal.

* **fiscal** having to do with government revenues, expenditures, and budgets.

fission splitting or breaking up; nuclear fission refers to the splitting of an atomic nucleus to release a vast quantity of energy.

fluctuation a series of movements up and down or back and forth.

foreclosure the act of a lender taking possession of mortgaged property from a borrower who is unable to make the required payments.

* **foreign aid** assistance in the form of money or goods supplied to a foreign country.

*** **foreign policy** a nation's policy in dealing with other nations.

* **Fourteen Points** President Wilson's plan for international peace presented to **Congress** on January 22, 1918.

franchise the right to vote; **suffrage**.

* **free enterprise** the freedom of private businesses to operate without undue government interference.

** **free trade** the freedom to exchange goods with other countries, especially without **tariffs**.

* **freedman** a freed slave, usually referring to a former slave freed by virtue of the Thirteenth Amendment.

* **freedom of religion** right of citizens to hold and practice religious beliefs without interference from government.

** **freedom of speech** right of citizens to say or write their views without regulation or reprisal from government; restricted in some cases, *see* **clear and present danger**.

* **freedom of the press** right of publishers to print material without prior approval by government; *see* **prior restraint**.

Freedom Riders civil rights advocates who traveled the South on buses to promote the desegregation of public facilities.

Free-Soil party political party before the Civil War opposed to the extension of slavery and the admission of slave states.

* **frontier** border region between two distinct areas, especially (in America) between settled and unsettled territory. In European usage, a frontier is the border between two countries.

Fugitive Slave Law federal law passed in 1850 that required Northern states to return escaped slaves to their owners in the South. It was widely opposed by a variety of legal and extra-legal means.

* **fundamental rights** *see* **natural rights**.

GAAT General Agreement on Tariffs and Trade signed by 132 countries to lower trade barriers.

gerrymandering drawing the boundaries of election districts to insure the victory of one party or faction by including or excluding neighborhoods of a particular ethnic or social class.

* **global** relating to the world as a whole; international; worldwide.

* **Good Neighbor policy** policy first announced by President Franklin Roosevelt to promote friendly relations with all Latin American nations.

*** **government** the institutions and people responsible for the conduct of public affairs.

Great Compromise agreement in the **Constitutional Convention** of 1787 to have two houses of **Congress**, one (the **Senate**) to represent the states equally and the other (the **House of Representatives**) to represent the people proportionately. Also known as the Connecticut Compromise.

** **Great Depression** period from the stock market crash of 1929 until the start of World War II during which industrial production declined and **unemployment** rose to over one fourth of the labor force.

* **Great Society** collective name for various social programs of President Lyndon Johnson, including the so-called War on Poverty and programs for job training, subsidized housing, and free medical care for the poor and aged.

green revolution the increase in agricultural crop yields brought about by the use of machinery, fertilizers, pesticides, and improved seeds.

greenhouse effect belief that excessive carbon dioxide in the atmosphere caused by burning fossil fuels will create a layer in the upper atmosphere that retains heat and will cause the earth's temperature to rise.

guerilla an active participant in a war who is not a member of the regular armed forces; a kind of warfare characterized by sabotage, harassment, and hit-and-run tactics.

* **habeas corpus** a writ or legal order directed to an official holding a person in custody, commanding the official to produce the person in court, show cause why the person has been confined, and prove that the person has not been deprived of liberty without **due process of law**.

* **Harlem Renaissance** a movement among black writers, artists, and musicians centered in Harlem, New York City, during the 1920s.

Head Start educational aid to preschool children from disadvantaged homes.

health maintenance organization (HMO) organization that provides health services such as hospitalization and doctors' fees to members who make a fixed monthly payment.

Hessians hired soldiers from the district of Hesse in Germany, employed by the British before and during the Revolutionary War.

* **heterogenous** composed of unlike parts; a society made up of different races, nationalities, or ethnic groups.

Holocaust originally, a burnt sacrificial offering; since World War II, it refers to the genocidal murders of millions of European Jews by the Nazis.

home front during a war, the area of a nation's domestic and civilian affairs.

* **Homestead Act** act passed by **Congress** in 1862 that gave 160 acres of Western land to any head of a family who agreed to cultivate it for five years; it encouraged the rapid settlement of the West by giving immigrants and Easterners free land.

* **homogenous** made up of similar elements; a society consisting primarily of the same race, nationality, or **ethnic** group.

hot line direct telephone link, especially between the White House and the Kremlin, always ready for instant communication.

** **House of Representatives** the half of **Congress** composed of representatives allotted among the states according to their population.

*** **immigration** act of moving into a country where one is not a native to become a permanent resident.

* **impeach** to bring formal charges against a public official for misconduct. The **House of Representatives** has the power to impeach federal officials, and the trial is held by the **Senate**.

** **imperialism** the practice of forming and maintaining an empire; possession of foreign territories or colonies for the benefit of the home country; the policy of seeking to dominate economically, politically, or militarily weaker areas of the world.

implementation   the means of accomplishing or carrying out a plan or program.

* **import quota**   a limit on the amount of a commodity that can be brought into the country.

* **inauguration**   a ceremonial beginning, especially the installing of an official at the beginning of a term.

* **incumbent**   person currently serving in political office, especially one seeking reelection.

* **Indians**   European term for the native inhabitants of the Americas; it was based on the mistaken belief that the continents were part of Asia or India.

indictment   a legal action to charge someone with a crime.

* **individualism**   doctrine that the rights and interests of individual persons are the most important source of values.

*** **industrialization**   economic transformation of society by the development of large industries, machine production, factories, and an urban workforce.

* **Industrial Revolution**   the transformation from an agricultural society to one based upon large-scale mechanized production and factory organization. It began in Europe (especially England) in the late eighteenth century and in America in the early nineteenth century.

* **infiltration**   gradual entrance or buildup with the intent of taking control.

* **inflation**   general and continuing rise in the price of goods, often due to the relative increase of available money and credit.

* **initiative**   process for the direct involvement of voters in the making of laws; by gathering enough signatures on a petition, a group can force a legislature to consider a proposal or require it to be placed on the ballot for public vote.

* **injunction**   order issued by a court directing someone to do or refrain from doing some specific act.

* **installment buying**   practice of buying a product through regular monthly or weekly payments; failure to pay gives the seller the right to repossess the product.

insurgency   an uprising or revolt against a government, short of actual war.

* **integration**   bringing together or making as one; unification; applied especially to blacks and whites.

* **interdependent**   depending on one another, such as nations that rely on each other's trade.
* **internal improvements**   roads, canals, and other means to assist transportation and commerce. In the first half of the nineteenth century, debate concerned who should fund internal improvements: the states or the federal government.
** **internationalism**   policy of cooperation among nations.
* **internment**   the detainment and isolation of **ethnic** groups for purposes of national security (such as Japanese Americans during World War II); this is now widely held to have been **unconstitutional**.

interposition   an argument that the states could legitimately object to acts of **Congress** if those acts exceeded **Congress**'s legitimate authority. Interposition fell short of **nullification**.

* **interpret**   to explain or determine the meaning.
* **interstate**   taking place across state lines; involving the citizens of more than one state.
* **Interstate Commerce Commission**   established by **Congress** in 1887 to regulate railroad rates and prevent abuses by railroads; it was later expanded to have **jurisdiction** over other forms of transportation.
* **intervention**   interference in the affairs of another country, including the use of force.

Intolerable Acts   series of acts of **Parliament** directed against the American colonies and intended to assert British authority and increase revenues from the colonies.

invalidate   to make null and void; to destroy the existence or effectiveness of, as, for example, a law.

Iran-Contra Affair   an illegal conspiracy by officials of the Reagan administration to provide funding for the anticommunist Contra rebels in Nicaragua by secretly selling missiles to Iran and diverting the money to the Nicaraguans.

Iron Curtain   the series of fortified borders separating Western Europe from Soviet-dominated Eastern Europe; the term was made popular by Winston Churchill.

** **isolationism**   policy of keeping a nation apart from alliances or other political relations with foreign nations.

* **Jim Crow laws**   laws enforcing **segregation** or control of blacks in such a way as to make them unequal.

* **joint resolution**   a legislative act that is the same in both houses of **Congress**.
* **judicial activism**   developing social policy through court decisions instead of through legislative action, often in response to changing values and circumstances.
* **judicial nationalism**   term used to describe the **Supreme Court** under the leadership of John Marshall, when its decisions consolidated the power of the federal government by centralizing responsibility for commerce, contracts, and finance.
* **judicial restraint**   the preference of a court to avoid upsetting existing law or practice.
** **judicial review**   power of the **Supreme Court** to void acts of **Congress** that are found to violate the **Constitution**.
* **judiciary**   the branch of government that interprets the law and tries cases; the system of courts.
  jurisdiction   authority of a court to interpret and apply the law; in general, the area of authority of a government.

* **Knights of Labor**   early labor union, formed in 1869.
  Kremlin   complex of government offices in Moscow; the center of government of Russia and the Soviet Union.
* **Ku Klux Klan**   secret organization founded in 1866 to intimidate freed slaves and keep them in conditions of servitude through threats and acts of violence; it later developed into a nativist organization opposed to Jews, Catholics, and immigrants, as well as African Americans.

** **laissez-faire**   doctrine opposing government interference or regulation of economic matters beyond what is necessary to maintain property rights and enforce contracts. *Laissez faire* is French for "let alone" or "let be."
  lame duck   an official who has not been reelected and is serving out the remainder of a term.
*** **League of Nations**   international organization of countries formed after World War I to promote world peace. It was supported by President Wilson, but the **Senate** refused to allow the United States to join. After World War II it was replaced by the **United Nations**.
** **legislature**   a body of persons elected to make laws for a nation or state; a congress or parliament.

* **levy**   to place and collect a tax; to draft persons for military service.

liberal   advocating political or social views that emphasize **civil rights**, democratic reforms, and the use of government to promote social progress.

* **liberty**   freedom; the power to do as one pleases.

life expectancy   statistical estimate of the average lifespan of a particular population.

* **limited government**   *see* **constitutionalism**.

* **line-item veto**   power of an **executive** to **veto** specific expenditures without vetoing the entire bill that contains them. Congress gave the **president** a limited line-item veto in 1996.

* **lobbying**   actions by private citizens or organizations seeking to influence (by legal means) the decisions of a **legislature** or **executive** department of government.

* **loose construction, loose interpretation**   reading of the **Constitution** that allows broad use of the **elastic clause** and **implied powers**.

* **Louisiana Purchase**   the purchase from France by the United States in 1803 for $15 million of the Louisiana Territory, stretching from New Orleans west to the Rocky Mountains, more than doubling the size of the United States.

Loyalists   American colonists who remained loyal to England during the American Revolution; also known as **Tories**.

* **Magna Carta**   agreement signed by King John I of England in 1215, granting certain rights (including trial by jury and **habeas corpus**) to the barons who had taken him prisoner.

majority   number greater than one half of the votes cast (simple majority); a "two-thirds majority" requires at least two thirds of the votes cast.

malaise   vague sense of unhappiness or discomfort.

* **Manifest Destiny**   belief, held by many Americans in the nineteenth century, that the United States was destined to control the continent between the Atlantic and Pacific Oceans.

* **market economy**   an economic system in which decisions about production and pricing are based on the actions of buyers and sellers in the marketplace; usually associated with capitalism.

* **Marshall Plan**   the program of U.S. aid to Europe following World War II to help those nations recover from the extensive damage to their cities, industries, and transportation.

materialism   valuing economic or material things more than spiritual or intellectual interests.

* **media**   the industries of mass communication, such as television, radio, and newspapers.

mediator   person who solves differences between two parties. Both sides do not usually agree beforehand to accept the decisions of the mediator, as they usually do with an arbitrator.

* **Medicaid**   federal government program to pay the hospital and medical costs for those on welfare or whose incomes are very low.

* **Medicare**   federal government program to pay the hospital costs of those over age 65 who pay a premium for additional coverage.

* **mercantilism**   the economic policies of European nations from the fifteenth century until the **Industrial Revolution**, based on mercantile (commercial, trading) activities and characterized by the acquisition of colonies and the establishment of a **favorable balance of trade**. The American colonies were established under the mercantile system.

* **middle class**   the members of a society having a socioeconomic position between the very wealthy and the poor.

* **migration**   the movement of people from one place to another.

militancy   aggressive opposition.

* **militaristic**   characterized by military discipline and aggressiveness.

military-industrial complex   the combined power of the Defense Department and the industries that supply it with equipment. The phrase was popularized by Eisenhower, who claimed that it worked for unnecessary increases in armaments.

militia   part-time soldiers who do not belong to the regular armed forces.

** **minority**   the portion of a group less than one half; an **ethnic** or racial group that is smaller than the dominant group and may be subjected to **discrimination**.

* **Miranda rights**   constitutionally guaranteed rights of those accused of crimes to be informed by the police that they have a right to remain silent, a right to an attorney, and a right to be supplied with legal counsel if they cannot afford a private attorney; established by *Miranda v. Arizona* (1966).

Missouri Compromise an agreement in 1820 between congressional advocates and opponents of the extension of **slavery** that preserved sectional balance. It included the simultaneous admission of the slave state Missouri and the free state Maine and the prohibition of slavery in the northern parts of the **Louisiana Purchase**.

** **monopoly** the exclusive control or ownership of an industry by a single person or company.

* **Monroe Doctrine** policy announced in 1823, during the presidency of James Monroe, that the United States would oppose European attempts to extend their control of the Western Hemisphere. It became and remains a basic principle of American foreign policy.

moratorium agreement to postpone payment of a debt or other obligation.

mortgage legal instrument specifying payments to be made on a loan for the purchase of property. Failure to make payments gives the mortgager the legal right to repossess the property.

* **muckraker** journalists in the late nineteenth and early twentieth centuries who reported on political or commercial corruption.

* **multicultural** different cultural beliefs and practices followed by different ethnic groups living in harmony within the same community.

multinational involving more than two nations.

municipality a city or local political unit.

munitions armaments and ammunition used in warfare.

NAFTA North American Free Trade Agreement (1993). An agreement ratified during President Clinton's first administration to eliminate trade barriers between the United States, Canada, and Mexico.

* **nationalism** (1) sense of pride in one's country; (2) extreme devotion to national interests.

* **National Labor Relations Board** federal agency established in 1935 to enforce laws against unfair labor practices.

* **National Origins Act** laws passed in 1921, 1924, and 1929 that limited **immigration** into the United States and established **quotas** for nations based on the number of persons from those

nations living in the United States according to an earlier **census**. It was regarded as **discriminatory** because it favored immigrants from Western Europe.

native   one who is connected with a place by birth; an original inhabitant as distinguished from immigrants or visitors.

** **Native Americans**   descendants of the original inhabitants of the Americas.

* **nativism**   in the United States, the policy of favoring native-born Americans and opposing immigrants.

* **natural rights**   rights or liberties to which one is entitled as a human being.

necessary and proper clause   portion of the **Constitution** granting **Congress** power to "make all Laws which shall be necessary and proper for carrying into Execution" its other powers.

** **neutrality**   policy of not helping either side in a war.

* **Neutrality Acts**   laws passed in 1935 and 1937 to avoid U.S. involvement in a war in Europe; they placed an embargo on arms sales to any nation engaged in war.

*** **New Deal**   name adopted by President Franklin Roosevelt for the reforms and social programs instituted by his administration, beginning in 1933.

* **New Freedom**   program of President Wilson to regulate banking and **currency** to influence the direction of the economy and to support stronger **antitrust** legislation.

* **New Nationalism**   program of President Theodore Roosevelt during his unsuccessful campaign for the presidency in 1912. It promised greater government supervision of the economy to balance the power of **big business**.

* **Nineteenth Amendment**   granted **suffrage** (the right to vote) to women; enacted in 1920.

* **nomination**   proposal of a candidate for an office.

nonintervention   policy of not becoming involved in the affairs of other nations.

* **nonpartisan**   not based on party interests or bias.

nonsectarian   not affiliated with any religious group.

* **nonviolence**   principle that all violence is to be avoided; the use of peaceful means for political ends.

* **normalcy**   the state of being normal; the term was applied to the era of the 1920s, following the disruptions of World War I.

* **North Atlantic Treaty Organization (NATO) collective security** military alliance formed in 1949 by the United States, Canada, and nations of Western Europe to oppose the threat posed by the Soviet Union and Warsaw Pact nations to Europe.

Northwest Territory federal administrative district west of the Allegheny Mountains, north of the Ohio River, south of the Great Lakes, and east of the Mississippi River, including the present states of Ohio, Indiana, Michigan, Illinois, and Wisconsin, and part of Minnesota. The Territory was organized by the **Continental Congress** in 1787 from lands claimed by several eastern states.

nullification argument or doctrine claiming that states could refuse to abide by acts of **Congress** if the states felt **Congress** had exceeded its enumerated powers. Used by states' rights advocates; championed by John C. Calhoun of South Carolina.

* **Nuremberg Tribunal** international military court held in Nuremberg, Germany, in 1945–46; top Nazi leaders were tried and convicted of crimes against humanity and violations of international law.

* **Open Door policy** an attempt by the United States in 1899 to preserve trade interests in China by asking European nations to respect the territorial integrity of China and to permit free access to ports they held in Asia.

ordinance a law or regulation, usually of a local municipality.

*** **organized labor** workers represented by labor unions.

original jurisdiction the first court with authority to consider and decide a case, as opposed to appellate jurisdiction.

* **overproduction** production of a commodity in excess of the demand for it; it usually results in falling prices.

* **parity** government support of prices for agricultural products to insure that farm income keeps pace with income in other economic sectors.

* **Parliament** the legislative body of Great Britain, consisting of the House of Commons and the House of Lords.

partition division of a country into two or more separate parts.

* **Peace Corps** U.S. government agency formed by President Kennedy in 1961; it sought to assist developing countries by sending American volunteers to teach and provide technical assistance.

penal having to do with punishment; liable to be punished.

Pentagon headquarters of the U.S. armed forces, near Washington, D.C.

* **per capita** the average per person for a particular population, as in per capita income.

perjury making a false statement under oath.

* **philanthropy** literally, the love of mankind; desire to help humankind, usually through gifts or endowments to charitable institutions.

* **picketing** method of demonstration by workers or political groups, usually taking place at the employer or the offices of the opposition; it includes notifying the public of the unfairness of the employer with signs and conversation.

plea bargaining pleading guilty to a lesser charge in order to avoid standing trial for a more serious one.

* **pluralistic** type of society in which diverse **ethnic**, racial, and national groups coexist while maintaining their own cultural heritage.

* **plurality** a number of votes greater than any other candidate but less than a majority of all the votes cast.

pocket veto an automatic veto that occurs if the **president** does not sign a bill passed by **Congress** during the last ten days of its session.

pogrom organized, officially encouraged persecution or massacre of a group.

political machine combination of party and political officials who maintain themselves in office, sometimes through corrupt means.

*** **politics** the practice of government; the art of winning control of public affairs.

* **poll tax** (1) a tax paid to register or vote in elections (prohibited under the Twenty-fourth Amendment). (2) a per-person or per-capita tax, not based on income or employment.

* **pollution** the contamination of the atmosphere by burning of automobile and smokestack emissions or the contamination of water by chemicals dumped into streams by factories or by fertilizers washed into water sources by rainfall.

popular sovereignty (1) doctrine in democratic forms of government that power ultimately derives from the people and that the consent of the governed is exercised through the vote; (2) in the years before the Civil War, a political position advocating that the legality of **slavery** in the western territories be decided by popular vote of the inhabitants; it was ridiculed by its opponents as "squatter sovereignty."

* **populism**   movement that began in agricultural areas in the late nineteenth century seeking government regulation to curb excesses and exploitation by big business.

pragmatism   belief in a practical (rather than an ethical or theoretical) approach to problems and affairs.

* **Preamble**   introductory part, especially the opening of the **Constitution**, which begins "We the people...."

precedence   the right to be first or have more authority.

precedent   rule or decision that serves as a guide for future actions or decisions; attorneys look for precedents to support their arguments when presenting a case in court.

* **prejudice**   a preconceived opinion or judgment, usually negative, not based on fact.

preside   to act as chairman.

*** **president**   the chief executive officer of the federal government.

* **press**   the news-gathering and publishing industry, including television, radio, magazines, and newspapers.

* **price supports**   government measures to maintain the price of a commodity at an artificially set level.

prior restraint   the prohibition of publication of an article, book, or story by a court order before the material is disclosed to the public. Permissable only in cases of obscenity or of **"clear and present danger."**

* **primary election**   election in which members of a political party choose their candidates for the coming general elections.

* **processing tax**   a tax on industries that convert raw materials into finished goods, such as cotton into cloth.

* **Progressive Era**   the period roughly from 1900 to 1920, marked by political, economic, and social reform movements.

* **progressive tax**   a tax that is higher for the wealthy than for the poor, such as income tax.

* **progressivism**   a broad reform movement during the late nineteenth and early twentieth centuries that sought to remedy the worst effects of industrialism and **urbanization** by imposing governmental controls on **big business**, improving social justice, and increasing direct democratic participation in politics.

* **prohibition** period from the enactment of the Eighteenth Amendment in 1919 until its repeal by the Twenty-first Amendment in 1933, during which the manufacture, sale, import, export, and transportation of alcoholic beverages was declared illegal.

proletariat the industrial working class, who sell their labor and do not own the means of production.

propaganda promotion of particular ideas and doctrines.

* **protective tariff** tax on imported goods intended to protect the interests of internal or domestic industries by raising the price of imports.

protectorate an area under the control and protection of a country that does not have full **sovereignty** over it.

proviso clause in a document or statute making some condition or provision.

* **purse** the power to authorize revenues and spending; in the federal government, **Congress** holds the power of the purse.

quarantine isolation of a person or country, usually to prevent spread of communicable diseases.

quartering forcibly housing soldiers in private residences.

* **quota** a maximum limit; a share or portion assigned to a group.

** **racism** belief that some races are inherently superior to others.
* **radical, radicalism** favoring extreme and fundamental changes.
*** **ratification** formal legal approval and adoption.
* **raw materials** products or resources not yet manufactured into their final state, as many agricultural products, lumber, or ores.

rearmament rebuilding of a nation's armed forces, often with new and better weapons.

* **recall** political reform procedure for removing a public official from office before the end of a term by popular vote; it is usually initiated by a petition.

** **Reconstruction** period from 1865 through 1876, when the Southern states were occupied by federal troops and under the direct control of the national government.

* **Red Scare** fears about the danger of **communist** subversion or invasion; especially after World War II, "Red Scare" tactics were used by Senator Joseph McCarthy and others for political purposes.

* **referendum** a proposal submitted to a popular vote before putting it into effect.

refinance to change the terms of a **mortgage** or loan to make it easier for the borrower to make the payments.

*** **reform** to improve or change, especially a social institution.

** **regulatory** enforcing the rules or laws.

rehabilitation restoration to a former or better condition.

* **relocation** the movement (sometimes by force) of a group of people to a new place.

* **reparations** payments imposed on nations defeated in war to help the victors recover the costs of war.

repercussion a widespread or indirect effect of an act.

** **representative** 1) a **delegate** or agent of another person or group of people; 2) a federal legislator; 3) a type of government by persons chosen from among the governed, usually by election.

* **Republican party** political party formed in the 1840s, opposed to the extension of **slavery**; Lincoln was the first Republican elected president (in 1860).

repudiate to disown or disavow.

* **reserved powers** powers not specifically granted to **Congress** or the federal government under the **Constitution**, and so held to be reserved to the states.

* **restraint of trade** language used in the **Sherman Antitrust Act** (1890) to describe combinations and activities of groups (businesses, labor unions) that were prohibited under the Act.

* **retaliatory** done in response to an attack or **aggression**; strong enough to deter an attack.

* **revenue** the income of governments from taxation, **tariffs**, fees, and other activities.

* **reverse discrimination** **discrimination** against whites or males.

* **revolution** rapid change, often accompanied by violence.

* **right to counsel** entitlement of an accused person to have an attorney present during questioning.

* **rights** individual liberties protected by the state or federal constitutions.

Rights of Englishmen an expression of the American colonists during their struggle with England; they claimed to want only the same liberties and privileges enjoyed by British subjects in England, as established by **Magna Carta**, common law, and the

English Bill of Rights, including **habeas corpus**, trial by jury, and representation in **Parliament**.

** **rights of the accused** include the Fifth Amendment guarantee against self-incrimination and the **right to counsel**; also known as **"Miranda rights,"** after the **Supreme Court** decision in the case of *Miranda v. Arizona* (1966).

* **Roaring Twenties** the 1920s, during which the United States returned to "normalcy" after World War I, with rapid economic expansion, changed social values, high spending for consumer goods, and the popularization of the automobile, radio, and motion pictures.

* **Roosevelt Corollary** supplement to the **Monroe Doctrine** asserted by President Theodore Roosevelt, who claimed the right of the United States to exercise international police power in the Western Hemisphere and to intervene in the affairs of Latin American nations.

* **"Rule of Reason"** term used by the **Supreme Court** in its decision in the case of *Standard Oil Co. v. United States* (1911), which held that only "bad" trusts were illegal.

* **ruling** an official decision.

** **SALT II** Strategic Arms Limitation Treaty signed by the United States and the Soviet Union to limit the number of bombers capable of carrying nuclear weapons; signed in 1979 as a major step in reducing the danger of nuclear war; a follow up to SALT I, which was the first step taken to slow the increase in nuclear weapons.

salutary neglect phrase describing the belief that the American colonies benefitted from lack of interest in their affairs by the British government during the period before 1763.

sanctuary place of refuge or protection.

satellite state a nation controlled by a more powerful nation.

* **Scopes trial** the trial of John T. Scopes in Dayton, Tennessee, in 1925 for violating a state law prohibiting the teaching of Darwinian evolution. The highly publicized trial featured William Jennings Bryan as prosecutor and Clarence Darrow for the defense. Scopes was found guilty and fined $100.

* **search and seizure** police power to look for and hold evidence in the investigation and prosecution of a crime; evidence from

unreasonable searches or searches without probable cause may be excluded from a trial.

* **secession** withdrawal of a member from a political group; withdrawal of a state from the Union.

* **second-class citizenship** condition of having fewer or inferior rights and privileges.

* **sectionalism** development of internal divisions based on geographic and economic alliances; rivalry between different areas of the country.

* **Securities and Exchange Commission** federal agency established in 1934 to regulate the stock market and to prevent the abuses practiced during the 1920s that led to the **stock market crash** of 1929.

security safety; freedom from danger.

sedition the act of stirring up rebellion against a government.

** **segregation** the isolation or separation of one group from another, usually applied to keeping whites and blacks apart.

*** **Senate** the half of the federal legislature made up of two members from each state.

** **separate but equal** legal doctrine established by the **Supreme Court** in the case of *Plessy v. Ferguson* (1896) that separate accommodations for blacks and whites did not violate the Fourteenth Amendment if the accommodations were of equal quality. Overruled by the later **Supreme Court** decision in *Brown v. Board of Education* (1954).

* **separation of church and state** doctrine that government may not restrict the free exercise of religious beliefs nor support any religious group or principle.

** **separation of powers** doctrine that liberty of the people is best assured by the division of government into separate branches. *See also* **checks and balances**.

* **sexual harassment** policy or practice of compelling female employees to submit to the sexual advances of male superiors or to endure verbal or physical harassment, in violation of the Civil Rights Act of 1964.

* **sharecroppers** tenant farmers who leased and cultivated pieces of land in exchange for a percentage of the crop.

Shays' Rebellion armed insurrection in western Massachusetts in the fall of 1786 led by Captain Daniel Shays and others in protest against economic policies and foreclosures of farms for failure to pay taxes. It was suppressed by the state **militia**, but it had a significant effect on the framing of the **Constitution** the following summer.

* **Sherman Antitrust Act**   passed in 1890 declaring combinations in restraint of trade to be illegal; it was passed to maintain competition in private industry and to correct abuses of companies that had gained **monopoly** power.

* **sit-in**   action of protesters in occupying a public place to force concessions; especially by **civil rights** advocates seeking **desegregation** of public facilities.

** **slavery**   system of holding persons against their will for involuntary servitude; in a system of "chattel slavery" the person held could be bought or sold as property. Slavery in the United States was abolished by the Thirteenth Amendment.

smokestack industries   heavy industries that burn large amounts of fossil fuels, such as steel-making or auto manufacturing.

social contract   the implied agreement among individuals in a community or between the people and their rulers.

* **socialism**   political philosophy advocating ownership and operation of the means of production (such as land, mines, factories) by society as a collective whole, with all members sharing in the work and benefits. Socialist economic systems usually include government ownership and operation of industries.

* **social mobility**   movement up or down the class scale within a society.

* **Social Security Act**   passed in 1935 to provide an income for persons who are disabled or aged and for families without a wage earner; it has become the basic means of support for retired persons who lack private pensions from employers.

** **social welfare**   organized services for helping disadvantaged people.

* **sovereign**   holding supreme authority.

* **sovereignty**   the ultimate power and authority to make laws, either directly or through representatives; in a democracy, sovereignty lies in the people.

space satellite   an object in space that orbits a planet or other body on a regular path.

* **special interest**   group or industry that seeks to influence government for its own benefit.

* **speculation** taking extreme risks in business or investing in hopes of earning large profits.

spoils system system wherein government positions and offices are awarded to political supporters on the basis of party loyalty or service rather than qualification or merit; based on the saying "To the victor go the spoils"; the system was replaced to some extent by the **Civil Service**, beginning in the 1880s.

stability the ability to remain unchanged or permanent.

* **Stamp Act** act enacted by **Parliament** in 1765 that required a tax stamp on all printed and legal documents. It was soon repealed due to American resistance.

* **START II** Strategic Arms Reduction Treaty signed in 1993 by the United States and Russia to reduce the number of nuclear warheads held by each nation by half; a follow-up to START I in 1991, which was the first agreement for each nation to scrap some of its nuclear weapons.

statehood condition of being a state and a full member of the United States; for example, Hawaii achieved statehood in 1959.

*** **states' rights** group of doctrines holding that the states retained the power to overrule, oppose, or withdraw from the federal government if they chose.

* **stock market crash** a rapid fall in the price of **stocks**. The great crash of 1929 was caused by overspeculation that increased stock prices far above their true value; prices started to fall when knowledgeable investors began to sell their shares; that forced speculators, who had invested with borrowed money, to sell as well, and the combined rush to sell caused a panic, which drove prices even lower.

* **stocks** certificates showing shares of ownership in a **corporation**.

strict construction doctrine that the **Constitution** limits governmental powers to those explicitly stated; *contrast with* **loose construction**.

** **strike** work stoppage by labor in an attempt to force the employer to make concessions.

* **subjugation** the act of bringing under control.

subpoena official written order commanding a person to appear in court or to produce specific items.

subsidiary in business, a company that is controlled by another company.

subterranean below the surface of the earth.

subversion the undermining, overthrowing, or destroying of an established institution, such as government.

** **suffrage** the right to vote.

supremacy the highest power or authority.

supremacy clause portion of the **Constitution** declaring it "the supreme law of the land" and overriding any state or local laws in conflict with it.

*** **Supreme Court** the highest court in the federal judicial branch.

surcharge an extra charge.

synthetic artificially produced or man-made by combinations of chemicals.

* **tariff** taxes on imports into a country to collect revenues or to protect domestic industries.

* **Teapot Dome** federal oil reserve in Wyoming that was secretly and illegally leased to a financial backer of President Harding.

** **technology** applied science used in production.

temperance moderation in the consumption of alcoholic beverages; a movement supporting governmental measures to curb alcohol consumption.

Tennessee Valley Authority federal public works project established in 1933 that constructed dams and reengineered waterways to control flooding and generate electricity in seven southern states.

tenure the act or right of holding an office.

* **term limits** legislation that limits elected officials to a set number of years in office, usually 8 to 12 years or 2 to 3 terms; a concept that has become popular in recent years and has been applied to elected officials in a number of states.

** **third parties** political parties existing at various times in the United States other than the two predominate political parties.

Third World the group of nations, especially in Asia and Africa, that were not aligned with either the communist **bloc** or the Western democracies.

* **three-fifths clause** clause in the **Constitution** saying that three fifths of the number of persons held as slaves be included in calculating representation in **Congress**, even though those persons were not citizens and were not entitled to vote. Superceded by the Fourteenth Amendment.

Tories   supporters of British rule during the Revolutionary War; also known as **Loyalists**. In England, the Tory party generally supported the king or conservative interests.

totalitarian   characterized by the state or government having total control over the lives of citizens.

town meeting   meeting of the citizens of a town as a legislative body.

* **trade deficit**   the amount by which imports exceed exports; how much is owed to other nations.

* **trade gap**   difference in amount between imports and exports.

treason   acts that intentionally endanger the security or **sovereignty** of one's own nation; waging war against one's country or giving aid to its enemies.

triangular trade   pattern of commerce pursued in the late eighteenth and early nineteenth centuries by New England merchants who carried sugar and molasses from the West Indies to New England, rum and manufactured goods from New England to Africa, and slaves from Africa to the West Indies.

* **Truman Doctrine**   policy announced by President Truman in 1947, stating that the United States would provide military and economic aid to nations threatened by subversion or invasion; it was established specifically to assist Greece and Turkey, which were threatened with communist takeover.

** **trust**   a combination of companies or industries established to reduce competition and increase profits.

* **turnout**   the number of eligible voters who participate in an election.

tyranny   absolute and arbitrary power without legal restraints.

unconditional surrender   total surrender without exceptions or conditions; the phrase was made popular by Ulysses S. Grant.

* **unconstitutional**   prohibited by or in opposition to the principles of the **Constitution**.

* **underclass**   class of the permanently poor.

** **unemployment**   being out of work; government compensation to people who have lost their jobs.

* **unicameral**   of a legislature, having only one house or chamber.

*** **union**   1) the political combination of the states; 2) the Northern and border states that opposed **secession** during the Civil War;

3) an organization of workers seeking **collective bargaining** with their employer.

** **United Nations (UN)**   international organization established in 1945 to preserve peace; currently has 185 members. Security Council made up of five permanent members (United States, Russia, China, Great Britain, and France) and ten nonpermanent members can cause military action, as it did during the Korean War and the Persian Gulf War, the deployment of peacekeeping forces to monitor cease-fire agreements, as it's done in the Middle East and Bosnia, and can impose economic sanctions, as it has done with Iraq, Yugoslavia, and South Africa.

* **universal suffrage**   the right of all citizens to vote, regardless of sex, race, or economic status.

* **Unwritten Constitution**   governmental practices and institutions not specifically set down in the **Constitution** but based upon custom and practice.

* **urbanization**   the growth of cities and the increasing concentration of population in them.

utilities   companies that furnish electric power, water, gas, or other services without competition and are regulated by law.

utopian   advocating impossibly idealistic or impractical forms of government or society.

* **Versailles Treaty**   peace treaty signed in 1919 between Germany and the Allies; it required Germany to give up its colonies, pay substantial reparations, and surrender territory to France, Poland, and Czechoslovakia.

* **veto**   action by an executive official preventing the enactment of a legislative act. A veto by the **president** can be overridden by a two-thirds majority of **Congress**.

VISTA   Volunteers in Service to America, a program of President Johnson's 1964 Economic Opportunity Act.

* **war crimes**   crimes against humanity; actions commited by armed forces against civilian populations during military conflicts, including genocide, murder, rape, extermination, deportation, enslavement, and persecutions on religious, racial, or political grounds; actions under jurisdiction of war crimes tribunals established under international law.

* **War on Poverty** President Johnson's domestic programs for social renovation, including the **VISTA**, Job Corps, and **Head Start** programs and the establishing of the Department of Housing and Urban Development.
* **War Powers Act** law passed in 1973 to limit the power of the **president** to use armed forces in combat without the authorization of **Congress**; it was adopted in response to the Vietnam War, in which millions of armed forces were sent to Vietnam without a declaration of war.
* **Watergate** hotel in Washington, D.C., where the national Democratic party headquarters were burglarized in 1972 by operatives of the Republican Committee to Reelect the President (Nixon). Attempts by the staff of the White House to cover up their links to the burglars eventually led to a widespread scandal and the resignation of President Nixon.
* **welfare** a government social support program to provide a limited income to people who are unemployable because of age or physical or mental condition or who are unemployed because they lack skills or initiative or because the economy has not created enough jobs; a program that has become more restrictive in recent years by limiting the number of people eligible to receive benefits or the number of years a person may receive benefits.
* **Whigs** in the United States from around 1800 until the Civil War, a political party opposed to the Jeffersonian Republicans and Jacksonian Democrats. Many of its supporters later joined the **Republican party**. In England, the Whig party generally opposed the extension of the king's power and supported the predominance of **Parliament**.
* **Whiskey Rebellion** armed insurrection in 1792 by settlers in western Pennsylvania and Virginia protesting federal excise tax on distilled spirits (whiskey). Suppressed by federal troops under Washington, who pardoned most of the participants.
* **Whitewater** (1994) name of an investigation in which legal questions arose regarding Arkansas land investments made by President and Mrs. Clinton. Attorney General Janet Reno appointed Kenneth Starr as independent counsel to investigate the charges. On Wednesday, September 20, 2000, Special Prosecutor Robert Ray concluded the investigation without

charging the Clintons with wrongdoing, saying there was insufficient evidence to prove they "knowingly participated in any criminal conduct."

work ethic   belief in the value and moral good of productive labor.

* **World Trade Organization (WTO)**   a specialized agency of the United Nations that is the most important organization supervising international trade; administers trade agreements, monitors trade policies and practices of nations, tries to settle trade disputes, and keeps track of statistics on trade.

Yalta Agreements   agreements reached between Roosevelt, Churchill, and Stalin at Yalta in February 1945, regarding the organization of post-war Europe in anticipation of the defeat of Germany. The agreements divided Germany and Berlin into temporary zones of occupation and established the basis for the **United Nations**.

yellow journalism   irresponsible, sensational, or misleading reporting of news.

Regents Examinations, Answers, Self-Analysis Charts, and Regents Specification Grids

Examination August 2008

United States History and Government

PART I: MULTIPLE CHOICE

Directions (1–50): For each statement or question, write in the space provided the *number* of the word or expression that, of those given, best completes the statement or answers the question.

Base your answers to questions 1 and 2 on the map below and on your knowledge of social studies. Each letter on the map represents a specific geographic feature.

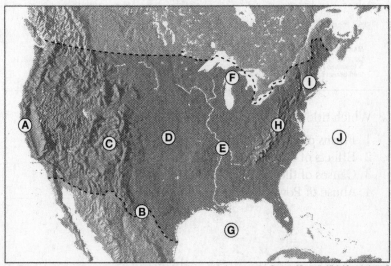

Source: *Mountain High Maps* (adapted)

1 Which geographic feature most limited the westward movement of American colonists before 1750?

1 *H*   3 *C*

2 *I*   4 *F*   1____

2 At the end of the Revolutionary War, which geographic feature became the western boundary of the United States?

1 *A*   3 *E*

2 *B*   4 *G*   2____

Base your answer to question 3 on the time line below and on your knowledge of social studies.

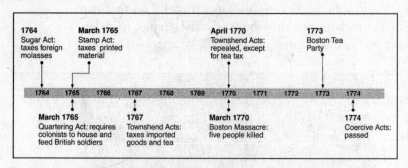

1764
Sugar Act:
taxes foreign
molasses

March 1765
Stamp Act:
taxes printed
material

April 1770
Townshend Acts:
repealed, except
for tea tax

1773
Boston Tea
Party

1764 1765 1766 1767 1768 1769 1770 1771 1772 1773 1774

March 1765
Quartering Act: requires
colonists to house and
feed British soldiers

1767
Townshend Acts:
taxes imported
goods and tea

March 1770
Boston Massacre:
five people killed

1774
Coercive Acts:
passed

3 Which title is most accurate for this time line?

1 Forms of Colonial Protest

2 Effects of British Navigation Laws

3 Causes of the American Revolution

4 Abuse of Power by Colonial Legislatures   3____

4 The Land Ordinance of 1785 and the Northwest Ordinance of 1787 are considered achievements under the Articles of Confederation because they

  1 established processes for settling and governing the western territories

  2 settled boundary disputes with Great Britain and Spain

  3 provided the basic methods of collecting taxes and coining money

  4 created a system of state and federal courts   4____

5 "The powers not delegated to the United States by the Constitution, nor prohibited by it to the States, are reserved to the States respectively, or to the people."

           — United States Constitution, 10th amendment

This part of the Bill of Rights was intended to

  1 give the people the right to vote on important issues

  2 reduce the rights of citizens

  3 limit the powers of the federal government

  4 assure federal control over the states   5____

6 The creation of the presidential cabinet and political parties are examples of

  1 the unwritten constitution

  2 separation of powers

  3 the elastic clause

  4 judicial review   6____

7 The term *supreme law of the land* refers to which document?

  1 Fundamental Orders of Connecticut
  2 Constitution of the United States
  3 Articles of Confederation
  4 Declaration of Independence   7 _____

8 Which principle of the United States Constitution is intended to ensure that no one branch of government has more power than another branch?

  1 checks and balances
  2 federalism
  3 limited government
  4 rule of law   8 _____

9 A geographic and economic motivation for the Louisiana Purchase (1803) was the desire to

  1 annex California
  2 secure land for the Erie Canal
  3 control the port of New Orleans
  4 own all of the Great Lakes   9 _____

10 The principal goal of the supporters of Manifest Destiny in the 1840s was to

  1 convince Canada to become part of the United States
  2 expand United States territory to the Pacific Ocean
  3 build a canal across Central America
  4 acquire naval bases in the Caribbean   10 _____

11 The climate and topography of the southeastern United States had a major impact on the history of the United States before 1860 because the region

  1 became the center of commerce and manufacturing

  2 developed as the largest domestic source of steel production

  3 was the area in which most immigrants chose to settle

  4 provided agricultural products that were processed in the North and in Europe   11____

12 Abolitionists in the pre–Civil War period were most likely to support the

  1 removal of the Cherokee Indians from Georgia

  2 passage of the Fugitive Slave Act

  3 activities of the Underground Railroad

  4 use of popular sovereignty in the territories   12____

13 Which Supreme Court decision created the need for a constitutional amendment that would grant citizenship to formerly enslaved persons?

  1 *Marbury* v. *Madison*

  2 *McCulloch* v. *Maryland*

  3 *Worcester* v. *Georgia*

  4 *Dred Scott* v. *Sanford*   13____

Base your answer to question 14 on the quotation below and on your knowledge of social studies.

. . . With malice toward none, with charity for all, with firmness in the right as God gives us to see the right, let us strive on to finish the work we are in, to bind up the nation's wounds, to care for him who shall have borne the battle and for his widow and his orphan, to do all which may achieve and cherish a just and lasting peace among ourselves and with all nations.

— Abraham Lincoln, Second Inaugural Address, March 4, 1865

14 This statement reveals President Lincoln's support for

1 a new peace treaty with Great Britain
2 universal male suffrage
3 a fair and generous peace
4 harsh punishment for Confederate leaders

14 _____

15 The passage of Jim Crow laws in the South after Reconstruction was aided in part by

1 a narrow interpretation of the 14th amendment by the United States Supreme Court
2 a change in the southern economy from agricultural to industrial
3 the growth of Republican-dominated governments in the South
4 the rise in European immigration to the South

15 _____

16 During the late 1800s, pools and trusts were used by big business in an effort to

1 increase imports
2 limit competition
3 improve working conditions
4 reduce corporate income taxes

16 _____

17 In the late 1800s, which group most often supported the views of the Populist Party?

   1 factory owners   3 farmers
   2 nativists   4 labor unions   17____

18 . . ."You are our employers, but you are not our
masters. Under the system of government we have
in the United States we are your equals, and we
contribute as much, if not more, to the success of
industry than do the employers." . . .

         — testimony, United States Congress, April 29, 1911

The point of view expressed in the quotation was
most likely that of a

   1 recent immigrant responding to discrimination
   2 government official campaigning for reelection
   3 woman demanding the right of suffrage
   4 labor leader speaking about the rights of workers   18____

19 In the late 1800s and early 1900s, many members
of Congress supported legislation requiring literacy
tests for immigrants in an attempt to

   1 stop illegal immigration from Latin America
   2 provide highly skilled workers for industry
   3 limit the power of urban political machines
   4 restrict immigration from southern and eastern
      Europe   19____

20 **"Hawaiian Planters Urge American Annexation"**

"U.S. and Germany Negotiate for Control of the Samoan Islands"

"U.S. Gains Control of Wake Island and Guam"

Which conclusion can best be drawn from these headlines?

1 The Anti-Imperialist League strongly influenced Congress.
2 Respect for native cultures motivated United States foreign policy.
3 United States territorial expansion increased in the Pacific Ocean.
4 Construction of a railroad to Alaska was a major policy goal. 20 _____

21 The Federal Reserve System was created in 1913 to

   1 protect endangered species
   2 reduce tariff rates
   3 collect income taxes
   4 regulate the nation's money supply 21 _____

22 The initiative and referendum are considered democratic reforms because they

   1 permit citizens to have a more direct role in law-making
   2 let all registered voters select their state's presidential electors
   3 extend the right to vote to 18-year-old citizens
   4 allow residents of one state to bring lawsuits against residents of another state 22 _____

23 During the early 1900s, the term *muckrakers* was used to describe

1 pacifists who demonstrated against war
2 writers who exposed the evils in American society
3 newspaper columnists who reported on celebrities
4 politicians who criticized Progressive Era presidents   23 _____

24 President Woodrow Wilson's policy of strict neutrality during the early years of World War I was challenged by

1 German violations of freedom of the seas
2 British disrespect for the Roosevelt corollary
3 attacks by Mexicans on United States border towns
4 the refusal of the League of Nations to supply peacekeepers   24 _____

25 What was a main result of national Prohibition during the 1920s?

1 Respect for the law decreased.
2 Woman's suffrage was restricted.
3 Racial prejudice increased.
4 Religious tolerance grew.   25 _____

26 Which foreign policy did Warren G. Harding support when he used the phrase "return to normalcy" during his presidential campaign of 1920?

1 appeasement   3 containment
2 internationalism   4 isolationism   26 _____

27 Which event led to the start of the Great Depression?

1 Red Scare (1919–1920)
2 election of President Herbert Hoover (1928)
3 stock market crash (1929)
4 passage of the Emergency Banking Act (1933)   27 ____

Base your answer to question 28 on the cartoon below and on your knowledge of social studies.

Until He Gets the Key the Door Cannot Be Opened

"The people in this country whose incomes are less than two thousand dollars a year buy more than two-thirds of the goods sold."
— President Roosevelt

Source: G. R. Spencer, *Omaha World-Herald*, 1934 (adapted)

28 Based on this cartoon, economic recovery would require

1 fewer regulations by the federal government
2 increased taxes on the working class
3 more money in the hands of lower-income families
4 protective tariffs on foreign goods   28 ____

Base your answers to questions 29 and 30 on the song below and on your knowledge of social studies.

Brother, Can You Spare a Dime?

They used to tell me I was building a dream
And so I followed the mob.
When there was earth to plow or guns to bear,
I was always there, right on the job.
They used to tell me I was building a dream
With peace and glory ahead —
Why should I be standing in line, just waiting
    for bread?

Once I built a railroad, I made it run,
Made it race against time.
Once I built a railroad, now it's done —
Brother, can you spare a dime? . . .

Once in khaki suits, gee, we looked swell
Full of that Yankee Doodle-de-dum.
Half a million boots went slogging through hell,
And I was the kid with the drum. . . .

— E. Y. Harburg and J. Gorney, 1932

29 Which statement most accurately expresses the main idea of this song?

  1   Railroad workers were often overpaid.
  2   The average wage in 1930 was 10 cents an hour.
  3   Soldiers never have difficulty finding jobs when they return from war.
  4   Hard times threaten economic opportunity.   29 ____

30 Which program was created to deal with the problem identified in this song?

  1   Interstate Commerce Commission (ICC)
  2   Works Progress Administration (WPA)
  3   Federal Trade Commission (FTC)
  4   Federal Deposit Insurance Corporation (FDIC)   30 ____

31 President Franklin D. Roosevelt's reelection in 1940 created a controversy that eventually led to

1 the Supreme Court declaring the election unconstitutional
2 the establishment of presidential term limits
3 an effort to increase voter participation
4 an attempt to increase the number of Justices on the Supreme Court   31 ____

Base your answers to questions 32 and 33 on the map below and on your knowledge of social studies.

Relocation Centers for Japanese Americans from the West Coast, 1942–1945

Source: National Park Service,
U.S. Department of the Interior (adapted)

32 Which statement is best supported by the information on the map?

1 Government officials used abandoned mining towns to house Japanese Americans.
2 Western states did not support the decision to create the relocation centers.
3 Relocation centers had to be placed near rivers.
4 The government considered Japanese Americans a threat to national security.   32 ____

33 The relocation camps shown on the map were mainly a reaction to the

  1 Japanese military attack on Pearl Harbor
  2 capture of Japanese war prisoners
  3 need to train Japanese Americans for military service
  4 attacks by Japanese Americans on United States military bases　　　　33____

34 The D-Day invasion in June 1944 was important to the outcome of World War II because it

  1 opened a new Allied front in Europe
  2 avoided use of the atomic bomb against civilian targets
  3 forced Italy to surrender
  4 stopped Soviet advances in eastern Europe　　　　34____

35 The Marshall Plan (1948–1952) was a United States effort to assist the nations of Europe by

  1 forming a strong military alliance
  2 providing economic aid
  3 sending United States troops to trouble spots
  4 continuing Lend-Lease aid to the Soviet Union　　　　35____

Base your answers to questions 36 and 37 on the statement below and on your knowledge of social studies.

. . . But this secret, swift, and extraordinary buildup of Communist missiles—in an area well known to have a special and historical relationship to the United States and the nations of the Western Hemisphere, in violation of Soviet assurances, and in defiance of American and hemispheric policy—this sudden, clandestine [secret] decision to station strategic weapons for the first time outside of Soviet soil—is a deliberately provocative and unjustified change in the status quo which cannot be accepted by this country, if our courage and our commitments are ever to be trusted again by either friend or foe. . . .

— President John F. Kennedy, October 22, 1962

36 This statement is most closely associated with the

   1 Bay of Pigs invasion
   2 Cuban missile crisis
   3 United States-Soviet space race
   4 nuclear test ban controversy   36 ____

37 What is a valid conclusion based on this statement?

   1 Strategic weapons of the United States should be stationed on foreign soil.
   2 An isolationist foreign policy is the most effective way to preserve peace.
   3 Presidential attempts were made to end military alliances.
   4 Geographic location plays an important role in determining foreign policy.   37 ____

38 **"Martin Luther King Jr. Delivers 'I Have a Dream' Speech to Civil Rights Demonstrators in D.C."**

"Rachel Carson Awakens Conservationists with Her Book, *Silent Spring*"

"Cesar Chavez Organizes Migrant Farm Workers"

A valid conclusion based on these headlines is that

1 individuals have a great impact on movements for change
2 social reforms progress faster with support from big business
3 the press discouraged efforts at reform in the 1960s
4 mass movements often continue without strong leaders   38 _____

Base your answers to questions 39 and 40 on the statement below and on your knowledge of social studies.

. . . In 1961, James Farmer orchestrated and led the famous Freedom Rides through the South, which are renowned for forcing Americans to confront segregation in bus terminals and on interstate buses. In the spring of that year, James Farmer trained a small group of freedom riders, teaching them to deal with the hostility they were likely to encounter using nonviolent resistance. This training would serve them well. . . .

— Senator Charles Robb, "A Tribute to an American Freedom Fighter," U.S. Senate

39 The principal goal of the activity described in this statement was to

1 achieve racial integration of public facilities
2 encourage change through violent means
3 expand voting rights for African Americans
4 force the president to send military troops into the South   39 _____

40 The activities described in this statement helped lead to

  1 President Harry Truman's order to desegregate the military

  2 passage of the Civil Rights Act of 1964

  3 ratification of the Equal Rights Amendment

  4 a decision by the Supreme Court to integrate public schools   40 ____

----

41 Which term is most commonly used to describe President Richard Nixon's foreign policy toward the Soviet Union?

  1 collective security   3 détente

  2 brinkmanship   4 neutrality   41 ____

42 Since the 1970s, many people have moved from the Midwest and Northeast to the South, Southwest, and West Coast. This migration has resulted in

  1 support for increasing the membership of Congress

  2 a decrease in immigration from Asia and Latin America

  3 increased pressure to eliminate the electoral college

  4 some states gaining and others losing seats in the House of Representatives   42 ____

Base your answer to question 43 on the cartoon below and on your knowledge of social studies.

Source: Dana Summers, *The Orlando Sentinel*, 1999

43 Which issue in the United States is the focus of this cartoon?

1 poor diets of many older Americans
2 high cost of many medicines
3 increased competition among drug manufacturers
4 government-controlled prices of prescription drugs

43 _____

Base your answer to question 44 on the cartoon below and on your knowledge of social studies.

Source: Etta Hulme, *The Fort Worth Star-Telegram,* 2004

44 The graduating student pictured in this cartoon is confronted by a problem caused in part by

1 cheaper foreign labor
2 increasing tariff rates
3 high-cost imports
4 lack of education   44 ____

45 **"Gasoline Prices Soar in 2008"**

"U.S. Oil Consumption and Imports Continue to Rise"

"OPEC Votes to Reduce Oil Production"

Which conclusion is most clearly supported by these headlines?

1 The United States exports more oil than it imports.
2 Energy policies are not affected by domestic events.
3 The demand for alternative energy sources is declining.
4 United States dependence on foreign oil is a major problem.   45 ____

Base your answer to question 46 on the graph below and on your knowledge of social studies.

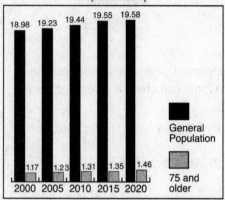

Projected New York State Population
(in millions)

Source: U.S. Bureau of the Census, 2005 (adapted)

46 Which generalization about the projected population in New York State is most clearly supported by the information on the graph?

1 The death rate will slowly increase by 2020.
2 The number of citizens 75 and older will double by 2020.
3 The number of citizens 75 and older will steadily decline by 2020.
4 The population of both groups shown on the graph will increase by 2020.

46 _____

47 The decision in *Gibbons* v. *Ogden* (1824) and the decision in *Wabash, St. Louis & Pacific Railroad* v. *Illinois* (1886) addressed the issue of

1 congressional privileges
2 regulation of interstate commerce
3 state taxation of federal property
4 contract rights

47 _____

48 Which economic policy argues that government should limit, as much as possible, any interference in the economy?

1 socialism   3 mercantilism
2 laissez-faire   4 protectionism   48____

49 Which pair of Supreme Court cases demonstrates that the Supreme Court can change an earlier decision?

1 *Schenck* v. *United States* and *United States* v. *Nixon*
2 *Korematsu* v. *United States* and *Miranda* v. *Arizona*
3 *Gideon* v. *Wainwright* and *Heart of Atlanta Motel* v. *United States*
4 *Plessy* v. *Ferguson* and *Brown* v. *Board of Education of Topeka*   49____

50 The disputed elections of 1876 and 2000 were similar because in both contests the

1 winner was chosen by a special electoral commission
2 states were required to hold a second election
3 winner of the popular vote did not become president
4 election had to be decided in the House of Representatives   50____

Answers to the essay questions are to be written on separate sheets of paper. In developing your answer to Part II, be sure to keep this general definition in mind:

> <u>discuss</u> means "to make observations about something using facts, reasoning, and argument; to present in some detail"

PART II: THEMATIC ESSAY

Directions: Write a well-organized essay that includes an introduction, several paragraphs addressing the task below, and a conclusion.

Theme: Government Role in the Economy

> Throughout history, the United States government has taken various actions to address problems with the nation's economy.

Task:

> Choose *two* actions that addressed a problem with the nation's economy and for *each*
> - Discuss the historical circumstance that led to the action
> - Discuss the impact of this action on the economy of the United States

You may use any example from your study of United States history. Some suggestions you might wish to consider include assumption of Revolutionary War debts, building the transcontinental railroad, passage of tariff laws, passage of the Interstate Commerce Act, creation of the Federal Deposit Insurance Corporation, adoption of the Social Security system, passage of federal minimum wage laws, Reagan Era tax cuts, and ratification of the North American Free Trade Agreement (NAFTA).

You are *not* limited to these suggestions.

Guidelines:

In your essay, be sure to
- Develop all aspects of the task
- Support the theme with relevant facts, examples, and details
- Use a logical and clear plan of organization, including an introduction and a conclusion that are beyond a restatement of the theme

In developing your answers to Part III, be sure to keep this general definition in mind:

> <u>discuss</u> means "to make observations about something using facts, reasoning, and argument; to present in some detail"

PART III: DOCUMENT-BASED ESSAY

This question is based on the accompanying documents. The question is designed to test your ability to work with historical documents. Some of the documents have been edited for the purposes of the question. As you analyze the documents, take into account the source of each document and any point of view that may be presented in the document.

Historical Context:

> The automobile has had an important influence on the United States since the early 20th century. Perhaps no other invention has had such a significant impact on production methods, the American landscape, the environment, and American values.

Task:

> Using information from the documents and your knowledge of United States history, answer the questions that follow each document in Part A. Your answers to the questions will help you write the Part B essay, in which you will be asked to
> • Discuss the political, economic, *and/or* social impacts of the automobile on the United States

Part A: Short Answer Questions

Directions: Analyze the documents and answer the questions that follow each document in the space provided.

Document 1

Length of Time an Average American Employee Must Work to Purchase a Car

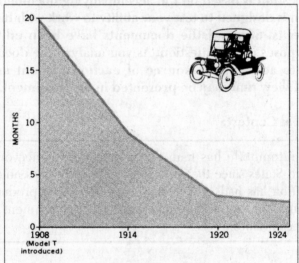

The Cost of a Model T Ford, 1908–1924   Henry Ford's mass production techniques cut the costs of production dramatically, and put the automobile within reach of the workingperson's purse. (Cost is shown in months of labor for an employee at the average national wage.)

Source: Bailey and Kennedy, *The American Pageant*, D.C. Heath and Company, 1987

1 According to Bailey and Kennedy, how did Henry Ford's mass production techniques influence the cost of the automobile? [1]

_____

_____

Document 2

> . . . The result [of buying a car] upon the individual is to break down his sense of values. Whether he will or no, he must spend money at every turn. Having succumbed [given in] to the lure of the car, he is quite helpless thereafter. If a new device will make his automobile run smoother or look better, he attaches that device. If a new polish will make it shine brighter, he buys that polish. If a new idea will give more mileage, or remove carbon, he adopts that new idea. These little costs quickly mount up and in many instances represent the margin of safety between income and outgo. The overplus [surplus] in the pay envelope, instead of going into the bank as a reserve-fund, goes into automobile expense. Many families live on the brink of danger all the time. They are car-poor. Saving is impossible. The joy of security in the future is sacrificed for the pleasure of the moment. And with the pleasure of the moment is mingled the constant anxiety entailed by living beyond one's means. . . .

Source: William Ashdown, "Confessions of an Automobilist,"
Atlantic Monthly, June 1925

2 According to William Ashdown, what were *two* negative impacts of automobile ownership in 1925? [2]

(1) _____

_____

(2) _____

_____

Document 3

> . . . Massive and internationally competitive, the automobile industry is the largest single manufacturing enterprise in the United States in terms of total value of products and number of employees. One out of every six U.S. businesses depends on the manufacture, distribution, servicing, or use of motor vehicles. The industry is primarily responsible for the growth of steel and rubber production, and is the largest user of machine tools. Specialized manufacturing requirements have driven advances in petroleum refining, paint and plate-glass manufacturing, and other industrial processes. Gasoline, once a waste product to be burned off, is now one of the most valuable commodities in the world. . . .

Source: National Academy of Engineering, 2000

3 Based on this article, state *two* ways the automobile industry has had an impact on the American economy. [2]

(1) _____

_____

(2) _____

_____

Document 4a

> . . . The automobile allowed a completely different pattern. Today there is often a semi-void of residential population at the heart of a large city, surrounded by rings of less and less densely settled suburbs. These suburbs, primarily dependent on the automobile to function, are where the majority of the country's population lives, a fact that has transformed our politics. Every city that had a major-league baseball team in 1950, with the exception only of New York—ever the exception— has had a drastic loss in population within its city limits over the last four and a half decades, sometimes by as much as 50 percent as people have moved outward, thanks to the automobile.
>
> In more recent years the automobile has had a similar effect on the retail commercial sectors of smaller cities and towns, as shopping malls and superstores such as the Home Depot and Wal-Mart have sucked commerce off Main Street and into the surrounding countryside. . . .

Source: John Steele Gordon, "Engine of Liberation,"
American Heritage, November 1996

4a According to John Steele Gordon, what has been *one* impact of the automobile on cities? [1]

_____

_____

Document 4b

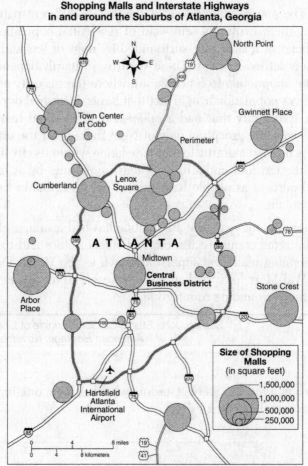

Shopping Malls and Interstate Highways
in and around the Suburbs of Atlanta, Georgia

Source: James M. Rubenstein, *The Cultural Landscape:
An Introduction to Human Geography,*
Pearson Prentice Hall, 2005 (adapted)

4b Based on the information on this map, what is **one** impact of
the automobile on suburbs? [1]

Document 5

> . . . What did the automobile mean for the housewife? Unlike
> public transportation systems, it was convenient. Located
> right at her doorstep, it could deposit her at the doorstep that
> she wanted or needed to visit. And unlike the bicycle or her
> own two feet, the automobile could carry bulky packages as
> well as several additional people. Acquisition of an automobile
> therefore meant that a housewife, once she had learned how
> to drive, could become her own door-to-door delivery service.
> And as more housewives acquired automobiles, more busi-
> nessmen discovered the joys of dispensing with [eliminating]
> delivery services—particularly during the Depression. . . .

Source: Ruth Schwartz Cowan, "Less Work for Mother?,"
American Heritage, September/October 1987

5 According to Ruth Schwartz Cowan, what was *one* way life
changed for the American housewife as a result of the automobile? [1]

_____

_____

Document 6

The Influence of the Automobile, 1923–1960 (Selected Years)

1923 Country Club Plaza, the first shopping center, opens in Kansas City.

1924 In November, 16,833 cars cross the St. John's River into Florida, the beginning of winter motor pilgrimages to Florida.

1930 Census data suggest that southern cities are becoming more racially segregated as car-owning whites move to suburbs that have no public transportation.

King Kullen, first supermarket, Queens, New York City. Supermarkets are an outgrowth of the auto age, because pedestrians cannot carry large amounts of groceries home.

1932 One-room rural schools decline because school districts operate 63,000 school buses in the United States.

1956 Car pools enable Montgomery, Alabama, blacks [African Americans] to boycott successfully the local bus company, beginning the modern civil rights movement.

National Defense and Interstate Highway Act passed. President Eisenhower argues: "In case of atomic attack on our cities, the road net [network] must allow quick evacuation of target areas."

1957 Sixty-six-year-old gas station operator Harlan Sanders, facing bankruptcy because the interstate has bypassed him, decides to franchise his Kentucky Fried Chicken restaurant.

1960 Organization of Petroleum Exporting Countries (OPEC) formed.

Source: Clay McShane, *The Automobile: A Chronology of Its Antecedents, Development, and Impact*, Greenwood Press, 1997 (adapted)

6a According to Clay McShane, what were **two** economic impacts of the automobile on the United States? [2]

(1) _____

_____

(2) _____

_____

b According to Clay McShane, what was **one** impact of the automobile on race relations in the United States? [1]

_____

_____

Document 7

Minor disruptions have begun to appear in the world oil trade in the wake of the renewal of hostilities between the Arabs and the Israelis, and industry executives and Government officials in many countries are waiting to see whether the Arab states will make a serious attempt to use oil as a weapon in the conflict or any political confrontation that follows. The Egyptians are reported to have attacked Israeli-held oil fields in the occupied Sinai, and if true it would be the most ominous event so far in the oil situation. It would be the first direct attack by either side on oil production facilities in any of the conflicts thus far. If the Israelis retaliate it could mean major disruptions of supplies. . . .

Source: William D. Smith, "Conflict Brings Minor Disruptions in Oil Industry: Arab States' Moves Studied for Clues to Intentions," *New York Times*, October 9, 1973

7 According to William D. Smith, what could be *one* impact of the conflicts in the Middle East on the United States? [1]

_____

_____

Document 8

WASHINGTON, July 17—President Reagan, appealing for cooperation in ending the "crazy quilt of different states' drinking laws," today signed legislation that would deny some Federal highway funds to states that keep their drinking age under 21.

At a ceremony in the White House Rose Garden, Mr. Reagan praised as "a great national movement" the efforts to raise the drinking age that began years ago among students and parents.

"We know that drinking, plus driving, spell death and disaster," Mr. Reagan told visitors on a sweltering afternoon. "We know that people in the 18–to–20 age group are more likely to be in alcohol-related accidents than those in any other age group."

Mr. Reagan indirectly acknowledged that he once had reservations about a measure that, in effect, seeks to force states to change their policies. In the past, Mr. Reagan has taken the view that certain matters of concern to the states should not be subject to the dictates of the Federal Government.

But in the case of drunken driving, Mr. Reagan said, "The problem is bigger than the individual states.". . .

Source: Steven R. Weisman, "Reagan Signs Law Linking Federal Aid to Drinking Age," *New York Times*, July 18, 1984

8 According to Steven R. Weisman, what was **one** reason President Reagan signed the law linking federal highway funds to the drinking age? [1]

Document 9

. . . After a long and bitter debate, lawmakers in California today [July 2, 2002] passed the nation's strongest legislation to regulate emissions of the main pollutant that can cause warming of the planet's climate, a step that would require automakers to sell cars that give off the least possible amount of heat-trapping gases. . . .

California is the largest market for automobiles in the United States, as well as the state with more serious air pollution problems than any other. Under federal clean air legislation, the state's air quality regulators are allowed to set standards for automobile pollution that are stricter than those imposed by federal law. In the past, many other states have followed California's lead in setting pollution rules on vehicles, and ultimately American automakers have been forced to build cars that meet California's standards and to sell them nation-wide. . . .

Source: John H. Cushman Jr., "California Lawmakers Vote to Lower Auto Emissions," *New York Times*, July 2, 2002

9 According to John H. Cushman Jr., what is **one** impact of the automobile on the United States? [1]

_____

_____

Part B: Essay

Directions: Write a well-organized essay that includes an introduction, several paragraphs, and a conclusion. Use evidence from *at least five* documents in the body of the essay. Support your response with relevant facts, examples, and details. Include additional outside information.

Historical Context:

The automobile has had an important influence on the United States since the early 20th century. Perhaps no other invention has had such a significant impact on production methods, the American landscape, the environment, and American values.

Task:

Using information from the documents and your knowledge of United States history, write an essay in which you
- Discuss the political, economic, *and/or* social impacts of the automobile on the United States

Guidelines:

In your essay, be sure to:
- Develop all aspects of the task
- Incorporate information from *at least five* documents
- Incorporate relevant outside information
- Support the theme with relevant facts, examples, and details
- Use a logical and clear plan of organization, including an introduction and a conclusion that are beyond a restatement of the theme

Answers
August 2008
United States History and Government

Answer Key

PART I

1. 1 or H	14. 3	27. 3	40. 2
2. 3 or E	15. 1	28. 3	41. 3
3. 3	16. 2	29. 4	42. 4
4. 1	17. 3	30. 2	43. 2
5. 3	18. 4	31. 2	44. 1
6. 1	19. 4	32. 4	45. 4
7. 2	20. 3	33. 1	46. 4
8. 1	21. 4	34. 1	47. 2
9. 3	22. 1	35. 2	48. 2
10. 2	23. 2	36. 2	49. 4
11. 4	24. 1	37. 4	50. 3
12. 3	25. 1	38. 1	
13. 4	26. 4	39. 1	

PART II: Thematic Essay   See answers explained section.

PART III: Document-Based Essay   See answers explained section.

Answers Explained

PART I (1–50)

1. **1** The geographic feature that most limited the westward movement of American colonists before 1750 was the Appalachian Mountains, represented by the letter *H* on the map. The Appalachian Mountain range runs from Georgia to Maine, and provided an effective barrier to large-scale movement westward. Before 1750, the lack of transportation routes beyond the Appalachian Mountains also inhibited western settlement. No navigable rivers extend from the Atlantic coast through the Appalachian Mountains, and trails through mountain passes were crude. After 1750, as land in the original colonies along the Atlantic became more expensive, a few settlers crossed over the Appalachian Mountains and established farms in the Mississippi and Ohio River valleys. These forays to the West led to conflicts with the French, who had earlier established outposts in the Ohio River valley. These conflicts contributed to the French and Indian War (1754–1763). After the war, the British passed the Proclamation Act (1763), forbidding colonists from venturing beyond the Appalachian Mountains. This act contributed to colonial resentment of British policies.

WRONG CHOICES EXPLAINED:
(2) The letter *I* appears to represent New England. New England was one of the population centers in colonial America and would not be considered an obstacle to westward movement.
(3) The letter *C* represents the Rocky Mountains. Colonists had not ventured that far west before 1750, so it would not be considered an obstacle to westward movement.
(4) The letter *F* represents the Great Lakes. Few colonists had ventured into the Great Lake region before 1750. In addition, the Great Lakes are navigable bodies of water. They would not be considered an obstacle to movement.

2. **3** At the end of the Revolutionary War, the western boundary of the United States became the Mississippi River, represented by the letter *E* on the map. The Treaty of Paris (1883) established the Mississippi River as the western boundary of the United States. The purchase of the Louisiana Territory in 1803 enlarged the territory of the United States and pushed the western boundary beyond the Mississippi River.

WRONG CHOICES EXPLAINED:
(1) The letter *A* represents the coast of the Pacific Ocean. This is the current western boundary of the continental United States, but it was not the

western boundary at the end of the Revolutionary War. The United States extended to the Pacific with the acquisition of Mexican Cession (1848) and the Oregon Territory (also 1848).

(2) The letter *B* represents the Rio Grande. This is the current boundary between the United States and Mexico. It was not a boundary at the end of the Revolutionary War. This boundary was established after the Mexican War (1848).

(4) The letter *G* represents the Gulf of Mexico. The coast of the Gulf of Mexico is the southern boundary of the United States today. It was part of the southern boundary, not western boundary, at the end of the Revolutionary War. The other part of the southern boundary of the United States at the end of the Revolutionary War was Florida, which was controlled by Spain until 1819.

3. **3** The most accurate title for the time line would be "Causes of the American Revolution." All the items on the time line reflect the growing tension between the British government and the American colonies in the period following the French and Indian War. After that war, which lasted from 1754 to 1763, the British government enacted a series of measures that many colonists found objectionable. The colonists were angered by a series of revenue or tax acts that the British imposed, in part to defray the costs of the war. The British believed their victory in the French and Indian War had been especially beneficial to the colonists. In return, the British reasoned it was fair for the colonists to assume some of the costs of the war and of continued protection.

The Stamp Act (1765), which imposed a tax on the paper used for various documents in the colonies, provoked the most intense opposition. This tax was solely a revenue raising measure as opposed to earlier taxes that were designed to regulate trade. Many colonists asserted that only representatives elected by them could enact taxes on the colonies. "No taxation without representation" became their rallying cry. The Stamp Act itself was rescinded, but a series of British moves and colonial responses in the coming years worsened the situation. The Townshend Acts (1767) imposed additional taxes on the colonists. In addition, the British stationed troops in Boston, forcing local residents to house and feed British troops (1765). The resentments between local residents and British troops resulted in a violent stand-off that led to British troops firing on a crowd of colonists (1770). This so-called massacre intensified colonial resentment of the British presence. In 1773, the British passed the Tea Act, which eliminated British tariffs from tea sold in the colonies by the British East India Company. This act actually lowered tea prices in Boston, but it angered many colonists who accused the British of doing special favors for a large company. The colonists responded by dumping cases of tea into the Boston harbor. The British responded to the Boston Tea Party by imposing a series of punitive measures known as the Coercive Acts (1774). Protests grew more intense and led to the colonies declaring their independence from Great Britain in 1776.

WRONG CHOICES EXPLAINED:

(1) "Forms of Colonial Protest" would not be an accurate title for the time line. The Boston Tea Party is the only colonial protest mentioned on the time line. The rest of the items are actions taken by the British.

(2) "Effects of British Navigation Laws" would not be an accurate title for the time line. Some of the items involve navigation laws, but the Quartering Act, the Stamp Act, and the Boston Massacre are not directly related to trade regulations.

(4) "Abuse of Power by Colonial Legislatures" would not be an accurate title for the time line. None of the items on the time line are actions taken by colonial legislatures. They are either acts of the British parliament or acts of resistance by crowds of colonists.

4. **1** The Land Ordinance (1785) and the Northwest Ordinance (1787) are considered achievements under the Articles of Confederation because they established processes for settling and governing the western territories. The two acts dealt with the Northwest Territory, the vast stretch of land north of the Ohio River, between the western border of Pennsylvania and the Mississippi River. The Confederation Congress persuaded the various states to give up their land claims in the region. Then it passed two significant pieces of legislation. The Land Ordinance provided for an orderly system of development for the Northwest Territory. It divided up the land and provided a plot in every town for public schools. The Northwest Ordinance spelled out the steps that these areas would have to go through to become states. In addition, the Northwest Ordinance banned slavery in the Northwest Territory. Although these acts are considered successes of the Confederation, historians have tended to focus on the problems of the period, such as inflation and lack of government revenues. In fact, the period is often labeled the *critical period*, in the sense of a patient being in critical condition.

WRONG CHOICES EXPLAINED:

(2) The two acts did not deal with boundary disputes with Great Britain and Spain. The United States had disputes with both countries during this period. The United States resented Spain for challenging its right to use the Mississippi River, and it resented Great Britain for refusing to evacuate forts in the western part of the United States and for interfering with its shipping in the Atlantic. Neither of these issues was dealt with satisfactorily by the Confederation Congress.

(3) The two acts did not deal with collecting taxes and coining money. Both of these issues posed problems for the Confederation Congress. The Articles did not give the national government the ability to exercise either of these basic governmental functions. As a result, both tax collection and the issuing of currency were carried out by the various states.

(4) The two acts did create a system of state and federal courts. Under the Articles of Confederation, states established their own court systems. There was no national court system.

5. **3** This part of the Bill of Rights was intended to limit the power of the federal government. The reading is the 10th Amendment to the Constitution. It assures the states that they can retain powers that are neither given to the federal government nor explicitly prohibited by the Constitution. The exact meaning of the amendment was the subject of a great deal of controversy, especially before the Civil War. Southern states insisted that this amendment prohibited the federal government from interfering in slavery. Generally, the 10th Amendment protects the right of states to regulate internal state affairs, such as education, commerce, and local government.

WRONG CHOICES EXPLAINED:

(1) The passage was not intended to give the people the right to vote on important issues. Voting rules are mainly left to the various states, as asserted in the 10th Amendment. Not all states allow people to vote directly on issues. It was not until the Progressive era of the early 20th century that some states created mechanisms for individuals to vote on important issues through the referendum process.

(2) The passage was not intended to reduce the rights of citizens. If anything, the passage would increase the rights of citizens by making clear that powers that are not expressly given to the federal or state government, nor expressly forbidden by law, are in the hands of the people.

(4) The passage was not intended to assure federal control over the states. The Supremacy Clause of the Constitution assures that the Constitution and federal laws and treaties are the "supreme law of the land."

6. **1** The creation of the presidential cabinet and political parties are examples of the unwritten constitution. The unwritten constitution refers to those traditions and practices that have become part of the American political system but were not mentioned in the Constitution. Many of these practices date back to the administration of George Washington. He first regularly convened a cabinet, comprising the heads of government departments, to advise him. Washington's administration also witnessed the development of political parties, a practice unforeseen by most of the founding fathers. For most of the nation's history, two major rival parties have existed. The political parties serve to focus debate in Congress, as members of Congress tend to support their party's position. The president is, by virtue of his office, the most prominent public voice of his party, and therefore acts as its leader (even though each party has a formal leader).

WRONG CHOICES EXPLAINED:

(2) The creation of the presidential cabinet and political parties are not examples of separation of powers. Separation of powers describes the basic structure of the government. The framers of the Constitution created a governmental system with three separate branches—the legislative, the executive, and the judicial—each with the ability to check the powers of the other two. The goal was to keep the three branches in balance. The framers were

very conscious of the problems of a government with limitless powers. After living under the British monarchy, they came to believe that a powerful government without checks was dangerous to liberty.

(3) The creation of the presidential cabinet and political parties are not examples of the elastic clause. The Constitution lists the specific powers of Congress. Some delegates feared that by listing specific powers, Congress could not exercise additional powers nor could it address unforeseen circumstances. They therefore pushed for the elastic clause, which stretched the powers of Congress by allowing it to "make all laws necessary and proper...."

(4) The creation of the presidential cabinet and political parties are not examples of judicial review. Judicial review is the power of the Supreme Court to review laws and determine if they are consistent with the Constitution. Laws declared unconstitutional by the court are immediately disallowed. The power was established by the court itself in the *Marbury* v. *Madison* decision (1803). This power of judicial review has been the main function of the Supreme Court since then and has been instrumental in maintaining balance between the three branches of the government.

7. **2** The term *supreme law of the land* refers to the Constitution. The framers of the Constitution grappled with the issue of where power should reside in the United States—on the national level or on the state level. While the Constitution left certain powers in the hands of the states, the Supremacy Clause of the Constitution states that the Constitution and federal laws and treaties are the "supreme law of the land." Therefore, state laws must operate within the bounds of the Constitution, as defined by the Supreme Court.

WRONG CHOICES EXPLAINED:
(1) The Fundamental Orders of Connecticut are not the "supreme law of the land" in the United States. The Fundamental Orders of Connecticut were adopted in 1638 and established the basic framework for government in the colony of Connecticut. It is considered to be one of the first written constitutions in the western world. For this reason, Connecticut is known as the Constitution State.

(3) The Articles of Confederation are not the "supreme law of the land" in the United States. The Articles guided the United States during the 1780s, before the ratification of the Constitution. Even then, the Articles would not have been considered the "supreme law of the land." The states kept many significant powers, including the power to tax, hampering the ability of the national government to rule.

(4) The Declaration of Independence is not the "supreme law of the land" in the United States. The Declaration was both a statement of intent and a propaganda piece, but it was not intended to be a governing document.

8. **1** The constitutional principle of checks and balances is intended to ensure that no one branch of the government has more power than another branch. The framers of the Constitution created three branches. The legislative

branch creates laws, the executive branch carries out laws, and the judicial branch interprets laws. The Constitution spells out the powers of each branch. The powers of Congress are listed in Article I, those of the president in Article II, and those of the Supreme Court in Article III. The framers were very conscious of the problems of a government with limitless powers. After living under the British monarchy, they came to believe that a powerful government without checks was dangerous to liberty. Therefore, they created a governmental system with three branches, each with the ability to check the powers of the other two. The goal was to keep the three branches in balance. An example of this concept of checks and balances is the president's ability to veto (or reject) bills passed by Congress, or the Supreme Court's ability to strike down laws that it deems unconstitutional.

WRONG CHOICES EXPLAINED:

(2) Federalism describes the relationship between the national government and state governments. While the word itself implies a loose league of states, in the American context federalism gives the strong national government supremacy over the state governments.

(3) Limited government describes a government structure in which restraints are placed on government intervention into people's private lives and into economic matters. It can be contrasted with a dictatorship or authoritarian government in which there are no restraints on the power of the governments. The United States has a limited government. The clearest expression of limits on the government can be found in the Bill of Rights.

(4) Rule of law describes a government structure in which power is exercised only within the bounds of written, publicly agreed upon laws and rules. Although United States government officials, including the president, have been known to operate, at times, outside the law, the United States is a country in which the rule of law is the norm. Rule of law can be contrasted with mob rule or dictatorial rule.

9. **3** A geographic and economic motivation for the Louisiana Purchase (1803) was the desire to control the port of New Orleans. During the administration of President Thomas Jefferson, the United States purchased the Louisiana Territory from France for $15 million. The purchase nearly doubled the size of the United States and gave the United States control of the Mississippi River and the port city of New Orleans. New Orleans became increasingly important as pioneers in the late 1700s and early 1800s crossed over the Appalachian Mountains and settled in the Mississippi and Ohio River Valleys and established farms. It was impractical to transport agricultural goods such as wheat and corn by overland routes to the population centers along the eastern seaboard. Roads were primitive and railroads had not yet been developed. Therefore, water routes down the Ohio and Mississippi Rivers to New Orleans and beyond became very important for the farmers.

WRONG CHOICES EXPLAINED:

(1) Annexing California was not a motivation for the Louisiana Purchase (1803). The United States did not acquire California until much later. It was part of the land ceded by Mexico in 1848 after the Mexican War.

(2) Securing land for the Erie Canal was not a motivation for the Louisiana Purchase (1803). The Erie Canal runs through upstate New York, land that the United States possessed from its founding.

(4) Owning all of the Great Lakes was not a motivation for the Louisiana Purchase. The United States already extended to the Great Lakes. The United States does not "own" the Great Lakes. Lake Michigan is within U.S. territory, but the other lakes form the U.S. border with Canada.

10. **2** The principal goal of supporters of Manifest Destiny in the 1840s was to expand U.S. territory to the Pacific Ocean. The term *Manifest Destiny* was coined in an 1845 newspaper article. It captured the fervor of the westward expansion movement, implying that it was God's plan that the United States take over and settle the entire continent. Americans who did settle out west were probably driven more by economic factors, such as cheap land or precious metals, than they were by a desire to fulfill God's plan. Supporters of Manifest Destiny achieved their goal of extending American territory to the Pacific Ocean with the acquisition of the Oregon Territory (1848) and the purchase of the Mexican Cession territory after the Mexican War (1848). Other noteworthy episodes in the history of the settlement of the West include Texas independence from Mexico (1836), the opening of the Oregon Trail (1841), and the Mormon exodus to Utah (1847). This movement was especially damaging for the Native Americans of the West, who were driven off their land and relegated to several western reservations.

WRONG CHOICES EXPLAINED:

(1) Supporters of Manifest Destiny might have dreamed of incorporating Canada into the United States, but that was never a principal goal of the movement.

(3) Manifest Destiny is associated with expansion across the North American continent. The push to build a canal across Central America came later. The Panama Canal was completed in 1914.

(4) Manifest Destiny is associated with expansion across the North American continent. The push to acquire naval bases in the Caribbean came in the 1890s as the United States became an imperialist power.

11. **4** The climate and topography of the southeastern United States had a major impact on the history of the United States before 1860 because the region provided agricultural products that were processed in the North and in Europe. The most important agricultural product was cotton. Cotton needs a long frost-free season, lots of sunshine, and moderate rainfall. These conditions are present in a broad swath of the South. Eli Whitney's cotton gin (1793) was instrumental in helping meet the growing demand for raw cotton.

A cotton gin separates the cotton seeds from the raw cotton strands. Southern plantation owners needed workers to plant, tend, and harvest the cotton crop. Thus, the institution of slavery saw a dramatic increase in the first half of the 1800s. From the 1830s onward, slavery became a contentious issue in American society. The issue intensified as the United States acquired more territory in the West. The question of whether these new territories would be slave or free became a central political issue in the 1850s and led to the Civil War (1861–1865).

WRONG CHOICES EXPLAINED:

(1) The southeastern United States was not the center of commerce and manufacturing, either before or after 1860. Throughout the 1800s, the northern states dominated these sectors of the economy.

(2) Steel production was not significant in the southeastern United States before 1860. Steel production was centered in Pennsylvania and Ohio, and became prominent only after the Civil War.

(3) The southeastern United States was not a magnet for immigrants, either before or after 1860. Throughout the 1800s, most immigrants to the United States settled in the cities of the northern states.

12. **3** Abolitionists in the pre-Civil War period were most likely to support the activities of the Underground Railroad. The Underground Railroad was an informal network of safe houses in which escaped slaves could find refuge. "Conductors" on the Underground Railroad guided these escaped slaves from one safe house to another at night to avoid detection by law enforcement authorities. The goal was to guide the escaped slaves to Canada. One of the important conductors on the Underground Railroad was Harriet Tubman. The movement to abolish slavery gained strength in the 1830s. A key early figure was William Lloyd Garrison, who began publishing *The Liberator* in 1831 to prod the public into challenging the institution of slavery.

WRONG CHOICES EXPLAINED:

(1) Abolitionists were not in favor of the removal of the Cherokee Indians from Georgia. Many of the proponents of Indian removal were motivated by a desire to expand cotton production, and slavery, in Georgia. The government passed the Indian Removal Act (1830), ordering the Cherokee to move west. The Cherokee got a short reprieve from the Supreme Court decision in *Worcester* v. *Georgia* (1832), which recognized the Cherokee people as a nation within the state of Georgia and ruled that they would not be subject to the Indian Removal Act. But the state of Georgia, with the support of President Andrew Jackson, began moving them to the West anyway.

(2) Abolitionists were opposed to the Fugitive Slave Act. One of the elements of the Compromise of 1850 was a stronger Fugitive Slave Act. White southern politicians welcomed this legislation because it gave slave catchers much greater latitude in retrieving runaway slaves in the North. Abolitionists despised it for the same reason.

(4) Abolitionists were opposed to the use of popular sovereignty in the territories. Popular sovereignty meant letting the people of a particular territory decide whether or not to allow slavery in that territory. The principle was applied to the newly created Kansas and Nebraska Territories under the Kansas-Nebraska Act (1854). Abolitionists opposed this act because it opened up those areas to the possibility of slavery. Previously, the Missouri Compromise (1820) closed that portion of the Louisiana Purchase territory to slavery.

13. **4** The Supreme Court decision in the case of *Dred Scott* v. *Sanford* created a need for a constitutional amendment that would grant citizenship to formerly enslaved persons. Dred Scott, a slave, sued to obtain his freedom on the grounds that he had lived for a time in territories where slavery was banned. The Supreme Court ruled against him and went further, declaring that no African Americans, not even free men and women, were entitled to citizenship in the United States because they were, according to the Court, "beings of an inferior order." The case alarmed African Americans and many white northerners. This principle was overturned with the ratification of the 14th Amendment (1868), which granted citizenship to all persons born in the United States.

WRONG CHOICES EXPLAINED:
(1) The case of *Marbury* v. *Madison* did not involve slavery or the status of formerly enslaved persons. The *Marbury* v. *Madison* decision (1803) is arguably the Supreme Court's most important decision. The decision established the Supreme Court's power to review laws and determine if they are consistent with the Constitution. Laws declared unconstitutional by the Court are immediately disallowed. This power of judicial review has been the main function of the Supreme Court since then and has been instrumental in maintaining balance between the three branches of the government.

(2) The case of *McCulloch* v. *Maryland* did not involve slavery or the status of formerly enslaved persons. In the *McCulloch* v. *Maryland* decision (1819), the Supreme Court prohibited Maryland from taxing the Bank of the United States. The case was significant because it declared federal power superior to state power.

(3) The case of *Worcester* v. *Georgia* did not involve slavery or the status of formerly enslaved persons. In the *Worcester* v. *Georgia* decision (1832), the Supreme Court recognized the Cherokee people as a nation within the state of Georgia and ruled that they would not be subject to the 1830 Indian Removal Act.

14. **3** The statement reveals President Lincoln's support for a fair and generous peace with the South after the Civil War. The phrase "with malice toward none; with charity for all" from his Second Inaugural Address (1865) reflects his desire to quickly restore the Union, rather than punish Southerners who took part in secession. His actions reflected this goal. In

1863, he announced his "10 percent plan" to quickly restore the Southern states after the war. If 10 percent of the 1860 voters in a Southern state took an oath of allegiance to the United States and promised to abide by emancipation, then that state could establish a new government and send representatives to Congress. In 1864, he vetoed the Wade-Davis Bill, which would have established much stricter standards for the Southern states to meet. Lincoln was assassinated less than a month after his second inauguration, so it is difficult to surmise how he would have negotiated the difficulties of the Reconstruction era.

WRONG CHOICES EXPLAINED:

(1) The statement does not address the issue of a new peace with Great Britain. The United States was not at war with Great Britain during Lincoln's administration, so there would have been no need for a peace treaty. Lincoln feared that Great Britain might join the Southern side in the Civil War. In fact, one of his motivations for issuing the Emancipation Proclamation (1863) was to prevent Great Britain from entering the war. He reasoned that Great Britain might join the South to protect its supply of raw cotton, but it would not join the South to protect the institution of slavery.

(2) The statement does not address the issue of universal male suffrage. Lincoln did not directly address this issue. In his attempt to quickly restore the Southern states to the United States, he did not bring up the contentious issue of extending the vote to African American males.

(4) The statement does not call for harsh treatment for Confederate leaders. The phrase "with malice toward none, with charity for all" indicates the lenient treatment Lincoln proposed for Confederate leaders. His desire was to quickly restore the Union, not punish Confederate leaders.

15. **1** The passage of Jim Crow laws in the South after Reconstruction was aided in part by a narrow interpretation of the 14th Amendment by the Supreme Court. Jim Crow laws segregated public facilities, such as railroad cars, bathrooms, and schools. These laws relegated African Americans to second-class status in the South. Advocates for civil rights for African Americans hoped that the 14th Amendment (ratified in 1868) would prevent the implementation of Jim Crow laws. The Amendment prevents states from making laws that limit the "privileges or immunities" of any U.S. citizen. It also insists that states provide all citizens with "equal protection under the law." But the Supreme Court interpreted this broad language in such a narrow way that it allowed for the implementation of Jim Crow laws. In the *Slaughterhouse* cases (1873), the Court made a distinction between national citizenship and state citizenship. It ruled that the 14th Amendment applied to national citizenship rights, such as the right to vote in national elections and the right to travel between states. The Court said that the Amendment did not apply to rights that derived from "state citizenship." Therefore, the 14th Amendment could not be used to prohibit state Jim Crow laws.

WRONG CHOICES EXPLAINED:

(2) The South did not experience a change in its economy from agriculture to industry after Reconstruction. Some Southerners in the post-Civil War period, notably Henry Grady, advocated that the South move beyond its old reliance on plantation agriculture and develop a mixed economy that would include industry. These "new South" advocates did not generally succeed in pushing the South toward industry. Only a few small pockets of industry emerged in the South before the second half of the 20th century.

(3) The Republican Party did not grow in the South after Reconstruction. The end of Reconstruction meant the end of Republican power in the South, as the Democratic Party reasserted dominance in the South.

(4) There was little European immigration to the South after Reconstruction. European immigrants moved to Northern and Midwestern cities, where industrial jobs were plentiful.

16. **2** During the late 1800s, pools and trusts were used by big business to limit competition. Trusts and pools are combinations of companies that came to dominate entire industries during the Gilded Age of the late 1800s. John D. Rockefeller established the first large trust in the oil processing industry. The formation of trusts was seen as harmful to the interests of consumers. The men who controlled the major industries in the United States came to be known as *robber barons*, a scornful title meant to call attention to their cutthroat business activities and their attempts to control the government. Critics of corporate power pushed the government to take steps to reign in these massive corporations. But their efforts often did not end up having the desired effect. The Sherman Antitrust Act was designed to break up trusts, but only a few trusts were challenged. Ironically, the act was used with equal vigor against unions, on the grounds that they were illegal formations that interfered with free trade.

WRONG CHOICES EXPLAINED:

(1) Pools and trusts were not used by business to increase imports. American business leaders of the late 1800s wanted to reduce imports because imported goods would compete with products produced by American companies.

(3) Pools and trusts were not used to improve working conditions. Working conditions of the late 1800s were often unsafe to the workers. American business leaders were not eager to put money into improving these conditions.

(4) Pools and trusts were not used to reduce corporate income tax. Business leaders are always eager to reduce their tax burden, but corporate income taxes were not levied until 1909.

17. **3** In the late 1800s, farmers most often supported the views of the Populist Party. The populist movement became a formidable force in the 1890s. The Populists grew angry at the concentration of wealth and power by Eastern industrialists. They supported a national income tax so that those

with higher incomes would pay more than the poor. They also supported free and unlimited coinage of silver. The Populist Party wanted the United States to get off the gold standard and to issue money backed by silver as well. This would increase the amount of money in circulation and would lead to inflation. Farmers supported inflationary policies so that the prices they received for their produce would increase. In 1896, the Populist Party endorsed William Jennings Bryan, a Democrat, because of his support for the free coinage of silver. In a famous speech, Bryan promised not to let the American people be crucified "upon a cross of gold." Finally, the populists supported the direct election of senators to make officials more accountable to the public.

WRONG CHOICES EXPLAINED:

(1) Factory owners would not have supported the views of the Populist Party. The Populists were very critical of the wealth and power that were concentrated in the hands of factory owners. They believed that such powerful economic interests had undermined democracy.

(2) There was some overlap between the Populist movement and the Nativist movement. Nativists were people who believed that immigration was dangerous to American society. Some Populist farmers were suspicious of urban people, including immigrants. However, other Populists thought it was important to create alliances among all producing people—farmers as well as urban factory workers.

(4) There was a great deal of overlap between the Populist movement and the Labor movement. Both movements championed the cause of the common man over the power of large corporations. However, the main support for the Populist movement came from farmers.

18. **4** The point of view expressed in the quotation was most likely that of a labor leader speaking about the rights of workers. The speaker was asserting that ordinary workers were equal, in terms of rights and privileges, to the owners of big corporations. The speaker was reminding the audience that ordinary workers actually produced the goods that were contributing much to the U.S. economy. At the time, labor leaders and their allies worried that the robber barons, as the owners of big corporations were derisively labeled, had come to dominate the political process in the United States.

WRONG CHOICES EXPLAINED:

(1) The speaker was not discussing immigration. Many of the workers at that time were immigrants, but the speaker was discussing their status as workers, not as immigrants.

(2) The speaker was not expressing the point of view of a government official on the campaign trail. The speaker identified himself or herself as a worker, not as a politician.

(3) The speaker was not discussing discrimination against women. There were certainly many women working in factories at the time, but the speaker was discussing the status of workers, not of women.

19. **4** In the late 1800s and early 1900s, many members of Congress supported legislation requiring literacy tests for immigrants in an attempt to restrict immigration from southern and eastern Europe. During this period a strong Nativist, or anti-immigrant, movement developed in the United States. Some members of the movement exhibited prejudice toward people who seemed "different." Others did not want immigrant workers to compete with Americans for jobs. Still others worried that the United States might become overpopulated. One strategy for restricting immigration was requiring immigrants to pass a literacy test before they would be admitted to the United States. Large numbers of immigrants were not literate in their native tongue, let alone English. Nativists failed to implement such a literacy test, but they were successful in the 1920s in restricting immigration. The United States passed the Emergency Quota Act (1921) and the National Origins Act (1924), both of which greatly reduced the number of new immigrants allowed into the United States. These acts set quotas for new immigrants based on nationality.

WRONG CHOICES EXPLAINED:

(1) Illegal immigration was not a major issue before the 1920s. In the 1920s, the United States passed laws drastically restricting the number of immigrants allowed into the country, based on complicated quota systems. Before the 1920s, however, the United States had virtually open borders. Therefore, one did not have to break the law to come into the United States.

(2) Literacy tests would be used to keep out immigrants, not to entice highly skilled workers into the United States. Further, by the early 1900s, there was much more demand for unskilled workers than for skilled workers. Mass production techniques required unskilled factory operatives, not skilled craftsmen.

(3) To participate in the electoral process, immigrants would have to become citizens of the United States. Reading, writing, and speaking English were prerequisites for citizenship.

20. **3** The three headlines indicate that U.S. territorial expansion increased in the Pacific Ocean. Hawaii, Samoa, Wake Island, and Guam are all Pacific islands that the United States has gained control over. With the annexation of Hawaii (1898) and victory in the Spanish-American War (also in 1898), the United States had acquired an empire and had become an imperialist power. In the Treaty of Paris, which ended the Spanish-American War, Spain ceded Puerto Rico, Guam, and the Philippines to the United States. Wake Island was annexed by the United States in 1898. It was uninhabited at the time. Samoa was divided as a result of negotiations between the United States and Germany in 1899. The negotiations followed several years of war in which the United States and Germany supported different sides. Some critics in the United States resisted the move toward empire. These critics wondered how the United States, a country born in an anti-colonial war, could acquire an empire of its own. The most prominent anti-imperialist was author Mark Twain.

WRONG CHOICES EXPLAINED:

(1) The headlines do not indicate that the Anti-Imperialist League strongly influenced Congress. The headlines describe imperialist acts on the part of the United States. If the Anti-Imperialist League was successful, such acts would not have occurred.

(2) The headlines do not indicate that United States foreign policy was motivated by respect for native cultures. The United States assumed that native cultures were inferior. It showed little respect for the desires of native people. In the case of Hawaii, the local leader, Queen Lilioukalani, hoped to restore Hawaii to native control and challenged American control. She was forced to surrender.

(4) The headlines all refer to incidents involving Pacific islands, far from the North American mainland.

21. **4** The Federal Reserve Bank was created in 1913 to regulate the nation's money supply. By regulating the amount of money in circulation, the Federal Reserve Bank (also known as the Fed) is able to regulate economic growth. For instance, if the economy is sluggish, the Fed will attempt to stimulate economic growth by putting more money in circulation. If inflation occurs, the Fed will attempt to slow down economic activity by taking money out of circulation. An important mechanism for regulating the amount of currency in circulation is raising or lowering the interest rate at which the Fed loans money to other banks. Other banks follow suit, raising or lowering the interest rates at which they loan money to the public. For example, by lowering interest rates, the Fed will encourage more people to take out loans and spend money on big-ticket items such as homes and cars. This has the effect of putting money in circulation. Conversely, if the Fed raises interest rates, people will be less likely to take out loans. More money would then stay in bank vaults instead of going into circulation.

WRONG CHOICES EXPLAINED:

(1) The Federal Reserve System was not created to protect endangered species. The United States passed the Endangered Species Act in 1973.

(2) The Federal Reserve System was not created to reduce tariff rates. A series of tariff acts throughout American history have either raised or lowered tariff rates.

(3) The Federal Reserve System was not created to collect income taxes. Federal income taxes were legally permitted with the ratification of the 16th Amendment, also in 1913.

22. **1** The initiative and referendum are considered democratic reforms because they permit citizens to have a more direct role in lawmaking. Progressive reformers in the first two decades of the 20th century sought to expand citizen participation in government by adopting the initiative and referendum. These reformers were concerned that government was being

taken over by corrupt and inefficient political machines. The muckraking journalist Lincoln Steffens exposed the underside of American municipal politics and the influence of wealthy businessmen in *The Shame of the Cities* (1902). Reformers hoped that by expanding democracy the power of these political machines would be lessened. The initiative would enable citizens to introduce a bill to the local or state legislature by petition. The referendum would allow people to vote directly on proposed legislation.

WRONG CHOICES EXPLAINED:

(2) The initiative and the referendum did not let all registered voters select their state's presidential electors. The Constitution states that each state shall determine the method for selecting electors. Currently, in all states the presidential electors are determined by the results of the popular vote in the state. Forty-eight states have a winner-take-all system for selecting electors.

(3) The initiative and the referendum did not extend the right to vote to 18-year-old citizens. The voting age was reduced from 21 to 18 by the 26th Amendment (1971).

(4) The initiative and referendum did not address the issue of lawsuits between residents of different states. There have never been any bans on residents of one state bringing lawsuits against residents of another state.

23. **2** During the early 1900s, the term *muckraker* was used to describe writers who exposed evils in American society. Muckrakers exposed wrongdoing by government officials, showed the negative side of industrialization, and let the world see a variety of social ills. Upton Sinclair exposed the dangerous and unhygienic conditions of the meat packing industry in his novel *The Jungle* (1906). Ida Tarbell wrote a scathing history of the Standard Oil Trust in 1904, detailing the underhanded tactics of John D. Rockefeller. Frank Norris wrote a novel called *The Octopus* (1901), which showed the unfair practices of the big railroad companies. Lincoln Steffens wrote *The Shame of Our Cities* (1902), which showed the corruption of urban political machines. These muckraking books inspired a generation of progressive reformers who pushed the government to intervene in these problems.

WRONG CHOICES EXPLAINED:

(1) Some muckrakers were critical of U.S. participation in World War I, but pacifism was not the defining feature of the muckraker journalists.

(3) Muckraking journalists did not, for the most part, report on celebrities. Starting in the 1920s, gossip columnists, such as Walter Winchell, became popular in newspapers.

(4) Muckraking journalists were not especially critical of Progressive Era presidents, such as Theodore Roosevelt (1901–1908) and Woodrow Wilson (1913–1921). The muckrakers welcomed many of the reforms championed by the progressive movement.

24. **1** President Woodrow Wilson's policy of strict neutrality during the early years of World War I was challenged by German violations of freedom of the seas. Freedom of the seas was a major reason for U.S. entrance into World War I. The United States initially assumed that it could stay neutral in World War I and maintain commercial ties to nations on both sides of the conflict. But quickly Great Britain successfully blockaded American ships from reaching Germany. Out of necessity, U.S. trade shifted to Great Britain exclusively. Germany responded by warning the United States that ships in the waters off of England would be subject to attack by U-boats, or submarines. The sinking of the British ocean liner *Lusitania* infuriated many Americans (128 Americans were among the dead). Germany, however, wanted to keep the United States out of the war and agreed in the Sussex Pledge (1916) to make no surprise submarine attacks on American ships. The United States took advantage of this pledge and traded extensively with Great Britain. In 1917, Germany rescinded the Sussex Pledge and declared that it would resume unrestricted submarine warfare; soon after, the United States declared war on Germany.

WRONG CHOICES EXPLAINED:

(2) The Roosevelt corollary to the Monroe Doctrine involved Latin America, not Europe. Further, the United States entered World War I on the side of Great Britain, so British "disrespect" of the United States would not contribute to America joining the war on the British side.

(3) There were no attacks by Mexicans on U.S. border towns. There was some concern about Mexico when the United States became aware of the Zimmerman note, in which German foreign secretary Arthur Zimmerman indicated that Germany would help Mexico regain territory it lost to the United States if Mexico joined the war on Germany's side. But Mexico stayed out of World War I.

(4) The League of Nations was not formed until after World War I.

25. **1** A main result of national Prohibition during the 1920s was that respect for the law decreased. Prohibition became national policy in 1919 when the 18th Amendment to the Constitution was ratified. The 18th Amendment, which went into effect on January 29, 1920, called for a ban on the manufacture, sale, and transportation of alcoholic beverages. The movement to ban alcohol from American society was one of the largest movements in the 19th century. There were several factors that contributed to the success of the temperance movement. Many women were troubled by the large amount of alcohol their husbands drank. Also, Nativists thought that the new immigrants, who were mostly non-Protestant, lacked the self-control of "proper," middle-class Protestant Americans. The final victory for the movement came as the United States entered World War I. The movement successfully equated the prohibition of alcohol with the quest to bring democracy to the world. Also, with wartime shortages of grain, it made sense to ban grain-based alcoholic beverages. The anti-German sentiment that

developed during World War I also played a role because many American breweries had German names. But the victory of the movement proved to be a hollow victory. While the per capita consumption of alcohol went down during the Prohibition era, the amount of lawlessness in America went up. Illegal bars, known as speakeasies, sprang up in cities across the country. Illegal producers and sellers of alcohol also proliferated. Criminal activity became so widespread that the nation agreed to ratify another Amendment, the 21st, which repealed Prohibition. The "noble experiment" of Prohibition demonstrated that it is difficult for the government to dramatically change individuals' behavior.

WRONG CHOICES EXPLAINED:

(2) National Prohibition did not result in the restriction of women's suffrage. Women gained the right to vote with ratification of the 19th Amendment, around the same time that Prohibition went into effect. The 19th Amendment was ratified in August 1920, seven months after Prohibition went into effect.

(3) There was a great deal of racial prejudice during the years of national Prohibition (1920–1933), but Prohibition would not be considered a cause of racial prejudice.

(4) The 1920s are known as a time of growing intolerance, not tolerance, with regard to religious issues.

26. **4** Warren G. Harding supported the foreign policy of isolationism when he used the phrase "return to normalcy" during his presidential campaign of 1920. Harding ran a conservative campaign. His call for a "return to normalcy" implied a rejection of the internationalist impulses that propelled the United States into World War I as well as a rejection of the reformist impulses of the Progressive era. Isolationism means retreating from world affairs. The policy of isolationism led to the Senate rejecting the Treaty of Versailles. Approval of the treaty by the Senate would have made the United States a member of the League of Nations. Harding signed into law the 1922 Fordney-McCumber Act, which dramatically raised tariff rates in order to keep out foreign goods. Isolationist sentiment in the 1920s also led to the enactment of legislation that dramatically restricted immigration into the United States.

WRONG CHOICES EXPLAINED:

(1) The foreign policy of appeasement is not associated with President Harding. The policy of appeasement is associated with the leaders of Great Britain and France in the 1930s, when they allowed Hitler to expand German territory.

(2) The foreign policy of internationalism is not associated with President Harding. Several presidents have pursued an internationalist foreign policy by urging greater U.S. involvement in international affairs. President Wilson ushered the United States into intervening in World War I, and President

Franklin Roosevelt pushed for greater United States involvement in World War II even before the Japanese attack on Pearl Harbor in 1941.

(3) The foreign policy of containment is not associated with President Harding. Containment, the policy of preventing the spread of communism beyond the countries in which it already existed, is associated with President Truman in the early years of the Cold War.

27. **3** The stock market crash (1929) led to the start of the Great Depression. In late October 1929, stock prices plummeted as investors went on a selling frenzy. When the market finally bottomed out, the Dow Jones Industrial Average, the major indicator of stock market trends, had dropped 89 percent from its peak. The crash of the stock market is attributed to excessive speculation on the part of the public. The stock market is built on the idea of speculation. At all times, people buy shares in a corporation with the hope that the price of the shares will rise. If there is strong demand for a particular company's stock, the price of a share rises. Normally, demand for a stock goes up if the company reports that it is doing well. But in the 1920s people bought stock without even considering the soundness of the company they were investing in. People figured the market would just go up and up indefinitely. Stock brokers provided easy access to credit so people could buy stock on margin, putting only a fraction of the cost of the stock down and promising to pay the rest on some future date. This whole system of wild speculation completely unraveled in October 1929 when investors lost confidence in the market. The stock market crash is cited as one of several causes of the Great Depression.

WRONG CHOICES EXPLAINED:

(1) The Red Scare (1919–1920) occurred a decade before the beginning of the Great Depression, so it would not be considered a cause of the depression. Also, the Red Scare was a political event, not an economic one. The Red Scare was the crusade against suspected communists, anarchists, and other radicals.

(2) The election of President Herbert Hoover (1928) is not considered a cause of the Great Depression. Some historians fault him for not responding to the economic crisis more vigorously, but the causes of the Great Depression are to be found in underlying economic problems of the 1920s.

(4) The Emergency Banking Act (1933) was a response to the Great Depression, not a cause of it. The act was part of President Franklin Roosevelt's New Deal and was designed to restore confidence in the banking system.

28. **3** Based on the cartoon, economic recovery would require more money in the hands of lower income families. The cartoon and the quote below it by President Franklin Roosevelt highlight one of the important philosophical underpinnings of Roosevelt's New Deal program. He saw that one of the causes of the Great Depression was that workers in the 1920s were

not able to purchase enough consumer goods to keep the economy growing. An important aspect of his New Deal was increasing workers' wages. Toward this end, President Franklin Roosevelt pushed for passage of the Wagner Act, which made it easier for workers to join unions so that their wages, and purchasing power, would rise. He also supported programs that would provide government jobs to unemployed people, such as the Works Progress Administration.

WRONG CHOICES EXPLAINED:

(1) The cartoon is not asserting that economic recovery would require fewer regulations by the federal government. The presence of Uncle Sam, helping "Mr. Small Income," indicates that the cartoonist would encourage greater government involvement in the economy, not less.

(2) The cartoon is not asserting that economic recovery would require increased taxes on the working class. The key to the "permanent recovery" door is labeled "increased purchasing power." President Franklin Roosevelt argued that workers were not able to purchase enough consumer goods to get the economy moving toward recovery. Increasing taxes on working people would not increase their purchasing power; it would diminish it.

(4) The cartoon is not asserting that economic recovery would require protective tariffs on foreign goods. The cartoon does not allude to trade at all. Roosevelt actually pushed to lower tariffs on foreign goods in order to boost trade.

29. **4** The main idea of the song is that hard times threaten economic opportunity. The famous song poignantly highlights the economic bind that many people were in during the Great Depression of the 1930s. The narrator of the song had participated in building the network of railroads that criss-crossed America and had fought to defend his country during World War I. Now he was reduced to asking for handouts to survive. The song makes clear that the unemployed during the Great Depression were not lazy; rather, there simply were no jobs available.

WRONG CHOICES EXPLAINED:

(1) The song does not assert that railroad workers were overpaid. The song is sympathetic to the men who built the network of railroads in the United States. It wonders why these hardworking men had no other option during the Great Depression than waiting in a bread line or asking for a handout.

(2) The song does not mention average wages in 1930. In fact, it notes that many hardworking men were unemployed during the Great Depression. The "dime" in the title refers to spare change that the narrator is asking passers-by for.

(3) The song does not assert that returning soldiers easily find work. Rather, it is noting the opposite. Many veterans of World War I were reduced to asking for handouts because they did not have jobs.

30. **2** The Works Progress Administration (WPA) was created to deal with the central problem identified in the song—widespread unemployment during the Great Depression of the 1930s. The WPA (1935) was a vast program of government projects that hired millions of unemployed workers. The WPA, for example, built schools, maintained highways, installed sewer lines, wrote guidebooks, and produced theatrical productions. Franklin Roosevelt took government in a new direction by asserting that the federal government should take some responsibility for the people. Previously, churches, settlement houses, and other private charities helped people in times of need. But the levels of poverty and unemployment during the Great Depression were unprecedented. Roosevelt believed that the government needed to take action. His series of government programs is called the New Deal.

WRONG CHOICES EXPLAINED:

(1) The Interstate Commerce Commission (ICC; 1887) was created to regulate trade between states, not to address the issue of unemployment. The impetus behind the ICC was widespread resentment at the practices of the large railroad companies. Many farmers believed the railroad companies were engaged in underhanded business practices and that the government should step in to regulate these giant corporations.

(3) The Federal Trade Commission (FTC; 1914) was created to regulate business practices, not to address the issue of unemployment. The FTC attempts to protect the consumers from unfair business practices.

(4) The Federal Deposit Insurance Corporation (FDIC; 1933) was created during the New Deal, but its focus was restoring people's confidence in the banking system, not helping the unemployed.

31. **2** President Franklin D. Roosevelt's reelection in 1940 created a controversy that eventually led to the establishment of presidential term limits. President George Washington established a precedent of serving only two terms. This tradition of serving for only two terms became such an ingrained part of the American political system that it was long described as being part of the "unwritten constitution" of the United States. Each president after Washington followed this tradition until President Franklin D. Roosevelt ran for a third term in 1940. He won that election, and he was even elected to a fourth term in 1944 before he died in office in 1945. After Roosevelt's death, many argued that the tradition of the two-term presidency should be added to the actual Constitution. These advocates argued that the power of the presidency gave an incumbent president an unfair advantage. In 1951, the 22nd Amendment to the Constitution was ratified, limiting to two the number of full terms a president may serve.

WRONG CHOICES EXPLAINED:

(1) The Supreme Court did not address the issue of presidential term limits. The Court did rule in 1995 that states could not impose term limits on their federal representatives.

(3) The controversy around President Franklin Roosevelt's decision to seek a third term did not involve the level of voter participation.

(4) The controversy around President Franklin Roosevelt's decision to seek a third term did not lead to him attempting to increase the number of justices on the Supreme Court. Roosevelt did attempt to increase the number of justices on the Supreme Court, but the "court packing" controversy occurred in 1937, three years before he ran for a third term.

32. **4** The map indicates internment camps where the government relocated Japanese Americans during World War II. This indicates that the government considered Japanese Americans a threat to national security. In 1942 President Roosevelt issued Executive Order 9066, authorizing the government to remove 120,000 people, two-thirds of them citizens, from West Coast states and relocate them to camps throughout the West. Most of their property was confiscated by the government. In the case of *Korematsu* v. *United States* (1944), the Supreme Court ruled that the relocation was acceptable on the grounds of national security. Much later, in 1988, the U.S. government publicly apologized to the surviving victims and extended $20,000 in reparations to each one. The Korematsu decision is one of several rulings by the Supreme Court that have curtailed civil liberties in times of war.

WRONG CHOICES EXPLAINED:
(1) The map does not indicate whether the camps were located in abandoned mining towns. Manzanar, one of the largest camps, was established at the site of an abandoned town that had been founded by ranchers and miners. Many of the camps were simply erected on open land out West.

(2) The map does not indicate whether Western states opposed the creation of the relocation centers. Anti-Japanese sentiment ran high during World War II, leading many people to support the move to relocate Japanese Americans.

(3) The map does not indicate whether the relocation centers were placed near rivers. Many were located in the desert and had to be supplied with water.

33. **1** The relocation camps shown on the map were mainly a reaction to the Japanese military attack on Pearl Harbor. The bombing of Pearl Harbor, Hawaii, by Japan (December 7, 1941) led the United States to enter World War II. Emotions ran high after this attack. Many Americans directed their anger at all Japanese people—even ones who had decided to immigrate to the United States. The United States asserted that these Japanese Americans posed a security risk, but the government never provided evidence of spying or sabotage by Japanese Americans.

WRONG CHOICES EXPLAINED:
(2) The relocation camps did not include Japanese war prisoners. The United States maintained prisoner-of-war camps in areas it controlled in the Pacific theater of operations.

(3) The relocation camps were not intended as military training centers for Japanese Americans. However, many Japanese Americans did volunteer to serve in the military during World War II. Despite the mistreatment they received at the hands of the U.S. government, Japanese Americans comprised the 442nd Regimental Combat Team, which fought with distinction in Europe.

(4) There were no attacks by Japanese Americans on U.S. military bases during World War II.

34. **1** The D-Day invasion in June 1944 was important to the outcome of World War II because it opened a new allied front in Europe. Until D-Day, most of the fighting against Germany was carried out by the Soviet Union in eastern Europe. Joseph Stalin, the leader of the Soviet Union, had been urging the United States and Great Britain to open a second western front in Europe against Germany. At a meeting in Tehran, Iran, in November 1943, President Franklin Roosevelt and British leader Winston Churchill assured Stalin that they would open up a second European front. In June 1944, allied troops landed on the beaches of Normandy, France, and began pushing Hitler's forces back toward Germany. By August 1944, allied forces had liberated Paris from Nazi occupation. Hitler made a last attempt to stop the allied assault in the winter of 1944–1945. German forces drove through allied lines into Belgium in the Battle of the Bulge before being stopped by allied forces. American and British troops approached Germany from the west as Soviet troops approached from the east. By April 1945, Soviet troops were on the outskirts of Berlin. On April 30, Hitler committed suicide, and on May 7, 1945, Germany surrendered, ending the war in Europe.

WRONG CHOICES EXPLAINED:

(2) The use of the atomic bomb was not an option for the United States and its allies in June 1944. The bomb had not yet been developed. It would take another year of frenzied research and development at Los Alamos, New Mexico, before the bomb was ready to use. In June 1945, this new deadly device was tested at the Alamogordo Air Base in New Mexico. In August 1945, an atomic bomb was used on the Japanese city of Hiroshima. Three days later, a second bomb was used on the Japanese city of Nagasaki. Within days of the dropping of the second bomb, Japan agreed to surrender.

(3) The D-Day invasion did not bring about the surrender of Italy. Italy surrendered after a long and bloody campaign against American and British forces just as the D-Day invasion was beginning in June 1944.

(4) The D-Day invasion was not intended to stop Soviet advances in eastern Europe. On the contrary, the strategy of the allies was to have two fronts in Europe against Hitler—the Soviets on the eastern front and the Americans and British on the western front.

35. **2** The Marshall Plan (1948–1952) was a U.S. effort to assist the nations of Europe by providing economic aid. The Marshall Plan (1948)

extended billions of dollars to war-torn western Europe after World War II. It was, in part, designed to strengthen the western democracies so that they would not turn to communism. The Marshall Plan was part of the U.S. policy of containment. The policy was developed after World War II when the wartime ally of the United States, the Soviet Union, became its rival and the two powers became entangled in an ongoing Cold War. The architects of the containment policy saw the Soviet Union as a predatory force, forcing its form of government on other countries. The reality was usually more complex, as Soviet pressure often combined with internal factors to push a country toward the communist camp.

WRONG CHOICES EXPLAINED:

(1) The Marshall Plan was an economic package, not a military alliance. As part of its strategy during the Cold War, the United States did encourage the formation of the North Atlantic Treaty Organization (NATO; 1949), a military alliance of nations opposed to the Soviet camp.

(3) The Marshall Plan was an economic package, not a military strategy. As part of the Cold War, the United States did send troops to trouble spots, most notably South Korea (1951–1953).

(4) The Marshal Plan did not extend aid to the Soviet Union. It was designed to strengthen nations so that they would not turn to communism. The Lend-Lease Act was the U.S. policy of extending aid to nations fighting Nazi aggression at the beginning of World War II.

36. **2** The statement is associated with the Cuban missile crisis. The Cuban Missile Crisis occurred in 1962 when a U.S. U-2 spy plane discovered that Cuba was preparing bases for Soviet nuclear missiles to be installed. President Kennedy felt that these missiles, in such close proximity to the United States, amounted to an unacceptable provocation and ordered Soviet Premier Nikita Khrushchev to halt the operation and dismantle the bases. Khrushchev insisted on the right of the Soviet Union to install the missiles. For about a week, the world stood on the brink of nuclear war. Finally, a deal was reached in which the Soviet Union would abandon its Cuban missile program and the United States would quietly remove missiles from Turkey.

WRONG CHOICES EXPLAINED:

(1) The statement is not associated with the Bay of Pigs invasion. The Bay of Pigs invasion (1961) did involve Cuba, but the statement refers specifically to "communist missiles" and "strategic weapons." The Bay of Pigs invasion was planned under the Eisenhower administration and implemented by President Kennedy. The plan called for the United States to train, arm, and aid a group of Cuban exiles opposed to the Communist government of Fidel Castro. The exiles landed at the Bay of Pigs in Cuba in April 1961, but they were quickly captured by Cuban forces.

(3) The statement is not associated with the United States-Soviet space race. The space race was the competition between the United States and the

Soviet Union to explore outer space. It began with the Soviet launch of the unmanned satellite *Sputnik* into space in 1957. The launching of *Sputnik* led the American government to devote more resources to teaching science and math to young people. The United States was the first nation to successfully land men on the moon in 1969.

(4) The statement is not associated with the nuclear test ban treaty. A Partial Test Ban Treaty was signed by the United States, the Soviet Union, and Great Britain in 1963. The ban exempted underground nuclear tests.

37. **4** Based on the statement, it is valid to conclude that geographic location plays an important role in determining foreign policy. The proximity of Cuba to the United States led President Kennedy to oppose the placement of missiles in that country. Throughout its history, the United States has taken a special interest in countries of the Western Hemisphere.

WRONG CHOICES EXPLAINED:
(1) The statement by President Kennedy did not mention the placement of U.S. strategic weapons.

(2) The statement by President Kennedy does not reflect an isolationist approach to foreign policy. By challenging the Soviet Union on behalf of the nations of the Western Hemisphere, Kennedy is demonstrating an interventionist approach to foreign policy.

(3) The statement by President Kennedy does not reflect a desire to end military alliances. By speaking out on behalf of the nations of the Western Hemisphere, he is asserting the importance of an alliance.

38. **1** The headlines support the conclusion that individuals have a great impact on movements for change. The three individuals mentioned all played pivotal roles in movements for change in the 1960s. Martin Luther King Jr., a reverend from Atlanta, Georgia, was a central figure in the civil rights movement of the 1950s and 1960s. King gained prominence in 1956 by being the leader of the Montgomery, Alabama, bus boycott. King supported directly challenging unjust practices through civil disobedience. In 1963, the civil rights movement held one of the biggest demonstrations in American history in Washington, D.C. More than 200,000 people gathered to march, sing, and hear speeches, including King's "I Have a Dream Speech." Rachel Carson was one of the first people to make the public aware of the damage being done to the environment by human practices. Her book *Silent Spring* (1962) detailed the harmful effects of toxic chemicals on the environment. Carson said that the big chemical companies spread false information about their products. Her book was especially critical of chemical pesticides such as DDT. *Silent Spring* shocked many people and was a catalyst for the environmental movement of the 1960s and 1970s. In the 1960s, Cesar Chavez brought the plight of migrant farm workers into the consciousness of the public. Chavez was one of the organizers of United Farm Workers. This organization organized strikes and boycotts of farm products to advance the cause of workers' rights. In the

1980s, Chavez was one of the organizers of a national boycott of grapes to protest the use of toxic chemicals used in growing grapes.

WRONG CHOICES EXPLAINED:

(2) The headlines do not indicate that social reforms progress faster with support from big business. The chemical industry vociferously opposed Carson's work and the agricultural industry opposed Chavez's effort.

(3) The headlines do not indicate that the press discouraged efforts at reform in the 1960s. The three items are all headlines from newspapers. This indicates that the press played a role in publicizing the issues raised by these individuals.

(4) The headlines do not indicate that mass movements often continue without strong leaders. The importance of leadership in mass movements is often debated by both historians and participants. But the three headlines all focus on strong individuals who led mass movements.

39. **1** The principal goal of the activity described in the statement was to achieve racial integration of public facilities. In 1960, the Supreme Court ruled that state laws separating the races on interstate transportation facilities were unconstitutional. Still, states maintained Jim Crow codes that separated African American from white passengers. In 1961, the Congress of Racial Equality (CORE) organized a series of bus rides, with African American as well as white passengers, through the South to challenge these local codes. The Freedom Riders met a great deal of resistance in the South. In Alabama, a mob slashed the tires of one bus and then firebombed it. President Kennedy finally sent federal marshals to Alabama to protect the Freedom Riders and to enforce federal law.

WRONG CHOICES EXPLAINED:

(2) The principal goal of the activity described in the statement was not to encourage change through violent means. Though the opponents of the Freedom Riders resorted to violence, the riders themselves practiced "nonviolent resistance."

(3) The principal goal of the activity described in the statement was not to expand voting rights for African Americans. Voting rights was a central goal of the civil rights movement, but the goal of the Freedom Riders was to integrate interstate bus lines.

(4) The principal goal of the activity described in the statement was not to force the president to send military troops into the South. President Kennedy did send federal marshals into Alabama after the riders were attacked by local mobs, but the goal of the Freedom Riders was to integrate interstate bus lines.

40. **2** The activities described in this statement helped lead to passage of the Civil Rights Act of 1964. Laws such as the ones separating the races on busses are known as Jim Crow laws. These laws relegated African Americans

to second-class status in the South. State and local Jim Crow laws first appeared in the South after Reconstruction ended (1877). Jim Crow laws became more prevalent after 1896 when the Supreme Court, in the case of *Plessy* v. *Ferguson*, accepted segregation as Constitutional as long as the facilities for both whites and African Americans were of equal quality. It was generally the case that the facilities for African Americans were substandard, but this "separate but equal" rule was the law of the land until the Supreme Court found segregated schools inherently unfair in the *Brown* v. *Board of Education* decision (1954). President Johnson extended this edict to all public facilities by signing the Civil Rights Act of 1964.

WRONG CHOICES EXPLAINED:

(1) The activities described in the passage did not lead to President Harry Truman's order to desegregate the military. Truman did issue Executive Order 9981 in 1948, desegregating the armed forces. This event, however, occurred well before the 1961 events described in the passage.

(3) The activities described in the statement did not lead to ratification of the Equal Rights Amendment. In fact, the Equal Rights Amendment was not ratified. The proposed amendment, which was intended to guarantee equal rights under the law regardless of sex, was passed by Congress in 1972 but failed to gain ratification by three-quarters of the states.

(4) The activities described in the statement did not lead to a decision by the Supreme Court to integrate public schools. The Supreme Court did issue such a decision, *Brown* v. *Board of Education* (1954), but that occurred before the activities described in the statement.

41. **3** The term most commonly used to describe President Richard Nixon's policy toward the Soviet Union is *détente*. *Détente* is the French word for loosening and refers to an easing of tensions in the Cold War and a warming of relations between the United States and the Soviet Union. The policy was carried out by President Nixon. It may seem ironic that a man who made a name for himself as a strong anti-communist—as a congressman, he pursued suspected Soviet spy Alger Hiss (1950)—was responsible for the détente policy. But Nixon's anti-Communist credentials enabled him to open relations with Communist nations without being accused of being "soft on communism." In 1972 Nixon became the first U.S. president to visit Communist China, and later in 1972 he held meetings with Soviet leaders in Moscow. The meetings produced several agreements, including an agreement to limit anti-ballistic missile systems (ABMs).

WRONG CHOICES EXPLAINED:

(1) President Nixon did not pursue a policy of collective security. For most of its history, the United States avoided the alliances and treaty organizations that would constitute collective security. This changed in 1949 when the United States participated in the formation of the North Atlantic Treaty Organization (NATO).

(2) President Nixon did not pursue a policy of brinksmanship. Brinksmanship refers to pushing a conflict to the verge of disaster. The goal is for one side to show the other that it means business and will not back down from a conflict. The policy is associated with President Eisenhower's Secretary of State John Foster Dulles.

(4) President Nixon did not pursue a policy of neutrality. Many U.S. presidents have attempted to remain neutral in respect to conflicts in various parts of the world. President Washington first urged the United States to maintain a policy of neutrality. The policy was debated and challenged in the lead-ups to U.S. participation in both of the World Wars. Since World War II, all U.S. presidents have embraced, to one degree or another, U.S. participation in world affairs.

42.   **4** The migration of many people from the Midwest and the Northeast to the South, Southwest, and West Coast since the 1970s has resulted in some states gaining and others losing seats in the House of Representatives. Representation in the House of Representatives is based on population. Every ten years, the government carries out a census to count the number of people in the United States and to determine which states and districts have grown with regard to population and which have shrunk. From these census figures, representation in the House of Representatives is adjusted. The total number of representatives is currently fixed at 435, so an increase in the number of representatives from one state would necessarily involve a decrease in another state. The demographic shift described in the question is associated with the deindustrialization of Northeastern and Midwestern cities in the last several decades. Large numbers of factories in Northeastern cities such as New York and Philadelphia, as well as Midwestern "rust belt" cities such as Pittsburgh, Cleveland, Detroit, and Chicago, have closed. People have left these cities to look for opportunities in the "sun belt" of the South, Southwest, and West Coast.

WRONG CHOICES EXPLAINED:
(1) There has not been a call to increase membership in Congress. An increase beyond the current number of representatives, 435, might make doing business unwieldy.

(2) There has not been a decrease in immigration from Asia and Latin America since the 1970s. In fact, there has been an increase.

(3) There have been calls by some people to eliminate the electoral college. Some have argued that the institution is flawed because it allows a situation in which a presidential candidate could win the national popular vote but could lose the election because he or she did not win the sufficient number of electoral votes. But these calls are unrelated to the demographic shift described in the question.

43.   **2** The focus of the cartoon is the high cost of many medicines. The woman in the cartoon is noting the price of a medication and is wryly suggesting that she and her husband would not be able to purchase food after

paying for the medication. The high cost of medications has been an important political issue recently. Many Americans have health insurance, which covers the costs of medication. But millions of Americans have no medical coverage and have to pay for medications out of pocket. Many prescription drugs are extremely expensive. Generally speaking, when a pharmaceutical company produces a new drug, it has a monopoly on selling it to the public as long as its patent is still in effect. Once the patent expires, other companies can make generic versions of the drug and sell them for considerably less. Many health care advocates argue that the prices of medications should be regulated so that helping the sick takes priority over corporate profits.

WRONG CHOICES EXPLAINED:

(1) The cartoon does not allude to poor diets of many older Americans. The woman in the cartoon jokes that perhaps the medication would have to replace dinner, but the point of the cartoon is the high costs of medications.

(3) The cartoon does not allude to increased competition among drug manufacturers. Many health care advocates argue that increased competition among drug manufacturers might lower drug costs. Currently, the holder of a patent to a particular medication has a monopoly on selling that medication.

(4) The cartoon does not allude to government-controlled prices of prescription drugs. Currently, the government does not regulate the prices of prescription drugs. Many health care advocates argue that the prices of prescription drugs should be regulated.

44. **1** The graduating student pictured in the cartoon is confronted by a problem caused by cheaper foreign labor. Currently, workers in many developing countries in Asia, Africa, and Latin America earn considerably less money than workers in the United States. Consequently, many American companies have outsourced jobs to foreign countries or have moved abroad altogether. Increasingly, many of the products Americans purchase, from automobiles to blue jeans, are produced abroad. This trend has led to a decrease in jobs in many fields in the United States. Politicians debate whether the government should attempt to protect American jobs or let the market take its course.

WRONG CHOICES EXPLAINED:

(2) The problem in the cartoon is not caused by increasing tariff rates. Most tariff rates have come down in recent years. Some advocates for American workers argue that America should increase tariff rates to keep out foreign goods and protect American jobs.

(3) The problem in the cartoon is not caused by high-cost imports. The goods from foreign countries tend to be lower in price, because the wages the workers earn in foreign countries tend to be lower.

(4) The problem in the cartoon is not caused by lack of education. The student pictured in the cartoon has just graduated. He has sufficient education. What he is lacking is job opportunities.

45. **4** The headlines support the conclusion that U.S. dependence on foreign petroleum is a major problem. The United States is the biggest consumer of petroleum, accounting for a quarter of all petroleum consumed in the world. Much of the oil that the United States purchases from abroad is from the Middle East. The oil-producing countries of the Middle East make up the majority of members of the Organization of Petroleum Exporting Countries (OPEC). The United States, as an importer of petroleum, has had to deal with changing policies of OPEC. In 1973, for example, the Middle Eastern OPEC nations cut exports to the United States, dramatically increasing the price of petroleum. These moves were in retaliation for U.S. support for Israel in the 1973 Yom Kippur War between Israel and its Arab neighbors. Supporters of American oil independence argue that such a move would free the United States from entanglements in Middle Eastern politics.

WRONG CHOICES EXPLAINED:

(1) The headlines do not indicate that the United States exports more oil than it imports. Two of the headlines refer to the importation of oil.

(2) The headlines do not indicate that energy policies are not affected by domestic events. Domestic events do affect energy policy. For example, an increase in oil consumption at home affects the options open to the United States with regard to energy policy.

(3) The headlines do not indicate that the demand for alternative energy is declining. If anything, we might infer that as petroleum prices soar, Americans will search for alternative energy sources.

46. **4** The information on the graph supports the conclusion that the population of both groups will increase by 2020. The increase among senior citizens is more pronounced than the increase among the general population. Between 2005 and 2020, the census expects the population of New Yorkers 75 and over to increase by about 11 percent. The increase in the general population in New York, on the other hand, is expected to be less than 2 percent. The "graying" of New York has implications for social policies.

WRONG CHOICES EXPLAINED:

(1) The graph does not support the conclusion that the death rate will slowly increase by 2020. The graph shows a steady increase in the number of people 75 and over by 2020. This increase in the population of older New Yorkers would not lead one to infer that the death rate is increasing.

(2) The graph does not support the conclusion that the number of people 75 and over will double by 2020. The increase is projected to be about 11 percent—considerably less than 100 percent.

(3) The graph does not support the conclusion that the number of people 75 and older will steadily decline by 2020. It will increase by about 11 percent by 2020.

47. **2** The decision in *Gibbons* v. *Ogden* (1824) and the decision in *Wabash, St. Louis and Pacific Railroad* v. *Illinois* (1886) addressed the issue of regulation of interstate commerce. In both cases, the Supreme Court affirmed that only the federal government can regulate trade between states. In *Gibbons* v. *Ogden*, the Court invalidated a monopoly given by New York State to a ferryboat company to navigate the Hudson River. The Court declared that because the river goes through two or more states, it is subject to the interstate commerce clause of the Constitution. Later, in the *Wabash* case, the Court ruled that Illinois could not regulate railroad rates on rail lines that crossed state boundaries, again citing the interstate commerce clause.

WRONG CHOICES EXPLAINED:

(1) The cases do not deal with congressional privileges. Members of Congress enjoy a wide array of privileges, such as franking privileges, which allows them to send mail to their constituents without postage stamps.

(3) The cases do not deal with state taxation of federal property. The Supreme Court addressed this issue in the case of *McCulloch* v. *Maryland* (1819). In that case, the Court prohibited Maryland from taxing the Bank of the United States.

(4) The cases do not deal with contract rights. The Supreme Court has issued two important decisions in which it upheld the legitimacy of contracts. In 1819, the state of New Hampshire attempted to turn Dartmouth College into a state college, despite the fact that Dartmouth had a charter to operate as a private college. In *Dartmouth College* v. *Woodward*, the Supreme Court upheld the original charter of Dartmouth College, asserting the importance of contracts. In *Fletcher* v. *Peck* (1810), the Supreme Court upheld a corrupt land deal between the state of Georgia and private individuals. The Court ruled that the deal might not have been in the public interest, but a contract should be upheld.

48. **2** The government policy of laissez-faire argues that government should limit, as much as possible, any interference in the economy. The French phrase *laissez-faire* means "to let alone." It describes a government policy that would take a hands-off approach with regard to economic activities. Throughout much of the history of the United States, Americans have been suspicious of government intervention in the economy. The founders of the United States had vivid memories of the overbearing, mercantilist policies of Great Britain. With the American economy growing by leaps and bounds in the 19th century, few challenged this doctrine. The term fit in well with the doctrine of social Darwinism, which gained many adherents in the late 19th century. Social Darwinists argued that government interference in the economy would hinder the evolution of the human species. The inequalities of wealth that characterized the late 1800s were part of the process of "survival of the fittest." But by the 20th century, the country began to face serious economic problems that called into question the laissez-faire doctrine. In the first decades of the 20th century, progressive reformers

called on the government to break up monopolies, regulate the food production industry, help the poor, and create peace between owners and workers. When the Great Depression struck the United States in the 1930s, Franklin D. Roosevelt argued more forcefully that the government must play an activist role. After Roosevelt won the presidential election in 1932, he initiated a sweeping array of programs known as the New Deal. Since the Great Depression, politicians have argued about the nature and degree of government economic intervention in the economy, but few today argue for a complete laissez-faire policy.

WRONG CHOICES EXPLAINED:

(1) Socialism is an economic policy that argues for government ownership of key sectors of the economy. It is the opposite of a laissez-faire approach of non-intervention by the government in the economy.

(3) Mercantilism is an economic policy that argues that the government should play an active role in the economy. Laissez-faire, by contrast, argues that the government should play no role in the economy. Mercantilist theory holds that governments should try to increase the wealth of a nation by maintaining colonies so as to have a steady and inexpensive source of raw materials. The theory guided Great Britain in maintaining its American colonies before the American Revolution.

(4) Protectionism is an economic policy that argues that the government should impose tariffs on goods imported into the United States. These tariffs would raise the prices of foreign-made goods and would make American goods comparatively more affordable. The tariffs would, in theory, protect American industry from foreign competition. Protectionism involves government intervention in the economy; laissez-faire implies no government intervention in the economy.

49. **4** The Supreme Court decisions in *Plessy* v. *Ferguson* and *Brown* v. *Board of Education of Topeka* demonstrate that the Supreme Court can change an earlier decision. To some degree, Supreme Court justices simply determine whether particular laws are consistent with the Constitution. But to some degree, the justices reflect the social values and ideals that are prevalent in the society they live in. So just as social values change over time, the Supreme Court can change its collective mind about a particular issue. In this case, the issue was Jim Crow laws and practices that relegated African Americans to second-class status in the South. These Jim Crow laws segregated public facilities, such as railroad cars, bathrooms, and schools. In the case of *Plessy* v. *Ferguson* (1896), the Supreme Court accepted segregation as constitutional as long as the facilities for both whites and African Americans were of equal quality. It was generally the case that the facilities for African Americans were substandard, but this "separate but equal" rule was the law of the land until the Supreme Court found segregated schools inherently unfair in the *Brown* v. *Board of Education* decision (1954).

WRONG CHOICES EXPLAINED:

(1) In the pair of Supreme Court decisions listed in this choice, one decision does not change an earlier decision. The two decisions deal with different issues. The decision in *Schenck* v. *United States* (1919) upheld the Espionage and Sedition Acts, passed during World War I to put limits on public expressions of antiwar sentiment. In *United States* v. *Nixon* (1974), the Supreme Court ordered Nixon to turn over tapes of conversations that were held in the White House Oval Office. Nixon had argued that executive privilege allowed him to keep the tapes.

(2) In the pair of Supreme Court decisions listed in this choice, one decision does not change an earlier decision. The two decisions deal with different issues. The decision in *Korematsu* v. *United States* (1944) upheld Executive Order 9066, issued by President Franklin Roosevelt during World War II, authorizing the government to remove more than 120,000 Japanese Americans from West Coast cities and relocate them to camps in the western United States. The *Miranda* v. *Arizona* (1966) decision revolved around the issue of self-incrimination. The 5th Amendment guarantees that people do not have to testify against themselves. But that right is meaningless if arrested people are not aware of it. In this decision, the Court ruled that arrested people must be read basic rights, now known as "Miranda rights," including the right to remain silent and the right to have a lawyer.

(3) In the pair of Supreme Court decisions listed in this choice, one decision does not change an earlier decision. The two decisions deal with different issues. In *Gideon* v. *Wainwright*, the Court ruled that the states must provide court-appointed attorneys to impoverished defendants. In the case of *Heart of Atlanta Motel* v. *United States* (1964), the Supreme Court upheld the 1964 Civil Rights Act and asserted that private businesses such as the Heart of Atlanta Motel cannot ban African American customers.

50. **3** The disputed elections of 1876 and 2000 were similar because in both contests the winner of the popular vote did not become the president. This fact highlights one of the criticisms of our present electoral system. The president is officially chosen by the electoral college, not by the results of the national popular vote. A president, therefore, can be selected by the electoral college without a majority of the popular vote. Whichever candidate wins the popular vote in a particular state gets *all* the electoral votes for that state. The number of electors for each state is equal to the number of members of Congress from that state. Bigger states, therefore, get more electors. Presently, there are 538 electoral votes. A candidate must win the majority, or 270 votes, to be declared the "president-elect." A situation could arise in which a candidate could win the popular vote while losing in the electoral college. If candidate A won the popular vote overwhelmingly in states whose electoral votes totaled 268 (just under the required majority), while candidate B just squeaked by in the remainder of the states, whose electoral votes totaled 270 (the majority), candidate B would be declared president-elect

even though he or she probably had less of the overall popular vote than candidate A. This scenario occurred in 1876 and 2000, as well as in 1824 and 1888. In 1876, Samuel J. Tilden won the majority of the popular vote but Rutherford B. Hayes became president. In 2000, Al Gore won the majority of the popular vote but George W. Bush became president.

WRONG CHOICES EXPLAINED:

(1) In 1876, the winner was chosen by a special electoral commission. The commission reached a compromise that allowed the Republican candidate, Rutherford B. Hayes, to win the presidency. In return, the Republicans agreed to end Reconstruction, paving the way for rule by the Democratic Party in the South. But in 2000, the winner was determined by the results of the electoral college vote. The final result in 2000 took several weeks to determine because the popular vote in Florida was so close that neither candidate could be declared victor immediately. The results of this state were crucial because neither candidate had reached the magic number of 270 in the electoral college without the electoral votes of Florida. Recounts of votes were occurring in several counties in Florida when the U.S. Supreme Court intervened and ordered the recount process to stop. At that moment, George Bush was slightly ahead in Florida and Florida's electoral votes therefore went to him.

(2) In neither case were states required to hold second elections.

(4) In neither case did the election have to be decided by the House of Representatives. In 1800 and 1824, the House of Representatives selected the president when no candidate received a majority in the electoral college.

PART II: THEMATIC ESSAY

Government Role in the Economy

The U.S. government has taken a variety of actions over the years to address problems with the nation's economy. Some of these actions have been more successful than others, but they have demonstrated that the government has rarely taken a purely laissez-faire, or hands-off, approach to the economy.

An early example of government intervention in the economy occurred in the 1790s. The nation's first secretary of the treasury, Alexander Hamilton, was troubled by a series of economic problems that were threatening the very existence of the United States. The U.S. government was in debt from fighting the American Revolution. Further, currency was in a great deal of flux. The various states and banks in the United States all issued their own currency. Commerce on a large scale was difficult, and no one quite trusted the value of any currency. Problems of currency and taxation flared up into full-scale rebellion in Shays's Rebellion in Massachusetts. This 1786 rebellion was one of the catalysts to convening the Constitutional Convention to address weaknesses in the U.S. government.

When Alexander Hamilton became the secretary of the treasury under President George Washington, he was determined to address these vexing economic issues. He proposed a series of economic measures meant to put the United States on sound economic footing. First, he pushed for the creation of a national bank, which would hold the government's tax revenues and act as a stabilizing force on the economy. This national bank would be 20 percent publicly controlled and 80 percent privately controlled. Hamilton thought it was important to get the wealthy people in the United States financially and psychologically invested in the new government. President Washington signed the bank into law in 1791.

Hamilton's economic plans included two other significant elements. He proposed an elaborate and controversial plan to deal with the new nation's substantial debt. He insisted that debts carried over from the war years be paid back, or funded, at full value. Many of the debt certificates had been sold by their holders. The original holders had little faith that the government would ever make good on the actual loans, so they sold the original certificates to speculators at a fraction of their original cost. Full funding meant a financial windfall for these speculators. In addition, Hamilton insisted that the government assume, or agree to pay back, state debts incurred during the war. The proposal met with strenuous opposition from states that either did not have a large debt or had already paid back their debts. To accomplish the goals of "funding" and "assumption," Hamilton prodded the government to take out new loans by selling government bonds. The final piece of Hamilton's financial program was to encourage manufacturing by imposing tariffs on foreign-made goods and subsidizing American industry.

These measures demonstrate that Hamilton was ready to use the power of the government to address economic issues. In the long-term, these measures proved to be successful. The bank provided stability to the U.S. economy. The "funding" and "assumption" of war debts let the world know that the United States was a good credit risk; it pays back its loans. Finally, Hamilton's support for manufacturing set the country on a course for a balanced economy with agriculture and manufacturing.

Another American leader who took action to address economic issues was President Ronald Reagan, who was in office from 1981 to 1989. His set of economic policy initiatives bears the name "Reaganomics." Reagan was a firm believer in supply-side economics. This approach to the economy stressed stimulating the supply-side of the economy—manufacturing firms, banks, insurance corporations. The idea is that if there is growth in the supply-side, there will be general economic growth and the benefits of that growth will reach everyone. The alternative approach is to stimulate the demand-side—consumers. Demand-side economics would emphasize government policies designed to increase workers' wages and expand social programs such as welfare and unemployment benefits. As a believer in supply-side economics, Reagan implemented policies that he thought would stimulate business. Reagan cut taxes for corporations and greatly reduced regulations on industry. He had all the unionized air traffic controllers fired in 1981 when they went on strike. This action broke their union and was consistent with helping the supply-side (the airline industry), rather than the demand-side (the unionized air traffic controllers).

Reagan's pro-business economic policies had mixed results. By cutting corporate taxes and taxes on wealthy individuals he cut government revenues. But, at the same time, he increased spending on armaments. This combination of increased spending and decreased revenues led to a doubling of the national debt from around $900 billion in 1980 to more than $2 trillion in 1986. A large debt is a problem because it requires large interest payments. By 1988, the interest on the national debt had reached 14 percent of total annual government expenditures. This huge debt has hindered economic growth to some degree since and forced future administrations to make difficult decisions with regard to keeping the debt under control.

The U.S. government often takes actions that address economic problems. Politicians might argue which specific action is most appropriate, but few political leaders today argue for a hands-off approach to the economy. These interventions into the economic realm can have differing results, sometimes aiding the economy, and sometimes hampering it.

PART III: DOCUMENT-BASED QUESTION

Part A: Short Answer

DOCUMENT 1

1. According to Bailey and Kennedy, Henry Ford's mass production techniques brought down the cost of an automobile.

This response receives full credit because it explains how Henry Ford's mass production techniques influenced the cost of the automobile.

DOCUMENT 2

2 (1). According to William Ashdown, one negative impact of the automobile was that it broke down the individual's sense of values.

2 (2). According to William Ashdown, another impact of the automobile is that it led people to spend more money than they earned.

These responses would receive full credit because they state two negative impacts of the automobile.

DOCUMENT 3

3 (1). Based on the article, one way the automobile industry has had an impact on the American economy is that it employed more people than any other industry in the United States.

3 (2). Another way the automobile industry has had an impact on the American economy is that it gave a boost to the steel and rubber industries.

These responses would receive full credit because they state two impacts the automobile industry has had on the American economy.

DOCUMENT 4

4a. According to John Steel Gordon, one impact of the automobile on cities is that many people have left cities to live in suburbs.

This response receives full credit because it describes one impact of the automobile on cities.

4b. Based on the information on the map, one impact of the automobile on suburbs is that it led to the development of shopping malls adjacent to interstate highways.

This response receives full credit because it describes one impact of the automobile on suburbs.

DOCUMENT 5

5. According to Ruth Schwartz Cowan, one way life changed for the American housewife as a result of the automobile is that women had to do more work picking up goods because businesses stopped doing deliveries.

This response receives full credit because it describes one way life changed for the American housewife as a result of the automobile.

DOCUMENT 6

6a (1). According to Clay McShane, one economic impact of the automobile on the United States is that cities became more racially segregated.

6a (2). Another economic impact of the automobile on the United States is that supermarkets began to replace smaller neighborhood markets.

These responses would receive full credit because they state two economic impacts of the automobile on the United States.

6b. According to Clay McShane, one economic impact of the automobile on race relations in the United States is that carpooling allowed African Americans to successfully boycott city buses in Montgomery, Alabama in 1956.

This response receives full credit because it states one impact of the automobile on race relations in the United States.

DOCUMENT 7

7. According to William D. Smith, one possible impact of Middle East conflicts on the United States is the disruption of the flow of oil into the country.

This response receives full credit because it states one impact the conflicts in the Middle East could have on the United States.

DOCUMENT 8

8. According to Steven R. Weisman, one reason Ronald Reagan signed the law linking federal highway funds to the drinking age is that he wanted to reduce the number of fatalities caused by drunken driving.

This response receives full credit because it states one reason President Reagan signed the law linking federal highway funds to the drinking age.

DOCUMENT 9

9. According to John H. Cushman, Jr., one impact of the automobile on the United States is that pollutants from automobiles have intensified global warming.

This response receives full credit because it states one impact of the automobile on the United States.

Part B: Document-Based Essay

The automobile has had a major impact on the United States since the early 20th century. The automobile has affected production methods, the American landscape, the environment, and even social values. Perhaps no invention has had such a profound impact on the United States.

Automobile production techniques ushered in the age of mass production. Certain mass production techniques, such as the use of interchangeable parts, existed before the automobile, but when Henry Ford began producing Model T cars in 1908, he created an entire production process based on the principles of mass production. Skilled craft workers were no longer needed at the Ford plant. A key innovation of Ford was the introduction of the conveyor belt. The conveyor belt brought the item being produced from worker to worker. Each worker performed a small task on each automobile. The conveyor belt-driven assembly line made work very efficient. On the negative side for the employees, work became somewhat monotonous. On the positive side, the efficiency of the process led to a steep drop in the price of an automobile. When the Model T was first introduced in 1908, an average American worker had to work approximately 20 months to earn enough money to purchase an automobile. By 1924, the Model T cost about the equivalent of two to three months' salary. The introduction of mass production techniques brought down the cost of the Model T so that it was within the reach of ordinary American workers. (Document 1)

Automobile production has influenced the entire American economy. One out of every six American businesses, according to the National Academy of Engineering, is directly dependent on the automobile. Furthermore, the industries that supply car manufacturers with raw materials, especially the steel industry and the rubber industry, have grown to be dependent on automobile production. Also, entire new industries have arisen to support the automobile industry, such as plate-glass manufacturers. (Document 3)

Perhaps the biggest economic impact of the automobile has been the rise of the petroleum industry. The petroleum industry has led to the rise of giant corporations, from Standard Oil a century ago to Exxon-Mobil today. More worrisome for the United States is the amount of petroleum purchased from the Middle East. The United States is often at odds politically with certain Middle Eastern oil-producing countries, notably Iran. Also, many of the Arab nations in the Middle East have been hostile toward Israel, our strongest ally in the region. In 1973, the Arab oil-producing countries, organized through the Organization of Petroleum Exporting Countries (OPEC), disrupted the flow of oil to the United States in retaliation for American support of Israel during the 1973 Arab-Israeli War. The dependence of the United States on petroleum from other countries has led to serious political and diplomatic problems for the United States. (Documents 3 and 7)

The automobile has had a tremendous impact on the American landscape. The biggest impact has been the decline of older American cities. Starting in the 1950s, middle-class Americans began moving out of urban centers and into suburbs because they were able to commute to work by automobile. Suburban superstores such as Wal-Mart and Home Depot have taken business away from older department stores and hardware stores in the urban core. We see the rise of suburban shopping malls near interstate highways and the decline of urban shopping districts. Many older cities such as Detroit and Pittsburgh have seen 50 percent of their residents move to surrounding suburbs or to other parts of the country. The division between urban and suburban has also become a division between African American and white. The neglected urban cores hold a high percentage of the nation's African American underclass, while many affluent suburbs are primarily white. Not only have cities declined, but the old one-room schools in small-town America have given way to large regional schools, as car-centered families are able to commute longer distances. (Documents 4a, 4b, and 6)

Perhaps the most subtle change brought about by the automobile has been the change in values. According to the author William Ashdown, writing in the 1920s, Americans have abandoned the frugality and moderation that characterized America for much of its history. With the automobile, Americans have become impulsive and present-minded. They no longer think about the future; they no longer put extra money in the bank. Americans have come to demand instant gratification. They want the next new thing, right now. These observations made in the 1920s seem to apply to many Americans today. (Document 2)

The automobile is in many ways a dangerous machine. In the short run, the rise of the automobile has led to the rise of automobile accidents. While driving itself is dangerous, the dangers are compounded when alcohol is brought into the mix. Drunk driving has become an epidemic in the United States. For this reason, President Ronald Reagan signed legislation in 1984 that put pressure on states to raise the drinking age from 18 to 21. (Document 8)

Drunk driving has come down somewhat in recent years, but another danger is on the horizon. Automobile emissions contribute to the greenhouse gasses that cause global warming. Already polar ice caps are receding, and more severe changes could be around the corner. Already, American society is making changes. California has passed legislation that would require automobiles to give off less damaging exhaust. Other communities are taking steps that include encouraging bicycling and mass transit. Hopefully, some of these changes will have an impact before it is too late. (Document 9)

The automobile has had profound impacts on American society. Some of the changes have been positive. The automobile has added a great deal of convenience to the lives of Americans. But with positive changes have come negative changes as well. We see the decline of cities and communities, the breakdown of social values, the rise of automobile accidents, and an increase in global warming. Americans must evaluate whether the positive impacts outweigh the negative impacts.

Topic	Question Numbers	*Number of Points
American political history	3, 4, 10, 14, 15, 22, 31, 32, 33 50	12
Economic theory/policy	16, 21, 27, 28, 43, 44, 45, 48	10
Constitutional principles	5, 6, 7, 8, 13, 47, 49	8
American foreign policy	20, 24, 26, 34, 35, 36, 37, 41	10
American studies—the American people	12, 17, 18, 19, 23, 25, 38, 39, 40, 42, 46	13
Social/cultural developments	29, 30	2
Geography	1, 2, 9, 11	5
Skills questions included in the above content areas		
Reading comprehension	5, 14, 20, 29, 30, 36, 37, 38, 39, 40, 45	
Graph/table interpretation	3, 43, 44, 46	
Cartoon/photo interpretation	28, 43, 44	
Map interpretation	1, 2, 32, 33	
Outlining skills	3	

*Note: The 50 questions in Part I are worth a total of 60 percent of the exam. Since each correct answer is worth 60/50 or 1.2 points, totals are shown to the nearest full point in each content category.

Part I
Multiple-Choice Questions by Standard

Standard	Question Numbers
1 — US and NY History	3, 4, 10, 12, 14, 15, 17, 19, 20, 23, 24, 25, 26, 30, 32, 33, 35, 39, 40, 41, 43, 47
2 — World History	34, 36
3 — Geography	1, 2, 9, 11, 37, 42, 46
4 — Economics	16, 18, 21, 27, 28, 29, 44, 45, 48
5 — Civics, Citizenship, and Government	5, 6, 7, 8, 13, 22, 31, 38, 49, 50

Parts II and III by Theme and Standard

	Theme	Standards
Thematic Essay	Change: Government: Role in the Economy; Presidential Decisions and Actions	Standards 1, 4, and 5: US and NY History; Economics; Civics, Citizenship, and Government
Document-based Essay	Impact of the Automobile on the United States; Factors of Production; Environment; Science and Technology; Culture and Intellectual Life; Places and Regions; Foreign Policy; Presidential Decisions	Standards 1, 2, 3, 4, and 5: US and NY History; World History; Geography; Economics; Civics, Citizenship, and Government

Examination
June 2009
United States History and Government

PART I: MULTIPLE CHOICE

Directions (1–50): For each statement or question, write in the space provided the *number* of the word or expression that, of those given, best completes the statement or answers the question.

1 Since the late 1700s, the Mississippi River has been a vital waterway because it

  1 divided the northern territories from the southern territories

  2 allowed American farmers direct access to Canadian markets

  3 connected the Great Lakes to the Atlantic Ocean

  4 provided farmers and merchants an outlet to the Gulf of Mexico   1 _____

2 During the first half of the 1800s, geographic factors influenced the economy of New England by

  1 encouraging the establishment of large plantations

  2 promoting the growth of trade and manufacturing

  3 increasing the region's reliance on slave labor

  4 supporting rice and indigo farming   2 _____

3 The British benefited from their mercantilist relationship with the American colonies primarily by

  1 supporting the growth of colonial industries
  2 prohibiting colonists from fishing and fur trading
  3 taking large amounts of gold and silver from the southern colonies
  4 buying raw materials from the colonies and selling them finished products   3____

4 The main reason Great Britian established the Proclamation Line of 1763 was to

  1 avoid conflicts between American colonists and Native American Indians
  2 make a profit by selling the land west of the Appalachian Mountains
  3 prevent American industrial development in the Ohio River valley
  4 allow Canada to control the Great Lakes region   4____

5 The Declaration of Independence (1776) has had a major influence on peoples throughout the world because it

  1 guarantees universal suffrage
  2 establishes a basic set of laws for every nation
  3 provides justification for revolting against unjust governments
  4 describes the importance of a strong central government   5____

6 One accomplishment of the national government under the Articles of Confederation was the passage of legislation establishing

1 a central banking system
2 a process for admitting new states to the Union
3 the president's right to put down rebellions
4 the ability of Congress to tax the states effectively   6____

7 Disagreement at the Constitutional Convention of 1787 over the Virginia and New Jersey plans was resolved by a compromise that

1 guaranteed continuation of the slave trade for at least twenty more years
2 limited the power of the federal government to wage war
3 provided for construction of a new national capital in the south
4 created a Congress made up of a Senate and a House of Representatives   7____

8 **"Presidential Candidates Skip Campaigning in Low-Population States"**
"Winner of Popular Vote Loses Election"

These headlines refer to controversial issues most directly related to

1 judicial review
2 the electoral college
3 impeachment
4 checks and balances   8____

9 "The United States shall guarantee to every state in this Union a republican form of government, and shall protect each of them against invasion; and on application of the legislature, or of the executive (when the legislature cannot be convened), against domestic violence."

—United States Constitution, Article IV, Section 4

According to this excerpt, a goal of the framers of the Constitution was to ensure that the United States

1 remained neutral during domestic conflicts involving the states
2 supported the right of each state to resist presidential decisions
3 provided for the common defense of every state
4 approved a bill of rights to protect citizens from government tyranny   9 _____

10 A major reason the Antifederalists opposed the ratification of the United States Constitution was because the Constitution

1 created a national bank
2 lacked a provision for a federal court system
3 failed to provide for the direct election of members of the House of Representatives
4 changed the balance of power between the state and national governments   10 _____

11 An example of the use of the unwritten constitution is the creation of the

1 presidential veto
2 United States Navy
3 federal postal system
4 president's cabinet   11 _____

12 President George Washington pursued a foreign
policy of neutrality during his administration primarily because he believed that

1 the United States needed time to gain economic
and military strength
2 treaties were prohibited by the Constitution
3 the United States should not expand by force
4 alliances should be established with both France
and England   12 _____

13 Many of the decisions made by the Supreme
Court while John Marshall was Chief Justice led
directly to

1 a reduction of federal influence in economic
affairs
2 an increase in the power of the federal government over the states
3 a greater role for Congress in foreign policy
4 a limitation on slavery in the states   13 _____

14 Manifest Destiny was used to justify an American
desire to

1 limit the number of immigrants entering the
country
2 control the area located east of the Appalachian
Mountains
3 expand the United States to the Pacific Ocean
4 warn European countries against colonizing
Latin America   14 _____

15 In the 1850s, the phrase "Bleeding Kansas" was used to describe clashes between

1 proslavery and antislavery groups
2 Spanish landowners and new American settlers
3 Chinese and Irish railroad workers
4 Native American Indians and white settlers

15 _____

16 In the 1850s, why did many runaway slaves go to Canada?

1 They feared being drafted into the Northern army.
2 The Fugitive Slave Act kept them at risk in the United States.
3 More factory jobs were available in Canada.
4 Northern abolitionists refused to help fugitive slaves.

16 _____

17 The Homestead Act, the mass killing of buffalo, and the completion of the transcontinental railroad are most closely associated with the

1 rise of organized labor
2 building of the Erie Canal
3 northern migration of African Americans
4 decline of the Plains Indians

17 _____

18 Many Southern States tried to limit the effects of Radical Reconstruction by

1 adopting federal laws mandating segregation
2 enacting Jim Crow laws
3 abolishing the Southern sharecropping system
4 securing passage of new amendments to the United States Constitution

18 _____

19 The mechanization of agriculture in the United States led directly to

1 an increase in production
2 less dependence on railroads by farmers
3 fewer agricultural exports
4 the decreasing size of the average farm   19 ____

20 News organizations were engaging in yellow journalism before the Spanish-American War when

1 publishers tried to prevent the war
2 articles about Cuba were fair and balanced
3 editors exaggerated events to build support for war
4 writers ignored the situation in Cuba   20 ____

21 The United States issued the Open Door policy (1899–1900) primarily to

1 bring democratic government to the Chinese people
2 secure equal trade opportunities in China
3 force China to change its immigration policies
4 use China as a stepping stone to trade with Japan   21 ____

22 Progressive Era authors such as Jacob Riis and Upton Sinclair are best known for

1 focusing attention on social conditions
2 fighting for the civil rights of African Americans
3 promoting the interests of the American farmer
4 supporting the goal of woman's suffrage   22 ____

23 Which type of federal tax was authorized by the 16th amendment in 1913?

1 excise   3 income
2 import   4 estate   23 _____

24 "... There's no chance of progress and reform in an administration in which war plays the principal part...."

—President-elect Woodrow Wilson, 1913

In this statement, President-elect Wilson was expressing the belief that

1 the United States should enter World War I immediately
2 reform movements are strengthened by war
3 the nation will require a change in leadership if it goes to war
4 the Progressive movement would be best served by continued peace   24 _____

25 In *Schenck* v. *United States* (1919), the Supreme Court decided that a "clear and present danger" to the country allowed the federal government to

1 establish a peacetime draft
2 restrict first amendment rights
3 suspend habeas corpus
4 limit minority voting rights   25 _____

26 One major reason the United States Senate refused to approve the Treaty of Versailles after World War I was that many senators

  1 were concerned about future United States obligations in foreign affairs

  2 rejected United States colonial practices in Asia

  3 wanted immediate repayment of war debts from France

  4 supported increased foreign aid to Germany   26 _____

27 National Prohibition, as authorized by the 18th amendment, stated that

  1 Americans must be 18 years old to purchase alcoholic beverages

  2 only imported alcoholic beverages would be sold

  3 alcoholic beverages could be sold only in government-run stores

  4 the manufacture and sale of alcoholic beverages was banned   27 _____

28 During the 1920s, Congress passed a series of immigration laws that were primarily designed to

  1 increase immigration from Asia

  2 expand the workforce for the growing economy

  3 limit immigration from southern and eastern Europe

  4 prohibit immigration from Latin America   28 _____

29 During the second half of the 1920s, which economic trend was a major cause of the Great Depression?

1 deficits in the federal budget
2 reductions in tariff rates
3 creation of national and state sales taxes
4 overproduction and underconsumption   29 ____

30 President Herbert Hoover's response to the Great Depression was often criticized because it

1 wasted money on new social programs
2 caused widespread rioting and looting in major cities
3 raised taxes on businesses and the wealthy
4 failed to provide direct relief for the neediest persons   30 ____

31 A major reason for creating the Tennessee Valley Authority (TVA) in 1933 was to

1 build and manage a turnpike in the valley
2 provide health care benefits for southerners
3 encourage African Americans to settle in the valley
4 improve economic conditions in a poor rural region   31 ____

Base your answer to question 32 on the cartoon below and on your knowledge of social studies.

All Set!

Source: Fred O. Seibel, *Richmond Times-Dispatch*,
January 4, 1936 (adapted)

32 Which statement about President Franklin D. Roosevelt's plans for a second term most accurately expresses the main idea of the cartoon?

1 Congress will give President Roosevelt a free hand to lead the nation.
2 The American people will trust Congress to control President Roosevelt.
3 President Roosevelt will seek direction from the people.
4 The Great Depression will no longer be a serious concern.

32 ____

Base your answer to question 33 on the quotation below and on your knowledge of social studies.

... I also ask this Congress for authority and for funds sufficient to manufacture additional munitions and war supplies of many kinds, to be turned over to those nations which are now in actual war with aggressor nations.

Our most useful and immediate role is to act as an arsenal for them as well as for ourselves. They do not need man power, but they do need billions of dollars worth of the weapons of defense.

The time is near when they will not be able to pay for them all in ready cash. We cannot, and we will not, tell them that they must surrender, merely because of present inability to pay for the weapons which we know they must have. ...

—President Franklin D. Roosevelt, Annual Message
to Congress, January 6, 1941

33 Which program was President Franklin D. Roosevelt proposing in this speech?

1 Fair Deal   3 Lend-Lease
2 Great Society   4 Cash and Carry   33____

Base your answer to question 34 on the cartoon below and on your knowledge of social studies.

Source: Dr. Seuss, *PM*, April 7, 1942

34 This World War II cartoon was used to encourage Americans to

1 buy war bonds
2 conserve natural resources
3 serve in the armed forces
4 work in war industries

34 _____

35 A major purpose of the GI Bill (1944) was to

1 replace the draft near the end of World War II
2 prohibit racial discrimination in the armed forces
3 provide federal funds for veterans to attend college
4 increase the number of women working in defense industries

35 _____

36 In the Truman Doctrine, President Harry Truman pledged to

1 support Greece in its fight against communist aggression
2 fight hunger in Africa and Asia
3 strengthen the United States nuclear arsenal
4 reject a policy of containment

36 _____

37 Which factor is most closely associated with McCarthyism?

1 buildup of Soviet missiles in Cuba
2 fear of communist influence in the United States
3 rise of the Communist Party in China
4 creation of the Warsaw Pact by the Soviet Union

37 _____

Base your answer to question 38 on the map below and on your knowledge of social studies.

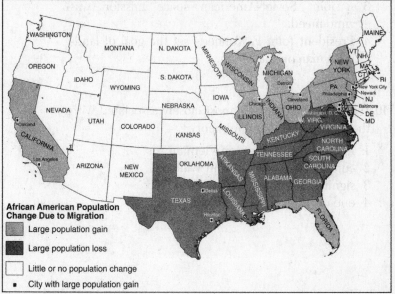

African American Migration, 1940–1970

Source: *Atlas of American History*, Rand McNally, 1999 (adapted)

38 The information on the map supports the conclusion that African American migration between 1940 and 1970 was mainly from the

  1   urban areas to rural areas
  2   south to the north
  3   Mountain states to the West Coast
  4   Sun Belt to the Great Plains   38 _____

39 Which development led to the other three?

  1 The United States government increased funding for science and math education.

  2 The Soviet Union launched the *Sputnik* satellite.

  3 A joint Soviet-American space mission was announced.

  4 President John F. Kennedy set the goal of landing a man on the Moon.   39 _____

40 Which development is most closely associated with the belief in the domino theory?

  1 military involvement in Vietnam

  2 construction of the Berlin Wall

  3 signing of the nuclear test ban treaty

  4 end of the Korean War   40 _____

Base your answer to question 41 on the cartoon below and on your knowledge of social studies.

New Library Section

Source: Herblock, *Washington Post*, December 4, 1975

41 Which statement most accurately describes the main idea of this 1975 cartoon?

1 The press should not publish materials that damage the reputation of public officials.
2 The government is improperly hiding information from the public.
3 Government should restrict the publication of sensitive materials.
4 Libraries are making too many government reports open to the public.

41 _____

42 The primary purpose of President Richard Nixon's policy of détente was to

1 expand United States military involvement in Southeast Asia
2 assure an adequate supply of oil from the Middle East
3 ease tensions between the United States and the Soviet Union
4 maintain a favorable balance of trade with China   42 _____

43 One way in which Andrew Jackson, Abraham Lincoln, and Woodrow Wilson are similar is that each

1 expanded presidential powers
2 reduced the size of the federal bureaucracy
3 faced congressional investigations over the handling of the military
4 used his power as commander in chief to send troops overseas to fight a war   43 _____

44 Which of these trials established the principle that leaders of a nation may be tried for crimes against humanity?

1 Scopes   3 Sacco and Vanzetti
2 Rosenberg   4 Nuremberg   44 _____

45 One similarity between the laws being challenged in the United States Supreme Court cases of *Plessy* v. *Ferguson* (1896) and *Korematsu* v. *United States* (1944) is that

1 specific groups of people were being targeted based on race or ethnicity
2 state laws were declared unconstitutional
3 immigrants were relocated to prison camps
4 federal laws segregating public transportation were upheld   45 _____

Base your answer to question 46 on the table below and on your knowledge of social studies.

Projected Change in House Seats in 2010, By State

State	House Seats	Projected House Seats	
	2000	2010	+/–
Arizona	8	9	+1
California	53	54	+1
Florida	25	27	+2
Georgia	13	14	+1
Illinois	19	18	–1
Massachusetts	10	9	–1
Missouri	9	8	–1
Nevada	3	4	+1
New York	29	27	–2
Ohio	18	16	–2
Pennsylvania	19	18	–1
Texas	32	35	+3

Source: Population Reference Bureau,
www.prb.org (adapted)

46 Information from the table supports the conclusion that the

1 population of the United States is increasing
2 center of population is moving eastward
3 distribution of House seats follows shifts in population
4 number of senators will soon increase

46 ____

47 **"Eisenhower Sends U.S. Troops to Protect Lebanon"**
"Kennedy Places Quarantine on Shipment of Soviet Missiles to Cuba"
"Johnson Increases U.S. Troop Strength in Vietnam by 125,000"

Which statement about the Cold War is illustrated by these headlines?

1 Rivalries between the superpowers often involved conflicts in other nations.
2 United States military support was most often deployed in Europe.
3 Communist forces were frequently victorious in Asia.
4 Summit talks frequently succeeded in limiting international tensions.   47_____

48 Which list of wars that involved the United States is in the correct chronological order?

1 Vietnam War → War on Terrorism → Korean War → World War II
2 Korean War → World War II → Vietnam War → War on Terrorism
3 World War II → Vietnam War → War on Terrorism → Korean War
4 World War II → Korean War → Vietnam War → War on Terrorism   48_____

Base your answers to questions 49 and 50 on the graph below and on your knowledge of social studies.

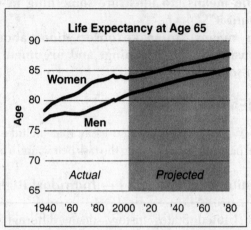

Source: *New York Times*, June 12, 2005 (adapted)

49 Which conclusion about life expectancy at age 65 is most clearly supported by the information in the graph?

1 Life expectancies for men and women are likely to remain the same.
2 Life expectancy rates for men show a steady decline since 1980.
3 By 2040, the life expectancy of men will exceed that of women.
4 Current life expectancy exceeds age 80 for both men and women.   49 ____

50 The changes shown between 1940 and 2000 are most likely the result of the

1 reduction in warfare
2 improvements in modern medicine
3 increase in the number of immigrants
4 decrease in obesity rates   50 ____

In developing your answer to Part II, be sure to keep these general definitions in mind:
  (a) <u>describe</u> means "to illustrate something in words or tell about it"
  (b) <u>discuss</u> means "to make observations about something using facts, reasoning, and argument; to present in some detail"

PART II: THEMATIC ESSAY

Directions: Write a well-organized essay that includes an introduction, several paragraphs addressing the task below, and a conclusion.

Theme: Constitutional Principles — Individual Rights

> Throughout United States history, many different groups have faced discrimination. The federal and state governments have taken actions that have either protected or limited the rights of these groups in American society.

Task:

> Select *two* different groups in American society who have faced discrimination and for *each*
> - Describe *one* specific example of discrimination faced by the group
> - Describe *one* action taken by the federal or state governments related to this example of discrimination
> - Discuss how the action taken by the federal or state governments either protected *or* limited the rights of the group

You may use any example from your study of United States history. Some groups you might wish to consider include Native American Indians, African Americans, Asian Americans, Hispanic Americans, women, the elderly, and the disabled.

You are *not* limited to these suggestions.

Guidelines:

In your essay, be sure to:
- Develop all aspects of the task
- Support the theme with relevant facts, examples, and details
- Use a logical and clear plan of organization, including an introduction and a conclusion that are beyond a restatement of the theme

In developing your answers to Part III, be sure to keep this general definition in mind:

> <u>discuss</u> means "to make observations about something using facts, reasoning, and argument; to present in some detail"

PART III: DOCUMENT-BASED ESSAY

This question is based on the accompanying documents. The question is designed to test your ability to work with historical documents. Some of the documents have been edited for the purposes of the question. As you analyze the documents, take into account the source of each document and any point of view that may be presented in the document.

Historical Context:

> Between the Civil War and the end of World War I, industrialization played an ever-increasing role in the economic, social, and political development of the United States.

Task:

> Using information from the documents and your knowledge of United States history, answer the questions that follow each document in Part A. Your answers to the questions will help you write the Part B essay, in which you will be asked to
> - Discuss the economic, social, *and/or* political effects of industrialization on the United States between the Civil War (1861–1865) and the end of World War I (1918)

Part A: Short-Answer Questions

Directions: Analyze the documents and answer the short-answer questions that follow each document in the space provided.

Document 1a

Selected Statistics Related to Industrialization

	Value of Manufactured Products	Employed in Manufacturing	
		Number of Males	**Number of Females**
1860	$1.9 billion	1.03 million	270,357
1870	$4.2 billion	1.61 million	323,506
1880	$5.3 billion	2.01 million	529,983
1890	$9.3 billion	2.86 million	503,089
1900	$12.9 billion	4.08 million	1.03 million
1910	$20.8 billion	8.84 million	1.82 million

Source: Inter-University Consortium for Political and Social Research, Ann Arbor, MI, and U.S. Census Bureau

Document 1b

United States Immigration 1861–1910

Decade	Total
1861–1870	2,314,824
1871–1880	2,812,191
1881–1890	5,246,613
1891–1900	3,687,564*
1901–1910	8,795,386

*Decline in numbers of immigrants due in part to the Depression of 1893.

Source: U.S. Immigration and Naturalization Service, *Statistical Yearbook of the Immigration and Naturalization Service, 1998,* U.S. Government Printing Office

1 Based on these charts, state *two* trends related to industrialization between 1861 and 1910.   [2]

(1) _____

(2) _____

Document 2a

Urbanization, Railroad Mileage, and Industrialization of the United States, 1860–1900

	1860	1870	1880	1890	1900
Urban Population (millions)	6.2	9.9	14.1	22.1	30.2
% Urban Population	20%	25%	28%	35%	40%
Number of Cities with Population of 10,000+	93	168	223	363	440
Railroad Mileage (thousands)	30.6	52.9	93.3	166.7	206.6

Source: Gary Fields, "Communications, Innovations, and Networks: The National Beef Network of G. F. Swift" (adapted)

Document 2b

Union Membership, 1870–1920

Year	Number of workers, age 10 and over (excluding agricultural workers)	Average annual union membership	Union membership as a percentage of the total number of workers outside agriculture
1870	6,075,000	300,000*	4.9%
1880	8,807,000	200,000*	2.3%
1890	13,380,000	372,000*	2.7%
1900	18,161,000	868,000	4.8%
1910	25,779,000	2,140,000	8.3%
1920	30,985,000	5,048,000	16.3%

*Figures for 1870, 1880, and 1890 are estimates.

Source: Irving Bartlett et al., *A New History of the United States*, Holt Rinehart and Winston, 1975 (adapted)

2 Based on these charts, state *two* effects of industrialization on the United States after the Civil War. [2]

(1) _____

(2) _____

Document 3

The resolutions below were proposed at the Populist [People's] Party National Convention.

---

4. *Resolved*, That we condemn the fallacy [myth] of protecting American labor under the present system, which opens our ports to the pauper [poor] and criminal classes of the world, and crowds out our wage-earners; and we denounce the present ineffective laws against contract labor [day laborers], and demand the further restriction of undesirable emigration.

5. *Resolved*, That we cordially sympathize with the efforts of organized workingmen to shorten the hours of labor, and demand a rigid enforcement of the existing eight-hour law on Government work, and ask that a penalty clause be added to the said law.

9. *Resolved*, That we oppose any subsidy or national aid to any private corporation for any purpose.

Source: People's Party National Platform, July 4, 1892

3 Based on this document, identify *one* reform proposed at the Populist Party Convention related to industrialization. [1]

_____

_____

Document 4

The excepts below are from an Illinois state law passed in 1893.

FACTORIES AND WORKSHOPS.

— —

INSPECTION

§ 1. Manufacture of certain articles of clothing prohibited in apartments, tenement houses and living rooms, except by families living therein. Every such work shop shall be kept clean, free from vermin [rodents], infectious or contagious matter and to that end shall be subject to inspection as provided in this act. Such work shops shall be reported to the board of health.

§ 2. If upon inspection such work shops shall be found unhealthy or infectious such orders shall be given and action taken as the public health shall require.

§ 4. Children under 14 years of age prohibited from being employed in any manufacturing establishment, factory or work shop in the state. Register of children under 16 years shall be kept. The employment of children between ages of 14 and 16 years prohibited unless an affidavit [legal document] by the parent or guardian shall first be filed in which shall be stated the age date and place of birth. Certificates of physical health may be demanded by the inspectors.

§ 5. No female shall be employed in any factory or workshop more than eight hours in any one day or forty-eight hours in any one week.

Source: "Factories and Workshops," *Laws of the State of Illinois, Passed by the Thirty-Eighth General Assembly*, 1893

4. Based on these excepts, identify *two* ways this 1893 Illinois state law addressed problems caused by industrialization.   [2]

(1) _____

    _____

(2) _____

    _____

Document 5

Hamlin Garland visited Homestead, Pennsylvania, and the Carnegie steel mills to write this article for *McClure's Magazine*.

> . . . The streets of the town were horrible; the buildings were poor; the sidewalks were sunken, swaying, and full of holes, and the crossings were sharp-edged stones set like rocks in a river bed. Everywhere the yellow mud of the street lay kneaded into a sticky mass, through which groups of pale, lean men slouched in faded garments, grimy with the soot and grease of the mills.
>
> The town was as squalid [dirty] and unlovely as could well be imagined, and the people were mainly of the discouraged and sullen type to be found everywhere where labor passes into the brutalizing stage of severity. It had the disorganized and incoherent effect of a town which has feeble public spirit. Big industries at differing eras have produced squads [groups] of squalid tenement-houses far from the central portion of the town, each plant bringing its gangs of foreign laborers in raw masses to camp down like an army around its shops.
>
> Such towns are sown thickly over the hill-lands of Pennsylvania, but this was my first descent into one of them. They are American only in the sense in which they represent the American idea of business. . . .

Source: Hamlin Garland, "Homestead and Its Perilous Trades–
Impressions of a Visit," *McClure's Magazine*, June 1894

5 Based on Hamlin Garland's observations, what is *one* impact of industrialization on Homestead, Pennsylvania? [1]

_____

_____

Document 6a

Clara Lemlich, a labor union leader, sparked the 1909 walkout of shirtwaist [blouse] makers with her call for a strike.

> First let me tell you something about the way we work and what we are paid. There are two kinds of work—regular, that is salary work, and piecework. The regular work pays about $6 a week and the girls have to be at their machines at 7 o'clock in the morning and they stay at them until 8 o'clock at night, with just one-half hour for lunch in that time.
>
> The shops. Well, there is just one row of machines that the daylight ever gets to—that is the front row, nearest the window. The girls at all the other rows of machines back in the shops have to work by gaslight, by day as well as by night. Oh, yes, the shops keep the work going at night, too. . . .

Source: Clara Lemlich, "Life in the Shop," *New York Evening Journal*,
November 28, 1909

Document 6b

Source: *Bain News Service*, New York, February 1910,
Library of Congress

6 Based on these documents, state *two* ways industrialization affected workers. [2]

(1) _____

(2) _____

Document 7a

THE TRUST GIANT'S POINT OF VIEW,
"What a Funny Little Government"

Source: Horace Taylor, *The Verdict*, January 22, 1900 (adapted)

7a What is the cartoonist's point of view concerning the relationship between government and industrialists such as John D. Rockefeller? [1]

_____

_____

Document 7b

Source: Clifford K. Berryman, *Washington Evening Star*, October 11, 1907 (adapted)

7b According to the cartoonist, what was President Theodore Roosevelt's policy toward trusts? [1]

_____

_____

Document 8

Although they sometimes used controversial methods to accumulate wealth, many industrialists, such as Andrew Carnegie, John D. Rockefeller, and J. P. Morgan, also gave away millions of dollars. This excerpt describes some of the charitable work of Andrew Carnegie.

> . . . But despite his wealth-getting, his wage-cutting, and his responsibility for a bloody labor dispute at his Homestead plant in 1892, Carnegie had not forgotten his heritage of concern for social justice. In his 1889 article "Wealth," he gloried in the cheap steel his leadership had given the American consumer but also proclaimed the moral duty of all possessors of great wealth to plow back their money into philanthropy [charity] with the same judgment, zeal, and leadership they had devoted to getting rich. And he lived up to that precept [principle], paying for thousands of library buildings, setting up trusts and foundations, endowing universities, building Carnegie Hall in New York and the Peace Palace at The Hague, and much more. He once wrote that the man who dies rich dies disgraced. He had some sins to answer for, and it took him a while, but in 1919 at eighty-three Andrew Carnegie died in a state of grace by his own agnostic [non-religious] definition. . . .

Source: Foner and Garraty, eds., "Andrew Carnegie," *The Reader's Companion to American History*, Houghton Mifflin, 1991

8 According to this document, how did Andrew Carnegie show his concern for social justice? [1]

_____

_____

Document 9

. . . The significance of the American entry into the conflict [World War I] was not at all a military one, at least for twelve to fifteen months after April 1917, since its army was even less prepared for modern campaigning than any of the European forces had been in 1914. But its productive strength, boosted by the billions of dollars of Allied war orders, was unequaled. Its total industrial potential and its share of world manufacturing output was two and a half times that of Germany's now overstrained economy. It could launch merchant ships in their hundreds, a vital requirement in a year when the U-boats were sinking over 500,000 tons a month of British and Allied vessels. It could build destroyers in the astonishing time of three months. It produced half of the world's food exports, which could now be sent to France and Italy as well as to its traditional British market.

In terms of economic power, therefore, the entry of the United States into the war quite transformed the balances, and more than compensated for the collapse of Russia at this same time. . . . the productive resources now arranged against the Central Powers were enormous. . . .

Source: Paul Kennedy, *The Rise and Fall of the Great Powers*, Random House, 1987

9 According to Paul Kennedy, what was *one* effect of United States industrialization on World War I? [1]

_____

_____

Part B: Essay

Directions: Write a well-organized essay that includes an introduction, several paragraphs, and a conclusion. Use evidence from *at least five* documents in your essay. Support your response with relevant facts, examples, and details. Include additional outside information.

Historical Context:

> Between the Civil War and the end of World War I, industrialization played an ever-increasing role in the economic, social, and political development of the United States.

Task:

> Using information from the documents and your knowledge of United States history, write an essay in which you
> - Discuss the economic, social, *and/or* political effects of industrialization on the United States between the Civil War (1861–1865) and the end of World War I (1918)

Guidelines:

In your essay, be sure to:
- Develop all aspects of the task
- Incorporate information from *at least five* documents
- Incorporate relevant outside information
- Support the theme with relevant facts, examples, and details
- Use a logical and clear plan of organization, including an introduction and conclusion that are beyond a restatement of the theme

Answers
June 2009
United States History and Government

Answer Key

PART I

1. 4	14. 3	27. 4	40. 1
2. 2	15. 1	28. 3	41. 2
3. 4	16. 2	29. 4	42. 3
4. 1	17. 4	30. 4	43. 1
5. 3	18. 2	31. 4	44. 4
6. 2	19. 1	32. 1	45. 1
7. 4	20. 3	33. 3	46. 3
8. 2	21. 2	34. 2	47. 1
9. 3	22. 1	35. 3	48. 4
10. 4	23. 3	36. 1	49. 4
11. 4	24. 4	37. 2	50. 2
12. 1	25. 2	38. 2	
13. 2	26. 1	39. 2	

PART II: Thematic Essay   See answers explained section.

PART III: Document-Based Essay   See answers explained section.

Answers Explained

PART I (1–50)

1. **4** Since the late 1700s, the Mississippi River has been a vital waterway because it provides farmers and merchants an outlet to the Gulf of Mexico. The Mississippi River, which flows all the way from Minnesota to the port city of New Orleans, has been an important resource for moving agricultural and manufactured goods. In the 19th century, many Americans began moving west to the fertile plains on either side of the Mississippi River. Before the development of railroads and trucking, the Mississippi River was a central artery for the movement of goods. The United States acquired full rights to the river when it purchased the Louisiana Territory from France in 1803.

WRONG CHOICES EXPLAINED:

(1) The Mississippi River does not divide the northern territories from the southern territories. The river runs in a north-south direction, from Minnesota to New Orleans. The Mason-Dixon line, along the southern border of Pennsylvania, has been the unofficial border between northern and southern states.

(2) The Mississippi River does not provide American farmers with direct access to Canadian markets. The origin of the river is in Minnesota; it does not extend into Canada.

(3) The Mississippi River does not connect the Great Lakes to the Atlantic Ocean. The Erie Canal, completed in 1825, connects the Great Lakes to the Atlantic Ocean, via the Hudson River.

2. **2** During the first half of the 1800s, geographic factors influenced the economy of New England by promoting the growth of trade and manufacturing. Rivers were especially important because they powered early textile factories and provided a means of transporting goods to coastal cities and beyond. An important early textile-manufacturing operation was built along the banks of the Merrimack River in Lowell, Massachusetts, in 1823. The owners of the mills recruited young women from the New England countryside to operate the machines. By 1830, eight mills employed more than 6,000 women. In addition to rivers, the coastal states of New England have several deep-water harbors that developed into important port cities, such as Boston, Massachusetts, and Newport, Rhode Island.

WRONG CHOICES EXPLAINED:

(1) During the first half of the 1800s, geographic features in New England did not encourage the establishment of large plantations. Large plantations require vast expanses of flat, fertile land. New England is known for its hilly terrain and rocky soil. Small-scale farming for local markets developed in New England, but large-scale plantations for national and international markets developed in the southern states.

(3) During the first half of the 1800s, geographic features in New England did not increase the region's reliance on slave labor. The hilly terrain of New England made it difficult to acquire the expansive plantations that characterized the southern agricultural economy. The smaller New England farms depended on family members, not on large numbers of slaves.

(4) During the first half of the 1800s, geographic features in New England did not support rice and indigo farming. Both crops depend on warmer climates than New England offers.

3. **4** The British benefited from their mercantilist relationship with the American colonies primarily by buying raw materials from the colonies and selling them finished products. Mercantilism is the economic theory that guided Great Britain's colonialist ventures. The theory held that if a nation could acquire raw materials from within its empire, it would not need to purchase them from competing nations. Wealth would be kept within the empire. Also, the colonies were seen as a captive market for the mother country's manufactured goods. According to the theory, colonies should not be allowed to develop manufacturing but should purchase manufactured goods from the mother country. England imposed several navigation laws on the American colonies to make sure the colonies fulfilled their role, but some of these laws were difficult to enforce.

WRONG CHOICES EXPLAINED:

(1) Mercantilism did not support the growth of colonial industries. The theory held that manufacturing should occur in the mother country, not in the colonies. The role of the colonies was to provide raw materials that would then be manufactured in the home country. Colonial manufacturing was discouraged because it would enable the colonies to exercise a degree of economic independence that was counter to the priorities of the mother country.

(2) Mercantilism did not prohibit the colonists from fishing and fur trading. These activities were encouraged by mercantilism. The theory held that the colonies would generate natural products that would be shipped to the home country.

(3) Mercantilism did not lead to the taking of large amounts of gold and silver from the southern colonies. In theory, mercantilism would encourage the extraction of natural resources from the colonies, especially valuable

resources such as gold and silver, but the southern colonies lacked these precious metals.

4. **1** The main reason Great Britain established the Proclamation Line of 1763 was to avoid conflicts between American colonists and Native American Indians. The Proclamation Line ran along the Appalachian Mountains. Great Britain prohibited the colonists from settling beyond the line. The line was established just after the conclusion of the French and Indian War (1754–1763), which was caused, in part, by colonial expansion into the land beyond the Appalachians. Before the war, a few settlers crossed over the Appalachian Mountains and established farms in the Ohio River valley. This expansion led to conflicts with the French, who had earlier established outposts in the area, and eventually to the French and Indian War. After the war, the British were determined to prevent skirmishes between the colonists and Native American Indians beyond the Appalachian Mountains. This act contributed to colonial resentment of British policies.

WRONG CHOICES EXPLAINED:
(2) Making a profit by selling land west of the Appalachian Mountains was not Great Britain's goal in establishing the Proclamation Line. The goal was to reduce settlement west of the Appalachian Mountains, not to increase it.

(3) Preventing American industrial development in the Ohio River valley was not Great Britain's goal in establishing the Proclamation Line. British mercantilist policies in general tried to prevent manufacturing in colonial America, but the Proclamation Line was not related to manufacturing.

(4) Transferring control of the Great Lakes region to Canada was not Great Britain's goal in establishing the Proclamation Line. Great Britain had just gained control of the region from France as a result of the French and Indian War (1754–1763) and was not eager to relinquish that control.

5. **3** The Declaration of Independence (1776) has had a major influence on peoples throughout the world because it provides justification for revolting against unjust governments. The Declaration of Independence, written by Thomas Jefferson and ratified by the Second Continental Congress in 1776, expressed the intent of the signers and the colonists they represented to be free of British control and to govern their own affairs. The document was addressed to the king but was also intended to convince cautious Americans to support independence. A major reason for independence was that the king of England failed to protect the natural rights of the American people. The preamble sets forth some of the natural rights that all people are born with. These include "life, liberty and the pursuit of happiness." The declaration goes on to assert that government gains its legitimacy from having "the consent of the governed." If a government violates people's natural rights, the people have the right "to alter or abolish it." The document is a

statement of principles more than a blueprint for government. The ideas in it have shaped democratic practices and have provided inspiration to those seeking to radically change the government they are living under.

WRONG CHOICES EXPLAINED:

(1) The Declaration of Independence did not guarantee universal suffrage. The document does not discuss the specifics of governance, such as voting guidelines.

(2) The Declaration of Independence does not establish a basic set of laws for every nation. The document does not even establish a basic set of laws for the United States.

(4) The Declaration of Independence does not describe the importance of a strong central government. Many of the members of the Continental Congress were suspicious of strong central government.

6. **2** One accomplishment of the national government under the Articles of Confederation was the passage of legislation establishing a process for admitting new states to the Union. The question of admitting new states arose as people began settling beyond the Appalachian Mountains in the 1780s. The Confederation Congress delineated the area of the United States north of the Ohio River, between the western border of Pennsylvania and the Mississippi River, as the Northwest Territory. The Northwest Ordinance (1787) spelled out the steps that unorganized areas would have to go through in order to become states. The law created a two-step process on the road to statehood. When a territory reached five thousand free-male inhabitants, it could create a bicameral legislature and send a nonvoting member to Congress. When it reached sixty thousand free-male inhabitants, it could apply for statehood. Earlier, the Confederation Congress persuaded the various states to give up their land claims in the region and then passed the Land Ordinance (1785), which divided up the land and provided a plot in every town for public schools. Although these acts are considered successes of the Confederation government, contemporaries and historians have tended to focus on the problems of the period, such as inflation and lack of government revenues. In fact, the period is often labeled the *critical period*, in the sense of a patient being in critical condition.

WRONG CHOICES EXPLAINED:

(1) The national government under the Articles of Confederation did not pass legislation establishing a central banking system. Under the Articles, most significant powers remained on the state level. The national government did not even have the power to directly levy taxes. After the ratification of the Constitution, the national government assumed additional powers, including the power to create the Bank of the United States (1791–1811).

(3) The national government under the Articles of Confederation did not pass legislation establishing the president's right to put down rebellions. In fact, the Articles of Confederation did not even provide for a president of the

nation. A major uprising, Shays's Rebellion (1786–1787), took place in Massachusetts for weeks before it was put down by state militia forces organized by the governor. This event convinced many Americans of the need for a stronger national government, with greater military powers.

(4) The national government under the Articles of Confederation did not pass legislation establishing the ability of Congress to tax states effectively. The national government was hampered by its inability to levy taxes. The power to levy import taxes was held onto by the states. When the national government tried to create a national import tax, the states with the most profitable ports, New York and Rhode Island, blocked it.

7. **4** Disagreement at the Constitutional Convention of 1787 over the Virginia and New Jersey plans was resolved by a compromise that created a Congress made up of a Senate and House of Representatives. This compromise, known as the Great Compromise, settled one of the main disagreements at the Constitutional Convention—how to create a representative system that met the desires of both the small states and the large states. The states with larger populations thought that they should have a larger voice in Congress. They rallied around the Virginia Plan, which would have created a legislature that pegged the number of representatives from each state to the population of the state. The small states feared that their voices would be drowned out in such a legislature. They countered with the New Jersey Plan, which called for a one-house legislature with each state getting one vote (similar to the Congress that existed under the Articles of Confederation). After much wrangling, the delegates agreed on the Great Compromise, which created the basic structure of Congress as it now exists. The plan called for a House of Representatives, in which representation is determined by the population of each state, and a Senate, in which each state gets two members.

WRONG CHOICES EXPLAINED:

(1) Disagreement at the Constitutional Convention over the Virginia and New Jersey plans was not resolved by a compromise that guaranteed continuation of the slave trade for at least twenty years. The convention did make such a decision, but the disagreement over the Virginia and New Jersey plans had to do with representation in Congress, not slavery.

(2) Disagreement at the Constitutional Convention over the Virginia and New Jersey plans was not resolved by a compromise that limited the power of the federal government to wage war. The convention placed the power to wage war in the hands of the federal government. A declaration of war must be passed by the Senate and signed by the president.

(3) Disagreement at the Constitutional Convention over the Virginia and New Jersey plans was not resolved by a compromise that provided for construction of a new national capital in the south. Such a compromise was worked out later. In 1781, Secretary of the Treasury Alexander Hamilton persuaded southern congressional leaders to support his plan for the national

government's assumption of state debts from the Revolutionary War by promising to locate the new national capital in the South.

8. **2** The headlines refer to controversial issues most directly related to the electoral college. The Constitution states the basic process for how the president would be elected in Article II. After the popular vote for president on Election Day, election boards determine which candidate won in each of the states. The winning candidate in a particular state gets all of that state's electoral votes. The number of electors for each state is equal to the number of members of Congress from that state. Bigger states, therefore, get more electors. This could lead to the situation alluded to in the first headline—candidates simply not campaigning in small states. The electors cast their votes 41 days after the popular vote. Presently, there are 538 electoral votes. A candidate must win the majority, or 270 votes, to be declared the "president-elect." The situation alluded to in the second headline, in which a candidate wins the popular vote while losing in the electoral college, could arise in the following way: If candidate A won the popular vote overwhelmingly in several states whose electoral votes totaled 268, while candidate B just squeaked by in the remainder of the states, whose electoral votes totaled 270, candidate B would win the electoral vote and be declared president-elect even though he or she probably had less of the overall popular vote than candidate A. This scenario is not so farfetched. In 1824, 1876, 1888, and 2000, the candidate who received the higher nationwide popular vote did not end up winning the presidency.

WRONG CHOICES EXPLAINED:
(1) The headlines do not refer to controversial issues related to judicial review. Judicial review is the Supreme Court's power to determine the constitutionality of laws. The power was assumed by the Supreme Court in its *Marbury* v. *Madison* decision (1803). Supreme Court decisions have often generated controversy.

(3) The headlines do not refer to controversial issues related to impeachment. Impeachment is the power of the House of Representatives to bring charges against the president. If impeached, the president must then be tried by the Senate. If found guilty of the charges, the president is then removed from office. Two presidents have been impeached—Andrew Johnson (1863) and Bill Clinton (1999). Both of these cases generated controversy, but neither president was removed from office.

(4) The headlines do not refer to controversial issues related to checks and balances. The system of checks and balances refers to the ability of each of the three branches of the government to limit, or check, the power of the other two. The goal is to keep the three branches in balance. Examples of this concept include the president's ability to veto (or reject) bills passed by Congress and the Supreme Court's ability to strike down laws that it deems unconstitutional. Controversies might arise if one branch tries to assume additional powers at the expense of another branch.

9.   **3**   According to the excerpt, a goal of the framers of the Constitution was to ensure that the United States provided for the common defense of every state. The framers of the Constitution believed that defense should not be left to the individual states. This concept was consistent with their general approach of strengthening the national government at the expense of the state governments. The mention of "domestic violence" in the Constitution might have been prompted by Shays's Rebellion (1786–1787). This uprising in Massachusetts convinced many Americans that a stronger national government was needed. Even the National Guard, which is composed of state units that can be called up by the various governors, is part of the United States military.

WRONG CHOICES EXPLAINED:

(1) The excerpt does not imply that the United States should remain neutral during domestic conflicts involving the states. The Constitution empowers the national government to settle disputes between states, such as border disputes. The national government, therefore, is not required to remain neutral in disputes between states.

(2) The excerpt does not imply that the United States supported the right of each state to resist presidential decisions. The Constitution states that the national government shall be the "supreme law of the land." States, therefore, do not have the right to resist the laws and decisions of the national government.

(4) The excerpt does not imply that the United States approved a bill of rights to protect citizens from government tyranny. The excerpt does not address the issues of rights and governmental tyranny. The Bill of Rights (1791) was ratified to protect the citizens from government intrusions, but this is not the subject of the excerpt.

10.   **4**   A major reason the Antifederalists opposed the ratification of the United States Constitution was because the Constitution changed the balance of power between the state and national governments. Under the Articles of Confederation, which governed the United States in the 1780s before the ratification of the Constitution, the states retained major powers, and the national government was given very limited powers. A central goal of the Constitution was to change this situation by giving the national government far more powers and declaring it the "supreme law of the land." The Antifederalists were distrustful of distant authority. The thirteen colonies had just emerged from under the thumb of the British Empire, so many colonists were eager to see power exercised locally. Eventually, many leading Antifederalists agreed to support ratification of the Constitution if a list of individual rights was added. This agreement led to the writing and ratification of the first ten amendments to the Constitution, known as the Bill of Rights.

WRONG CHOICES EXPLAINED:

(1) Antifederalist opposition to the Constitution was not centered on the creation of a national bank. In fact, the Constitution does not provide for the creation of a national bank. After ratification of the Constitution, Secretary of the Treasury Alexander Hamilton pushed for the creation of a national bank. Secretary of State Thomas Jefferson opposed the idea, arguing that the Constitution did not permit the government to create such an institution. Hamilton won the dispute; the Bank of the United States existed from 1791 to 1811.

(2) Antifederalist opposition to the Constitution was not centered on the lack of a provision for a federal court system. The Constitution did empower Congress to establish a federal court system.

(3) Antifederalist opposition to the Constitution was not centered on the method of electing members of the House of Representatives. The Constitution did provide for the direct election of members of the House of Representatives. Senators, however, were selected by the various state legislatures, not by direct election. This changed with the ratification of the 17th Amendment (1913), which provided for the direct election of senators.

11. **4** An example of the use of the unwritten constitution is the creation of the president's cabinet. The unwritten constitution refers to those traditions and practices that have become part of the American political system, but are not mentioned in the Constitution. Many of these practices date back to the administration of George Washington. He first regularly convened a cabinet, comprised of the heads of government departments, to advise him. He also set the precedent of serving for no more than two terms. This tradition became law with the ratification of the 22nd Amendment (1951), ratified after Franklin Roosevelt broke tradition and won the presidency four times. Washington's administration also witnessed the development of political parties, a practice unforeseen by most of the founding fathers and not mentioned in the written Constitution.

WRONG CHOICES EXPLAINED:

(1) (2) and (3) All of these choices are governmental powers specifically mentioned in the Constitution, so they are not part of the "unwritten constitution." Article I, which outlines the powers and procedures of Congress, mentions the president's ability to sign or veto legislation. Article I also gives Congress the power to "provide and maintain a navy" as well as the power to "establish post offices."

12. **1** President George Washington pursued a foreign policy of neutrality during his administration primarily because he believed that the United States needed time to gain economic and military strength. President Washington is closely identified with the idea of neutrality. He issued the 1793 Neutrality Act and in his Farewell Address he urged the United States to avoid "permanent alliances" with foreign powers. He did not want the

newly independent nation, on precarious footing, to be drawn into the seemingly endless conflicts of Europe. The particular circumstances of the 1793 Neutrality Act grew out of the French Revolution, which began in 1789. Americans were divided over France's revolution. The debates took on greater significance after France and England went to war in 1793. Many Americans felt that the United States had an obligation to help France because France had helped the United States in the Revolutionary War. A treaty between the two countries (1778) committed the United States to help France if it were under attack. Others argued that the United States should stay out. After all, the treaty was made with a French government that no longer existed, and the French Revolution had devolved from a democratic movement into a bloodbath. The latter position won Washington's support. His calls for neutrality have been invoked by isolationists throughout American history, especially preceding United States entrance into both World Wars.

WRONG CHOICES EXPLAINED:

(2) President Washington's calls for a foreign policy of neutrality were not motivated by his belief that the Constitution prohibited treaties. In fact, the Constitution explicitly gives the president the ability to "make treaties," which then must be approved by the Senate.

(3) President Washington's calls for a foreign policy of neutrality were not motivated by his belief that the United States should not expand by force. Washington neither supported nor opposed the idea of expansion. During Washington's tenure as president, the question of expansion was not on the table.

(4) President Washington's calls for a foreign policy of neutrality were not motivated by his belief that alliances should be established with both England and France. In fact, in his Farewell Address, he specifically warned against permanent alliances with European powers.

13. **2** Many of the decisions made by the Supreme Court while John Marshall was Chief Justice led directly to an increase in the power of the federal government over the states. Marshall was the Chief Justice of the Supreme Court from 1801 to 1835. Decisions of the Marshall Court consistently expanded federal power at the expense of state power. *McCulloch* v. *Maryland* (1819), for example, prohibited Maryland from taxing the Bank of the United States and declared federal power superior to state power. *Gibbons* v. *Ogden* (1824) invalidated a monopoly on ferry transportation between New York and New Jersey that had been granted by New York, and asserted that only the federal government could regulate interstate trade.

WRONG CHOICES EXPLAINED:

(1) Decisions by the Marshall Court did not lead to a reduction of federal influence in economic affairs. In fact, Marshall Court decisions did

the opposite. In several cases, the Supreme Court intervened in economic transactions to assert the validity of contracts. In the case of *Fletcher* v. *Peck* (1810), the Supreme Court upheld a corrupt land deal between the state of Georgia and private individuals. The Court ruled that the deal might not have been in the public interest, but a contract should be upheld.

(3) Decisions by the Marshall Court did not directly have an impact on the role of Congress in foreign policy.

(4) Decisions by the Marshall Court did not directly have an impact on slavery.

14. **3** Manifest Destiny was used to justify an American desire to expand to the Pacific Ocean. The term *Manifest Destiny* was coined in an 1845 newspaper article. It captured the fervor of the westward expansion movement, implying that it was God's plan that the United States should take over and settle the entire continent. Americans who did settle out West were probably driven more by economic factors, such as cheap land or precious metals, than they were by a desire to fulfill God's plan. The history of the settlement of the West includes many noteworthy episodes: Texas independence from Mexico (1836), the opening of the Oregon Trail (1841), the Mexican War (1846–48), the Mormon exodus to Utah (1847), and the California gold rush (1849). This movement was especially damaging for the Native Americans of the West who were driven off their land and relegated to several western reservations.

WRONG CHOICES EXPLAINED:

(1) Manifest Destiny was not used to justify an American desire to limit the number of immigrants entering the country. The movement to limit immigration into the United States is called nativism. This movement gained adherents in the 1850s, as immigration from Ireland expanded. Supporters of Manifest Destiny did not have a unified position on immigration.

(2) Manifest Destiny was not used to justify an American desire to control the area located east of the Appalachian Mountains. This area was already controlled by the United States; it was part of the original territory of the United States.

(4) Manifest Destiny was not used to justify an American desire to warn European countries against colonizing Latin America. It was the Monroe Doctrine (1823) that specifically warned the European powers against furthering their colonial activities in the Americas.

15. **1** In the 1850s, the phrase "Bleeding Kansas" was used to describe clashes between pro-slavery and anti-slavery groups. The term refers to the violence that broke out in Kansas following passage of the Kansas-Nebraska Act (1854). The Kansas-Nebraska Act allowed for the possibility of slavery in the territories of Kansas and Nebraska—areas that had been closed to slavery by the Missouri Compromise (1820). The act mandated that the question of slavery in these territories be decided by popular sovereignty. Popular

sovereignty called for settlers in new territories to vote on the issue of slavery. Many Northerners were angry at the act and at the sponsor of the act, Senator Stephen A. Douglas. Violence erupted in Kansas as pro-slavery and anti-slavery men fought for control of the state. "Bleeding Kansas" can be seen as a dress rehearsal for the Civil War. The question of slavery in Kansas was unresolved when the Civil War began. After Southern secession, Kansas quickly joined the Union as a free state in 1861.

WRONG CHOICES EXPLAINED:

(2) The clashes in "Bleeding Kansas" were not between Spanish landowners and new American settlers. Spanish settlement had not reached as far north as Kansas. Clashes between Spanish-speaking landowners and new American settlers occurred in the 1850s in California, following the 1849 discovery of gold deposits.

(3) The clashes in "Bleeding Kansas" were not between Chinese and Irish railroad workers. Such clashes would have occurred further west, as the transcontinental railroad neared completion in 1869.

(4) The clashes in "Bleeding Kansas" were not between Native American Indians and white settlers. Such clashes occurred throughout American history, from the earliest days of the Jamestown, Virginia, settlement (1607) until the end of organized Native American resistance to encroachment by white settlers at Wounded Knee, South Dakota, in 1890. However, the specific clashes at "Bleeding Kansas" revolved around the question of slavery.

16. **2** In the 1850s, many runaway slaves went to Canada because the Fugitive Slave Act kept them at risk in the United States. Slavery was illegal in Canada, and slave catchers from the United States were not permitted to cross the border in search of escaped slaves. Before 1850, many escaped slaves settled in the free states of the northern United States. However, after 1850, this option became more difficult. The United States government passed a more stringent Fugitive Slave Act, forcing Northern state officials and individuals to cooperate with Southern slave catchers, as part of the Compromise of 1850. This compromise evolved following California's application for statehood in 1850. The most important elements of the Compromise of 1850 were the admittance of California as a free state, which pleased Northern politicians, and a more stringent Fugitive Slave Law, which pleased Southern politicians.

WRONG CHOICES EXPLAINED:

(1) The reason that many runaway slaves went to Canada in the 1850s was not fear of being drafted into the Northern army. The Civil War (1861–1865) had not yet begun in the 1850s, so there was no danger of being drafted into the United States Army in the 1850s.

(3) The reason that many runaway slaves went to Canada in the 1850s was not the availability of factory jobs in Canada. Industrial jobs were not

prevalent in either Canada or United States before the Civil War. After the Civil War, industrialization occurred at a rapid pace in the United States and at a slower pace in Canada.

(4) The reason that many runaway slaves went to Canada in the 1850s was not that abolitionists refused to help fugitive slaves. Abolitionists were more than eager to do whatever they could to help fugitive slaves, but it was simply too dangerous for fugitive slaves to settle in the free North after the passage of the Fugitive Slave Act.

17. **4** The Homestead Act, the mass killing of buffalo, and the completion of the transcontinental railroad are most closely related to the decline of the Plains Indians. The Plains Indians are the Native American Indian nations, including the Cheyenne, Comanche, and Sioux nations, that lived in the Great Plains region of the United States. The Great Plains is the huge area of relatively flat land between the Mississippi River and the Rocky Mountains. Much of this area has rich soil and a long growing season, making it desirable for white settlers. The government encouraged development of the region by passing the Homestead Act (1862), which provided free land in the region to settlers who were willing to farm it. Hundreds of thousands of people applied for and were granted homesteads. The expansion of railroads into the west, leading to the completion of a transcontinental railroad in 1869, also encouraged white settlement in the Great Plains. The railroads provided an economic lifeline for these new settlers. Freight trains brought crops and cattle from the Great Plains states to cities such as Chicago. This increased economic activity led to Native American Indians being pushed off their land. The railroads also brought sportsmen out West who shot at buffalo herds from their passing train cars. Although these buffalo were sport for white travelers, they were a means of sustenance for many Plains Indians. These factors all led to the decline of the Plains Indians.

WRONG CHOICES EXPLAINED:

(1) The factors listed in the question are not related to the rise of organized labor. The Homestead strike (1892), unrelated to the Homestead Act, was a brutal episode in the history of organized labor.

(2) The factors listed in the question are not related to the building of the Erie Canal. Soon after the canal's completion (1825), railroads began to provide a faster and cheaper alternative for moving goods. However, the building of the Erie Canal is unrelated to the completion of the transcontinental railroad (1869).

(3) The factors listed in the question are not related to the northern migration of African Americans. This migration, often referred to as the Great Migration, occurred in the 1910s and 1920s. It was caused by bad economic conditions in the cotton-growing South, the persistence of racist violence and Jim Crow laws in southern states, and job opportunities in factories in the North.

18. **2** Many southern states tried to limit the effects of Radical Reconstruction by enacting Jim Crow laws. Radical Reconstruction (1867–1877) began when Republicans in Congress took the reins of reuniting and rebuilding the nation following the Civil War. It involved sweeping changes in the South, including the military occupation of the rebellious southern states and assurances that African Americans in the South would finally get some basic rights. The modest gains for African Americans were short lived. Reconstruction came to an end after the election of 1876. The enacting of Jim Crow laws was part of the strategy to undo the limited advances African Americans achieved during the Radical Reconstruction period. These laws, which segregated public facilities, such as railroad cars, bathrooms, and schools, once again relegated African Americans to a second-class status in the South. Jim Crow laws became more prevalent after 1896 when the Supreme Court, in the case of *Plessy* v. *Ferguson*, accepted segregation as constitutional as long as the facilities for both white and African Americans were of equal quality. It was generally the case that the facilities for African Americans were substandard, but this "separate but equal" rule was the law of the land until the Supreme Court found segregated schools inherently unfair in the *Brown* v. *Board of Education* decision (1954).

WRONG CHOICES EXPLAINED:
(1) Southerners opposed to Reconstruction did not adopt federal laws mandating segregation. Although they generally supported the goal of segregating the races, Southerners did not have enough power to push through legislation on the federal level during the Reconstruction period. Their efforts were on the state level, not the federal level.

(3) Southerners opposed to Reconstruction did not abolish the Southern sharecropping system. In the sharecropping system, which developed after the Civil War, African Americans (and poor whites) would farm a few acres of a large estate and give a share, often half, of the crops to the owner as rent. Since cotton production continued, Southern foes of Reconstruction did not oppose the sharecropping system.

(4) Southerners opposed to Radical Reconstruction would not have worked to secure passage of the new amendments to the Constitution that were passed during the Reconstruction period. These amendments were the 13th Amendment (1865), which outlawed slavery; the 14th Amendment (1868), which provided citizenship and due process of law to African Americans; and the 15th Amendment (1870), which prevented discrimination in voting based on race. These amendments were all designed to extend legal and political rights to former slaves.

19. **1** The mechanization of agriculture in the United States led directly to an increase in production. By the late 1800s, mechanization was rapidly transforming American agriculture. Expensive, motorized machinery, such as the mechanical reaper and the combine harvester, replaced hand-held tools. Mechanization had both positive and negative effects for American farmers.

Mechanization increased overall agricultural production, and it reduced the man-hours needed for agricultural tasks. At the same time, it worked to undermine small-scale family farms. First, the overall increase in production lowered the prices that farmers received per bushel of corn or wheat. Second, many farmers could not afford the new equipment. By the late 1800s and into the 1900s, large-scale farms came to dominate agriculture in the United States.

WRONG CHOICES EXPLAINED:

(2) The mechanization of agriculture in the United States did not lead to less dependence on railroads by farmers. Large-scale mechanized farming created greater dependence on railroads because the crops were destined for distant urban centers rather than local markets.

(3) The mechanization of agriculture in the United States did not lead to fewer agricultural exports. The increases in output allowed for increases in agricultural exports.

(4) The mechanization of agriculture in the United States did not lead to the decreasing size of the average farm. Farm size increased with mechanization as farmers realized that they could operate far bigger farms with the same number of man-hours.

20. **3** News organizations were engaging in yellow journalism before the Spanish-American War when editors exaggerated events to build support for war. There were several causes for the United States' declaration of war on Spain in 1898. Spain controlled Cuba at the time, but an independence movement was trying to break Cuba's ties to Spain. Many Americans wanted the United States to intervene on Cuba's side in this struggle. Some Americans saw parallels between the Cuban struggle for independence from Spain and America's struggle for independence from England. Also, some American businessmen were angered by the interruption of the sugar harvest by the fighting between Cuban rebels and Spanish forces. The event that led directly to the Spanish-American War was the destruction of a United States warship, the USS *Maine*, in the harbor of Havana, Cuba. Many in the United States thought that the destruction of the ship was the work of Spain, especially after American newspapers bluntly accused Spain of the crime, despite the scarcity of evidence. This sensationalistic, irresponsible coverage of events is known as yellow journalism. These newspapers breathlessly followed events in Cuba, with lurid accounts of Spanish wrongdoing.

WRONG CHOICES EXPLAINED:

(1) Yellow journalism did not involve publishers trying to prevent the Spanish-American War. Publishers practicing yellow journalism seemed eager to incite war, knowing that images of bloodshed and destruction would sell more newspapers.

(2) Yellow journalism did not involve fair and balanced coverage of affairs in Cuba before the Spanish-American War. Practitioners of yellow journalism

generally divided the world into good and evil, leaving little room for fair and balanced coverage. This was the case in regard to Cuba in the lead-up to the Spanish-American War. The Cubans were presented as innocent victims and the Spanish as savage monsters.

(4) Yellow journalism did not ignore the situation in Cuba before the Spanish-American War. Practitioners of yellow journalism routinely covered the situation in Cuba in a way that created sympathy for the Cuban people and hostility toward Spain.

21. **2** The United States issued the Open Door policy (1899–1900) primarily to secure equal trade opportunities. The Open Door policy was put forth by President McKinley's Secretary of State John Hay. In the 1890s the major European powers had established spheres of influence in China. These nations each declared that they had exclusive trading privileges in their sphere of influence. The United States asserted that all of China should be open to trade with all nations. The European nations begrudgingly accepted this concept.

WRONG CHOICES EXPLAINED:
(1) The Open Door policy was not intended to bring democratic government to the Chinese people. In recent years, United States foreign policy has attempted to prod China toward improvements in human rights while at the same time maintaining favorable trade status with China.

(3) The Open Door policy was not intended to force China to change its immigration policies. The United States has not attempted to influence China's immigration policies.

(4) The Open Door policy was not intended to make China a stepping stone for trade with Japan. The United States pursued opening up both Japan and China to American trade, but independently of one another.

22. **1** Progressive Era authors such as Jacob Riis and Upton Sinclair are best known for focusing attention on social conditions. The term *muckraker* was applied to authors such as Riis and Sinclair who exposed wrongdoing by government officials, showed the negative side of industrialization, and let the world see a variety of social ills. Upton Sinclair wrote *The Jungle* (1906), a stirring book about the unsanitary conditions in the meat packing industry. Jacob Riis's book of photography and text, *How the Other Half Lives* (1890), documented the squalid conditions of the urban poor. Muckraking books inspired a generation of Progressive reformers to push the government to intervene in societal problems. A whole host of reforms were implemented by Progressive reformers and their allies in the 1900s and 1910s.

WRONG CHOICES EXPLAINED:
(2) The Progressive Era authors such as Jacob Riis and Upton Sinclair are not known for fighting for the civil rights of African Americans. In general, Progressive Era reformers and authors turned a blind eye toward the plight

of African Americans. A significant exception was Ida B. Wells, who wrote about the injustices carried out against African Americans in the South.

(3) Progressive Era authors such as Jacob Riis and Upton Sinclair are not known for promoting the interests of the American farmer. The Progressive movement was primarily an urban movement. The interests of farmers were promoted by the Populist movement in the late 1800s.

(4) Progressive Era authors such as Jacob Riis and Upton Sinclair are not known for supporting the goal of women's suffrage. There was certainly a great deal of overlap between the Progressive movement and the woman's suffrage movement, but woman's suffrage was not the focus of Riis's and Sinclair's work.

23. **3** The 16th Amendment (1913) authorized the federal income tax. Previously the federal government gained its revenues almost entirely from import tariffs. The creation of an income tax was a reform championed by both the Populist movement and the Progressive movement. Reformers argued that a national income tax would create a more equitable society by shifting the burden of taxation onto the shoulders of those most able to pay. The income tax in the United States is a progressive income tax, meaning that those at the highest end of the income scale pay a significantly higher percentage of their income in taxes than those at the lowest end of the income scale. As incomes increase, tax rates progressively increase. The income tax remains the federal government's primary means of collecting revenues.

WRONG CHOICES EXPLAINED:

(1) The 16th Amendment did not authorize an excise tax. An excise tax is simply a sales tax on a commodity or a service. Excise taxes exist primarily on the state level in the United States, although there are federal excise taxes on gasoline and cigarettes.

(2) The 16th Amendment did not authorize an import tax. Federal import taxes, or duties, are allowed for in the Constitution and have existed throughout United States history.

(4) The 16th Amendment did not authorize an estate tax. An estate tax is a tax on the material wealth that one inherits upon the death of a donor. Congress adopted a federal estate tax in 1916.

24. **4** In the statement, President-elect Woodrow Wilson was expressing the belief that the Progressive movement would be best served by continued peace. Wilson believed that militarism shifted a nation's priorities away from domestic reform. He was therefore opposed to United States participation in World War I when it began in 1914. Wilson initially assumed that the United States could stay neutral in World War I and maintain commercial ties to nations on both sides of the conflict. However, England successfully blockaded American ships from reaching Germany. Out of necessity, United States trade shifted to England exclusively. Germany became increasingly

belligerent toward the United States as the war progressed. When Wilson ran for reelection in 1916, he still maintained an antiwar position but, after reelection, became increasingly convinced that United States participation in World War I was necessary to make the world "safe for democracy." Wilson's shift to a prowar stance divided Progressives. The United States finally entered the war in 1917.

WRONG CHOICES EXPLAINED:

(1) In the statement, Wilson was not expressing the sentiment that the United States should enter World War I immediately. He adopted such a position in 1917, but in 1913 he was against United States entrance into the war.

(2) In the statement, Wilson was not expressing the sentiment that reform movements are strengthened by war. In fact, he is expressing the opposite sentiment. He is arguing that war would shift priorities away from Progressive reform.

(3) In the statement, Wilson was not expressing the sentiment that the nation will require a change in leadership if it goes to war. He was arguing against the advisability of going to war, but he was not commenting on his ability to lead the nation in war.

25. **2** In *Schenck* v. *United States* (1919), the Supreme Court decided that a "clear and present danger" to the country allowed the federal government to restrict 1st Amendment rights. The decision upheld the Espionage and Sedition Acts, passed during World War I to put limits on public expressions of antiwar sentiment. Charles Schenck and other members of the Socialist Party had been arrested under the Espionage Act for printing and distributing flyers opposing the war and urging young men to resist the draft. The defense argued that distributing antiwar literature was protected by the 1st Amendment. The Supreme Court decided that the government is justified in limiting certain forms of speech during wartime. The Court argued that certain utterances pose a "clear and present danger." By analogy the Court reasoned that one is not allowed to falsely shout "Fire!" in a crowded theater. The *Schenck* decision is one of several instances in United States history in which the Supreme Court decided that the government could limit certain rights during time of war.

WRONG CHOICES EXPLAINED:

(1) The *Schenck* decision did not address the question of whether the federal government could establish a peacetime draft. The federal government has never attempted to establish a peacetime draft, but the Constitution does not prevent it from doing so.

(3) The *Schenck* decision did not address the question of whether the federal government could suspend habeas corpus. Habeas corpus is the constitutional provision for taking legal action to free someone who is unlawfully detained by the authorities. During the Civil War, President

Lincoln suspended habeas corpus and allowed the federal government to imprison suspected rebels, draft resisters, and anyone else deemed disloyal.

(4) The *Schenck* decision did not address the question of whether the federal government could limit minority voting rights. Although the Supreme Court has never explicitly given its approval to practices that limit minority voting rights, it has generally left it to the states to determine voting procedures. During the 19th and 20th centuries, states often implemented voting procedures that limited minority voting rights.

26. **1** One major reason the United States Senate refused to approve the Treaty of Versailles after World War I was that many senators were concerned about future United States obligations in world affairs. The Senate's rejection of the treaty was a blow to President Woodrow Wilson. The treaty stipulated that the nations who signed it would be participants in the new League of Nations. Therefore, the Senate's rejection of the treaty also meant rejection of United States membership in the League. The League of Nations was dear to President Wilson. He included the concept in his Fourteen Points program for the postwar world and he campaigned vigorously for it in Europe and the United States. Some senators, however, wanted to isolate the United States from world affairs and opposed membership in the League. They feared that membership in the League might obligate the United States to participate in future wars.

WRONG CHOICES EXPLAINED:
(2) Senate rejection of the Treaty of Versailles was not caused by opposition to United States colonial practices in Asia. Nothing in the treaty condemned or condoned United States colonial practices.

(3) Senate rejection of the Treaty of Versailles was not caused by concerns about repayment of war debts from France. The issue of repayments of war debt from France and England surfaced in the 1920s as part of the Dawes Plan (1924).

(4) Senate rejection of the Treaty of Versailles was not related to increased foreign aid to Germany. The treaty stipulated that Germany must pay war reparations.

27. **4** National Prohibition, as authorized by the 18th Amendment, stated that the manufacture and sale of alcoholic beverages was banned. The ratification of the 18th Amendment (1919) was the result of a long national dialogue in the United States about the role of alcoholic beverages in daily life. In the early 19th century, the temperance movement urged individuals to pledge not to consume alcohol. Later in the century, the Prohibition movement went further, urging the government to outright prohibit the production, sale, and consumption of alcohol. Women were well represented in these movements. The final victory for the Prohibition movement came as the United States entered World War I. With wartime shortages of grain, it made sense to ban grain-based alcoholic beverages. The anti-German sentiment

that developed during World War I also played a role; many American breweries had German names. These factors led to the ratification of the 18th
Amendment, which banned alcohol production, sale, and consumption as of
January 1, 1920. The experiment in Prohibition reduced the overall quantity
of alcohol consumed, but it also turned otherwise upstanding citizens into
outlaws, as many ordinary Americans continued to find ways to procure alcoholic beverages. Prohibition ended with the ratification of the 21st
Amendment (1933).

WRONG CHOICES EXPLAINED:
(1) (2) and (3) National Prohibition was an outright ban on the production,
sale, and consumption of alcoholic beverages. It did not set the drinking age
at 18, ban the sale of domestically produced alcoholic beverages, or mandate
that alcohol be sold in government-run stores.

28. **3** During the 1920s, Congress passed a series of immigration laws
that were primarily designed to limit immigration from southern and eastern
Europe. The two most important pieces of legislation were the Emergency
Quota Act (1921) and the National Origins Act (1924). These acts greatly
reduced the number of immigrants allowed into the United States by establishing quotas for different nations based on the numbers of each national
group present in the United States decades earlier. Eastern and southern
Europeans were especially hard hit by these quotas. Opposition to immigration, or Nativism, rose steeply in the years after World War I. There are
several reasons Nativists resented the new wave of immigrants that arrived in
the United States between 1880 and 1920. Some Nativists focused on the fact
that most of the new immigrants were not Protestant. Poles and Italians
tended to be Catholic; Russians and Greeks tended to be Eastern Orthodox;
and Jewish immigrants came from several countries in eastern Europe. Some
Nativists objected to the cacophony of languages heard on the streets of New
York or Chicago. Some Americans were anti-European after the trauma of
World War I. Some Nativists associated the immigrants with either radical
movements or drunkenness. Finally, some working-class people feared that
low-wage immigrant laborers would take jobs from native-born American
workers.

WRONG CHOICES EXPLAINED:
(1) The immigration laws of the 1920s were not designed to increase
immigration from Asia. In fact, Nativists tended to harbor an intense resentment of Asian immigrants. Asian immigration was effectively cut off
even before the passage of the immigration laws of the 1920s. In 1882,
Congress passed the Chinese Exclusion Act. In 1907, President Theodore
Roosevelt worked out the "Gentlemen's Agreement" with the leaders of
Japan. Roosevelt agreed to undo anti–Japanese American legislation
in California in exchange for Japan agreeing to limit emigration into the
United States.

(2) The immigration laws of the 1920s were not designed to expand the workforce for the growing economy. In fact, the immigration laws of the 1920s had the opposite effect, reducing the flow of potential new laborers into the United States to a trickle.

(4) The immigration laws of the 1920s were not designed to prohibit immigration from Latin America. The laws did not prohibit immigration from any nation or region. Rather, they set quotas for different nations.

29. **4** During the second half of the 1920s, overproduction and under-consumption were major causes of the Great Depression. Mass production techniques, such as the assembly line, led to an overall increase in the production of consumer goods, but ordinary Americans found it increasingly difficult to purchase these consumer goods. Wages did not rise significantly in the 1920s. One reason for low wages among workers was a weak union movement. The Red Scare of the late 1910s and early 1920s intimidated people from organizing unions. Also, in the 1910s and 1920s, lower-paid unskilled assembly line workers were replacing higher-paid skilled craft workers. If workers had received higher wages in the 1920s, they might have been able to absorb more of the consumer goods that were piling up in warehouses from 1927 onward.

WRONG CHOICES EXPLAINED:
(1) The Great Depression was not caused by deficits in the federal budget. In the 1920s and earlier, the federal government generally did not have deficits except during times of war. Large peacetime federal deficits first appeared during the 1930s, as President Franklin D. Roosevelt's New Deal programs cost more money than was being brought in from tax revenues.

(2) The Great Depression was not caused by reductions in tariff rates. In fact, tariff rates were high in the 1920s, as isolationist senators attempted to limit United States interactions with Europe. These high tariff rates contributed to the Great Depression by causing some of America's trading partners to implement retaliatory tariffs, thus reducing Americans exports.

(3) The Great Depression was not caused by the creation of national and states sales taxes. States sales taxes existed before, during, and after the Great Depression. Certain products, such as gasoline and cigarettes, are subject to federal excise taxes.

30. **4** President Herbert Hoover's response to the Great Depression was often criticized because it failed to provide direct relief for the neediest persons. Hoover was a believer in supply-side economics. This approach to the economy stressed stimulating the supply side of the economy—manufacturers, banks, and insurance corporations. The theory is that if there is growth in the supply side, there will be a general economic revival and the benefits of a robust economy will trickle down to everyone. The alternative approach is to stimulate the demand side—consumers. Demand-side economics would emphasize government policies designed to increase

workers' wages and benefits, such as welfare and unemployment benefits. As a believer in supply-side economics, Hoover implemented policies that he thought would stimulate business. One of Hoover's major initiatives was the Reconstruction Finance Corporation. This agency extended loans to manufacturers and banks. Hoover resisted extending relief programs to individuals in need, believing that direct relief would make people dependent on the government rather than on their own resolve.

WRONG CHOICES EXPLAINED:

(1) Hoover's response to the Great Depression was not criticized for wasting money on new social programs. In fact, Hoover's critics leveled the opposite criticism against him. They argued that he should spend more on social programs designed to help the neediest.

(2) Hoover's response to the Great Depression was not criticized for causing widespread rioting and looting in major cities. There is one instance of large-scale violence associated with Hoover's decisions. In June 1932, a group of World War I veterans, who called themselves the Bonus Expeditionary Force, marched into Washington, D.C., to demand a bonus that they had been promised for their service in the military. After several days, Hoover ordered the army to break up the encampment. A riot ensued, resulting in several injuries and a death.

(3) Hoover's response to the Great Depression was not criticized for raising taxes on businesses and the wealthy. As a believer in supply-side economics, Hoover did not raise taxes on businesses and the wealthy. His idea was to stimulate the supply side—banks, manufacturers, and other businesses—with lower taxes so that the benefits would trickle down to everyone.

31. **4** A major reason for creating the Tennessee Valley Authority (TVA) in 1933 was to improve economic conditions in a poor rural region. The TVA was part of Franklin D. Roosevelt's New Deal. This set of programs and agencies was designed to address the poverty and economic dislocation caused by the Great Depression. Roosevelt tried a variety of approaches to put the economy on sound footing. The TVA was a set of development projects in the Tennessee River area, which includes the states of Kentucky, Virginia, North Carolina, Tennessee, Georgia, Alabama, and Mississippi. The region was especially hard hit by the Great Depression. Even before the Depression, poverty was pervasive; most homes in the region were without electricity. The TVA included major infrastructure projects, including electricity-generating dams along the Tennessee River. The strategy was to provide jobs and electricity to people in the region. The TVA was largely successful, and still exists, despite initial resistance from competing utility companies.

WRONG CHOICES EXPLAINED:

(1) The TVA was not designed to build and manage a turnpike in the valley. New Deal projects included new roads, but the TVA focused on electricity-generating projects.

(2) The TVA was not designed to provide health care benefits for Southerners. Access to health care was not a major focus of the New Deal. Later, in the 1960s, President Lyndon Johnson's Great Society programs included Medicare and Medicaid. Access to health care remains a contentious issue that government officials continue to address.

(3) The TVA was not designed to encourage African Americans to settle in the valley. The program was designed to help existing residents in the region, not bring in new ones.

32. **1** The main idea of the cartoon is that Congress will give President Franklin D. Roosevelt a free hand to lead the nation during his second term. President Roosevelt won a resounding endorsement from the American people when he ran for reelection in 1936. He won over 60 percent of the popular vote and carried every state except for the Republican strongholds of Vermont and Maine. The cartoonist is interpreting such a landslide as a mandate for Roosevelt's New Deal program—a mandate that Congress would not dare to challenge. The president is depicted as confidently steering the sled, labeled "New Deal legislation." Congress is depicted as deferring to the president when asked by the American people about the direction of the New Deal legislation sled.

WRONG CHOICES EXPLAINED:
(2) The main idea of the cartoon is not that the American people will trust Congress to lead the nation. In the cartoon, Congress is literally taking a back seat to the president. When asked about the direction of New Deal legislation, Congress is depicted as deferring to the president.

(3) The main idea of the cartoon is not that President Roosevelt will seek direction from the people. Roosevelt is depicted as confidently steering the sled, while the people ask meekly, "Where we goin' this time?"

(4) The main idea of the cartoon is not that the Great Depression will no longer be a serious concern. The sled represents New Deal legislation. Roosevelt is still steering the sled forward, indicating his intention to continue pushing for programs to address the Depression.

33. **3** President Franklin D. Roosevelt is proposing the Lend-Lease Act in the speech. The speech makes a direct appeal to Congress to militarily aid those nations fighting against fascism, even if those nations are unable to pay for that aid. Between the start of World War II (1939) and the Japanese attack on Pearl Harbor (1941), United States foreign policy shifted from neutrality to military support for the Allies. When World War II began in Europe, many Americans, including President Roosevelt, were sympathetic to the Allies (England and France), but isolationist sentiment was strong in the United States. Congress passed several neutrality acts starting in 1935. A 1939 neutrality act stipulated that the United States could sell weaponry to the Allies but only on a "cash and carry" basis. In early 1941 Roosevelt was able to make military supplies more readily available to the Allies with the

Lend-Lease Act. This act demonstrated the commitment of the United States to the Allies, but it was not until the attack on Pearl Harbor on December 7, 1941, that the United States entered the war.

WRONG CHOICES EXPLAINED:

(1) The speech is not proposing the Fair Deal. The Fair Deal was a set of domestic initiatives put forth by President Franklin D. Roosevelt's successor, Harry Truman.

(2) The speech is not proposing the Great Society. The Great Society was a set of domestic initiatives put forth by President Lyndon B. Johnson.

(4) The speech is not proposing the Cash and Carry policy. The Cash and Carry policy (1939) was put forth by President Franklin D. Roosevelt and was designed to provide weaponry to the foes of fascism, but the speech makes clear that Roosevelt is breaking with the Cash and Carry policy. In the Cash and Carry policy, the United States demanded that other nations pay for weapons up front, in cash, before they are delivered. In this speech, Roosevelt does not want to let other nations' "inability to pay" prevent the United States from providing needed weaponry.

34.　**2**　The cartoon was used to encourage Americans to conserve natural resources. The cartoonist is asserting that the fuel used by American motorists could be better used by tanks fighting abroad. There was a government-sponsored public campaign to conserve natural resources during World War II. A famous poster encouraged carpooling by showing a driver in a car with Hitler in the passenger seat. The caption read, "When you drive alone, you drive with Hitler." The campaign asserted that wasting resources hurt the war effort and helped the enemy.

WRONG CHOICES EXPLAINED:

(1) (3) and (4) The cartoon was not used to encourage Americans to buy war bonds, serve in the armed forces, or work in war industries. The government did encourage Americans to do all of these things, but that was not the purpose of this cartoon.

35.　**3**　A major purpose of the GI Bill (1944) was to provide federal funds for veterans to attend college. The GI Bill, formally known as the Servicemen's Readjustment Act, provided low-interest loans for veterans to purchase homes and extended funds for college education. The intent of the GI Bill was to help the veterans of World War II adjust to life during peacetime. The program was very successful. It helped millions of veterans advance economically. A college education and home ownership have been seen as key components of entrance into the middle class.

WRONG CHOICES EXPLAINED:

(1) The purpose of the GI Bill was not to replace the draft near the end of World War II. Throughout World War II, the military depended on draftees as well as volunteers to staff the armed forces.

(2) The purpose of the GI Bill was not to prohibit racial discrimination in the armed forces. President Harry Truman issued an executive order prohibiting discrimination in the military in 1948.

(4) The purpose of the GI Bill was not to increase the number of women working in defense industries. The government did attempt to increase the number of women working in defense-related industries through a public relations campaign that featured the fictional character, Rosie the Riveter.

36. **1** In the Truman Doctrine, President Harry Truman pledged to support Greece in its fight against communist aggression. The issuing of the Truman Doctrine is one of several important events in the history of the Cold War. The United States and the Soviet Union emerged as rival superpowers in the Cold War. After the close of World War II, the Soviet Union left its troops in the nations of eastern Europe, turning these nations into Soviet satellites. The United States was worried that the Soviet Union would try to push into western Europe. The leader of the Soviet Union, Joseph Stalin, insisted that he only wanted to have Allied nations on the border of the Soviet Union. In order to block any further aggression by the Soviet Union, Truman issued the Truman Doctrine (1947), in which he said that the goal of the United States would be to contain communism. Toward this end, the United States extended military aid to Greece and Turkey. The United States made it clear that it would be involved in world affairs even in peacetime.

WRONG CHOICES EXPLAINED:
(2) The Truman Doctrine was not a pledge to fight hunger in Africa and Asia. The United States has provided foreign aid to nations experiencing food shortages, but the Truman Doctrine was part of the strategy to contain communism.

(3) The Truman Doctrine was not a pledge to strengthen the United States nuclear arsenal. In the 1950s, the United States did attempt to strengthen its nuclear arsenal in order to close the so-called missile gap between the United States and the Soviet Union. The missile gap proved to be illusory, but the perception of a gap influenced United States nuclear policy. The Truman Doctrine, however, was part of the strategy to contain communism.

(4) The Truman Doctrine was not a pledge to reject the policy of containment. On the contrary, the Truman Doctrine was part of the strategy to contain communism.

37. **2** McCarthyism is associated with the fear of communist influence in the United States. Senator Joseph McCarthy, a Republican from Wisconsin, was such a central figure in the anticommunist movement in the early 1950s that the movement bears his name. McCarthy rose to national prominence in 1950 when he announced that he had a list of "known communists" who had infiltrated the State Department. This and similar claims, mostly baseless, created a name for McCarthy and set the stage for a

host of measures to halt this perceived threat. Congress established committees to investigate Communist Party infiltration in different sectors of society. Congress especially targeted the entertainment industry, fearing that communists would subtly get their message out through television and movies. Leading members of the party were arrested under the anti-espionage Smith Act. Loyalty oaths became commonplace for public sector employees. Critics asserted that these measures violated people's constitutional right to freedom of speech. Finally McCarthy went too far, accusing members of the military establishment of being communists. The Senate voted to censure him in 1954, thus ending the worst excesses of what many people referred to as a witch-hunt.

WRONG CHOICES EXPLAINED:
(1) McCarthyism is not closely associated with the buildup of Soviet missiles in Cuba. In 1962, the United States discovered that Cuba was preparing bases for Soviet nuclear missiles to be installed. This move was challenged by President John F. Kennedy. After a tense standoff between the Soviet Union and the United States, the Soviet Union agreed to halt its plans, and the United States quietly agreed to remove nuclear missiles from Turkey. These events occurred eight years after McCarthy was censured by the Senate and five years after his death.

(3) McCarthyism is not closely associated with the rise of the Communist Party in China. The Communist Party in China, led by Mao Zedong, established the People's Republic of China in 1949 after a protracted civil war. This occurred the year before McCarthy rose to national prominence. Although events in China contributed to the rise of anticommunist sentiment in the United States, McCarthy is more closely associated with the fear of domestic communism.

(4) McCarthyism is not closely associated with the creation of the Warsaw Pact by the Soviet Union. The Warsaw Pact was a military alliance that the Soviet Union created in 1955 with the communist nations of eastern and central Europe. Although the creation of the Warsaw Pact was part of the Cold War, McCarthy is more closely associated with the fear of domestic communism.

38. **2** The information on the map supports the conclusion that African American migration between 1940 and 1970 was mainly from the south to the north. Approximately five million African Americans left the South during this period. Historians often label this migration the Second Great Migration. The First Great Migration of African Americans out of the South occurred between 1910 and 1930. There were several important reasons for the migration of African Americans from the rural South to the urban North that apply to both periods. A basic factor was the mistreatment that African Americans received in the South. White Southerners created a series of Jim Crow laws that separated African Americans from whites in schools, busses, trains, and other facilities. A rigid system of segregation

persisted in the South well into the 20th century and constantly reminded African Americans of their second-class status. In addition, African Americans were excluded from the political system in the South. A series of obstacles, such as literacy tests and poll taxes, limited their ability to vote. African Americans who spoke out against this were targets of violence and even death. Finally, many African Americans in both periods were drawn north by jobs. By the turn of the 20th century, the industrial revolution was in full swing in northern cities such as New York and Chicago. During the first period of migration, production for World War I made the need for factory workers especially acute. World War II served the same function during the second period.

WRONG CHOICES EXPLAINED:

(1) The information on the map does not support the conclusion that African American migration between 1940 and 1970 was mainly from urban areas to rural areas. The map does not indicate population changes in cities or rural areas. In actuality, the migration was mainly from rural areas to urban areas.

(3) The information on the map does not support the conclusion that African American migration between 1940 and 1970 was mainly from the Mountain states to the West Coast. The map indicates that there was "little or no population change" in Mountain states such as Colorado, Wyoming, and Montana.

(4) The information on the map does not support the conclusion that African American migration between 1940 and 1970 was mainly from the Sun Belt to the Great Plains. The map shows that some Sun Belt states, such as Florida and California, experienced a "large population gain," but most of the states of the Great Plains, from Oklahoma to the Dakotas, experienced "little or no population change."

39. **2** The Soviet launch of the *Sputnik* satellite led to the other three developments mentioned in the question. When the Soviet Union launched the unmanned satellite *Sputnik* into space in 1957, many Americans were caught off guard. America had assumed that it was technologically superior to the Soviet Union. The launching of *Sputnik* alarmed United States government officials because they realized that the same type of rocket that launched the satellite could also be used to quickly deliver atomic weapons to any location on earth. The launching of *Sputnik* led the American government to devote more resources to teaching science and math to young people. The launching also initiated a space race with the Soviet Union. In 1961, President John F. Kennedy announced the goal of landing a man on the moon before the close of the 1960s. This goal was accomplished, as the United States was the first nation to successfully land men on the moon in 1969. After two decades of the space race, the Soviet Union and the United States began several cooperative space ventures. The first joint mission was the Apollo-Soyuz Project in 1975. This and subsequent joint missions

were symbolic of an easing of tensions, known as *détente*, between the two superpowers.

WRONG CHOICES EXPLAINED:
(1) (3) and (4) These choices were not the cause of the other developments mentioned in the question. All three developments occurred in the period of space exploration between the 1950s and 1970s, but it was the launching of the *Sputnik* satellite that led to these developments.

40. **1** The domino theory is closely associated with American military involvement in Vietnam. The domino theory asserts that when a nation becomes communist, its neighbors will be more likely to also become communist. The name of the theory alludes to the game of lining up dominos in a row, so that when the first domino is pushed over, each successive domino in the row will in turn be knocked over. The theory presumes that communism is imposed on a country from the outside—that it does not develop as a result of internal conditions. The Vietnam War began in 1959 as communist rebels in South Vietnam, aided by communist North Vietnam, challenged the government of South Vietnam. The United States feared that South Vietnam would become a communist nation as North Vietnam had. The United States sent military advisors and assistance to the government of South Vietnam in the 1950s. Large-scale American involvement in the Vietnam War began with the Tonkin Gulf Resolution (1964). Despite the presence of over half a million United States troops and the fire power of the U.S. military, President Johnson was not able to declare victory over the communists rebels in South Vietnam. As the war dragged on, and as the United States suffered more casualties, many Americans began to question the wisdom of American policies in Vietnam. United States involvement in Vietnam continued until 1973, when President Richard Nixon withdrew the last American troops. In 1975, the government of South Vietnam became communist.

WRONG CHOICES EXPLAINED:
(2) The domino theory is not closely associated with the construction of the Berlin Wall. The communist government of East Germany built the Berlin Wall in 1961 to completely encircle West Berlin and separate it from East Germany. Berlin had been divided when Germany was divided into East Germany and West Germany in 1949. Berlin was located completely within East German territory, so West Berlin was physically separate from the rest of West Germany. Before construction of the wall, many residents of East Germany escaped to the west through West Berlin.

(3) The domino theory is not closely associated with the signing of the nuclear test ban treaty. The treaty, which banned test detonations of nuclear weapons except for underground tests, was negotiated between the United States and the Soviet Union in 1963.

(4) The domino theory is not closely associated with the end of the Korean War. The Korean War (1951–1954) began when communist North Korea invaded South Korea. The domino theory is designed to prevent possible future aggression, rather than to respond to actual aggression.

41. **2** The main idea of the cartoon is that the government is improperly hiding information from the public. The patron in the library seems puzzled that the government has classified so much information as "dangerous" for the public to see. The cartoon is a response to the varied efforts by President Richard Nixon to prevent damaging or critical information from reaching the public. The cartoonist is asserting that President Nixon attempted to classify so much information that it could fill an entire section of a library. The Nixon administration vigorously attempted to suppress information about the Vietnam War that did not present the administration's efforts in a positive light. It also attempted to keep secret various CIA and FBI actions that might be viewed as illegal or unethical. The most important dispute over secrecy occurred when Nixon attempted to prevent the *New York Times* and the *Washington Post* from publishing the *Pentagon Papers*, a secret study of the Vietnam War written by the Defense Department. The study revealed official deception and secrecy. It was leaked to the press by Daniel Ellsberg, a Pentagon official critical of the direction the Vietnam War was taking. Initially, the Nixon administration obtained an injunction against publication, but the Supreme Court, in the case of *New York Times* v. *United States* (1971), overruled the injunction and upheld the right of the newspapers to publish the information.

WRONG CHOICES EXPLAINED:
(1) The cartoonist is not asserting that the press should refrain from publishing materials that damage the reputation of public officials. The criticism is aimed at the government's obsession with secrecy, not at the press's criticism of public officials. The right of the press to criticize public officials is firmly established in the United States.

(3) The cartoonist is not asserting that the government should restrict the publication of sensitive materials. The library patron is alarmed at the large amount of information already deemed "dangerous" by the government.

(4) The cartoonist is not asserting that libraries are making too many government reports open to the public. The concern in the cartoon is that the reports are deemed "dangerous" by the government, not that they are open to the public.

42. **3** The primary purpose of President Richard Nixon's policy of *détente* was to ease tensions between the United States and the Soviet Union. *Détente* is the French word for "loosening" and refers to an easing of tensions in the Cold War and a warming of relations between the United States and the Soviet Union. It may seem ironic that a man who made a name for himself as a strong anticommunist came to be responsible for the *détente*

policy. However, Nixon's anticommunist credentials enabled him to open relations with communist nations without being accused of being "soft on communism." In 1972 Nixon became the first United States president to visit Communist China and later that year he held meetings with Soviet leaders in Moscow. The meetings produced several agreements, including an agreement to limit anti-ballistic missile systems (ABMs).

WRONG CHOICES EXPLAINED:

(1) The policy of *détente* was not intended to expand United States military involvement in Southeast Asia. Nixon did expand United States military involvement in Southeast Asia, but *détente* is associated with moves toward peace, not toward war.

(2) The policy of *détente* was not intended to assure an adequate supply of oil from the Middle East. This has been a goal of United States foreign policy since the 1950s, but *détente* is associated with relations between the United States and the Soviet Union.

(4) The policy of *détente* was not intended to maintain a favorable balance of trade with China. Concerns about the balance of trade between the United States and China have emerged in the 2000s, as China has become the leading manufacturer of consumer goods in the world. The United States has a large and growing trade deficit with China, but *détente* is associated with relations between the United States and the communist world during the Cold War.

43. **1** One way in which Andrew Jackson, Abraham Lincoln, and Woodrow Wilson are similar is that each expanded presidential powers. President Jackson (1829–1837) expanded presidential power in several ways. After South Carolina asserted its intent to nullify the Tariff Act of 1828, Jackson challenged and prevented the move. Later, when the Supreme Court, in the case of *Worcester* v. *Georgia* (1832), ruled that the Cherokee people were not subject to the 1830 Indian Removal Act, Jackson and the state of Georgia began moving them to the West anyway. Finally Jackson destroyed the Second Bank of the United States in the 1830s. His critics labeled him King Andrew in response to these heavy-handed measures. In the heat of an all-encompassing Civil War, President Lincoln (1861–1865) greatly expanded presidential power. During the war, Lincoln had several secessionist-minded members of the Maryland legislature arrested to prevent it from voting to secede. He also suspended the constitutional right to a writ of habeas corpus during the war, allowing authorities to keep opponents of the war in jail without charges being filed. Finally, President Wilson (1913–1921) expanded presidential powers during World War I. Wilson created several new government departments to organize the war effort. The Committee on Public Information organized prowar propaganda; the War Industries Board directed industrial production. These and other boards were under the direction of the White House.

WRONG CHOICES EXPLAINED:

(2) The three presidents mentioned in the question did not work to reduce the size of the federal bureaucracy. The federal bureaucracy has grown fairly consistently from the thousand employees in the Washington administration in 1790 to the 2.6 million employees today.

(3) The three presidents mentioned in the question did not face congressional investigations over the handling of the military. There were no congressional investigations in regard to Jackson or Lincoln. There were congressional investigations into the handling of World War I, but they were well after the war and after Wilson's death. The Senate's Nye committee (1934–1937) uncovered evidence that certain American corporations greatly profited from World War I.

(4) All three of the presidents mentioned in the question did not send troops overseas. Only President Wilson did; he sent troops to participate in World War I.

44. **4** The Nuremburg War Crimes trials established the principle that leaders of a nation may be tried for crimes against humanity. After World War II, a series of trials was held in the German city of Nuremberg in response to the Holocaust. The Holocaust was the systematic murder by the Nazis of six million European Jews and other "undesirables." In 1939 the German dictator Adolf Hitler and other leading Nazis developed the "final solution," a plan to eliminate the Jewish population. After German forces took over most of continental Europe during World War II, this plan went from being the scheming of a madman to a horrible, deadly reality. The plan also included other groups such as gypsies and homosexuals. After the end of World War II, the full extent of Nazi crimes became known. The victorious nations set up an international tribunal to try leading Nazis for committing crimes against humanity. At these trials, about 30 American judges participated. The chief justice of the United States Supreme Court was a lead lawyer for the prosecution. Many of the Nazis defended themselves by claiming that they were merely following orders. The charge of crimes against humanity has been used by international tribunals in more recent cases; the Khmer Rouge leaders of Cambodia in the 1970s and Charles Taylor of Liberia have both been charged with crimes against humanity.

WRONG CHOICES EXPLAINED:

(1) The Scopes trial did not involve the charge of crimes against humanity. The Scopes trial (1925) involved the teaching of evolution in the public schools. John Scopes, a Tennessee biology teacher, was arrested for violating a state law forbidding the teaching of evolution. The trial pitted rural, traditional, religious values against science.

(2) The Rosenberg trial did not involve the charge of crimes against humanity. Ethel and Julius Rosenberg were an American couple who were accused of passing secrets of the nuclear bomb to the Soviet Union. The Rosenbergs, who were members of the Communist Party, insisted on their

innocence but were sent to the electric chair in 1953. Evidence has emerged since the end of the Cold War that suggests that Julius had been involved in some sort of espionage on behalf of the Soviet Union.

(3) The Sacco and Vanzetti trial did not involve the charge of crimes against humanity. Nicola Sacco and Bartolomeo Vanzetti were accused of robbing and killing a payroll clerk in Massachusetts in 1920. The evidence against them was sketchy, and the judge was openly hostile to the two men, who were not only Italian immigrants but also anarchists. After they were found guilty, many Americans protested the verdict and wondered if an immigrant, especially with radical ideas, could get a fair trial in the United States. Despite protests, the two men were executed in 1927.

45. **1** One similarity between the laws being challenged in the Supreme Court cases of *Plessy* v. *Ferguson* (1896) and *Korematsu* v. *United States* (1944) is that specific groups of people were being targeted based on race and ethnicity. In the *Plessy* case, the laws that were being challenged were Jim Crow laws, which southern states implemented to segregate African Americans from whites. The specific law that came under scrutiny was a Louisiana law that required segregation on trains that passed through the state. The Supreme Court accepted that segregation was constitutional as long as the facilities for both whites and African Americans were of equal quality. It was generally the case that the facilities for African Americans were substandard, but this "separate but equal" rule was the law of the land until the Supreme Court found segregated schools inherently unfair in the *Brown* v. *the Board of Education* decision (1954). In the *Korematsu* case, the law that was being challenged was Executive Order 9066 (1942), issued by President Franklin D. Roosevelt during World War II. The order authorized the government to remove over 100,000 Japanese Americans from West Coast states and relocate them to camps in the interior of the West. Their property was confiscated by the government. The Supreme Court ruled that the relocation was acceptable on the grounds of national security. Much later, in 1988, the United States government publicly apologized to the surviving victims and extended $20,000 in reparations to each one.

WRONG CHOICES EXPLAINED:

(2) In neither case were state laws declared unconstitutional. In the *Plessy* case, a state law was upheld. The *Korematsu* case dealt with a federal order.

(3) In neither case were immigrants relocated to prison camps. The *Plessy* case dealt with the issue of segregation. The *Korematsu* case dealt with the relocation of Japanese Americans to internment camps, not prison camps. Further, most (62 percent) of those who were relocated were American-born citizens, not immigrants.

(4) In neither case were federal laws segregating public transportation upheld. In the *Plessy* case, it was a state, not a federal, segregation law that was upheld. The *Korematsu* case dealt with the relocation of Japanese Americans.

46. **3** Information from the table supports the conclusion that the distribution of House seats follows shifts in population. Each state's delegation in the House is determined by its population. California currently has the largest delegation with 53 members; six states have only one member each. The total number of voting representatives is currently fixed at 435, so an increase in the number of representatives from one state would necessarily involve a decrease in another state. The table shows that the biggest gains projected in the House are in the Sun Belt states of Florida and Texas. The biggest losses projected are in northern states. The demographic shift described in the question is associated with the deindustrialization of northeastern and midwestern cities in the last several decades. Large numbers of factories in northern cities such as New York, Philadelphia, Pittsburgh, Cleveland, Detroit, and Chicago have closed. People have left these cities and looked for opportunity in the Sun Belt of the South, Southwest, and West Coast.

WRONG CHOICES EXPLAINED:

(1) The information in the table does not support the conclusion that the population of the United States is increasing. The number of voting members of the House is fixed at 435. Therefore, gains and losses in the House delegations are caused by relative changes in the populations of the various states, not by an overall change in the population of the United States. The population of the United States is increasing, but that is not indicated in the chart.

(2) The information in the table does not support the conclusion that the center of population is moving eastward. All of the eastern states listed in the chart, except for Florida, are predicted to lose House seats in 2010. The chart supports the conclusion that the center of population is moving southward and westward.

(4) The information in the table does not support the conclusion that the number of senators will soon increase. The chart deals with the House of Representatives, not the Senate. Each state has two members of the Senate, so the only way for the number of senators to increase is for new states to be admitted into the United States.

47. **1** These Cold War era headlines illustrate that rivalries between the superpowers often involved conflicts in other nations. The Cold War, a period of conflict, rivalry, and tension between the United States and the Soviet Union, began almost immediately after the close of World War II. The Cold War ended with the collapse of the Soviet Union in 1991. During the Cold War, many conflicts throughout the world were seen through the lens of the Cold War. In 1958, the pro-Western government of Lebanon, led by Camille Chamoun, a Christian, was challenged by a rebellion of Sunni Muslims who wanted Lebanon to have closer ties with other Arab nations. The United States sent troops to Lebanon to prevent these rebels from gaining power. In 1962, the United States discovered that Cuba was preparing bases for Soviet nuclear missiles to be installed. The communist leader of Cuba, Fidel Castro,

and Soviet Premier Nikita Khrushchev agreed to install nuclear missiles on Cuban soil as a deterrent to hostile actions by the United States. President Kennedy saw these bases, in such close proximity to the United States, as an unacceptable provocation and ordered the Soviet Union to halt the operation and dismantle the bases. For about a week, the world stood on the brink of nuclear war. Finally, a deal was reached in which the Soviet Union would abandon its Cuban missile program and the United States would quietly remove missiles from Turkey. In 1964, the United States became heavily involved in the Vietnam War after Congress gave President Johnson a blank check with the Tonkin Gulf Resolution. As the war dragged on, and as the United States suffered more casualties, many Americans began to question the wisdom of American policies in Vietnam. United States involvement in Vietnam ended in 1973. In 1975, after communist forces achieved victory in South Vietnam, Vietnam was reunited as a communist nation.

WRONG CHOICES EXPLAINED:

(2) The three headlines do not reveal that United States military support was most often deployed in Europe. The United States maintained a military presence in Europe throughout the Cold War, especially in West Germany, but the major military engagements of the Cold War era occurred outside of Europe.

(3) The three headlines do not all illustrate that communist forces were frequently victorious in Asia. Communist forces were ultimately victorious in Vietnam, but in the case of Lebanon, there was no victory by communist forces. Cuba is not in Asia.

(4) The three headlines do not all illustrate that summit talks frequently succeeded in limiting international tensions. In the case of the Cuban missile crisis, talks between American and Soviet leaders did diffuse a potentially disastrous situation. In the case of the Vietnam War, the Paris Peace Accord led to the withdrawal of United States forces from the region, but the accord would not be labeled a success. By 1973, the United States was simply eager to end its engagement in Vietnam after nine years of war. Talks did not occur in Lebanon.

48. **4** The correct chronology for the events listed in the question is the following: World War II (1939–1945), Korean War (1950–1953), Vietnam War (1959–1975), and War on Terrorism (2001–present). World War II began in 1939, when Nazi-controlled Germany attacked Poland. England and France quickly declared war on Germany. The United States remained neutral until the Japanese attack on the United States base at Pearl Harbor, Hawaii, on December 7, 1941. United States involvement in the European theater of war was limited until D-Day in June 1944. Most of the American effort was focused on the Asian theater. The war ended in 1945. The decisive blow against Japan was the dropping of two atomic bombs in August 1945. The Korean War began in June 1950, when North Korean troops invaded South Korea. President Truman decided to commit troops to support South

Korea, and managed to secure United Nations sponsorship. North Korean forces were joined by China. After intense fighting, the two sides settled into positions on either side of the thirty-eighth parallel. By 1953, an armistice was reached accepting a divided Korea. The Vietnam War began in 1959 as communist rebels in South Vietnam, aided by communist North Vietnam, challenged the government of South Vietnam. The United States became heavily involved in the Vietnam War after Congress gave President Johnson a blank check with the Tonkin Gulf Resolution (1964). Despite the presence of over half a million United States troops and the fire power of the military, the United States was not able to declare victory over the communists rebels in South Vietnam. As the war dragged on, many Americans began to question the wisdom of American policies in Vietnam. United States involvement in Vietnam ended in 1973. In 1975, after communist forces achieved victory in South Vietnam, Vietnam was reunited as a communist nation. The War on Terrorism began after the September 2001 terrorist attacks on the United States. On the morning of September 11, 2001, 19 terrorists working with the al-Qaeda organization hijacked four domestic airplanes. One plane was flown into the Pentagon, inflicting heavy damage, and one plane crashed in a field after the hijackers were overtaken by passengers. The other two airplanes did the most damage, destroying the two towers of the World Trade Center in New York City. Approximately 3,000 people died from the four incidents. The War on Terrorism has involved several important developments. In 2001 the United States overthrew the Taliban regime in Afghanistan, which had given refuge to al-Qaeda. Also in 2001 Congress passed the Patriot Act, which greatly expanded the government's authority in the fight against terrorism. Some critics have said that it impinges on people's civil liberties. In 2003 a United States-led coalition invaded Iraq and toppled the government of Saddam Hussein in Iraq. United States troops have been engaged in Iraq since then. President George W. Bush asserted that this action was part of the War on Terrorism, but critics contended that connections between Saddam Hussein and the al-Qaeda terrorists were never established.

WRONG CHOICES EXPLAINED:
    (1) (2) and (3) These choices do not contain the correct chronological order of the four events listed.

    49. **4** The information in the graph supports the conclusion that current life expectancy at age 65 for both men and women exceeds age 80. The graph charts the average expected age of men and women in the United States who have already reached the age of 65. These figures exclude people who died before the age of 65. Life expectancy for both men and women in the United States has risen steadily since 1940 and is projected to continue to rise through 2080. The reasons for these increases include improvements in diet, in medical care, and in public health measures. In general, wealthier countries have a higher life expectancy than poorer countries. Average life expectancy at birth in many African nations is considerably lower than in the United States. The chart also illustrates that women tend to live longer than

men. There is not general agreement in regard to the reasons for this discrepancy. Some experts attribute the discrepancy to social and cultural factors. Men are more likely to engage in dangerous activities, such as war, industrial work, and consumption of tobacco, alcohol, and illegal drugs. Other experts focus on biological differences between men and women.

WRONG CHOICES EXPLAINED:

(1) The information in the graph does not support the conclusion that life expectancies for men and women are likely to remain the same. Figures for both men and women have changed since 1940, and are predicted to change in the future. In each year, the figures for men and women are different. Women can expect to live about five years longer than men.

(2) The information in the graph does not support the conclusion that life expectancy rates for men show a steady decline since 1980. The graph indicates that life expectancy for men has increased steadily since 1940 and is expected to increase into the future.

(3) The information in the graph does not support the conclusion that by 2040, the life expectancy of men will exceed that of women. The life expectancy rates for women have been higher than those for men since at least 1940 and are expected to be higher into the future.

50. **2** The changes shown between 1940 and 2000 are most likely the result of the improvements in modern medicine. Doctors today can use sophisticated diagnostic tools that were simply unavailable before 1940 to identify diseases and conditions. The medical field has not found outright cures to major diseases such as cancer and heart disease, but it has developed procedures and medicines to greatly improve a patient's chances of prolonging life. Although the medical field has made great strides in treating individuals, public health measures have had a greater impact on society as a whole. Public health officials have pushed for greater availability of vaccinations and have initiated campaigns to encourage hand washing and condom use and discourage smoking and taking illegal drugs.

WRONG CHOICES EXPLAINED:

(1) The changes in the graph between 1940 and 2000 are not due to a reduction in warfare. Life expectancy has increased, but warfare has continued and even intensified. Americans suffered significant casualties in World War II, the Korean War, and the Vietnam War.

(3) The changes in the graph between 1940 and 2000 are not due to an increase in the number of immigrants. Immigrants have tended to push down overall life expectancy figures, but the graph shows an increase in life expectancy. Immigrants tend to come from poorer countries with a lower average life expectancy.

(4) The changes in the graph between 1940 and 2000 are not due to a decrease in obesity rates. Obesity is seen today by public health officials as a major health problem. This period has seen an increase in obesity rates, while the graph indicates an increase in life expectancy.

PART II: THEMATIC ESSAY

Constitutional Principles—Individual Rights

Many different groups have faced discrimination throughout United States history. At times federal and state governments have taken actions that have limited the rights of these groups. At other times federal and state governments have taken actions that protected the rights of these groups. In the decades around the middle of the 20th century, the federal government took different actions that had different impacts on discriminated groups. In 1942, the federal government ordered the internment of Japanese Americans, limiting their rights. A mere 15 years later, in 1957, the federal government intervened in a crisis in Arkansas to ensure that African Americans would be allowed to attend the main high school in Little Rock. In this case, the federal government acted to protect the rights of a discriminated group.

In regard to Japanese Americans, the federal government took actions during World War II that many people thought were unfair. Later, in the 1980s, the federal government apologized for its actions during the war. The United States entered World War II in 1941, immediately after Japanese planes attacked the United States base at Pearl Harbor, Hawaii. Not only did the United States enter the war, but a wave of anti-Japanese sentiment swept over America. This anti-Japanese sentiment did not emerge out of nowhere. In the late 1800s, many Japanese people immigrated to the West Coast of the United States. In California, these

Japanese immigrants often suffered discrimination. Many white Californians harbored resentment for their new neighbors. In the early years of the twentieth century, California passed legislation ordering "Orientals" to be segregated from white students in the public school system. When Japan protested, President Theodore Roosevelt and Japanese leaders negotiated a "Gentlemen's Agreement" in which Roosevelt agreed to reverse this legislation and Japan agreed to limit the number of emigrants coming into the United States. However, on the eve of World War II, anti-Japanese sentiment still existed in California and elsewhere in the United States.

This sentiment was certainly enflamed by the attack at Pearl Harbor. Many Americans became convinced that Japanese Americans, many of whom were American citizens born in the United States, would be more loyal to Japan than to the United States. With no evidence, the United States military asserted to President Franklin D. Roosevelt that Americans of Japanese descent might act as spies on the United States for Japan. Roosevelt took this assertion seriously and in 1942 issued Executive Order 9066, less than three months after the attack on Pearl Harbor. This order authorized government officials to round up and remove over 100,000 Japanese Americans from California and other West Coast cities and towns, and relocate them to camps in the interior of the West. These Americans of Japanese descent were forced to spend the rest of the war in these internment camps. To add to the woes of the Japanese Americans, most of their property was confiscated by the government. When the relocation was ordered, the Supreme Court upheld the federal government. In the case of *Korematsu* v. *United States*, the Court ruled that the relocation was acceptable because the country was at war and during war, civilian authorities should defer to the wishes of the military.

During the context of war, the federal government took an action that limited the rights of a particular group, but only a few years later, in the context of the civil rights movement, the federal government took an action that protected another group's rights. The federal action was in response to a crisis that had developed in Little Rock, Arkansas. The local school board had decided to allow a group of African American students to enter the previously all-white Central High School. Little Rock was like virtually all communities in the South at the time—schools were rigidly segregated by race. A series of Jim Crow laws enforced segregation throughout the various southern states. White southerners created the system to put African Americans in a second-class status. The Jim Crow system was dealt a serious blow in 1954, when the Supreme Court issued its landmark decision in the case of *Brown* v. *Board of Education of Topeka*. This decision declared segregated schools inherently unfair and ordered states and communities to take measures to undo this system.

The school board in Little Rock, Arkansas, decided to begin the desegregation of Central High School at the beginning of the 1957 school year by admitting nine African American students. The plan developed without much controversy, but just before the beginning of the school year, Arkansas Governor Orville Faubus decided to send the National Guard to ring the school and not permit the nine African American students to enter the building. The news of Faubus's action prompted a large crowd of prosegregation whites to also come out. Faubus had instigated a mob to enforce white supremacy in Little Rock.

It was at this point that the federal government acted. President Dwight D. Eisenhower was not a strong supporter of the civil rights movement, but he was alarmed to see the Arkansas governor directly challenge federal authority. At first, Eisenhower urged the governor to comply with the segregation plan. Governor Faubus gave Eisenhower his word that he would withdraw the National Guard troops from the school. He did withdraw the National Guard, but he made no provisions for the safety of the nine African American students. The students had to confront an angry mob of white people, with only a contingent of local police to protect them. At that point, President Eisenhower sent in federal troops to guarantee the safety of the students and to ensure that Little Rock High School would comply with the *Brown* decision. Some of the troops remained at the school for the entire school year.

We see that at times the federal government has taken actions that have limited the rights of particular groups, and at other times, it has sought to protect those rights. The federal government functions within the context of the larger society and sometimes changes its stance in response to the changing context.

PART III: DOCUMENT-BASED QUESTION

Part A: Short Answer

DOCUMENT 1A AND DOCUMENT 1B

1 (1). According to the charts, one trend related to industrialization

between 1861 and 1910 is that the value of products manufactured in the

United States increased dramatically by approximately ten times.

1 (2). According to the charts, another trend related to industrialization

between 1861 and 1910 is that the number of immigrants coming into the

United States increased dramatically by approximately four times.

These answers receive full credit because they state two trends related to industrialization between 1861 and 1910.

DOCUMENT 2A AND DOCUMENT 2B

2 (1). Based on the charts, one effect of industrialization on the United

States after the Civil War is that the percentage of people living in cities

doubled from 20 percent of the population to 40 percent of the population.

2 (2). Based on the charts, one effect of industrialization on the United

States after the Civil War is that the percentage of nonfarm workers in

unions tripled.

These answers would receive full credit because they state two effects of industrialization on the United States after the Civil War.

DOCUMENT 3

3. Based on this document, one reform proposed at the Populist Party National Convention related to industrialization was that immigration into the United States should be limited in order to benefit American workers.

This answer would receive full credit because it identifies one reform proposed at the Populist Party Convention related to industrialization.

DOCUMENT 4

4 (1). Based on the excerpt, one way the 1893 Illinois state law addressed problems caused by industrialization is that it prohibited children under 14 years of age from working in any manufacturing establishment, factory, or workshop.

4 (2). Based on the excerpt, another way the 1893 Illinois state law addressed problems caused by industrialization is that it limited to eight the number of hours a female factory worker could be employed in one day.

These answers would receive full credit because they identify two ways the 1893 Illinois state law addressed problems caused by industrialization.

DOCUMENT 5

5. Based on Hamlin Garland's observations, one impact of industrialization on Homestead, Pennsylvania, is that the town had become dirty and squalid.

This answer receives full credit because it describes one impact of industrialization on Homestead, Pennsylvania.

DOCUMENT 6A AND DOCUMENT 6B

6 (1). According to the documents, one way industrialization affected workers is that they had to work long hours, sometimes from 7 o'clock in the morning until 8 o'clock at night.

6 (2). According to the documents, another way industrialization affected workers is that they went on strike to improve their conditions.

These answers would receive full credit because they state two ways industrialization affected workers.

DOCUMENT 7A

7a. The cartoonist's point of view is that industrialists such as John D. Rockefeller completely control the government.

This answer receives full credit because it states the cartoonist's point of view concerning the relationship between the government and industrialists such as John D. Rockefeller.

DOCUMENT 7B

7b. According to the cartoonist, President Theodore Roosevelt's policy toward trusts is that he wanted to destroy trusts that were destructive to society, but he wanted to simply restrain trusts that were beneficial to society.

This answer receives full credit because it states President Theodore Roosevelt's policy toward trusts.

DOCUMENT 8

8. According to the document, Andrew Carnegie showed his concern for

social justice by contributing millions of dollars to charity.

This answer receives full credit because it states how Andrew Carnegie showed his concern for social justice.

DOCUMENT 9

9. According to Paul Kennedy, one effect of industrialization on World

War I was to provide enough military equipment to prevent the Central

Powers from achieving victory.

This answer receives full credit because it states one effect of industrialization on World War I.

Part B: Document-Based Essay

The United States underwent a sweeping industrial revolution during the second half of the 19th century. Between the Civil War and the end of World War I, this industrial revolution transformed the production process, as mass production replaced craft production and unskilled work replaced skill work. The average size of manufacturing firms grew, the relationship between owners and workers changed, and the very nature of work changed. This industrial revolution had a huge impact on the United States. The changes brought by industrialization—economic, political, and social—would transform life in the United States.

The most obvious transformations brought about by industrialization were economic. Between 1860 and 1910, the value of products manufactured in the United States went up an astonishing ten times, from just under two billion dollars to over 20 billion dollars. Also, the number of people employed in industrial processes went up dramatically. The number of men employed in manufacturing climbed from just over a million to well over eight million. Even women were brought into the industrial sector. (Document 1a) The value of the output of the meatpacking industry went up by 12 times in just the 30 years between 1870 and 1900. In 1860, there were 30 thousand miles of railroad track; by 1900 there were well over 200 thousands miles of track. In 1860 only 270,000 women were employed in manufacturing; by 1910, the figure climbed to 1.8 million. (Document 1a) These figures vividly demonstrate the rapid economic growth of the United States during the industrial revolution. In fact, it was the industrial might of the United States that turned the tide of World War I and led to the defeat of the Central Powers. (Document 9)

However, the benefits of this economic growth were not evenly distributed. Although the owners of big industrial firms, often referred to as "robber barons" by their critics, grew wealthy, the typical factory operative struggled to make ends meet. Female shirtwaist workers, for instance, made approximately $6 a week in 1909 for working a 13-hour day. (Document 6a) To rectify this situation, workers formed unions to collectively press for higher wages and better working conditions. Annual union membership in the United States rose from 300,000 in 1870 to over five million by 1920. (Document 2b) One of the most important tools that unions had at their disposal was the strike. A strike would involve workers ceasing work until certain demands were met. Typically, striking workers would picket outside their place of work, both to publicize their cause and to try to prevent replacement workers, known as "scabs" in the labor movement, from entering the premises. One of the most spectacular strikes in the period was an industry-wide strike of garment workers in New York City, known as "the uprising of twenty thousand." One of the leaders of the strike, Clara Lemlich, vividly described the low wages, long hours, and inhumane conditions associated with garment work. (Document 6a) This strike of mostly female workers in 1909-1910 did much to advance the cause of unionism in New York City. (Document 6b)

Occasionally these strikes became violent. One of the most violent incidents was at Homestead, Pennsylvania, in 1892 as steel workers protested a wage cut at the Carnegie Steel Mills. Dozens of striking steel workers died in clashes with Pinkerton guards hired by owner Andrew Carnegie. Two years after the altercation, a journalist noted the squalid conditions at Homestead. (Document 5)

These economic changes were accompanied by profound social changes. In response to the demand for labor caused by industrialization, the United States became a major destination for immigrants. During the 1860s, a little over two million new residents entered the United States. That figure jumped to nearly nine million for the first decade of the twentieth century. (Document 1b) These new immigrants settled primarily in the growing industrial cities of the Northeast and the Midwest, such as New York, Philadelphia, Cleveland, and Chicago. Rapid industrialization and immigration led to another important social change—urbanization. Between 1860 and 1900, the number of Americans who lived in cities jumped from 6.2 million to over 30 million, which amounted to a shift in the urban population from 20 percent of the total population to 40 percent. (Document 2a) Without industrialization, the multiethnic urban centers that came to define America in the 20th century would probably not have existed.

Finally, industrialization had significant political impacts on the United States. For one, we see in America the rise of the "robber barons" in terms of their political influence. Industrialists such as John D. Rockefeller and J. P. Morgan were able to greatly influence the political process through their wealth and connections. Some industrialists tried to mitigate their bad reputations by contributing significant sums to charitable causes. Andrew Carnegie was a leader on this front, elevating charitable work to a religious calling. (Document 8) However, many people still feared that the power wielded by these industrial giants would undermine democracy altogether. A cartoon from 1900 presented Rockefeller as a giant with a tiny government in the palm of his hand. The government is portrayed as his plaything. (Document 7a)

In response to the political power exercised by the "robber barons," reformers worked to check this power. The Populist Party, for example, attempted to put the priorities of working men and women on the political stage. Although this movement originated among farmers, its 1892 national platform included calls for better working conditions for laborers and for the eight-hour day. (Document 3) Agitation by the Populist Party and other workers' parties yielded results. In 1893, for instance, Illinois passed a law outlawing child labor, mandating inspections of factories, and limiting the number of hours that women could work. (Document 4) On the national level, the Sherman Antitrust Act (1890) empowered the federal government to limit monopolistic practices. The act was not enforced with a great deal of enthusiasm until the presidency of Theodore Roosevelt. He made a point of using the act to pursue "bad trusts"—ones that interfered with commerce. One of his targets was the Northern Securities Company, a railroad holding company. (Document 7b)

The far-reaching changes brought about by industrialization have dramatically reshaped American society. The benefits of industrialization made the United States a wealthy country. At the dawn of the 21st century, the United States is still wrestling with the legacies of industrialization, from environmental destruction to communities impacted by deindustrialization, as factories and jobs migrate abroad.

Topic	Question Numbers	*Number of Points
American political history	4, 6, 14, 15, 16, 17, 18, 20, 24, 30, 31, 32, 37, 41, 43	18
Political theory	5	1
Economic theory/policy	3, 19, 29	4
Constitutional principles	7, 8, 9, 10, 11, 13, 23, 25, 27, 45	12
American foreign policy	12, 21, 26, 33, 34, 36, 39, 40, 42, 44, 47, 48	14
American studies—the American people	22, 28, 35, 38, 46, 49, 50	8
Geography	1, 2	2
Skills questions included in the above content area		
Reading comprehension	8, 9, 24, 33, 47	
Graph/table interpretation	32, 34, 46, 49, 50	
Cartoon/photo interpretation	41	
Map interpretation	38	
Chronological sequencing	48	
Cause-effect relationship	39	

*Note: The 50 questions in Part I are worth a total of 60 percent of the exam. Since each correct answer is worth 60/50 or 1.2 points, totals are shown to the nearest full point in each content category.

Part I
Multiple-Choice Questions by Standard

Standard	Question Numbers
1 — US and NY History	4, 10, 12, 15, 16, 17, 18, 20, 21, 22, 24, 26, 27, 30, 32, 33, 34, 35, 37, 40, 42, 45, 48, 50
2 — World History	5, 36, 39, 44, 47
3 — Geography	1, 14, 28, 38, 49
4 — Economics	2, 3, 19, 23, 29, 31
5 — Civics, Citizenship, and Government	6, 7, 8, 9, 11, 13, 25, 41, 43, 46

Parts II and III by Theme and Standard

	Theme	Standards
Thematic Essay	Constitutional Principles; Individual Rights	Standards 1, 3, 4, and 5; US and NY History; Geography; Economics; Civics, Citizenship, and Government
Document-based Essay	Change: Factors of Production; Government; Immigration and Migration; Reform; Environment; Foreign Policy	Standards 1, 2, 3, 4, and 5; US and NY History; World History; Geography; Economics; Civics, Citizenship, and Government

Examination
August 2009

United States History and Government

PART I: MULTIPLE CHOICE

Directions (1–50): For each statement or question, write in the space provided the *number* of the word or expression that, of those given, best completes the statement or answers the question.

1 Farmers in the Ohio River valley gained the greatest economic benefit when the United States acquired the

1 Oregon Territory
2 Gadsden Purchase
3 Louisiana Territory
4 Mexican Cession   1 ____

2 The Mayflower Compact, New England town meetings, and the Virginia House of Burgesses are examples of

1 early colonial efforts in self-government
2 colonial protests against British taxation
3 governments imposed by Parliament
4 attempts to limit democracy   2 ____

3 The main purpose for writing the Declaration of Independence was to

  1 declare war on Great Britain
  2 force France to support the Revolutionary War
  3 convince Great Britain to abolish slavery
  4 state the colonists' reasons for separating from Great Britain   3____

4 At the Constitutional Convention of 1787, which problem was solved by the Great Compromise?

  1 developing the method of electing a president
  2 designating control of interstate commerce
  3 outlining the structure of the federal court system
  4 establishing the formula for representation in Congress   4____

5 In the United States Constitution, the power to impeach a federal government official is given to the

  1 House of Representatives
  2 president
  3 state legislatures
  4 Supreme Court   5____

6 A constitutional power specifically delegated to the federal government is the power to

  1 regulate marriage and divorce
  2 establish education standards
  3 declare war
  4 issue driver's licenses   6____

7 To win a presidential election, a candidate must win a

  1 two-thirds vote of the state legislatures
  2 two-thirds vote in Congress
  3 majority of the popular vote
  4 majority of the electoral college vote   7 ____

8 One goal of Alexander Hamilton's financial plan was the establishment of a

  1 stock exchange
  2 national sales tax
  3 federal income tax
  4 national bank   8 ____

9 What was one outcome of the Supreme Court decision in *Marbury* v. *Madison* (1803)?

  1 State governments could now determine the constitutionality of federal laws.
  2 The principle of judicial review was established.
  3 Congress expanded its delegated powers.
  4 A method to approve treaties was developed.   9 ____

10 The Louisiana Purchase initially presented a dilemma for President Thomas Jefferson because he believed it would

  1 lead to war with Great Britain
  2 bankrupt the new nation
  3 force Native American Indians off their lands
  4 violate his strict constructionist view of the Constitution   10 ____

11 Which statement about the Missouri Compromise (1820) is most accurate?

   1 Slavery was banned west of the Mississippi River.

   2 Unorganized territories would be governed by the United States and Great Britain.

   3 The balance between free and slave states was maintained.

   4 The 36°30′ line formed a new boundary between the United States and Canada.   11 _____

12 Which 19th-century event supported the movement for women's rights?

   1 Seneca Falls Convention

   2 *Dred Scott* decision

   3 formation of the Republican Party

   4 Lincoln-Douglas debates   12 _____

Base your answer to question 13 on the poster below and on your knowledge of social studies.

---

100 DOLLARS REWARD!

Ranaway from the subscriber on the 27th of July, my Black Woman, named

EMILY,

Seventeen years of age, well grown, black color, has a whining voice. She took with her one dark calico and one blue and white dress, a red corded gingham bonnet; a white striped shawl and slippers. I will pay the above reward if taken near the Ohio river on the Kentucky side, or THREE HUNDRED DOLLARS, if taken in the State of Ohio, and delivered to me near Lewisburg, Mason County, Ky.

THO'S H. WILLIAMS.

August 4, 1853.

Source: Ohio Historical Center Archives (adapted)

13 Prior to the Civil War, abolitionists reacted to the situation described in the poster by

   1 supporting the Underground Railroad

   2 opposing the Emancipation Proclamation

   3 banning freed slaves from Northern states

   4 proposing a stricter fugitive slave law   13 _____

14 Literacy tests and poll taxes were often used to

  1 enforce constitutional amendments added after the Civil War

  2 limit voter participation by African Americans

  3 promote equal educational opportunities for minority persons

  4 provide job training for freedmen   14____

Base your answers to questions 15 and 16 on the song below and on your knowledge of social studies.

> We mean to make things over,
> we are tired of toil for naught,
> With but bare enough to live upon,
> and never an hour for thought;
> We want to feel the sunshine,
> and we want to smell the flowers,
> We are sure that God has will'd it,
> and we mean to have eight hours.
> We're summoning our forces
> from the shipyard, shop and mill,
>
>   Chorus.
> Eight hours for work, eight hours for rest,
> eight hours for what we will!
> Eight hours for work, eight hours for rest,
> eight hours for what we will!
>
> —I.G. Blanchard, "Eight Hours," 1878

15 During the late 1800s, the ideas expressed in these lyrics were the goals of

  1 organizers of labor unions

  2 sharecroppers following the Civil War

  3 Grangers demanding railroad regulation

  4 owners of big businesses   15____

16 In the 1890s, which political party incorporated the chief concern expressed in this song into its platform?

1 Know-Nothing   3 Whig
2 Populist   4 Bull Moose   16____

17 Society advances when its fittest members are allowed to assert themselves with the least hindrance.

The idea expressed in this statement is most consistent with the
1 principles of Social Darwinism
2 concept of assimilation
3 goals of the Progressive movement
4 melting pot theory of American culture   17____

18 During the late 1800s, many North American Indian tribes were sent to reservations that were located

1 along the major rivers and lakes of the Midwest
2 near large cities in the Northwest
3 in sparsely populated regions of the West
4 east of the Mississippi River   18____

19 The closing of the frontier and the growth of industry in the late 1800s are two factors often associated with the

1 reduction of exports to Asian nations
2 restoration of a plantation economy in the South
3 formation of alliances with other nations
4 rise of United States imperialism   19____

20 Yellow journalists created support for the Spanish-American War by writing articles about the

  1 political popularity of William Jennings Bryan
  2 efforts of the United States to control Mexico
  3 destruction of United States sugar plantations by Hawaiians
  4 sinking of the United States battleship *Maine* in Havana Harbor   20____

21 Muckrakers Ida Tarbell and Upton Sinclair influenced the federal government to

  1 grant citizenship to people who had entered the country illegally
  2 pass legislation to correct harmful business practices
  3 force individual states to regulate monopolies
  4 end racial discrimination in the workplace   21____

Base your answers to questions 22 and 23 on the speakers' statements below and on your knowledge of social studies.

Speaker A: Nature should be left as it is found. All unsettled land should be off limits to future settlement or development.

Speaker B: Natural resources should be controlled by big business to ensure the economic strength of the United States. Our abundance of land gives us a great advantage for competing in world markets.

Speaker C: The natural resources of the United States should be used wisely. We must conserve them for future generations while also using them to serve the people of today.

Speaker D: No man or institution owns the land. It is to be shared by everyone and everything in the best interest of all who depend upon its offerings.

22 Which speaker best expresses the environmental views of President Theodore Roosevelt?

1 *A*   3 *C*
2 *B*   4 *D*   22 _____

23 The statement of *Speaker D* is most like views expressed by

1 Native American Indians
2 western farmers
3 railroad companies
4 European immigrants   23 _____

24 Many United States senators refused to support membership in the League of Nations because they believed that it would

1 endanger United States economic growth
2 force the United States to give up its colonies
3 grant the president the power to annex new territory
4 involve the United States in future foreign conflicts   24 _____

25 Immigration laws passed during the 1920s changed United States policy by

1 establishing immigration quotas
2 allowing only skilled workers into the country
3 favoring immigration from Asia
4 encouraging an increase in immigration to the United States   25 _____

26 Henry Ford's use of the assembly line in the production of automobiles led directly to

1 a decrease in the number of automobiles available
2 a decrease in the cost of automobiles
3 an increase in the unemployment rate
4 an increase in the time needed to produce a single automobile   26 _____

27 The convictions of Sacco and Vanzetti in the 1920s most closely reflected the

1 increase in nativist attitudes
2 federal government's war on crime
3 corruption of political machines
4 rise in labor unrest   27 _____

28 What was one cause of the stock market crash of 1929 and the Great Depression that followed?

1 Costs associated with World War I had bankrupted the economy.
2 Speculators had purchased shares of stock on margin with borrowed funds.
3 Federal tax cuts had caused high inflation.
4 Low farm production had weakened banks.   28 _____

29 During the Great Depression, one way New Deal programs tried to stimulate economic recovery was by

1 raising tariff rates
2 increasing interest rates
3 creating public works jobs
4 lowering the minimum wage

29 _____

Base your answer to question 30 on the cartoon below and on your knowledge of social studies.

Let's Harmonize!

Source: Gene Elderman, *Washington Post*, January 7, 1937
(adapted)

30 The cartoonist is commenting on President Franklin D. Roosevelt's efforts to

1 win congressional approval for his Supreme Court nominees
2 gain Supreme Court support for his legislative program
3 set up a retirement plan for Supreme Court Justices
4 keep members of Congress off the Supreme Court

30 _____

31 Which geographic area is most closely associated with the Dust Bowl of the 1930s?

   1 Great Lakes basin
   2 Mississippi River valley
   3 Appalachian Mountains
   4 Great Plains   31 ____

32 Which series of events leading to World War II is in the correct chronological order?

   1 Neutrality Acts → Japanese attack on Pearl Harbor → Lend-Lease Act → United States declaration of war on Japan
   2 Lend-Lease Act → Neutrality Acts → United States declaration of war on Japan → Japanese attack on Pearl Harbor
   3 United States declaration of war on Japan → Japanese attack on Pearl Harbor → Lend-Lease Act → Neutrality Acts
   4 Neutrality Acts → Lend-Lease Act → Japanese attack on Pearl Harbor → United States declaration of war on Japan   32 ____

33 Which change in American society occurred during World War II?

   1 African Americans were granted equality in the armed forces.
   2 Women were allowed to enter combat units for the first time.
   3 Congress enacted the first military draft.
   4 Women replaced men in essential wartime industries.   33 ____

34 Which action was taken by the United States government to help Europe's economic recovery after World War II?

1 forming the Alliance for Progress
2 sending troops to Turkey
3 creating the Marshall Plan
4 joining the North Atlantic Treaty Organization   34 _____

35 Issuing the Truman Doctrine, defending South Korea, and sending military advisors to Vietnam were actions taken by the United States to

1 encourage membership in the United Nations
2 promote American business in Asia
3 limit the spread of communism
4 gain additional overseas colonies   35 _____

36 The president acted as commander in chief in response to which event of the civil rights movement?

1 refusal of the governor of Arkansas to obey a federal court order to integrate public schools in Little Rock
2 desegregation of the city bus system in Montgomery, Alabama
3 arrest of Martin Luther King Jr. during protests in Birmingham, Alabama
4 assassination of Medgar Evers in Mississippi   36 _____

37 Lunch counter sit-ins and the actions of freedom riders are examples of

  1 steps taken in support of the Americans with Disabilities Act

  2 programs dealing with affirmative action

  3 violent acts by the Black Panthers

  4 nonviolent attempts to oppose segregation   37____

38 One way in which President John F. Kennedy's Peace Corps and President Lyndon Johnson's Volunteers in Service to America (VISTA) are similar is that both programs attempted to

  1 increase domestic security

  2 support United States troops fighting overseas

  3 improve the quality of people's lives

  4 provide aid to immigrants coming to the United States   38____

39 The Supreme Court cases of *Gideon* v. *Wainwright* (1963) and *Miranda* v. *Arizona* (1966) dealt with the constitutional principle of

  1 freedom of religion

  2 freedom from unreasonable search

  3 separation of powers

  4 rights of the accused   39____

Base your answers to questions 40 and 41 on the cartoon below and on your knowledge of social studies.

The Odd Couple

Source: Bill Mauldin, *Chicago Sun-Times*, 1973 (adapted)

40 The cartoonist is commenting on which Cold War foreign policy?

1 détente
2 brinkmanship

3 the domino theory
4 collective security

40 _____

41 Which United States foreign policy decision most clearly reflects the relationship shown in the cartoon?

1 issuance of the Eisenhower Doctrine
2 quarantine of Cuba
3 support of Israel in the Six Day War
4 negotiation of the Strategic Arms Limitation Treaty (SALT)

41 _____

42 President Ronald Reagan's supply-side economic policy was successful in

   1 increasing government spending on social programs

   2 lowering tax rates on personal and business income

   3 reducing defense spending

   4 enforcing stricter environmental regulations   42____

43 The rapid westward migration caused by the discovery of gold in California led directly to

   1 the start of the Civil War

   2 the adoption of the Compromise of 1850

   3 increased trade through the Panama Canal

   4 control of the United States Senate by the slave states   43____

Base your answer to question 44 on the statement below and on your knowledge of social studies.

... With a profound sense of the solemn and even tragical character of the step I am taking and of the grave responsibilities which it involves, but in unhesitating obedience to what I deem my constitutional duty, I advise that the Congress declare the recent course of the Imperial German Government to be in fact nothing less than war against the government and people of the United States; that it formally accept the status of belligerent which has thus been thrust upon it, and that it take immediate steps not only to put the country in a more thorough state of defense but also to exert all its power and employ all its resources to bring the Government of the German Empire to terms and end the war. ...

44 Which presidential action is the focus of this statement?

1 William McKinley's request for war in 1898
2 Theodore Roosevelt's support for the Panamanian revolt in 1903
3 William Howard Taft's decision to send troops to Latin America in 1912
4 Woodrow Wilson's response to unrestricted submarine warfare in 1917

44____

Base your answers to questions 45 and 46 on the table below and on your knowledge of social studies.

Congressional Bills Vetoed: 1961 to 1993

Period	President	Total vetoes	Regular vetoes	Pocket vetoes	Vetoes upheld	Bills passed over veto
1961–63	John F. Kennedy	21	12	9	21	0
1963–69	Lyndon Johnson	30	16	14	30	0
1969–74	Richard Nixon	43	26	17	36	7
1974–77	Gerald Ford	66	48	18	54	12
1977–81	Jimmy Carter	31	13	18	29	2
1981–89	Ronald Reagan	78	39	39	69	9
1989–93	George H. W. Bush	44	29	15	43	1

Source: U.S. Senate

45 Which statement is accurate about congressional bills vetoed between 1961 and 1993?

1 Congress was usually able to override a presidential veto.
2 Pocket vetoes were used more often than regular vetoes.
3 The majority of presidential vetoes were upheld.
4 The use of the veto increased steadily between 1961 and 1993.   45 _____

46 The data in the table illustrate the operation of

1 executive privilege
2 checks and balances
3 congressional immunity
4 federal supremacy   46 _____

47 The Pacific [Transcontinental] Railway Act (1862) and the Interstate Highway Act (1956) are both examples of

1 federally supported internal improvement projects linking the nation
2 regional construction projects coordinated by southern and western states
X3 military projects required to meet the needs of the defense industry
✗4 transportation legislation designed to encourage foreign trade   47____

48 Mark Twain, Langston Hughes, and John Steinbeck made their most important contributions to the United States in the field of

1 music   3 literature
2 politics   4 business   48____

49 One way in which the New Deal, the Fair Deal, and the Great Society are similar is that these programs

1 promoted the idea of "rugged individualism"
2 increased government commitment to the well-being of the people
3 reduced the amount of money spent on domestic programs
4 encouraged the states to take a more active role in national defense   49____

Base your answer to question 50 on the graphs below and on your knowledge of social studies.

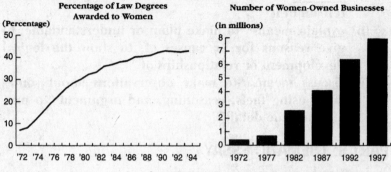

Source: "Feminism's Future," *The CQ Researcher*, February 1997 (adapted)

50 Data from the graphs most clearly support the conclusion that by the mid-1990s, American women as a group

  1 surpassed men in the number of businesses owned and law degrees received

  2 had given up marriage in favor of careers outside the home

  3 had gained more opportunities in professional areas

  4 earned more than men in the legal profession   50 _____

In developing your answer to Part II, be sure to keep these general definitions in mind:
   (a) <u>describe</u> means "to illustrate something in words or tell about it"
   (b) <u>explain</u> means "to make plain or understandable; to give reasons for or causes of; to show the logical development or relationships of"
   (c) <u>discuss</u> means "to make observations about something using facts, reasoning, and argument; to present in some detail"

PART II: THEMATIC ESSAY

Directions: Write a well-organized essay that includes an introduction, several paragraphs addressing the task below, and a conclusion.

Theme: Government — Supreme Court Decisions

> The United States Supreme Court has played a major role in United States history. The Court's decisions have had a significant impact on many aspects of American society.

Task:

> Select *two* Supreme Court cases that have had an impact on American society and for *each*
> - Describe the historical circumstances surrounding the case
> - Explain the Supreme Court's decision in the case
> - Discuss an impact this decision has had on American society

You may use any appropriate Supreme Court case from your study of United States history. Some suggestions you might wish to consider include *Worcester* v. *Georgia* (1832), *Dred Scott* v. *Sanford* (1857), *Northern Securities Co.* v. *United States* (1904), *Korematsu* v. *United States* (1944), *Brown* v. *Board of Education of Topeka* (1954), *Heart of Atlanta Motel* v. *United States* (1964), *Miranda* v. *Arizona* (1966), *Roe* v. *Wade* (1973), *and United States* v. *Nixon* (1974).

You are *not* limited to these suggestions.

Guidelines:

In your essay, be sure to:
- Develop all aspects of the task
- Support the theme with relevant facts, examples, and details
- Use a logical and clear plan of organization, including an introduction and a conclusion that are beyond a restatement of the theme

In developing your answers to Part III, be sure to keep these general definitions in mind:

(a) <u>describe</u> means "to illustrate something in words or tell about it"

(b) <u>explain</u> means "to make plain or understandable; to give reasons for or causes of; to show the logical development or relationships of"

(c) <u>discuss</u> means "to make observations about something using facts, reasoning, and argument; to present in some detail"

PART III: DOCUMENT-BASED ESSAY

This question is based on the accompanying documents. The question is designed to test your ability to work with historical documents. Some of the documents have been edited for the purposes of the question. As you analyze the documents, take into account the source of each document and any point of view that may be presented in the document.

Historical Context:

> Historians who have evaluated presidential leadership have generally agreed that **George Washington, Abraham Lincoln,** and **Franklin D. Roosevelt** were great presidents because each successfully addressed a critical challenge faced by the nation during his administration.

Task:

Using information from the documents and your knowledge of United States history, answer the questions that follow each document in Part A. Your answers to the questions will help you write the Part B essay, in which you will be asked to

Select *two* presidents mentioned in the historical context and for *each*
- Describe a challenge that faced the nation during his administration
- Explain an action taken by the president to address this challenge
- Discuss the impact of this action on the United States

Part A: Short-Answer Questions

Directions: Analyze the documents and answer the short-answer questions that follow each document in the space provided.

Document 1

At daybreak on July 16, 1794, about fifty men armed with rifles and clubs marched to the house of John Neville, regional supervisor for collection of the federal excise tax in western Pennsylvania. They demanded that Neville resign his position and turn over to them all records associated with collection of the tax on domestically distilled spirits. He refused. Shots were fired. In the ensuing battle five of the attackers fell wounded. One of them later died. Neville and his slaves, who together had defended the premises from secure positions inside the house, suffered no casualties. The mob dispersed. . . .

The Whiskey Rebellion, as it is traditionally known and studied, had begun. Before it was over, some 7000 western Pennsylvanians advanced against the town of Pittsburgh, threatened its residents, feigned [pretended] an attack on Fort Pitt and the federal arsenal there, banished seven members of the community, and destroyed the property of several others. Violence spread to western Maryland, where a Hagerstown crowd joined in, raised liberty poles, and began a march on the arsenal at Frederick. At about the same time, sympathetic "friends of liberty" arose in Carlisle, Pennsylvania, and back-country regions of Virginia and Kentucky. Reports reached the federal government in Philadelphia that the western country was ablaze and that rebels were negotiating with representatives of Great Britain and Spain, two of the nation's most formidable European competitors, for aid in a frontier-wide separatist movement. In response, President Washington nationalized 12,950 militiamen from New Jersey, Pennsylvania, Maryland, and

Virginia—an army approximating in size the Continental force that followed him during the Revolution—and personally led the "Watermelon Army"* west to shatter the insurgency [rebellion]. . . .

Source: Thomas P. Slaughter, *The Whiskey Rebellion: Frontier Epilogue to the American Revolution*, Oxford University Press, 1986

*Watermelon Army was a nickname by whiskey tax rebels mocking the physical fitness and fighting skills of federal troops, particularly those from New Jersey.

1 According to Thomas P. Slaughter, what was *one* problem that resulted from the collection of the federal excise tax in western Pennsylvania? [1]

_____

_____

Document 2

To Major-General Lee

Sir:—I have it in special instruction from the President [George Washington] of the United States, now at this place, to convey to you the following instructions for the general direction of your conduct in the command of the militia army, with which you are charged.

The objects [reasons] for which the militia have been called forth are:

1st. To suppress the combinations [groups] which exist in some of the western counties in Pennsylvania, in opposition to the laws laying duties upon spirits distilled within the United States, and upon stills.

2nd. To cause the laws to be executed.

These objects are to be effected in two ways:

1. By military force.

2. By judiciary process and other civil proceedings.

The objects of the military force are twofold:

1. To overcome any armed opposition which may exist.

2. To countenance [approve] and support the civil officers in the means of executing the laws. . . .

Your obedient servant,
Alexander Hamilton

Source: Alexander Hamilton to Major-General Henry Lee, October 20, 1794, Henry Cabot Lodge, ed., *The Works of Alexander Hamilton*, Volume VI, G.P. Putnam's Sons (adapted)

2a According to Alexander Hamilton, what action is President George Washington ordering in response to the Whiskey Rebellion? [1]

_____

_____

2b According to Alexander Hamilton, what is **one** reason President Washington gave this order? [1]

_____

_____

Document 3

> . . . The [whiskey] rebellion has long been interpreted as a milestone in the creation of federal authority, and in most respects that is its chief significance. Certainly to the Federalists, who had long been striving for a strong national government, it was a major test: the new government successfully crushed organized and violent resistance to the laws. As Hamilton put it, the rebellion "will do us a great deal of good and add to the solidity [stability] of every thing in this country." . . .

Source: Richard H. Kohn, "The Washington Administration's Decision to Crush the Whiskey Rebellion," *The Journal of American History*, December 1972

3 According to Richard H. Kohn, what was the significance of the Whiskey Rebellion? [1]

_____

_____

Document 4

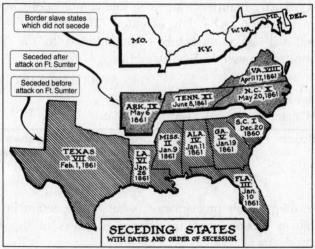

Source: Kennedy and Bailey, eds., *The American Spirit, Volume I: To 1877*, Houghton Mifflin, 2002 (adapted)

4 Based on the information on this map, state *one* problem the United States faced under President Abraham Lincoln. [1]

_____

_____

Document 5

April 15, 1861
By the President of the United States
A Proclamation.

Whereas, the laws of the United States have been for some time past, and now are opposed, and the execution thereof obstructed [interfered with], in the States of South Carolina, Georgia, Alabama, Florida, Mississippi, Louisiana and Texas, by combinations too powerful to be suppressed by the ordinary course of judicial proceedings, or by the powers vested in the Marshals by law,

Now therefore, I, Abraham Lincoln, President of the United States, in virtue of the power in me vested by the Constitution, and the laws, have thought fit to call forth, and hereby do call forth, the militia of the several States of the Union, to the aggregate [total] number of seventy-five thousand [75,000], in order to suppress said combinations, and to cause the laws to be duly executed. The details, for this object, will be immediately communicated to the State authorities through the War Department. . . .

ABRAHAM LINCOLN

By the President
William H. Seward, Secretary of State.

Source: Roy P. Basler, ed., *The Collected Works of Abraham Lincoln*,
Volume IV, Rutgers University Press (adapted)

5 According to this proclamation, what is *one* action President Abraham Lincoln took to enforce the laws of the United States? [1]

_____

_____

Document 6

. . . The greatest names in American history are Washington and Lincoln. One is forever associated with the independence of the States and formation of the Federal Union; the other with universal freedom and the preservation of that Union. Washington enforced the Declaration of Independence as against England; Lincoln proclaimed its fulfillment not only to a downtrodden race in America, but to all people for all time, who may seek the protection of our flag. These illustrious men achieved grander results for mankind within a single century—from 1775 to 1865—than any other men ever accomplished in all the years since first the flight of time began. Washington engaged in no ordinary revolution. With him it was not who should rule, but what should rule. He drew his sword, not for a change of rulers upon an established throne, but to establish a new government, which should acknowledge no throne but the tribune [authority] of the people. Lincoln accepted war to save the Union, the safeguard of our liberties, and re-established it on "indestructible foundations" as forever "one and indivisible." To quote his own grand words:

"Now we are contending that this Nation under God, shall have a new birth of freedom; and that government of the people, by the people, for the people, shall not perish from the earth." . . .

Source: William McKinley, Speech at the Marquette Club,
Chicago, February 12, 1896, Nicolay and Hay, eds.,
Complete Works of Abraham Lincoln

6 According to William McKinley, what is **one** impact of President Abraham Lincoln's actions on the United States? [1]

_____

_____

Document 7

Interview with Aaron Barkham, a coal miner
in West Virginia

. . . It got bad in '29. The Crash caught us with one $20 gold piece. All mines shut down—stores, everything. One day they was workin', the next day the mines shut down. Three or four months later, they opened up. Run two, three days a week, mostly one. They didn't have the privilege of calling their souls their own. Most people by that time was in debt so far to the company itself, they couldn't live.

Some of them been in debt from '29 till today [c. 1970], and never got out. Some of them didn't even try. It seem like whenever they went back to work, they owed so much. The company got their foot on 'em even now. . . .

Source: Studs Terkel, *Hard Times: An Oral History of the Great Depression*,
Pantheon Books

7 According to this interview with coal miner Aaron Barkham, what was ***one*** problem faced by mine workers during the Great Depression? [1]

_____

_____

Document 8a

> . . . In the consistent development of our previous efforts toward the saving and safeguarding of our national life, I have continued to recognize three related steps. The first was relief, because the primary concern of any Government dominated by the humane ideals of democracy is the simple principle that in a land of vast resources no one should be permitted to starve. Relief was and continues to be our first consideration. It calls for large expenditures and will continue in modified form to do so for a long time to come. We may as well recognize that fact. It comes from the paralysis that arose as the after-effect of that unfortunate decade characterized by a mad chase for unearned riches and an unwillingness of leaders in almost every walk of life to look beyond their own schemes and speculations. In our administration of relief we follow two principles: First, that direct giving shall, wherever possible, be supplemented by provision for useful and remunerative [paid] work and, second, that where families in their existing surroundings will in all human probability never find an opportunity for full self-maintenance, happiness and enjoyment, we will try to give them a new chance in new surroundings. . . .

Source: Franklin D. Roosevelt, Address of the President,
"Review of the Achievements of the Seventy-third
Congress," June 28, 1934, FDR Library

8a According to President Franklin D. Roosevelt, what was **one** action needed to safeguard the life of the nation? [1]

_____

_____

Document 8b

Source: Clifford Berryman, *Washington Star*, January 5, 1934, Library of Congress

8b According to this document, what was *one* step taken by President Franklin D. Roosevelt to solve the problems of the Great Depression? [1]

_____

_____

Document 9

... But was the New Deal answer really successful? Did it work? Other scholarly experts almost uniformly praise and admire Roosevelt, but even the most sympathetic among them add a number of reservations. "The New Deal certainly did not get the country out of the Depression," says Columbia's William Leuchtenburg, author of *Franklin D. Roosevelt and the New Deal*. "As late as 1941, there were still 6 million unemployed, and it was really not until the war that the army of the jobless finally disappeared." "Some of the New Deal legislation was very hastily contrived [planned]," says Williams College's James MacGregor Burns, author of a two-volume Roosevelt biography. Duke's James David Barber, author of *The Presidential Character*, notes that Roosevelt "was not too open about his real intentions, particularly in the court-packing episode." ...

After all the criticisms, though, the bulk of expert opinion agrees that Roosevelt's New Deal changed American life substantially, changed it permanently and changed it for the better. While the major recovery programs like the NRA and AAA have faded into history, many of Roosevelt's reforms—Social Security, stock market regulation, minimum wage, insured bank deposits—are now taken for granted. ...

But what actually remains today of the original New Deal? Alexander Heard, 64, who is retiring soon as chancellor of Vanderbilt University, remembers working in the CCC as a youth, remembers it as a time when a new President "restored a sense of confidence and morale and hope—hope being the greatest of all." But what remains? "In a sense," says Heard, "what remains of the New Deal is the United States."

Source: Otto Friedrich, "F.D.R.'s Disputed Legacy,"
Time, February 1, 1982 (adapted)

9 According to this document, what were **two** effects of President Franklin D. Roosevelt's New Deal policies on the nation? [2]

(1)_____

_____

(2)_____

_____

Part B: Essay

Directions: Write a well-organized essay that includes an intro-duction, several paragraphs, and a conclusion. Use evidence from *at least four* documents in your essay. Support your response with relevant facts, examples, and details. Include additional outside information.

Historical Context:

> Historians who have evaluated presidential leadership have generally agreed that **George Washington, Abraham Lincoln,** and **Franklin D. Roosevelt** were great presidents because each successfully addressed a critical challenge faced by the nation during his administration.

Task:

> Using information from the documents and your knowledge of United States history, write an essay in which you
>
> Select *two* presidents mentioned in the historical context and for *each*
> - Describe a challenge that faced the nation during his administration
> - Explain an action taken by the president to address this challenge
> - Discuss the impact of this action on the United States

Guidelines:

In your essay, be sure to:
- Develop all aspects of the task
- Incorporate information from *at least four* documents
- Incorporate relevant outside information
- Support the theme with relevant facts, examples, and details
- Use a logical and clear plan of organization, including an introduction and conclusion that are beyond a restatement of the theme

Answers
August 2009

United States History and Government

Answer Key

PART I

1. 3	14. 2	27. 1	40. 1
2. 1	15. 1	28. 2	41. 4
3. 4	16. 2	29. 3	42. 2
4. 4	17. 1	30. 2	43. 2
5. 1	18. 3	31. 4	44. 4
6. 3	19. 4	32. 4	45. 3
7. 4	20. 4	33. 4	46. 2
8. 4	21. 2	34. 3	47. 1
9. 2	22. 3	35. 3	48. 3
10. 4	23. 1	36. 1	49. 2
11. 3	24. 4	37. 4	50. 3
12. 1	25. 1	38. 3	
13. 1	26. 2	39. 4	

PART II: Thematic Essay   See answers explained section.

PART III: Document-Based Essay   See answers explained section.

Answers Explained

PART I (1–50)

1. **3** Farmers in the Ohio River valley gained the greatest economic benefit when the United States acquired the Louisiana Territory. In the late 1700s and early 1800s, pioneers crossed over the Appalachian Mountains and established farms in the Ohio River valley. It was impractical to transport agricultural goods such as wheat and corn by overland routes to the population centers along the eastern seaboard. Roads were primitive and railroads had not yet been developed. Therefore, water routes down the Ohio River, into the Mississippi River, and then to New Orleans and beyond became very important for these farmers. The United States controlled the land up to the Mississippi River, but not the land on the western bank of the river. That land, along with the port city of New Orleans, was controlled by Spain, which repeatedly closed the Mississippi River to American shipping. Spain ceded control of this land back to France in 1800, and in 1803 France sold this huge piece of land, known as the Louisiana Territory, to the United States, giving the United States control of both sides of the Mississippi River and of New Orleans. This was a boon to American settlers along both the Ohio River and the Mississippi River.

WRONG CHOICES EXPLAINED:
(1) The acquisition of the Oregon Territory was not especially beneficial to farmers in the Ohio River valley. The Oregon Territory was incorporated into the United States in 1848, following the resolution of a border dispute with Great Britain. The two nations agreed that the border would be along the 49th parallel. The Oregon Territory included the entire future states of Oregon, Washington, and Idaho, as well as parts of Montana and Wyoming.
(2) The acquisition of the Gadsden Purchase was not especially beneficial to farmers in the Ohio River valley. The Gadsden Purchase was acquired from Mexico in 1853, five years after the Mexican War. It added an additional area to the vast swath of land obtained by the United States following the war. The Gadsden Purchase was sought by the United States as a possible southern route for the transcontinental railroad.
(4) The acquisition of the Mexican Cession was not especially beneficial to farmers in the Ohio River valley. The Mexican Cession was the vast swath of land that the United States acquired from Mexico following the Mexican War in 1848. The region includes the present-day states of California, Nevada, and Utah, as well as portions of present-day Arizona, New Mexico, Wyoming, and Colorado. The purchase of this region was part of the Treaty of Guadalupe Hidalgo.

2. **1** The Mayflower Compact, New England town meetings, and the Virginia House of Burgesses are examples of early colonial efforts in self-government. These early attempts at self-government can be seen as laying the groundwork for eventual independence from Great Britain. The Mayflower Compact was a document written and signed by the Pilgrims on board the *Mayflower* before it touched land at Plymouth, Massachusetts, in 1620. The king had granted the Pilgrims land further south in Virginia. To give themselves a sense of legitimacy in an area in which they had no legal status, the Pilgrims agreed in this document to set up a government and obey its laws. New England town meetings were face-to-face decision-making assemblies that were open to all free male residents of a town. This form of direct democracy allowed for a high degree of citizen participation in decision making. The House of Burgesses was created by the Virginia Company in 1619. The company had founded the colony of Virginia in 1607 as a profit-generating venture. The company saw the need for some sort of body to govern the inhabitants of the colony and created this representative assembly. All free adult men could vote for representatives. Later, voting was limited to wealthy men. After Virginia came under the jurisdiction of the crown, instead of the Virginia Company (1624), the king allowed the Houses of Burgesses to continue.

WRONG CHOICES EXPLAINED:

(2) The three institutions mentioned in the question are not examples of colonial protests against British taxation. Such protests did occur, especially after the French and Indian War (1754–1763). The colonists engaged in a variety of protests, from boycotts to destruction of property, to oppose British taxes and to insist upon "no taxation without representation."

(3) The three institutions mentioned in the question are not examples of governments imposed by Parliament. The British government did impose many governmental bodies upon the colonists. Generally, the governor of each colony was appointed by the monarch of Great Britain.

(4) The three institutions mentioned in the question are not examples of attempts to limit democracy. Democratic expression was relatively free in colonial America for free, male, white citizens. Of course, it is difficult to call colonial America democratic, in the contemporary sense of the word, with the existence of slavery, indentured servitude, rigid gender roles, and property qualifications for voting.

3. **4** The main purpose for writing the Declaration of Independence was to state the colonists' reasons for separating from Great Britain. The Declaration of Independence, written by Thomas Jefferson and ratified by the Second Continental Congress in 1776, expressed the intent of the signers and the colonists they represented to be free of British control and to govern their own affairs. In justifying this bold move, Jefferson asserted broad concepts about equality and the rights of "life, liberty, and the pursuit of

happiness" that all men are born with. The document asserts that the major purpose of government is to protect these natural rights of the people. The document was addressed to the king but was also intended to convince cautious Americans to support independence.

WRONG CHOICES EXPLAINED:

(1) The Declaration of Independence was not a declaration of war on Great Britain. A state of war already existed between the colonies and Great Britain. Fighting began at Lexington and Concord, Massachusetts, in April 1775.

(2) The Declaration of Independence was not intended to force France to support the Revolutionary War. The American colonies were in no position to impose their will upon France. France did decide to support the rebellious colonists after their victory over the British at the Battle of Saratoga (1777). France's motivation was animosity toward Great Britain, not affinity with the ideas of the Declaration of Independence.

(3) The Declaration of Independence was not intended to convince Great Britain to abolish slavery. The goal of the document was to justify breaking away from Great Britain, not to change British policies. An early draft of the Declaration of Independence included a paragraph condemning the king for imposing the slave trade on the colonies. The statement was not strictly true; colonists participated in the slave trade for economic reasons, not because they were ordered to by the king. In any case, it was removed from the final draft because of opposition from southern slave-holding delegates to the Second Continental Congress.

4. **4** At the Constitutional Convention of 1787, the Great Compromise established a formula for representation in Congress. One of the main disagreements at the Constitutional Convention was how to create a representative system that met the desires of both the small states and the large states. The states with larger populations thought that they should have a larger voice in Congress. They rallied around the Virginia Plan, which would have created a bicameral legislature that based the number of representatives from each state on the population of the state. The small states feared that their voices would be drowned out in such a legislature. They countered with the New Jersey Plan, which called for a one-house legislature with each state getting one vote (similar to the existing Congress under the Articles of Confederation). After much wrangling, the delegates agreed on the Great Compromise, which created the basic structure of Congress as it now exists. The plan called for a House of Representatives, in which representation would be determined by the population of each state, and a Senate, in which each state would get two members.

WRONG CHOICES EXPLAINED:

(1) The Great Compromise did not establish a method of electing a president. The Constitutional Convention did establish a method of electing a president. The electoral college was created to elect the president. The number of electors from each state was based on the size of the congressional delegation of that state, giving larger states more power in determining the outcome.

(2) The Great Compromise did not designate control of interstate commerce. The Constitutional Convention decided that Congress would have the power to control interstate commerce. This designation is included in Article I of the Constitution.

(3) The Great Compromise did not outline the structure of the federal court system. The Constitutional Convention decided that there should be a federal court system, including a Supreme Court. The structure of the system was spelled out in subsequent legislation.

5. **1** In the United States Constitution, the power to impeach a federal government official is given to the House of Representatives. Impeachment is the act of bringing charges against a federal official. It is parallel to indictment in the criminal court system. Impeachment occurs when the House of Representatives passes "articles of impeachment," charging a federal official with "treason, bribery, or other high crimes and misdemeanors." Once impeached, a federal official is then tried by the Senate, with the chief justice of the Supreme Court presiding over the trial. The only punishment for conviction is removal from office. Two presidents, Andrew Johnson and Bill Clinton, and several federal judges have been impeached. In Johnson's case (1868), impeachment was the culmination of tensions that grew between the Democratic president and congressional Republicans over Reconstruction. Clinton's impeachment (1998) stemmed from the aftermath of a sexual affair he had with a twenty-one-year-old intern. In both cases, partisan tensions drove the impeachment process, and in both cases the Senate ultimately found the president not guilty.

WRONG CHOICES EXPLAINED:

(2) (3) and (4) Neither the president, state legislatures, nor the Supreme Court has the power to impeach a federal government official.

6. **3** A constitutional power specifically delegated to the federal government is the power to declare war. The Constitution specifically grants Congress this power. Congress has formally declared war on five separate occasions—The War of 1812, The Mexican-American War (1846), the Spanish-American War (1898), World War I (1917), and World War II (1941). On numerous occasions in American history, the United States has engaged in military activities without a formal declaration of war.

WRONG CHOICES EXPLAINED:

(1) The Constitution does not specifically delegate to the federal government the power to regulate marriage and divorce. This power is exercised by the various states. This power has become a source of contention in recent years as several states have granted the right to marry to same-sex couples.

(2) The Constitution does not specifically delegate to the federal government the power to establish education standards. This power is exercised by the various states. The federal government has begun to play a greater role in guiding state standards with the passage of the No Child Left Behind Act (2001).

(4) The Constitution does not specifically delegate to the federal government the power to issue driver's licenses. This power is exercised by the various states.

7. **4** To win a presidential election, a candidate must win a majority of the electoral vote. The Constitution states the basic process for how the president would be elected. After the popular vote for president on Election Day, election boards determine which candidate won in each of the states. The winning candidate in a particular state gets all of that state's electoral votes. The number of electors for each state is equal to the congressional delegation from that state. Bigger states, therefore, get more electors. The electors cast their votes 41 days after the popular vote. Presently, there are 538 electoral votes. A candidate must win the majority, or 270 votes, to be declared the "president-elect." The system has its detractors and defenders. Detractors site the fact that candidates put most of the energy into states that can go either way—the so-called swing states. Candidates tend to ignore states that are solidly for one or the other political parties. In addition, a scenario can unfold in which a candidate could win the overall popular vote, but lose in enough states to not attain the majority of the electoral vote. In such a scenario, the winner of the popular vote would not win the presidency. This scenario occurred in 1824, 1876, 1888, and 2000. Defenders of the system note that many smaller states get attention from the candidates that they would not get if there were just a national popular vote.

WRONG CHOICES EXPLAINED:

(1) (2) and (3) The methods described in these choices are not used in presidential elections. The electoral college has always been used in presidential elections in the United States.

8. **4** One goal of Alexander Hamilton's financial plan was the establishment of a national bank. This national bank would be 20% publicly controlled and 80% privately controlled. Hamilton thought it was important to have wealthy investors financially and psychologically invested in the new government. The proposal to create a national bank became a major source of disagreement between Hamilton and Secretary of State Thomas Jefferson.

Jefferson argued that the Constitution did not permit Congress to create a national bank. It was not among the congressional powers listed in the Constitution. Hamilton countered that the elastic clause in the Constitution, which lets Congress do what it considered "necessary and proper," implicitly allowed for the creation of a national bank. Jefferson insisted that the elastic clause should be invoked only in cases of genuine national emergencies. President Washington agreed with Hamilton and signed the bank law in 1791.

WRONG CHOICES EXPLAINED:

(1) Alexander Hamilton did not propose establishing a stock exchange. The first stock exchange, the Philadelphia Stock Exchange in the United States (1790), was established by private individuals, not by the government.

(2) Alexander Hamilton did not propose creating a national sales tax. He did propose an excise, or sales, tax on whiskey. This led to protests in western Pennsylvania, known as the Whiskey Rebellion (1794).

(3) Alexander Hamilton did not propose a federal income tax. The federal income tax did not come in existence until 1913 with the ratification of the 16th Amendment.

9. **2** One outcome of the Supreme Court decision in *Marbury* v. *Madison* (1803) was that the principle of judicial review was established. The *Marbury* v. *Madison* decision is arguably the Supreme Court's most important decision. The details of the decision have to do with the seating of judges that had been appointed in the last days of the John Adams administration. But more importantly, the decision established the Supreme Court's power to review laws and determine if they are consistent with the Constitution. Laws declared unconstitutional by the Court are immediately struck down. This power of judicial review has been the main function of the Supreme Court since then and has been instrumental in maintaining balance between the three branches of the government.

WRONG CHOICES EXPLAINED:

(1) The *Marbury* v. *Madison* decision did not establish that state governments could determine the constitutionality of federal laws. In the late 18th and early 19th century, several prominent public figures asserted the right of states to strike down, or nullify, federal laws that they determined were unconstitutional. Thomas Jefferson and James Madison, for example, asserted the state power of nullification after President John Adams signed the Alien and Sedition Acts into law (1798). But it is only the Supreme Court that has the power to strike down unconstitutional federal legislation.

(3) The *Marbury* v. *Madison* decision did not allow Congress to expand its delegated powers. Congress's delegated powers are those powers specifically listed in the Constitution. Only a change to the Constitution could expand these delegated powers.

(4) The *Marbury* v. *Madison* decision did not establish a method to approve treaties. The method for approving treaties—a two-thirds vote by the Senate—was established in the Constitution.

10. **4** The Louisiana Purchase initially presented a dilemma for President Thomas Jefferson because he believed it would violate his strict construction-ist view of the Constitution. The Louisiana Territory was long held by France until France ceded it to Spain in 1763 following the French and Indian War. France then regained the territory in 1801. The ambitious French leader Napoleon Bonaparte, in need of cash to fund war with England, was ready to sell the Louisiana Territory at a reasonable price. American negotiators quickly agreed to a price of $15 million. Jefferson was at first reluctant to approve the deal because the Constitution did not allow for the acquisition of additional lands. Jefferson had long held a strict constructionist view of the Constitution, asserting that the government's power was limited to what was explicitly allowed for in the Constitution. But if Jefferson waited for a consti-tutional amendment specifically allowing Congress to acquire new lands, Napoleon could rescind his offer. So Jefferson violated his stated principle and quickly presented the offer to Congress, which assented and appropri-ated the money. For $15 million the United States bought this vast expanse of land and nearly doubled its size.

WRONG CHOICES EXPLAINED:
(1) Jefferson was not concerned that the purchase of the Louisiana Territory would lead to war with Great Britain. Tensions existed at the time between the United States and Great Britain, but these were over trade, not over the Louisiana Territory. These tensions eventually led to the War of 1812.

(2) Jefferson was not concerned that the purchase of the Louisiana Territory would bankrupt the new nation. The price of the territory was rela-tively cheap ($15 million).

(3) Jefferson was not concerned that the purchase of the Louisiana Territory would force Native American Indians off their land. Jefferson's views on Native Americans changed over time. At one point, he argued that Native Americans should assimilate with mainstream culture. Later, he supported removal plans. But these views did not present a dilemma for Jefferson in regard to the Louisiana Purchase.

11. **3** The Missouri Compromise (1820) maintained the balance between free and slave states. Controversy arose between the slave-holding states and the free states in 1820 when Missouri applied for statehood as a slave state. At the time, there were 11 slave and 11 free states. The admission of Missouri would have upset that balance. A compromise that allowed for the admission of two new states—Missouri as a slave state and Maine as a free state—was reached. It also divided the remaining area of the Louisiana

Territory at 36°30′ north latitude. Above that line, slavery was not permitted (except for in Missouri); below the line, it was permitted.

WRONG CHOICES EXPLAINED:

(1) The Missouri Compromise did not ban slavery west of the Mississippi River. It did ban slavery in part of the land west of the Mississippi. Under the Missouri Compromise, slavery would not be permitted in the northern part of the Louisiana Territory, above the 36°30′ north latitude line.

(2) The Missouri Compromise did not stipulate that unorganized territories would be governed by the United States and Great Britain. Between 1818 and 1846, the United States and Great Britain agreed to "joint occupancy" of the Oregon Country. In 1846, a boundary line was established in the Oregon Country between American and British territory.

(4) The Missouri Compromise did create a new boundary between the United States and Canada at the 36°30′ line. That line of latitude was part of the Missouri Compromise. It divided the Louisiana Territory into areas that would include slavery (south of the line) and those that would ban slavery (north of the line).

12. **1** The Seneca Falls Convention (1848) supported the movement for women's rights. In fact, it is often considered the birth of the women's rights movement. The convention was organized by Lucretia Mott and Elizabeth Cady Stanton. The genesis of the convention was their exclusion from an abolitionist conference in London in 1840. Mott and Stanton began thinking not only about the abolition of slavery but also about the conditions of women in the United States. The laws of the country relegated women to a second-class status. Women could not vote or sit on juries. Women were not entitled to protection against physical abuse by their husbands. When women married, any property they owned became the property of their husbands. Society defined women as intellectually inferior and insisted that the proper role for women was maintaining the house and caring for children. This "cult of domesticity" prevented women from participating in public life. The convention issued a Declaration of Sentiments modeled after the Declaration of Independence. The document declared, "All men and women are created equal."

WRONG CHOICES EXPLAINED:

(2) The *Dred Scott* decision (1857) did not involve women's rights. The decision involved slavery. It declared that Dred Scott was not free even though he had lived in a free state with his owner. It also declared that African Americans are not entitled to citizenship rights and that Congress does not have the power to ban slavery in the territories. It was a blow to opponents of slavery and one of the events that precipitated the Civil War.

(3) The formation of the Republican Party was not directly related to the women's rights movement. The founders of the Republican Party were

united in their opposition to the expansion of slavery into the new territories of the United States. They did not have a united position in regard to women's rights, although there was certainly overlap between the anti-slavery movement and the women's rights movement.

(4) The Lincoln-Douglas debates were not about women's rights. The debates, which occurred between Abraham Lincoln and Stephen Douglas during their race for the Senate in 1858, revolved around the issue of slavery.

13. **1** Prior to the Civil War, abolitionists reacted to the situation described in the poster by supporting the Underground Railroad. The poster is a runaway slave ad. A slave owner is offering a reward for the return of one of his slaves who had escaped. The Underground Railroad was an informal network of safe houses in which escaped slaves could find refuge. "Conductors" on the Underground Railroad guided these escaped slaves from one safe house to another at night to avoid detection by law enforcement authorities. The goal was to guide the escaped slaves to Canada. An important "conductor" on the Underground Railroad was Harriet Tubman.

WRONG CHOICES EXPLAINED:
(2) Abolitionists would not have opposed the Emancipation Proclamation. The Emancipation Proclamation was issued by President Abraham Lincoln during the Civil War. The document declared that as of January 1, 1863, slaves held in Confederate territory would be free. Of course, United States laws were not enforceable in Confederate territory, but the Emancipation Proclamation had the important effect of turning the Civil War into a war for the liberation of the enslaved population of the South.

(3) Abolitionists would not have banned freed slaves from Northern states. Abolitionists were, for the most part, in favor of equality and justice for African Americans.

(4) Abolitionists would not have proposed a stricter fugitive slave law. A stricter fugitive slave law was part of the Compromise of 1850. It gave slave catchers far greater latitude to retrieve escaped slaves in Northern states. It made it a federal crime to interfere with these slave catchers or to aid escaped slaves. Abolitionists were deeply troubled by the new law.

14. **2** Literacy tests and poll taxes were often used to limit voter participation by African Americans. After the Civil War, three amendments to the Constitution were ratified to extend legal and political equality to African Americans. The 15th Amendment (1870) declared that the right to vote shall not be denied on the basis of race. Following the ratification of the 15th Amendment, Southern states adopted a variety of measures to prevent African Americans from voting. These measures included instituting poll taxes and literacy tests. Poll taxes required people to pay a tax in order to vote. Literacy tests required people to demonstrate their ability to read before they were allowed to vote. These laws effectively prevented the vast majority of African Americans in the South from voting from the 1800s until passage of the Voting Rights Act in 1965.

WRONG CHOICES EXPLAINED:

(1) Literacy tests and poll taxes were not used to enforce constitutional amendments added after the Civil War. In fact, they were used to circumvent the 15th Amendment (1870), which was intended to prevent racial discrimination in voting.

(3) Literacy tests and poll taxes were not used to promote equal educational opportunities for minority persons. The measures were related to voting, not education, and they promoted inequality, not equality.

(4) Literacy tests and poll taxes were not used to provide job training for freedmen. The measures were related to voting, not employment, and they limited options for freedmen rather than expanding them.

15. **1** During the late 1800s, the ideas expressed in these lyrics were the goals of the organizers of labor unions. Labor unions formed after the Civil War to increase the bargaining power of workers as they dealt with owners. Many workers thought they had a better chance to gain concessions from owners if they banded together in unions. Unions made demands for better wages, improved conditions, or shorter hours. They could call a strike if their demands were not met by management. A significant early union was the Knights of Labor, founded in 1869. This union welcomed all members, regardless of race, sex, or level of skill. A second early union was the American Federation of Labor (1886), which included only skilled workers, the "aristocracy of labor." It was known as a craft union, in distinction from the Knights, which was an industrial union. The eight-hour day was a common demand for both craft unions and industrial unions. The song asserts the demand for a shorter workday, but it also embodies the utopian idea that life should be about more than work and mere survival; even working people should be able to "feel the sunshine" and "smell the flowers."

WRONG CHOICES EXPLAINED:

(2) The song does not express the goals of sharecroppers following the Civil War. Sharecroppers were landless farmers who used a landowner's property, paying rent with a share of the crop. The demand for an eight-hour day was made by factory workers not agricultural workers.

(3) The song does not express the goals of Grangers demanding railroad regulation. The lyrics are about the eight-hour workday, not about railroad regulation. The Grange is a farmers' organization that was founded in 1867 and continues to exist. During the 1800s, the Grange often expressed its solidarity with urban laborers, but it focused on agrarian issues.

(4) The song does not express the goals of the owners of big business. Owners of big business wanted to maximize the number of hours that their workers worked. The song, on the other hand, is advocating limiting the workday to eight hours.

16. **2** In the 1890s, the Populist Party incorporated the demand for an eight-hour day into its platform. The Populist Party was organized in 1892. It grew out of the populist movement, an assortment of groups and individuals that advanced the goals of struggling farmers. The movement resented the concentration of wealth and power among eastern industrialists and bankers. The Populist Party wanted the United States to get off the gold standard and to issue money backed by silver as well. Also, the party pushed for greater democracy, supporting the direct election of senators. Finally, the platform called for better treatment of industrial workers and for the eight-hour day.

WRONG CHOICES EXPLAINED:

(1) The Know-Nothing Party did not incorporate the demand for an eight-hour day into its platform. The Know-Nothing Party existed in the 1840s and 1850s. It was primarily an anti-immigrant party.

(3) The Whig Party did not incorporate the demand for an eight-hour day into its platform. The Whig Party existed from the 1830s to 1850s. It developed in opposition to President Andrew Jackson and the Democratic Party. It was interested in economic modernization, but it was not a champion of workers' rights. In fact, working-class men were more likely to vote for the Democratic Party at the time.

(4) The Bull Moose Party, formally known as the Progressive Party, did not incorporate the demand for an eight-hour day into its platform in the 1890s. The party was formed to support the independent candidacy of Theodore Roosevelt in 1912. It existed until 1916. Progressives were sympathetic to the demand for an eight-hour day, but the Bull Moose Party did not exist in the 1890s.

17. **1** The idea expressed in this statement is most consistent with the principles of Social Darwinism. This school of thought gained popularity during the industrial revolution of the late 1800s. Social Darwinism was an attempt to apply Charles Darwin's ideas about the natural world to social relations. The theory was popularized in the United States by William Graham Sumner. Sumner was attracted to Darwin's ideas about competition and "survival of the fittest." Social Darwinists argued against any attempt at government intervention into the economic and social spheres. Interference, they argued, would hinder the evolution of the human species. The inequalities of wealth that characterized the late 1800s, they argued, were part of the process of "survival of the fittest." This hands-off approach to economic activities is known by the French phrase *laissez faire*. Social Darwinism appealed to owners of large corporations, because it both justified their wealth and power and warned against any type of regulation or reform.

WRONG CHOICES EXPLAINED:

(2) The idea expressed in the statement is not consistent with the concept of assimilation. Assimilation refers to minority groups adopting the customs and attitudes of the prevailing culture. The concept has been used in relation to both Native American Indians and to immigrants. The statement does not endorse or condemn assimilation.

(3) The idea expressed in the statement is not consistent with the goals of the Progressive movement. The statement encourages a hands-off approach to society. Progressives, on the other hand, encouraged government intervention in social issues, such as child labor, women's rights, and environmental conservation.

(4) The idea expressed in the statement is not consistent with the melting pot theory of American culture. The melting pot theory entails a vision of the United States in which the different races and ethnicities that comprise the country shed their old habits and customs and collectively build a new, distinctively American, society. The statement does not endorse or condemn the melting pot theory.

18. **3** During the late 1800s, many North American Indian tribes were sent to reservations that were located in sparsely populated regions of the West. This strategy of moving Native Americans to reservations involved a shift in policy away from the dictates of the Dawes Act (1887), which called for the assimilation of Native Americans into mainstream society.

WRONG CHOICES EXPLAINED:
(1) (2) and (3) Native Americans were not sent to these areas because these areas were already densely settled by non-Native Americans.

19. **4** The closing of the frontier and the growth of industry in the late 1800s are two factors often associated with the rise of United States imperialism. Both factors are seen by historians as causes of the United States embarking on an imperialist path. The frontier was, in the 19th century, the unofficial boundary line between settled and sparsely settled or unsettled lands. The frontier line shifted further and further west as more and more of the United States became settled. Some public thinkers, such as historian Frederick Jackson Turner, saw this closing of the frontier as a call for the United States to look for new lands, and new opportunities, abroad. Their thinking contributed to public enthusiasm for an imperialist policy. Also contributing to the push for imperialism was the unprecedented growth of American industry. Imperial holdings would provide American industry with important raw materials, as well as markets for the growing output of consumer products that American industry was turning out.

WRONG CHOICES EXPLAINED:
(1) The closing of the frontier and the growth of industry are not associated with a reduction of exports to Asian nations. In fact, exports to Asian countries increased in the late 1800s as American industry expanded.

(2) The closing of the frontier and the growth of industry are not associated with the restoration of a plantation economy in the South. In fact, there was not a restoration of the Southern plantation economy. The era of the large Southern plantation ended with the destruction of slavery during the Civil War.

(3) The closing of the frontier and the growth of industry are not associated with the formation of alliances with other nations. In fact, the United

States was very reluctant to form alliances with other nations throughout most of its history. It was only after World War II that the United States agreed to participate in a permanent alliance—the North Atlantic Treaty Organization (1949).

20. **4** Yellow journalists created support for the Spanish-American War by writing articles about the sinking of the United States battleship *Maine* in the Havana harbor. In 1898, the *Maine* exploded and sunk in the harbor of Havana, Cuba. Many in the United States thought that the destruction of the ship was the work of Spain, especially after American newspapers bluntly accused Spain of the crime, despite the scarcity of evidence. This sensationalistic, irresponsible coverage of events is known as *yellow journalism*. The coverage of the sinking of the *Maine* was one of several causes of the war. Spain controlled Cuba at the time, but a Cuban independence movement was trying to break its ties to Spain. Many Americans wanted the United States to intervene on Cuba's side in this struggle. Some Americans saw parallels between the Cuban struggle for independence from Spain and America's struggle for independence from England. Also, some American businessmen were angered by the interruption of the sugar harvest by the fighting between Cuban rebels and Spanish forces. American newspapers breathlessly followed events in Cuba, with lurid accounts of Spanish wrongdoing.

WRONG CHOICES EXPLAINED:
(1) The political popularity of William Jennings Bryan was unrelated to the Spanish-American War. Bryan was in the headlines in 1896 when he ran for president on the Democratic ticket. His "cross of gold" speech during the campaign was widely reprinted. Bryan was in the headlines again in 1925 when he became a special prosecutor in the Scopes trial. John Scopes was put on trial for teaching evolution, in violation of Tennessee law.

(2) Efforts by the United States to control Mexico were unrelated to the Spanish-American War. President Wilson did send troops to Mexico in 1916 to pursue Mexican revolutionary Pancho Villa.

(3) The destruction of United States sugar plantations by Hawaiians was unrelated to the Spanish-American War. The United States did intervene in Hawaii in 1893 to protect American businessmen who had toppled the regime of the local ruler, Queen Lili'uokalani.

21. **2** Muckrakers Ida Tarbell and Upton Sinclair influenced the federal government to pass legislation to correct harmful business practices. The term *muckraker* was applied to journalists who wrote magazine articles and books that exposed wrongdoing by government officials, showed the negative side of industrialization, and let the world see a variety of social ills. Upton Sinclair exposed the underside of the meat-packing industry in the novel *The Jungle* (1906). The novel follows a Lithuanian immigrant family through the

stockyards of Chicago. The public uproar that followed the publication of the book led Congress to pass the Meat Inspection Act (1906) and the Pure Food and Drug Act (also 1906), which established the Food and Drug Administration. Ida Tarbell's book, *The History of the Standard Oil Company* (1904), exposed the ruthlessness of John D. Rockefeller's oil company. Her book contributed to the government breaking up the Standard Oil Trust in 1911. These muckraking books inspired a generation of Progressive reformers to push the government to intervene in these problems. A whole host of reforms were implemented by Progressive reformers and their allies in the 1900s and 1910s.

WRONG CHOICES EXPLAINED:

(1) Ida Tarbell and Upton Sinclair did not influence the federal government to grant citizenship to people who had entered the country illegally. Neither writer focused on the question of immigration and citizenship.

(3) Ida Tarbell and Upton Sinclair did not influence the federal government to force individual states to regulate monopolies. Both writers urged the federal government itself, rather than state governments, to take action.

(4) Ida Tarbell and Upton Sinclair did not influence the federal government to end racial discrimination in the workplace. Many of the muckraking journalists of the Progressive era shared the racial attitudes of much of mainstream white society at the time. Few challenged the pervasive racism of American society. One exception was Ida B. Wells, an African American muckraking journalist who challenged the mistreatment of African Americans in the country.

22. **3** *Speaker C* best expresses the environmental views of President Theodore Roosevelt. *Speaker C* reflects the views of an environmental conservationist. This view endorses using natural resources in a responsible way so that these resources continue to exist for future generations. This view can be contrasted with the views of an environmental preservationist. The preservationist view is reflected in the statement by *Speaker A*. Preservationists want society to have a hands-off approach in regard to the remaining relatively untouched natural areas. An early preservationist was John Muir, one of the founders of the Sierra Club (1892). Both conservationists and preservationists were concerned about the rapid disappearance of natural areas in the United States. Logging and mining operations were taking a toll on forested areas starting in the late 1800s. Roosevelt (1901–1909), an avid outdoorsman, set aside millions of acres as protected areas. These include six national parks.

WRONG CHOICES EXPLAINED:

(1) *Speaker A* does not reflect the environmental views of President Theodore Roosevelt. *Speaker A* reflects the views of an environmental preservationist. A preservationist wants to preserve remaining wilderness

areas in the state they are currently in. Conservationists, like Roosevelt, would allow for some limited economic activity in wilderness areas. An early preservationist was John Muir, one of the founders of the Sierra Club (1892).

(2) *Speaker B* does not reflect the environmental views of President Theodore Roosevelt. *Speaker B* reflects the views of the owners of big businesses who saw the environment as a source of income, rather than as an intrinsic good that should be conserved.

(4) *Speaker D* does not reflect the environmental views of President Theodore Roosevelt. *Speaker D* reflects views usually associated with Native American Indians. Many Native American Indians thought of the land as a common good, not as something that could be owned.

23. **1** The statement of *Speaker D* is most like the views expressed by Native American Indians. Many Native Americans held the view that the land was a common good, not something to be bought and sold. Native American Indians tended to live in harmony with the natural world to a greater degree than the majority of Americans do today. Native Americans tended to view humans as part of nature, not separate from nature. Of course, it is also important to remember that Native American Indians were not all of one mind in regard to attitudes toward nature. A variety of attitudes, ideas, and practices in regard to the natural world existed among the various Native American Indian nations of North America.

WRONG CHOICES EXPLAINED:

(2) (3) and (4) The statement of *Speaker D* does not reflect the views of most western farmers, railroad companies, or European immigrants. All three of these groups tended to see nature as something that can be owned, used, and profited from, not as something that should be respected and shared.

24. **4** Many United States senators refused to support membership in the League of Nations because they believed that it would involve the United States in future foreign conflicts. The issue emerged after World War I, as the United States Senate debated whether to ratify the Treaty of Versailles. By approving the Treaty of Versailles, the Senate would have also made the United States a member of the League of Nations. President Woodrow Wilson had championed the idea of an organization of the world's nations in his Fourteen Points document. The victorious powers in Europe after World War I largely ignored Wilson's idealistic vision for a post-war world, but they agree to create the League of Nations. Wilson pushed for United States approval of the Treaty of Versailles, so that the United States would be a participant in this new organization. But some senators wanted to isolate the United States from world affairs and opposed membership in the league. These isolationists announced that they would vote to reject the treaty. Some senators took a middle position; they would agree to vote to approve the

treaty, if the Senate put certain conditions on United States participation in the League of Nations. Wilson refused to compromise with these senators and urged his allies in the Senate to reject any conditions. Without these senators in the middle, the Treaty of Versailles was rejected by the Senate, and the United States did not join the League of Nations.

WRONG CHOICES EXPLAINED:

(1) Opposition to United States membership in the League of Nations was not based on economic concerns. The main concern was that League membership would entail the United States being dragged into foreign conflicts.

(2) Opposition to United States membership in the League of Nations was not based on the belief that membership in the League would force the United States to give up its colonies. There was no mandate that League members give up their colonies. The colonial powers that joined the League continued to hold onto their colonies.

(3) Opponents of United States membership in the League of Nations did not believe that League membership would grant the president the power to annex new territories. Annexations of additional territories must be approved by Congress.

25. **1** Immigration laws passed in the 1920s changed United States policy by establishing immigration quotas. The Emergency Quota Act (1921) and the National Origins Act (1924) greatly reduced the number of immigrants allowed into the United States. These acts set quotas for new immigrants based on nationality. The first act set the quota for each nationality at 3% of the total number of that nationality that was present in the United States in 1910. The second act reduced the percentage to 2% and moved the year back to 1890. This had the effect of setting very low quotas for many of the "new immigrants"—people from eastern and southern Europe. The laws were passed in response to a large nativist, or anti-immigrant, movement. These quotas were largely in place until the Immigration and Nationality Act of 1965 ended the quota system.

WRONG CHOICES EXPLAINED:

(2) The immigration laws of the 1920s did not restrict immigration into the United States to only skilled workers. A 1952 change in immigration policy kept the 1924 national quotas in place, but did make some exceptions for certain skilled workers.

(3) The immigration laws of the 1920s did not favor immigration from Asia. In fact, the laws specifically banned most Asians from immigrating into the United States.

(4) The immigration laws of the 1920s did not encourage an increase in immigration into the United States. In fact, it did the opposite. The immigration laws of the 1920s effectively shut the door to immigration.

26. **2** Henry Ford's use of the assembly line in the production of automobiles led directly to a decrease in the cost of automobiles. Ford introduced the assembly line at his auto plant in order to tap into the large number of unskilled immigrants who were flooding into the United States after 1880. Ford and other manufacturers wanted to move away from having their products built by skilled craftsmen. Skilled workers took time to train and once trained could demand higher wages. Ford's goal was to recreate the production process so that his automobiles would no longer be built by highly trained mechanics, but instead would be assembled by unskilled workers. The assembly line, first introduced in 1908, broke down the production process into small steps. No longer would a worker need to know how to assemble an entire automobile. Now, he would simply have to know how to turn a bolt or weld a piece of metal. The impact of the assembly line on the United States was profound. Ford's assembly line was a key component in the mass-production revolution of the late 19th and early 20th century. With mass production, ordinary people could afford goods that were previously beyond their reach. Another impact of the assembly line was on the workers themselves. Many workers found working at an assembly line incredibly boring. Gone was the sense of pride that skilled workers had carried with them into the shop. Aside from the loss of pride, was the loss of income. Assembly line workers found that they were paid far less per hour than their skilled counterparts from a generation earlier.

WRONG CHOICES EXPLAINED:

(1) Henry Ford's assembly line did not lead to a decrease in the number of automobiles available. It did the opposite. It greatly increased the number of automobiles produced and sold in the United States.

(3) Henry Ford's assembly line did not lead to an increase in the unemployment rate. It did the opposite. The great success of Ford's plants necessitated an increase in the number of workers employed.

(4) Henry Ford's assembly line did not lead to an increase in the time needed to produce a single automobile. It did the opposite. It greatly reduced the amount of time need to produce an automobile.

27. **1** The convictions of Sacco and Vanzetti in the 1920s most closely reflected the increase in nativist attitudes. Nicola Sacco and Bartolomeo Vanzetti were two working-class Italian immigrants who were accused of robbing and killing a payroll clerk in Massachusetts in 1920. The evidence against them was sketchy, and the judge was openly hostile to the two men, who were not only immigrants but anarchists. After they were found guilty, many Americans protested the verdict and wondered if an immigrant, especially with radical ideas, could get a fair trial in the United States. Despite the protests, the two men were executed in 1927. Anti-immigrant sentiment ran very high in the 1920s. The United States passed the Emergency Quota Act (1921) and the National Origins Act (1924), both of which greatly reduced the number of new immigrants allowed into the United States.

WRONG CHOICES EXPLAINED:

(2) The convictions of Sacco and Vanzetti did not reflect the federal government's war on crime. The two men were tried in state court, not federal court. Most of the federal government's anti-crime activities in the 1920s dealt with prohibition and organized crime.

(3) The convictions of Sacco and Vanzetti did not reflect corruption of political machines. Sacco and Vanzetti were not accused of political corruption. Political corruption was rampant in the 1920s. The most famous case was the Teapot Dome scandal (1921–1923), during the Warren Harding administration, involving bribery and public oil lands.

(4) The convictions of Sacco and Vanzetti did not reflect a rise in labor unrest. Though there was a spike in labor unrest immediately following World War I, in 1918 and 1919, labor was fairly quiet in the 1920s.

28. **2** One cause of the stock market crash of 1929 and the Great Depression that followed was that speculators had purchased shares of stock on margin with borrowed funds. Stockbrokers provided easy access to credit so people could buy stock on margin, putting only a fraction of the cost of the stock down and promising to pay the rest by some future date. The general public assumed that the stock market would go up indefinitely and many stockbrokers agreed. Indeed, such enthusiasm for stocks drives prices up; prices of shares in a company are determined by the level of demand for its stock. But, these confident investors in the 1920s often ignored the soundness of the companies they were investing in. This whole system of wild speculation completely unraveled in October 1929, when investors lost confidence in the market and a selling frenzy overtook Wall Street, sending stock prices down to a mere fraction of their high prices. There were several other causes of the Great Depression. The distribution of wealth in the United States became more skewed in the 1920s. The unequal distribution of wealth weakened the manufacturing sector. Consumption just could not keep up with production. Manufacturers made the logical decision of beginning layoffs. Of course, unemployed workers had even less ability to purchase goods. The agricultural sector also suffered. Farmers expanded production through mechanization, but this ultimately pushed down commodity prices and farm income.

WRONG CHOICES EXPLAINED:

(1) The stock market crash and the Great Depression were not caused by the costs associated with World War I. Wartime spending usually stimulates economic growth. Spending on World War II was one of the causes of the United States climbing out of the Great Depression.

(3) The stock market crash and the Great Depression were not caused by federal tax cuts causing high inflation. Inflation was not high in the 1920s. In fact, the overproduction and under-consumption of the 1920s produced falling prices, not inflation.

(4) The stock market crash and the Great Depression were not caused by low farm production. Farm production in the 1920s was high. Mechanization allowed farmers to put more acres under cultivation and to increase yields per acre. But this development was not good news for farmers; high yields depressed commodity prices and farm income.

29. **3** During the Great Depression, one way New Deal programs tried to stimulate economic recovery was by creating public works jobs. The most well-known jobs programs were the Civilian Conservation Corps (1933), which sent young men to remote areas to work in parks and forests, and the vast Works Progress Administration (1935), which consisted of a myriad of public projects. The WPA built schools, installed sewer lines, wrote guide-books, and produced theatrical productions. President Franklin D. Roosevelt argued that one of the causes of the Great Depression was that workers in the 1920s were not able to purchase enough consumer goods to keep the economy growing. An important aspect of his New Deal was increasing work-ers' wages and purchasing power. This approach to economic growth is often referred to as demand-side economics, in that it focuses on stimulating consumer demand by getting more money into ordinary people's pockets. The alternative approach is to stimulate the supply side of the economy— manufacturing firms, banks, insurance corporations. Supply-side economists believe that if there is growth in the supply side, there will be general economic growth, and the benefits of that growth will reach everyone. Republican presidents, such as Herbert Hoover in the 1920s and Ronald Reagan in the 1980s, subscribed to supply-side economics.

WRONG CHOICES EXPLAINED:
(1) The New Deal did not try to stimulate economic growth by raising tariff rates. Earlier, the Republican presidents of the 1920s believed in raising tariff rates. President Hoover pushed for the Hawley-Smoot Tariff (1930), which created the highest tariff in United States history on imported agricul-tural goods. President Franklin D. Roosevelt later saw these high tariffs as counterproductive and lowered tariffs to stimulate international trade.

(2) The New Deal did not try to stimulate economic growth by increasing interest rates. The government tried to keep interest rates down in order to stimulate borrowing and spending.

(4) The New Deal did not try to stimulate economic growth by lowering the minimum wage. A national minimum wage did not exist before the New Deal. Roosevelt actively pushed for a minimum wage law. The National Industrial Recovery Act (1933) included a minimum wage as one of its stan-dards. After the Supreme Court invalidated the act, the Fair Labor Standards Act (1938), another New Deal program, set a minimum wage. A minimum wage law has existed since then.

30. **2** The cartoonist is commenting on President Franklin D. Roosevelt's efforts to gain Supreme Court support for his legislative program. The cartoonist is implying that Roosevelt had been heavy-handed in forcing Congress to support his programs. His statement to the Supreme Court, "Let's Harmonize!," seems to be a call for cooperation and collaboration, but the cartoonist intends these words to be taken ironically. The reader of the cartoon is supposed to imagine that Roosevelt will use the same bullying techniques with the Supreme Court that he had already used with Congress. The cartoon is commenting on President Roosevelt's much-criticized plan to increase the number of justices on the Supreme Court. By the end of 1936, Roosevelt had grown increasingly frustrated with the Supreme Court after it shot down the National Recovery Act in *Schecter* v. *United States* (1935) and the Agricultural Adjustment Act in *Butler* v. *United States* (1936). After winning reelection in 1936, he announced a plan to increase the number of justices on the Supreme Court, to as many as 15. He said that some of the older justices had difficulty keeping up with the heavy workload. But it was clear that he was trying to create a Supreme Court friendlier to his New Deal programs. The Senate rejected Roosevelt's "court packing" scheme in 1937 because the plan would have threatened the principle of checks and balances by making the Supreme Court a rubber stamp for New Deal legislation.

WRONG CHOICES EXPLAINED:

(1) President Roosevelt did try to win congressional support for his Supreme Court nominees, but that is not what the cartoon is commenting on. The cartoon shows him trying to "harmonize" with, or gain the support of, the Supreme Court, as it was comprised at the time. He is not depicted as trying to gain support for new nominees.

(3) President Roosevelt did not try to set up a retirement plan for Supreme Court justices. When he announced his plan to expand the number of Supreme Court justices, he said that some of the older justices had trouble keeping up with the heavy workload, but he did not insist that they retire.

(4) President Roosevelt did not try to keep members of Congress off the Supreme Court. His problem was with justices who were already on the Supreme Court, not with potential future justices.

31. **4** The Great Plains was the area most closely associated with the Dust Bowl of the 1930s. The Dust Bowl was the name given to that portion of the Great Plains that was afflicted by a devastating draught and unsustainable overfarming. The natural grass cover of the region, which includes parts of Oklahoma and Texas as well as smaller parts of neighboring states, had been removed in the years leading up to the Dust Bowl, as wheat farmers increased the number of acres under cultivation. With this natural root system gone, the fertile topsoil simply blew away when drought struck from 1934 to 1937. The government, through the Soil Conservation Service, encouraged farmers to replant trees and grass and purchased land to be kept out of cultivation. The Dust Bowl promoted some significant cultural

responses, such as the Dust Bowl ballads of the folk singer Woody Guthrie and the novel *The Grapes of Wrath* by John Steinbeck. These cultural responses chronicled the plight of Dust Bowl refugees, including the "Okies" who fled from Oklahoma.

WRONG CHOICES EXPLAINED:

(1) (2) and (3) The Dust Bowl did not include the Great Lakes basin, the Mississippi River valley, or the Appalachian Mountains. All of these regions were affected by the economic dislocation of the Great Depression, but the Dust Bowl was restricted to the southern portion of the Great Plains.

32. **4** The correct chronological order for the events listed in the question is the following: Neutrality Acts (1935–1939), The Lend-Lease Act (1940), Japanese attack on Pearl Harbor (December 7, 1941), and United States declaration of war on Japan (December 8, 1941). The events chart a shift in United States foreign policy in the 1930s and 1940s, from isolationism to interventionism. In the 1930s, many Americans, including President Roosevelt, were alarmed at the aggressive actions taken by Germany, Italy, and Japan, but isolationist sentiment was strong in the United States. In this atmosphere, the first Neutrality Act was passed in 1935. Additional neutrality acts were passed in the coming years. One stipulated that the United States could sell weaponry, but only on a "cash and carry" basis. When World War II began (1939), many began to see Hitler as a threat to world peace and democracy. In early 1941 Roosevelt was able to make military supplies more readily available to Hitler's opponents with the Lend-Lease Act. This act demonstrated the commitment of the United States to the Allies but it was not until the attack on Pearl Harbor on December 7, 1941, that the United States entered the war (December 8, 1941).

WRONG CHOICES EXPLAINED:

(1) (2) and (3) These choices do not contain the correct chronological order of the four events listed.

33. **4** During World War II, a change occurred in American society as women replaced men in essential wartime industries. Women were needed because factories were working around the clock producing military goods and much of the male work force was in the military. Many images were produced by the government, usually through the Office of War Information, showing women in industrial settings. The fictional "Rosie the Riveter" was often featured in this public relations campaign. These female workers were presented in a positive light—helping the nation as well as the men in combat abroad. Such a campaign was needed because prewar societal mores discouraged women from doing industrial work. During the Great Depression of the 1930s, women were encouraged to leave the job market so that there would be enough jobs available for male "bread winners." The campaign was successful. By 1945, one-third of the work force was female.

WRONG CHOICES EXPLAINED:

(1) African Americans were not granted equality in the armed forces during World War II. For the vast majority of the war, African Americans served in segregated units. In 1948, President Harry Truman issued Executive Order 9981, which ordered the desegregation of the armed forces.

(2) Women were not allowed to enter combat units during World War II. Women have continued to serve in the armed forces in a variety of capacities. Over 40,000 women served in the Gulf War (1991), but did not participate in ground engagements. Women, mostly serving as military police, have been involved in combat in the war with Iraq (2003–present).

(3) Congress did not enact the first military draft during World War II. The federal government first drafted men to serve in the military during the Civil War. During the American Revolution, states occasionally drafted men to serve in state Continental Army units.

34. **3** After World War II, the United States created the Marshall Plan in order to help Europe's economic recovery. The Marshall Plan (1948) extended billions of dollars to war-torn Western Europe after the war. It was designed to strengthen the Western democracies so that they would not turn to communism. The Marshall Plan was part of the United States policy of containment. The policy was developed after World War II when the wartime ally of the United States, the Soviet Union, became its rival and the two powers became entangled in an ongoing Cold War. The Cold War lasted from the end of World War II (1945) to the collapse of the Soviet Union (1991). At times, the conflict was nothing more than a rivalry; at other times, the two nations were at the brink of war.

WRONG CHOICES EXPLAINED:

(1) The Alliance for Progress was not designed to help Europe's economic recovery after World War II. The Alliance for Progress was another Cold War–era initiative. It was founded by President John F. Kennedy in 1961 to foster greater economic cooperation between North and South America. It was created in the wake of Cuba becoming a communist nation.

(2) The United States did not send troops to Turkey. In 1947, the United States provided $400 million in military aid to Greece and Turkey to prevent those countries from becoming communist. This action was part of the United States' policy of containment, the Cold War-era policy of preventing the spread of communism.

(4) The decision by the United States to join the North Atlantic Treaty Organization (NATO) was not made to help Europe's economic recovery after World War II. NATO was created in 1949 by the United States and its allies. NATO was part of the Cold War, but it was a military alliance, not an economic development program.

35. **3** Issuing the Truman Doctrine, defending South Korea, and sending military advisors to Vietnam were actions taken by the United States to limit the spread of communism. The idea of limiting the spread of communism, or containing it, was central to United States foreign policy during the Cold War. The Cold War was a period of tensions between the United States and the Soviet Union that lasted from the end of World War II (1945) to the collapse of the Soviet Union (1991). The Truman Doctrine made it clear that the goal of the United States would be to contain communism. Toward this end, President Harry S. Truman extended military aid to Greece and Turkey in 1947 and economic aid to the war ravaged nations of Western Europe, in the form of the Marshall Plan (1948). The United States again acted to limit the spread of communism when it sent troops to South Korea to defend it from North Korea. In June 1950, North Korean troops invaded South Korea, beginning the Korean War. President Truman decided to commit troops to support South Korea, and managed to secure United Nations sponsorship. United Nations forces were led by U.S. General Douglas MacArthur. The United States began sending military advisors to the government of South Vietnam after Vietnam was divided in 1954. The United States feared that South Vietnam would become a communist nation, as North Vietnam had. The United States became heavily involved in the Vietnam War after Congress gave President Johnson a blank check with the Tonkin Gulf Resolution (1964).

WRONG CHOICES EXPLAINED:

(1) The Truman Doctrine and American actions in Korea and Vietnam were not intended to encourage United Nations membership. Most countries of the world eagerly joined the United Nations. The United States made efforts during the Cold War to prevent communist countries from joining the organization. Communist-run China, for example, was barred from United Nations membership until 1971.

(2) The Truman Doctrine and American actions in Korea and Vietnam were not directly intended to promote American business in Asia. Critics of United States policy during the Cold War claimed that United States opposition to communism was driven by a desire to extend American business interests rather than to promote democracy. However, the stated, direct goal of the actions was to limit the spread of communism.

(4) The Truman Doctrine and American actions in Korea and Vietnam were not intended to gain additional overseas colonies. During the Cold War and beyond, the United States has not attempted to gain overseas colonies. The United States has put more effort into promoting friendly governments abroad, and isolating unfriendly ones, than it has in turning foreign countries into American colonies.

36. **1** The president acted as commander-in-chief in response to the refusal of the governor of Arkansas to obey a federal court order to integrate public schools in Little Rock. President Dwight D. Eisenhower sent federal

troops to Little Rock in 1957 to provide protection to the first group of African American students to enter the previously all-white Central High School. Local authorities in Little Rock had decided to allow nine African American students to enter Central High School at the beginning of the school year in 1957. This move was in response to the Supreme Court decision in *Brown* v. *Board of Education of Topeka* (1954), which prohibited segregation in public schools. At first Governor Orval Faubus, hoping to shore up support among anti-segregationist white voters, sent the National Guard to block the African American students from entering the building. This overt flaunting of federal authority troubled President Eisenhower who directly urged the governor to comply with the segregation plan. Governor Faubus withdrew the National Guard but made no provisions for the safety of the nine African American students. The students had to confront an angry mob of white people, with only a contingent of local police to protect them. At that point, President Eisenhower exercised his power as commander-in-chief and sent in federal troops, some of whom remained at the school for the entire school year.

WRONG CHOICES EXPLAINED:

(2) The president did not intervene in the attempts to desegregate the city bus system in Montgomery, Alabama. The Montgomery bus boycott, which lasted about a year (1955–1956), began when Rosa Parks refused to give up her seat to a white person. It ended without violence, with the bus company ending its policy of making African Americans give up their seats to whites. It was during the boycott that Martin Luther King Jr. became nationally known.

(3) The president did not intervene in the civil rights protests in Birmingham, Alabama, nor did he attempt to have Martin Luther King Jr. arrested. Civil rights protests in Birmingham gained national attention in 1963 when the police commissioner of Birmingham, "Bull" Connor, took extreme measures against the civil rights protesters. He had the police shoot fire hoses into a crowd of young people, and he let police dogs loose on nonviolent protestors.

(4) The president did not intervene in the assassination of Medgar Evers. Evers was a prominent civil rights activist who was killed in his driveway in 1963. The suspect in the Evers' murder was tried in state court, twice, without a guilty verdict. Later, in 1994, he was retried and found guilty.

37. **4** Lunch counter sit-ins and the actions of the freedom riders are examples of nonviolent attempts to oppose segregation. Both actions are part of the civil rights movement to challenge racist practices and create a more egalitarian society. The two actions both occurred in the early 1960s, as some members of the movement grew frustrated with simply protesting and pushed the movement to take direct action to challenge and defy racist practices. The lunch counter sit-ins began in 1960 in Greensboro, North

Carolina, when four African American students challenged the "whites only" policy of Woolworth's lunch counter and sat at the counter. The lunch counter sit-ins spread to other cities, including Nashville, Tennessee. They put the practice of segregation of public facilities on the front pages of newspapers and eventually pressured companies to end the practice. Segregation of public facilities became illegal with the passage of the Civil Rights Act (1964). The Freedom Rides occurred in 1961. The previous year, the Supreme Court had ruled that state laws separating the races on interstate transportation facilities were unconstitutional. Still, states maintained Jim Crow codes that separated African American from white passengers. In 1961, the Congress on Racial Equality (CORE) organized a series of bus rides, with African American as well as white passengers, through the South to challenge these local codes. The Freedom Rides met a great deal of resistance in the South. In Alabama, a mob slashed the tires of one bus and then firebombed it. President Kennedy finally sent federal marshals to Alabama to protect the freedom riders and to enforce federal law.

WRONG CHOICES EXPLAINED:

(1) Lunch counter sit-ins and the freedom riders were not part of the movement to support the Americans with Disabilities Act. The Americans with Disabilities Act was passed in 1990 after Americans with disabilities and their allies organized a campaign of awareness and protest, in many ways gaining inspiration from the civil rights movement of the 1950s and 1960s.

(2) Lunch counter sit-ins and the freedom riders were not part of the movement to support programs dealing with affirmative action. The movement for affirmative action occurred after the civil rights movement successfully pushed for an end to legal segregation. In many ways, affirmative action was the next step in the struggle for civil rights. The idea was that employers and colleges would take race into consideration when looking at applicants in an attempt to rectify past discrimination.

(3) Lunch counter sit-ins and the freedom riders were not violent acts by the Black Panthers. The Black Panthers Party was formed in 1966, several years after the two events occurred. The Black Panthers grew out the "Black Power" movement, and embraced self-defense and militant rhetoric. Initially, the Back Panthers focused on community organizing, but their activities grew increasingly confrontational.

38. **3** President John F. Kennedy's Peace Corps and President Lyndon Johnson's Volunteers in Service to America (VISTA) are similar in that both programs were attempts to improve the quality of people's lives. Kennedy created the Peace Corps (1961) in order to give support to developing nations in fields such as education, agriculture, and health care. The program depends on volunteers, often recent college graduates, to work on development projects in poor countries. The Peace Corps reflected a sense of optimism that many saw in the Kennedy administration and in the era of the

1960s. It was also an attempt by the United States, in the midst of a Cold War with the Soviet Union, to shed negative perceptions of its role in foreign countries. The Peace Corps still exists. President Johnson created VISTA in 1964 to be a domestic version of the Peace Corps. The program was part of Johnson's War on Poverty. VISTA volunteers often worked in the field of education and vocational training in poverty-stricken areas. Under President Bill Clinton, VISTA was absorbed into the AmeriCorps program.

WRONG CHOICES EXPLAINED:

(1) The Peace Corps and VISTA were not intended to increase domestic security. The Federal Bureau of Investigation and local law enforcement authorities exist to maintain domestic security.

(2) The Peace Corps and VISTA were not intended to support United States troops fighting overseas. The United Service Organization (USO), a private organization, provides entertainment and recreational activities for United States troops stationed abroad.

(4) The Peace Corps and VISTA were not intended to provide aid to immigrants coming into the United States. A series of organizations and agencies have performed that function. The settlement house movement in the late 1800s and early 1900s provided aid to immigrants.

39. **4** The Supreme Court cases of *Gideon* v. *Wainwright* (1963) and *Miranda* v. *Arizona* dealt with the constitutional principle of rights of the accused. The Bill of Rights lists many rights of the accused, such as the right to a trial by jury and the right to a lawyer, but since its passage (1791), circumstances have arisen which have required clarification by the Supreme Court. The Gideon case dealt with Clarence Earl Gideon, who had been accused of breaking into a poolroom and stealing money from the cash register. The state court rejected his demand for a state-appointed lawyer. After defending himself and being found guilty, he appealed, eventually bringing the case to Supreme Court. In *Gideon* v. *Wainwright*, the Court ruled that the states must provide impoverished defendants with court-appointed attorneys. The *Miranda* v. *Arizona* (1966) decision involved the issue of self-incrimination. The 5th Amendment guarantees that people do not have to testify against themselves. But that right is meaningless if arrested people are not aware of it. People might blurt out incriminating information without knowing about the 5th Amendment. In this decision, the court ruled that when people are arrested, they must be read basic rights, now known as Miranda rights, including the right to remain silent and the right to have a lawyer. These decisions were issued by the Supreme Court under the leadership of Earl Warren (who was chief justice from 1953 to 1969). Conservatives have accused the Warren Court of getting in the way of proper law enforcement and letting criminals go free. Liberals have generally welcomed Warren Court decisions as promoting equal treatment in the legal system for all people, regardless of race or class.

WRONG CHOICES EXPLAINED:

(1) The two cases did not deal with the constitutional principle of free-dom of religion. Numerous Supreme Court decisions have attempted to clar-ify the limits of religious freedom, especially when certain religious practices might involve activities that are illegal or that might infringe on other people's rights. In the case of *West Virginia State Board of Education* v. *Barnette*, for instance, the Supreme Court ruled that it was unconstitutional to compel students to recite the Pledge of Allegiance because reciting it violated the religious freedom of Jehovah's Witnesses, who are not allowed to pledge allegiance to anyone or anything other than God.

(2) The two cases do not deal with the constitutional principle of freedom from unreasonable search and seizure. The 4th Amendment allows for searches if law enforcement authorities first obtain a search warrant. The Supreme Court has issued several decisions that have attempted to clarify this right to privacy, especially if it runs counter to the ability of law enforce-ment authorities to carry out their responsibilities.

(3) The two cases do not deal with the constitutional principle of separa-tion of powers. This principle deals with maintaining a balance of power among the three braches of government—the executive, the legislative, and the judiciary. The Supreme Court has issued several decisions limiting the powers of one of the three branches of government if it finds that one branch is infringing on the power of another branch. In *Schecter* v. *United States* (1935), for instance, the Court shot down the National Industrial Recovery Act (NIRA) on the grounds that the president had assumed legislative powers in creating NIRA regulations.

40. **1** The cartoonist is commenting on the Cold War policy of *détente*. The cartoon depicts the United States (the eagle) and the Soviet Union (the bear) proudly pushing their newborn child—peace (a dove with an olive branch in its mouth). The title of the cartoon, "The Odd Couple," implies that this development was unexpected. *Détente* is the French word for loos-ening and refers to an easing of tensions in the Cold War and a warming of relations between the United States and the Soviet Union. The policy was carried out by President Nixon. In 1972 Nixon became the first United States president to visit Communist China and later that year he held meetings with Soviet leaders in Moscow. It may seem especially odd that Richard Nixon, a man who made a name for himself as a strong anti-communist, was responsi-ble for the détente policy. But Nixon's anti-communist credentials enabled him to open relations with communist nations without being accused of being "soft on communism."

WRONG CHOICES EXPLAINED:

(2) The cartoonist is not commenting on the foreign policy of brinksman-ship. Brinksmanship refers to pushing a conflict to the verge of disaster. The goal is for one side to show the other that it means business and will not back

down from a conflict. The policy is associated with President Eisenhower's Secretary of State John Foster Dulles.

(3) The cartoonist is not commenting on the foreign policy of the domino theory. The domino theory is closely associated with American military involvement in Vietnam. The domino theory asserts that when a nation becomes communist, its neighbors will be more likely to become communist.

(4) The cartoonist is not commenting on the foreign policy of collective security. For most of its history, the United States avoided the alliances and treaty organizations that would constitute collective security. This changed in 1949 when the United States participated in the formation of the North Atlantic Treaty Organization (NATO).

41. **4** The warming of relations between the Soviet Union and the United States, known by the French word *détente*, that is depicted in the cartoon resulted in the negotiation of the Strategic Arms Limitation Treaty (SALT). Many Americans had become increasingly fearful of the massive nuclear arsenals that both the United States and the Soviet Union had developed. These weapons programs were also a drain on the resources of both countries. Starting in 1969, negotiations between the two nations began to limit future weapons production. The United States and the Soviet Union signed SALT in 1972. This treaty called for a slight curb in production of nuclear weapons.

WRONG CHOICES EXPLAINED:

(1) The warming of relations between the Soviet Union and the United States in the early 1970s did not result in the issuance of the Eisenhower Doctrine. In 1957 President Eisenhower made clear that the United States would provide economic and military aid to any Middle Eastern nation resisting communist aggression. The Eisenhower Doctrine asserted United States resolve to challenge aggression, not a move toward peaceful coexistence.

(2) The warming of relations between the Soviet Union and the United States in the early 1970s did not result in the quarantine of Cuba. The United States did block shipping into Cuba when, in 1962, a U-2 spy plane discovered that Cuba was preparing bases for Soviet nuclear missiles to be installed. President Kennedy felt that these missiles, in such close proximity to the United States, amounted to an unacceptable provocation and ordered the project stopped. For about a week, the world stood on the brink of nuclear war. Finally a deal was reached in which the Soviet Union would abandon its Cuban missile program and the United States would quietly remove missiles from Turkey.

(3) The warming of relations between the Soviet Union and the United States in the early 1970s did not result in American support for Israel in the Six Day War. The Six Day War occurred in 1967 between Israel and the neighboring states of Egypt, Syria, and Jordan. The United States did support Israel in this conflict; the Soviet Union supported the Arab side.

42. **2** President Reagan's supply-side economic policy was successful in lowering tax rates on personal and business income. Reagan's set of supply-side economic policy initiatives bears the name "Reaganomics." This approach to the economy stressed stimulating the supply side of the economy—manufacturing firms, banks, insurance corporations. The idea is that if there is growth in the supply side, there will be general economic growth, and the benefits of that growth will reach everyone. The alternative approach is to stimulate the demand side—consumers. Demand-side economics would emphasize government policies designed to increase workers' wages and expand social programs such as welfare and unemployment benefits. As a believer in supply-side economics, Reagan implemented policies that he thought would stimulate business. Reagan cut taxes for corporations and greatly reduced regulations on industry. Reagan's pro-business economic policies had mixed results. By cutting corporate taxes and taxes on wealthy individuals, he cut government revenues. But, at the same time, he increased spending on armaments. This combination of increased spending and decreased revenues led to a doubling of the national debt from around $900 billion in 1980 to over $2 trillion in 1986.

WRONG CHOICES EXPLAINED:

(1) President Reagan's supply-side economic policies did not involve increasing government spending on social programs. Reagan cut spending on social programs. Supporters of demand-side economics, like President Franklin D. Roosevelt, increased spending on social programs.

(3) President Reagan's supply-side economic policies did not involve reducing defense spending. Reagan pursued an aggressive foreign policy in regard to the Soviet Union. This entailed increasing defense spending.

(4) President Reagan's supply-side economic policies did not involve enforcing stricter environmental regulations. Reagan believed that government regulations stymied economic growth. He eliminated many environmental regulations.

43. **2** The rapid westward migration caused by the discovery of gold in California led directly to the adoption of the Compromise of 1850. The Gold Rush began when gold was discovered at Sutter's Mill in California in 1848. Earlier that year, California became a United States territory as a result of the Mexican War. As word spread, thousands of people came to California to try to strike it rich. A large percentage of the 300,000 people who migrated to California came in 1849, thus their nickname, "forty-niners." By 1850, California had enough people to form a state. Californians wrote up a constitution to submit to Congress in which slavery would be illegal. Southern senators objected to the admission of an additional free state. Senate negotiators worked out a series of measures that became known as the Compromise of 1850. The most important elements of the compromise were the admittance of California as a free state, which pleased Northern politicians, and a more stringent Fugitive Slave Law, which pleased Southern politicians.

WRONG CHOICES EXPLAINED:

(1) The California Gold Rush did not directly lead to the Civil War. Over a decade passed between the discovery of gold in California (1848) and the beginning of the Civil War (1861). The controversy sparked by California's application for statehood subsided after 1850. It was new issues related to slavery that led to the political divisions that immediately preceded the Civil War.

(3) The California Gold Rush did not directly lead to increased trade through the Panama Canal. The Panama Canal did not open until 1914, 75 years after the discovery of gold in California. The two events are too far apart chronologically to assert a direct causal link.

(4) The California Gold Rush did not lead to control of the United States Senate by the slave states. The admission of California had the opposite effect; it provided the free states with two additional senators.

44. **4** The statement is part of Woodrow Wilson's response to unrestricted submarine warfare. Wilson is addressing Congress, asking it to declare war against Germany. Congress supported Wilson's request and issued a declaration of war in 1917. When World War I began in 1914, Wilson initially assumed that the United States could stay neutral and maintain commercial ties with nations on both sides of the conflict. But quickly Great Britain successfully blocked American ships from reaching Germany. Out of necessity, United States trade shifted to Great Britain exclusively. Germany responded by warning that American ships in the waters off of Great Britain would be subject to attack by U-boats, or submarines. The sinking of the British ocean liner *Lusitania* infuriated many Americans (128 Americans were among the dead). Germany, however, wanted to keep the United States out of the war and agreed in the Sussex Pledge (1916) to make no surprise submarine attacks on American ships. The United States took advantage of this pledge and traded extensively with Great Britain. In 1917, Germany rescinded the Sussex Pledge and declared that it would resume unrestricted submarine warfare; soon after, the United States declared war on Germany.

WRONG CHOICES EXPLAINED:

(1) William McKinley's request for war in 1898 is not the focus of the statement in the question. The statement declares Germany to be the enemy. In 1898, the United States went to war with Spain.

(2) Theodore Roosevelt's support for the Panamanian revolt in 1903 is not the focus of the statement in the question. The statement declares Germany to be the enemy. The Panamanian revolt, which the United States did support, was against the government of Colombia.

(3) William Howard Taft's decision to send troops to Latin America in 1912 is not the focus of the statement in the question. The statement declares Germany to be the enemy. In 1912, Taft sent troops to Nicaragua to prop up the conservative president Adolfo Diaz.

45. **3** The table indicates that the majority of presidential vetoes between 1961 and 1993 were upheld. The Constitution gives presidents the power to veto, or reject, legislation they find objectionable. The president vetoes a bill by returning it to Congress within ten days of having received it. The president must also submit in writing his or her objections to the bill. If the president simply does not sign the bill within those ten days, it becomes law. However, a situation might occur in which the president does not sign a bill, but Congress adjourns before the ten-day period is up. In such a scenario, the bill does not become law. In that scenario, the president has carried out a pocket veto (in effect, he has put the bill in his pocket, rather than returning it to Congress). In either case—a regular veto or a pocket veto—Congress has the power to override the veto with a two-thirds majority vote in both houses. In the case of a congressional override, the bill becomes law without the president's signature. The table indicates that very few presidential vetoes have been overridden by Congress. None of President John F. Kennedy's or Lyndon Johnson's vetoes were overridden. President Gerald Ford had the largest number of his vetoes overridden (12). Even in his case, that amounts to only 18% of his vetoes being overridden.

WRONG CHOICES EXPLAINED:
(1) Between 1961 and 1993, Congress was not usually able to override presidential vetoes. Only 11% of presidential vetoes were overridden.
(2) Between 1961 and 1993, pocket vetoes were not used more than regular vetoes. Five of the presidents listed in the table used regular vetoes more than pocket vetoes. One, President Ronald Reagan, used the same number of regular and pocket vetoes. Only President Jimmy Carter used more pocket vetoes than regular vetoes.
(4) Between 1961 and 1993, the use of the veto did not increase steadily. The use of the veto varied considerably with each president. There is not a notable trend evident in the table.

46. **2** The data in the table illustrate the operation of checks and balances. Both the presidential veto and the congressional override illustrate the concept of checks and balances. Each of the three branches has the ability to check the powers of the other two. The goal was to keep the three branches in balance. The framers of the Constitution were very conscious of the problems of a government with limitless powers. After living under the British monarchy, they came to believe that a powerful government without checks was dangerous to liberty. Therefore, they created a governmental system with three branches, each with the ability to check the powers of the other two. The goal was to keep the three branches in balance. Additional examples of the concept of checks and balances are the Supreme Court's ability to strike down laws that it deems unconstitutional and the Senate's power to approve or reject presidential nominees for Supreme Court justices and ambassadors, as well as its power to reject or approve treaties.

WRONG CHOICES EXPLAINED:

(1) The data in the table do not illustrate the operation of executive privilege. Executive privilege is the power claimed by the president and other members of the executive branch to resist certain search warrants and other steps that might be taken by the legislative and judicial branches.

(3) The data in the table do not illustrate the operation of congressional immunity. Congressional immunity is the right of members of Congress to be free from arrest by the executive branch, except in extreme cases. The idea is to prevent the president from arresting members of the legislature in order to prevent them from voting on a particular item.

(4) The data in the table do not illustrate the operation of federal supremacy. Federal supremacy is contained in the supremacy clause of the Constitution, which states that the Constitution and federal laws and treaties are the "supreme law of the land."

47. **1** The Pacific [Transcontinental] Railroad Act (1862) and the Interstate Highway Act (1956) are both examples of federally supported internal improvement projects linking the nation. The completion of the transcontinental railroad at Promontory Summit, Utah, in 1862 was a milestone in the development of a network of railroad lines that connected the far reaches of the country. Railroads sped up the movement of goods and expanded markets. The government encouraged this expansion of the railroad network by giving railroad companies wide swaths of land. These generous land grants totaled more than 180 million acres, an area equal to the size of Texas. The railroad companies built rail lines on this land and also sold land adjacent to the tracks. Nearly a century later, automobiles and trucks replaced railroads for much of the nation's transportation needs. The federal government hastened this development with the Interstate Highway Act (1956). The act initiated the biggest public works project in United States history, a nationwide network of superhighways. The federal government paid 90% of the costs of construction, with the states paying the other 10%. Between 1956 and 1966, the federal government spent $25 billion to build 40,000 miles of highways. Initiated during the Cold War, the government also saw the act as a defense measure. The highways would allow for quick movement of troops and heavy military equipment.

WRONG CHOICES EXPLAINED:

(2) The Pacific [Transcontinental] Railroad Act and the Interstate Highway Act are not examples of regional construction projects coordinated by southern and western states. Both were federal initiatives that affected the entire nation.

(3) The Pacific [Transcontinental] Railroad Act and the Interstate Highway Act are not examples of military projects required to meet the needs of the defense industry. Proponents of the Interstate Highway Act, passed during the Cold War, emphasized the role interstate highways could

play in the movement of troops and military equipment. But both initiatives were primarily transportation projects, not military projects.

(4) The Pacific [Transcontinental] Railroad Act and the Interstate Highway Act are not examples of transportation legislation designed to encourage foreign trade. Both projects facilitated trade within the United States, not with foreign nations.

48. **3** Mark Twain, Langston Hughes, and John Steinbeck made their most important contributions to the United States in the field of literature. Mark Twain was one of the most popular writers in American history and is considered one of the best. He wrote from the 1860s to the 1900s. His most famous novels, *The Adventures of Tom Sawyer* (1876) and *The Adventures of Huckleberry Finn* (1884) captured the rhythms and customs of the Mississippi River region. Twain was a scathing critic of American society. *The Adventures of Huckleberry Finn* is, in many ways, an attack on the prevailing racist attitudes of the day. Huck comes to see the humanity he shares with the escaped slave, Jim. Langston Hughes was an influential poet whose career lasted from the 1920s to the 1960s. He was part of the Harlem Renaissance, a cultural movement that grew out of the African American community in the 1920s. Hughes's most well-known poems include "The Negro Speaks of Rivers," (1921), "I, Too" (1926), and "Harlem" (1951). John Steinbeck was a major novelist who chronicled the lives of working people and the downtrodden. His most well-known novel, *The Grapes of Wrath* (1939), chronicled the plight of Dust Bowl refugees.

WRONG CHOICES EXPLAINED:

(1) (2) and (4) Mark Twain, Langston Hughes, and John Steinbeck all made their most important contributions in the field of literature, not music, politics, or business.

49. **2** The New Deal, the Fair Deal, and the Great Society are similar in that these programs increased government commitment to the well-being of the people. The New Deal was the set of programs proposed by the administration of President Franklin D. Roosevelt (1933–1945) to address the poverty and dislocation of the Great Depression of the 1930s. Roosevelt's initiatives were unprecedented in their scope and direction. The Roosevelt administration provided direct relief, or what would be known as welfare today, to millions of families. In addition, the New Deal included jobs programs such as Civilian Conservation Corps (1933), which focused on young men, and the vast Works Progress Administration (1935), which consisted of a myriad of public projects. The WPA built schools, installed sewer lines, wrote guidebooks, and produced theatrical productions. Also, the New Deal addressed the welfare of retired people and people with disabilities by creating the Social Security system in 1935. The Fair Deal was the set of programs created by the administration of President

Harry S. Truman (1945–1953). In many ways, the Fair Deal continued the direction of the New Deal in using the power of the government to ensure the well-being of the people. Truman faced greater opposition than Roosevelt in implementing sweeping change. Truman failed to implement universal health care, but he did get the Housing Act of 1949 passed and was able to desegregate the armed forces. President Lyndon Johnson was more success-ful than Truman on many fronts. His Great Society agenda, also known as the War on Poverty, refers to a series of domestic programs that Johnson pushed through Congress in 1964 and 1965. Great Society programs include the development of Medicare to provide health insurance for the elderly and Medicaid to provide health insurance for welfare recipients. Johnson sought to improve education for poor students with the Head Start program, which created preschool programs, and the Elementary and Secondary Education Act. Other initiatives included creating welfare programs, expanding civil rights for African Americans, and building public housing projects. The programs had mixed results. Medicare and Medicaid have proved to be highly successful, but the cycle of poverty proved to be too difficult to break in a short period of time. In addition, the Vietnam War became increasingly costly, diverting billions of dollars that could have been used for anti-poverty programs.

WRONG CHOICES EXPLAINED:
(1) The New Deal, the Fair Deal, and the Great Society did not promote the idea of "rugged individualism." President Herbert Hoover (1929–1933) encouraged people affected by the Great Depression to rely on their "rugged individualism," believing that direct relief would make people dependent on the government.
(3) The New Deal, the Fair Deal, and the Great Society did not reduce the amount of money spent on domestic programs. The programs in all three of the agendas involved an increase in amount of money spent on domestic programs.
(4) The New Deal, the Fair Deal, and the Great Society did not encour-age the states to take a more active role in national defense. The three agen-das consisted of federal, not state, programs, and they were designed to improve the well-being of the people, not bolster national defense.

50. **3** Data from the graphs most clearly support the conclusion that by the mid-1990s, American women as a group had gained more opportunities in professional areas. Between 1972 and 1994, the percentage of law degrees awarded to women rose from less than 10% to over 40%. As of 1994, men still received more of the law degrees awarded (nearly 60%) than women, but the four-fold leap for women in a little over two decades is astounding. A law degree opens doors in the legal profession, as well as in politics and business. In regard to women-owned businesses, the jump from 1972 to 1994 was also astounding. In 1972, there were less than half a million women-owned busi-

nesses. In 1997, that figure had jumped to approximately 8 million. The increased opportunities for women in professional areas can be seen as a success of the women's liberation movement of the 1960s and 1970s. The women's liberation movement challenged the notion that the only measure of success for women is getting married and becoming a stay-at-home mother. The movement encouraged society, and women themselves, to imagine a variety of options open to women—including fulfilling professional careers.

WRONG CHOICES EXPLAINED:

(1) The data from the graphs does not support the conclusion that by the mid-1990s American women as a group surpassed men in the number of businesses owned and law degrees received. The graph on the right only notes the number of women-owned businesses. It does not indicate the number of male-owned businesses or the total number of businesses in the United States. It is, therefore, impossible to ascertain whether women owned more businesses than men. The graph on the left indicates that by 1994, women received about 40% of law degrees. Men still received more—approximately 60%.

(2) The data from the graphs does not support the conclusion that by the mid-1990s American women as a group had given up marriage in favor of careers outside the home. Neither graph indicates marriage rates. It would be an incorrect presumption to assert that women can only become successful professionals if they forego marriage.

(4) The data from the graphs does not support the conclusion that by the mid-1990s American women as a group earned more than men in the legal profession. Neither chart indicates incomes.

PART II: THEMATIC ESSAY
Government—Supreme Court Decisions

Several Supreme Court decisions have had a major impact on different aspects of American society. To some degree, Supreme Court decisions are made with a great deal of independence and objectivity. After all, once Supreme Court justices are confirmed, they hold their position for life; they do not need to worry about losing an election. But to some degree, Supreme Court decisions are deeply embedded in contemporary society. The justices do not develop their ideas and values in isolation. They often share the convictions, the prejudices, the hopes, and the fears of their fellow citizens. These pivotal court decisions have all had their detractors and their defenders, but their impact on American society is undeniable.

An important 19th-century Supreme Court decision was issued in the case of *Dred Scott* v. *Sanford* (1857). The case intensified the rift between pro-slavery and anti-slavery Americans and, in many ways, pushed the nation a bit closer to Civil War. The case involved the fate of a slave named Dred Scott. Scott was owned by a doctor serving in the United States army. Scott and his wife, along with their owner, lived for a time in the state of Illinois and in the Wisconsin Territories, areas in which slavery had been banned by the Northwest Ordinance. Years after returning to Missouri, Scott sued for his and his wife's freedom on the grounds that they had lived for a time in free areas, and that made them free. The Supreme Court did not find Dred Scott's arguments persuasive.

First, the court ruled that Scott was still a slave and did not even have the right to initiate a lawsuit. That could have been the end of the decision. But the court went further. In regard to the issue of free territories, the Supreme Court ruled that Congress had overstepped its bounds in declaring the northern portion of the Louisiana Purchase territory off limits to slavery. It therefore invalidated the Missouri Compromise of 1820.

The Court went even further than that. Not only did Dred Scott not have standing to file suit, the Court declared that no African Americans, not even free men and women, were entitled to citizenship in the United States because they were, according to the Court, "beings of an inferior order."

The impact of the case on sectional relations cannot be overstated. Of course, the decision was welcomed by pro-slavery forces in the South. But it shocked many Northerners. By ruling that Congress could not ban slavery in the territories, the Court dealt a blow to those who sought to use the power of the federal government to prevent the spread of slavery into America's new territories. It infuriated abolitionists who were working for an end to slavery altogether. In addition, it alarmed many moderate Northerners who were hoping that the two sections could deal with their differences with compromise and negotiation. By invalidating the Missouri Compromise, the Court cast future negotiations between the regions in doubt. The case pushed more and more Northerners into the ranks of the new Republican Party. As a party avowedly against the spread of slavery in the country, the Republicans grew as an entirely regional party. At the same time, the Democratic Party closed ranks around a more expressly pro-slavery position, lauding the reasoning behind the Dred Scott decision. It, too, became, essentially a regional party. As the major parties became regional in nature, they hardened their positions, not needing to appeal to voters throughout the nation. In 1860, the Republican Party won the presidency, leading to Southern secession and then to Civil War.

A second decision that had a major impact on American society is the decision in the case of *Brown* v. *Board of Education of Topeka*. This 1954 decision concerned segregated schools. After the Civil War, a rigid Jim Crow system in the Southern states of the United States created separate facilities for African Americans and white people. These included separate waiting rooms at train stations, separate drinking fountains, and separate schools. In many cases, African Americans were simply barred from certain public facilities. This Jim Crow system was challenged in the Supreme Court case, *Plessy* v. *Ferguson* (1896), but the Supreme Court ruled that separate facilities were allowable, as long as the facilities for both races were of equal quality. Even though the facilities for African Americans were routinely of inferior quality, this "separate but equal" doctrine was the law of the land until the middle of the 20th century.

After World War II, African Americans began challenging the Jim Crow system of segregation. Many African Americans felt a sense of empowerment after having served in the armed forces during World War II and were ready to fight for democracy at home. These early activists pushed civil rights onto the national agenda. President Harry Truman was somewhat receptive to their call for greater equality in the United States. Truman and other political leaders also found it difficult to defend the Jim Crow system during the height of the Cold War. After all, the United States consistently criticized the Soviet Union for denying basic freedoms to the Soviet people; it seemed hypocritical when the United States denied basic rights to many of its own people.

In this context, the Supreme Court heard the case of *Brown* v. *Board of Education* in 1954. The lead lawyer for the plaintiffs, Thurgood Marshall, who worked with the National Association for the Advancement of Colored People, argued that segregated schools were inherently unfair and stigmatized young African American children. The Court unanimously agreed with Marshall. Schools districts across America had to take steps to end segregation, to abolish "whites only" schools, and to create a new integrated education system.

In many towns and cities in the South, officials quietly began to dismantle segregated schools. But, in Little Rock, Arkansas, the process did not proceed smoothly. The local school board made plans to desegregate Central High School in 1957 by admitting nine African American students. This modest plan was about to go into effect, but on the evening before school was to start, the governor of Arkansas, Orval Faubus, announced that he was sending the National Guard to Central High School to keep it a "whites only" school. These guardsmen were ordered to circle the school and only admit white students. With encouragement from the governor, many white residents of Little Rock and the surrounding area took up the cause of keeping Central High School segregated. The news from Little Rock shocked many Americans and troubled President Eisenhower. At first, Eisenhower met quietly with Governor Faubus and requested that the governor end the standoff and allow the African American students to attend Central High School. Faubus did call off the National Guard, but that left no one to protect the African American students from the white mob. Local police were not able to maintain order. At this point Eisenhower took definitive action. He sent United States troops to protect the students. These troops were ordered to usher the students into the building and to guarantee their safety as they went from class to class.

The Supreme Court, with the backing of the president and the enforcement power of the army, helped usher in a new era in education and, ultimately, a new era in American society. The Court's decision in *Brown* v. *Board of Education* in the 1950s and its decision in *Dred Scott* v. *Sanford*, a century earlier, both demonstrate the profound impact the Supreme Court can have on American society.

PART III: DOCUMENT-BASED QUESTION

Part A: Short Answer

DOCUMENT 1

I. According to Thomas P. Slaughter, one problem that resulted from the collection of the federal excise tax in western Pennsylvania is that 700 men took up arms to rebel against the tax.

This answer receives full credit because it states one problem that resulted from the collection of the federal excise tax in western Pennsylvania.

DOCUMENT 2A AND DOCUMENT 2B

2a. According to Alexander Hamilton, President George Washington is ordering the militia to suppress the Whiskey Rebellion.

This answer receives full credit because it states one action President George Washington ordered in response to the Whiskey Rebellion.

2b. One reason President Washington ordered the suppression of the Whiskey Rebellion is that he wanted to ensure that the laws of the land, in this case the excise tax, were properly executed.

This answer receives full credit because it states one reason that President George Washington gave the order to suppress the Whiskey Rebellion.

DOCUMENT 3

3. According to Richard H. Kohn, the Whiskey Rebellion was significant because it demonstrated the resolve of the federal government to put down organized and violent resistance to the laws.

This answer receives full credit because it states the significance of the Whiskey Rebellion.

DOCUMENT 4

4. Based on the information on the map, one problem the United States faced under President Abraham Lincoln is that many states in the South seceded from the United States.

This answer receives full credit because it states one problem the United States faced under President Abraham Lincoln.

DOCUMENT 5

5. According to the proclamation, one action President Abraham Lincoln took to enforce the laws of the United States was to call forth 75,000 men to serve in state militias to suppress the secession of several Southern states.

This answer receives full credit because it states one action President Abraham Lincoln took to enforce the laws of the United States.

DOCUMENT 6

6. According to William McKinley, one impact of President Abraham Lincoln's actions on the United States was that he ended slavery and demonstrated that all races are entitled to the same rights and protections.

This answer receives full credit because it states one impact of President Abraham Lincoln's actions on the United States.

DOCUMENT 7

7. According to the interview with coal miner Aaron Barkham, one problem faced by mine workers during the Great Depression was that many coal mines shut down.

This answer receives full credit because it states one problem faced by mine workers during the Great Depression.

DOCUMENT 8A AND DOCUMENT 8B

8a. According to President Franklin D. Roosevelt, one action needed to safeguard the life of the nation was to provide relief to poor people so they would not starve.

This answer receives full credit because it states one action needed to safeguard the life of the nation.

8b. According to the document, one step taken by President Franklin D. Roosevelt to solve the problems of the Great Depression was to create new programs.

This answer receives full credit because it states one step taken by President Franklin D. Roosevelt to solve the problems of the Great Depression.

DOCUMENT 9

9 (1). According to the document, one effect of President Franklin D. Roosevelt's New Deal policies on the nation was the creation of lasting programs such as Social Security and insurance for bank deposits.

9 (2). According to the document, another effect of President Franklin D. Roosevelt's New Deal policies was the restoration of confidence and hope among the people.

These answers receive full credit because they state two effects of President Franklin D. Roosevelt's New Deal policies on the nation.

Part B: Document-Based Essay

The few presidents who have been consistently categorized as "great presidents" by historians have earned that label because they have successfully addressed critical challenges that have confronted the nation. Abraham Lincoln and Franklin D. Roosevelt both faced serious crises and both dealt with them successfully. Lincoln faced secession and Civil War and Roosevelt faced the Great Depression. Both of these presidents showed resolve and wisdom in guiding the nation through these crises, earning the designation "great president."

Abraham Lincoln faced the most daunting challenge in the nation's history. In 1860, Lincoln, under the banner of the new Republican Party, won the presidency. The Republican Party was critical of slavery. While Lincoln vowed that he would not attempt to challenge slavery where it already existed, he stated that he was opposed to the expansion of slavery into the new territories out west. Lincoln's electoral victory alarmed many defenders of slavery from the South, to the point that leading political figures in the South were ready to secede. Even before Lincoln was inaugurated, seven Southern states seceded. After Lincoln's inauguration and the first shots of the Civil War at Fort Sumter, an additional four upper-south states seceded. (Document 4)

Lincoln reacted to this situation with resolve. In April 1961, he issued a proclamation calling up 75,000 troops to "cause the laws to be duly executed." (Document 5) Soon, the United States and the seceded

Southern states, calling themselves the Confederate States of America, were at war. The war lasted almost exactly four years, from April 1861 to April 1864. Lincoln's greatness is evident in his leadership during this bloody conflict. Lincoln made a series of decisions that proved to be timely and wise. He fired several generals to lead the army before settling on Ulysses S. Grant. But perhaps Lincoln's greatest wartime achievement was playing a key role in the liberation of the slaves. Lincoln did not achieve this historic goal on his own—abolitionists, Radical Republicans, and, of course, the slaves themselves all pushed the envelope and put the issue of liberation on the wartime agenda. But Lincoln was able to usher in this historic event while guiding the country through a wrenching war. He issued the Emancipation Proclamation without pushing the border states into the rebel camp. He was able to convince a reluctant country that ending slavery was consistent with the most basic American rights.

The most serious economic crisis faced by the United States was the Great Depression of the 1930s. This crisis tested the leadership of President Franklin D. Roosevelt. The crisis began before Roosevelt's election. In October 1929, the stock market crashed, devastating many people's investments. The stock market crash was the most visible and dramatic cause of the Great Depression. Other causes can be seen in economic trends of the 1920s. The gap between the rich and the poor widened. Wages for industrial workers stagnated as the decade dragged on. This trend was damaging to the economy because the masses of

Americans simply could not afford the bounty of products that mass production was making available. Producers took the only logical step when they saw their inventories growing—they laid off workers. Factory workers, miners, and store clerks were all affected by these layoffs. (Document 7) Matters were even worse for farmers. Throughout the 1920s mechanization of farming increased production, but it also pushed down commodity prices. Farmers were not getting a high enough price for a bushel of corn to make ends meet. Finally, the banking sector was in crisis. Depositors panicked upon hearing rumors of bank collapses. They ran to the bank and withdrew all their money. The rumors became self-fulfilling prophecies.

After three years of depression, voters abandoned the Republican leadership of President Herbert Hoover and embraced the reassuring Democratic candidate, Franklin D. Roosevelt. Hoover stubbornly held onto an ideology that saw government aid to the poor, or "relief" as it was called, as wrong. He encouraged people to rely on "rugged individualism," not government relief programs. Roosevelt on the other hand, saw government relief programs as a "human ideal." (Document 8a) He was ready to experiment with different approaches to the problems of poverty, hunger, and unemployment. He wanted relief to be accompanied by useful work, but he would not remain idle while Americans starved. (Document 8b)

Upon inauguration in 1933, Roosevelt went on an unprecedented flurry of activity. He created a series of programs to address the problems associated with the Great Depression. These programs were known as the New Deal. The Roosevelt administration created relief programs that aided millions of families. In addition, the New Deal included several public works programs. The Civilian Conservation Corps focused on young men, and the Works Progress Administration created hundreds of public projects. The WPA built schools, installed sewer lines, wrote guidebooks, and produced theatrical productions. Also, the New Deal addressed the welfare of retired people and people with disabilities by creating the Social Security system in 1935. While this array of programs did not end the Great Depression, Roosevelt was able to convey to the American people that the government was on their side. The New Deal and Roosevelt's assuring tone lessened the fears of many Americans during the Great Depression. (Document 9)

Both Lincoln and Roosevelt were able to guide the nation through difficult times. They were excellent leaders, demonstrating resolve and wisdom in the face of crises. For this reason they usually head the list of great American presidents.

Topic	Question Numbers	*Number of Points
American political history	3, 8, 11, 14, 15, 16, 21, 30, 38, 43, 45, 47, 49	16
Political theory	2	1
Economic theory/policy	26, 28, 29, 42	5
Constitutional principles	4, 5, 6, 7, 9, 10, 39, 44, 46	11
American foreign policy	19, 20, 24, 32, 34, 35, 40, 41	10
American studies—the American people	12, 13, 18, 25, 31, 33, 36, 37, 50	11
Social/cultural developments	17, 22, 23, 27, 48	6
Geography	1	1
Skills questions included in the above content area		
Reading comprehension	13, 15, 16, 17, 22, 23, 44	
Graph /table interpretation	45, 46, 50	
Cartoon/photo interpretation	30, 40, 41	
Chronological sequencing	32	

*Note: The 50 questions in Part I are worth a total of 60 percent of the exam. Since each correct answer is worth 60/50 or 1.2 points, totals are shown to the nearest full point in each content category.

Part I
Multiple-Choice Questions by Standard

Standard	Question Numbers
1—US and NY History	2, 3, 10, 11, 12, 13, 14, 17, 20, 21, 22, 25, 27, 30, 32, 37, 38, 43, 44, 48
2—World History	34, 35, 40, 41
3—Geography	1, 18, 31, 47
4—Economics	8, 15, 16, 19, 23, 26, 28, 29, 33, 42, 49, 50
5—Civics, Citizenship and Government	4, 5, 6, 7, 9, 24, 36, 39, 45, 46

Parts II and III by Theme and Standard

	Theme	Standards
Thematic Essay	Supreme Court Decisions: Citizenship; Constitutional Principles; Civic Values	Standards 1 and 5: US and NY History; Civics, Citizenship, and Government
Document-based Essay	Presidential Decisions and Actions; Constitutional Principles; Government; Change	Standards 1, 3, 4, and 5: US and NY History; Geography; Economics; Civics, Citizenship, and Government

Examination June 2010

United States History and Government

PART I: MULTIPLE CHOICE

Directions (1–50): For each statement or question, write in the space provided the *number* of the word or expression that, of those given, best completes the statement or answers the question.

Base your answer to question 1 on the map below and on your knowledge of social studies.

Source: Education Place: http://www.eduplace.com,
Houghton Mifflin Co., 2002 (adapted)

1 This map shows the western limit on colonial settlement that resulted from the

    1 founding of Jamestown
    2 Proclamation of 1763
    3 Monroe Doctrine
    4 Compromise of 1850   1____

_____

2 Climatic conditions in the southern colonies most directly influenced the development of

    1 democratic institutions
    2 a canal system
    3 the plantation system
    4 the coal industry   2____

3 Which heading best completes the partial outline below?

> I. _____
>
>   A. Magna Carta
>   B. House of Burgesses
>   C. Town meetings
>   D. John Locke

    1 Ideas of Social Darwinism
    2 Basis of British Mercantilism
    3 Contribution to American Literature
    4 Influences on United States Constitutional
      Government   3____

4 The main reason the Articles of Confederation were replaced as the basis of the United States government was that they

1 lacked provision for a national congress
2 declared that political protests were unconstitutional
3 placed too many restrictions on the activities of state governments
4 failed to give the central government enough power to govern effectively   4 ___

Base your answers to questions 5 and 6 on the passage below and on your knowledge of social studies.

We the people of the United States, in order to form a more perfect union, establish justice, insure domestic tranquility, provide for the common defense, promote the general welfare, and secure the blessings of liberty to ourselves and our posterity, do ordain and establish this Constitution for the United States of America.

—Preamble to the United States Constitution

5 In this passage, the authors are stating that

1 both men and women should have equal voting rights
2 state governments created the United States government
3 sovereignty belongs to the people of the nation
4 people obtain their rights from their monarch   5 ___

6 Which two groups debated the ratification of the new Constitution?

  1 loyalists and revolutionaries
  2 Federalists and Antifederalists
  3 Democratic Party and Whig Party
  4 executive branch and judicial branch   6____

7 Which heading best completes the partial outline below?

> I. _____
>   A. National nominating conventions
>   B. Political parties
>   C. Congressional committees

  1 Articles of Confederation
  2 Constitutional Compromises
  3 Jeffersonian Democracy
  4 Unwritten Constitution   7____

8 The amendment process was included in the Constitution to
  1 allow for change over time
  2 expand the powers of the president
  3 increase citizen participation in government
  4 limit the authority of the United States Supreme Court   8____

9 Which situation best illustrates the practice of lobbying?

1 Congress decides to reduce the number of military bases in California.
2 The federal government cancels a defense contract with a company in New York State.
3 A senator from Pennsylvania and a senator from New Jersey agree to support each other's bill in Congress.
4 Several environmental groups try to persuade members of Congress to vote for the Clean Air Act.

9 ____

10 A major purpose of the president's cabinet is to

1 offer advice on important issues
2 nominate ambassadors
3 conduct impeachment trials
4 regulate the amount of money in circulation

10 ____

11 The Louisiana Purchase (1803) was a foreign policy success for the United States primarily because it

1 secured full control of Florida from Spain
2 ended French control of the Mississippi River
3 ended British occupation of forts on American soil
4 eliminated Russian influence in North America

11 ____

12 Under Chief Justice John Marshall, the Supreme Court strengthened its authority by

  1 applying judicial review to state and national laws
  2 changing the operation of the electoral college
  3 increasing the number of Justices on the Court
  4 expanding the freedoms included in the first amendment

12 ____

13 Which action is most closely associated with the term *Manifest Destiny*?

  1 declaring independence from Great Britain
  2 deciding to end the War of 1812
  3 acquiring territory from Mexico in 1848
  4 annexing Hawaii and the Philippines

13 ____

14 Most Southern political leaders praised the Supreme Court decision in *Dred Scott* v. *Sanford* (1857) because it

  1 granted citizenship to all enslaved persons
  2 upheld the principle of popular sovereignty
  3 supported the right of a state to secede from the Union
  4 protected the property rights of slave owners in the territories

14 ____

15 Before the former Confederate states could be readmitted to the Union, the congressional plan for Reconstruction required them to

  1 ratify the 14th amendment
  2 imprison all former Confederate soldiers
  3 provide 40 acres of land to all freedmen
  4 help rebuild Northern industries

15 ____

16 In the late 1800s, southern state governments used literacy tests, poll taxes, and grandfather clauses to

1 ensure that only educated individuals voted
2 require African Americans to attend school
3 prevent African Americans from voting
4 integrate public facilities   16____

17 Which statement best expresses the melting pot theory as it relates to American society?

1 Only European immigrants will be allowed into the United States.
2 All immigrant groups will maintain their separate cultures.
3 Different cultures will blend to form a uniquely American culture.
4 Immigrant ghettos will develop in urban areas.   17____

18 In passing the Sherman Antitrust Act (1890), Congress intended to

1 prevent large corporations from eliminating their competition
2 distinguish good trusts from bad trusts
3 regulate rates charged by railroads
4 force large trusts to bargain with labor unions   18____

19 A high protective tariff passed by Congress is intended to affect the United States economy by

1 promoting free trade
2 limiting industrial jobs
3 encouraging American manufacturing
4 expanding global interdependence

19 _____

20 Which government action is most closely associated with the efforts of muckrakers?

1 ratification of the woman's suffrage amendment
2 approval of the graduated income tax
3 creation of the National Forest Service
4 passage of the Meat Inspection Act

20 _____

21 In the early 1900s, Progressive Era reformers sought to increase citizen participation in government by supporting the

1 expansion of the spoils system
2 direct election of senators
3 creation of the electoral college
4 formation of the Federal Reserve system

21 _____

Base your answers to questions 22 and 23 on the cartoon below and on your knowledge of social studies.

The First Spadeful

Source: W. A. Rogers, *A World Worthwhile*, Harper & Bros.

22 The cartoon illustrates the actions of President Theodore Roosevelt in

1 securing the land to build the Panama Canal
2 leading troops in the Spanish-American War
3 ending the war between Russia and Japan
4 improving diplomatic relations with Latin American nations   22 _____

23 Critics of the actions shown in this cartoon claimed President Theodore Roosevelt was

  1 causing environmental damage
  2 requiring massive tax increases
  3 following a policy of imperialism
  4 producing major trade deficits with China   23 _____

24 A major reason the United States entered World War I was to

  1 maintain freedom of the seas
  2 stop impressment of United States sailors
  3 protect United States cities from foreign attacks
  4 counter a German invasion of Latin America   24 _____

25 Isolationists in the Senate objected to the United States joining the League of Nations because they opposed

  1 creation of the Security Council
  2 colonialism in Africa and Asia
  3 membership in the League by Germany
  4 involvement in future foreign wars   25 _____

26 In the mid-1920s, the immigration policy of the United States was mainly designed to

  1 deport illegal immigrants
  2 continue the traditional policy of open immigration
  3 establish quotas to limit immigration from certain nations
  4 favor immigrants from southern and eastern Europe   26 _____

27 What was the major problem facing American farmers during the 1920s?

1 shortage of fertile land
2 overproduction of crops
3 low prices of imported farm products
4 limited labor supply   27 ____

28 The contributions of Langston Hughes and Duke Ellington illustrate the importance of the Harlem Renaissance to

1 economic growth
2 educational reform
3 the creative arts
4 political leadership   28 ____

29 The Civilian Conservation Corps (CCC) and the Works Progress Administration (WPA) were both New Deal programs developed to address the problem of

1 excessive stock market speculation
2 high unemployment
3 increased use of credit
4 limited income of senior citizens   29 ____

30 A major reason that President Franklin D. Roosevelt proposed adding Justices to the Supreme Court in 1937 was to

1 make the Court processes more democratic
2 end corruption and favoritism in handling cases
3 influence Court decisions related to New Deal programs
4 ensure the appointment of members of minority groups   30 ____

31 Which event led to the other three?

  1 migration of 300,000 people to California to find work
  2 development of Dust Bowl conditions on the Great Plains
  3 passage of New Deal legislation to conserve soil
  4 publication of John Steinbeck's novel *The Grapes of Wrath*   31 _____

32 In 1939, President Franklin D. Roosevelt responded to the start of World War II in Europe by

  1 asking Congress to enter the war
  2 urging continued appeasement of aggressor nations
  3 attempting to negotiate a peaceful settlement of the hostilities
  4 selling military supplies to the Allied nations   32 _____

33 Which statement about the United States economy during World War II is most accurate?

  1 Federal economic controls increased.
  2 The manufacturing of automobiles increased.
  3 Worker productivity declined.
  4 Prices fell rapidly.   33 _____

Base your answers to questions 34 and 35 on the time line below and on your knowledge of social studies.

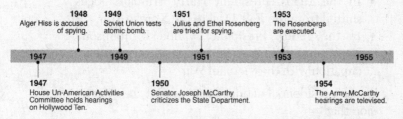

| 1948 | 1949 | 1951 | 1953 |
| Alger Hiss is accused of spying. | Soviet Union tests atomic bomb. | Julius and Ethel Rosenberg are tried for spying. | The Rosenbergs are executed. |

1947 — 1949 — 1951 — 1953 — 1955

| 1947 | 1950 | 1954 |
| House Un-American Activities Committee holds hearings on Hollywood Ten. | Senator Joseph McCarthy criticizes the State Department. | The Army-McCarthy hearings are televised. |

Source: *The American Journey: Time Line Activities*, Glencoe/McGraw-Hill (adapted)

34 The events shown on the time line are most closely associated with

1 the bombing of Pearl Harbor
2 the launching of *Sputnik*
3 a need for collective security
4 a fear of communism

34 _____

35 Which civil liberty was most seriously threatened during the period shown on the time line?

1 freedom of speech
2 freedom of religion
3 the right to bear arms
4 the right to petition the government

35 _____

36 • In the 1940s, President Franklin D. Roosevelt made winning World War II a priority over extending the New Deal.
  • In the 1950s, President Harry Truman's focus shifted from the Fair Deal to the Korean War.
  • In the 1960s, President Lyndon B. Johnson's attention to the Great Society gave way to preoccupation with the Vietnam War.

These presidential actions best support the conclusion that

1 presidents prefer their role as commander in chief to that of chief legislator
2 domestic programs are often undermined by the outbreak of war
3 Presidents Roosevelt, Truman, and Johnson were not committed to their domestic initiatives
4 large domestic reform programs tend to lead nations toward involvement in foreign wars   36 ____

37 The United Nations was created mainly to

1 prevent globalization
2 work for international peace
3 stop the spread of disease
4 establish democratic governments   37 ____

38 The United States policy of détente can best be described as an effort to

1 reduce tensions with the Soviet Union
2 negotiate peace agreements with North Korea
3 halt the arms race with China
4 end an embargo against Cuba   38 ____

Base your answers to questions 39 and 40 on the photograph below and on your knowledge of social studies.

Source: Warren K. Leffler, *U.S. News & World Report Magazine Photograph Collection*, Library of Congress

39 Which leader is most closely associated with the approach to reform illustrated in this photograph?

   1 Malcolm X of the Black Muslims
   2 Huey Newton of the Black Panthers
   3 Booker T. Washington of the Tuskegee Institute
   4 Martin Luther King Jr. of the Southern Christian
      Leadership Conference   39____

40 The activity shown in the photograph can best be described as an example of

   1 labor unrest
   2 judicial activism
   3 nonviolent protest
   4 affirmative action   40____

41 President Richard Nixon's decision to resign from the presidency in 1974 was based primarily on

  1 developments in the Watergate investigation
  2 backlash from his policies toward China and the Soviet Union
  3 protests against his secret military actions during the Vietnam War
  4 accusations of trading arms for hostages   41 ____

Base your answers to questions 42 and 43 on the cartoon below and on your knowledge of social studies.

Source: Gary Brookins, *The Richmond Times-Dispatch*, 1985

42 What is the main topic of this 1985 cartoon?

  1 quality of Japanese products
  2 imbalance in Japanese-United States trade
  3 outsourcing of American jobs to Japan
  4 relocation of American companies to Japan   42 ____

43 If this 1985 cartoon were to be redrawn today, which country would most likely replace Japan as the subject of the cartoon?

  1 China
  2 Brazil
  3 Germany
  4 Russia   43 ____

44 Which event of Bill Clinton's presidency best illustrates the use of checks and balances?

  1 hosting peace talks between Israelis and Palestinians
  2 reelection to a second term
  3 selection of Al Gore as vice president
  4 impeachment for alleged perjury and obstruction of justice   44 ____

Base your answer to question 45 on the letter below and on your knowledge of social studies.

THE WHITE HOUSE
WASHINGTON

A monetary sum and words alone cannot restore lost years or erase painful memories; neither can they fully convey our Nation's resolve to rectify injustice and to uphold the rights of individuals. We can never fully right the wrongs of the past. But we can take a clear stand for justice and recognize that serious injustices were done to Japanese Americans during World War II.

In enacting a law calling for restitution and offering a sincere apology, your fellow Americans have, in a very real sense, renewed their traditional commitment to the ideals of freedom, equality, and justice. You and your family have our best wishes for the future.

Sincerely,

G. Bush

Source: Letter of President George H. W. Bush, 1990,
A More Perfect Union, Smithsonian National Museum
of American History

45 Which event is President George H. W. Bush referring to in this letter?

  1 the bombing of Pearl Harbor during World War II
  2 the military service of Japanese Americans during World War II
  3 the internment of Japanese Americans during World War II
  4 a ban on Japanese immigration to the United States after World War II   45____

46 The terrorist attacks of September 11, 2001, led the federal government to create the

  1 Environmental Protection Agency
  2 Department of Homeland Security
  3 Central Intelligence Agency
  4 Federal Bureau of Investigation   46____

47 In which case did the United States Supreme Court rule that segregated public facilities were constitutional?

  1 *Worcester* v. *Georgia*
  2 *Plessy* v. *Ferguson*
  3 *Brown* v. *Board of Education of Topeka*
  4 *Miranda* v. *Arizona*   47____

48 The Supreme Court decision in *Schenck* v. *United States* (1919) and the USA Patriot Act of 2001 both dealt with the power of the federal government to

1 suspend the writ of habeas corpus
2 restrict freedom of religion
3 deny civil rights to those who lack citizenship
4 limit civil liberties for reasons of national security   48____

49 President Jimmy Carter's decision to criticize South Africa's apartheid policy and President Bill Clinton's decision to send troops to Bosnia were both responses to

1 human rights abuses
2 civil wars
3 immigration policies
4 trade agreement violations   49____

50 The Supreme Court rulings in *Roe* v. *Wade* (1973) and *Planned Parenthood of Southeastern Pennsylvania, et al.* v. *Casey* (1992) are similar in that both cases dealt with a woman's right to

1 privacy
2 medical insurance
3 equal pay for equal work
4 participate in school sports   50____

In developing your answer to Part II, be sure to keep this general definition in mind:

> <u>discuss</u> means "to make observations about something using facts, reasoning, and argument; to present in some detail"

PART II: THEMATIC ESSAY

Directions: Write a well-organized essay that includes an introduction, several paragraphs addressing the task below, and a conclusion.

Theme: Technology

> Technological developments have had both positive and negative effects on the United States economy and on American society.

Task:

> Identify *two* different technological developments and for *each*
> * Discuss the positive *and/or* negative effects of the technological development on the United States economy *or* on American society.

You may use any technological developments from your study of United States history. Some suggestions you might wish to consider include the cotton gin, steam-powered engines, the assembly line, nuclear power, the automobile, television, and computers.

You are *not* limited to these suggestions.

Guidelines:

In your essay, be sure to:
- Develop all aspects of the task
- Support the theme with relevant facts, examples, and details
- Use a logical and clear plan of organization, including an introduction and a conclusion that are beyond a simple restatement of the theme

In developing your answers to Part III, be sure to keep these general definitions in mind:

   (a) <u>describe</u> means "to illustrate something in words or tell about it"

   (b) <u>discuss</u> means "to make observations about something using facts, reasoning, and argument; to present in some detail"

PART III: DOCUMENT-BASED ESSAY

This question is based on the accompanying documents. The question is designed to test your ability to work with historical documents. Some of the documents have been edited for the purposes of the question. As you analyze the documents, take into account the source of each document and any point of view that may be presented in the document.

Historical Context:

> Reform movements developed during the 19th century and early 20th century to address specific problems. These included the *women's rights movement*, the *temperance movement*, and the *movement to end child labor*. These movements met with varying degrees of success.

Task:

> Using information from the documents and your knowledge of United States history, answer the questions that follow each document in Part A. Your answers to the questions will help you write the Part B essay, in which you will be asked to
>
> Choose *two* reform movements mentioned in the historical context and for *each*
> - Describe the problems that led to the development of the movement
> - Discuss the extent to which the movement was successful in achieving its goals

Part A: Short-Answer Questions

Directions: Analyze the documents and answer the short-answer questions that follow each document in the space provided.

Document 1

Lucy Stone and Henry Blackwell signed this document before they were married in 1855. They were protesting laws in which women lost their legal existence upon marriage.

While acknowledging our mutual affection by publicly assuming the relationship of husband and wife, yet in justice to ourselves and a great principle, we deem it a duty to declare that this act on our part implies no sanction of, nor promise of voluntary obedience to such of the present laws of marriage, as refuse to recognize the wife as an independent, rational being, while they confer upon the husband an injurious [harmful] and unnatural superiority, investing him with legal powers which no honorable man would exercize [exercise], and which no man should possess. We protest especially against the laws which give to the husband:

1. The custody of the wife's person.
2. The exclusive control and guardianship of their children.
3. The sole ownership of her personal [property], and use of her real estate, unless previously settled upon her, or placed in the hands of trustees, as in the case of minors, lunatics, and idiots.
4. The absolute right to the product of her industry [work].
5. Also against laws which give to the widower so much larger and more permanent an interest in the property of his deceased wife, than they give to the widow in that of the deceased husband.
6. Finally, against the whole system by which "the legal existence of the wife is suspended during marriage," so that in most States, she neither has a legal part in the choice of her residence, nor can she make a will, nor sue or be sued in her own name, nor inherit property. . . .

Source: Laura A. Otten, "Lucy Stone and Henry Blackwell: Marriage Protest," *Women's Rights and the Law*, Praeger, 1993

1 According to this document, what were *two* rights denied to women in 1855? [2]

(1) _____

_____

(2) _____

_____

Document 2

> . . . The woman ballot will not revolutionize the world. Its results in Colorado, for example, might have been anticipated. First, it did give women better wages for equal work; second, it led immediately to a number of laws the women wanted, and the first laws they demanded were laws for the protection of the children of the State, making it a misdemeanor to contribute to the delinquency of a child; laws for the improved care of defective children; also, the Juvenile Court for the conservation of wayward boys and girls; the better care of the insane, the deaf, the dumb [unable to speak], the blind; the curfew bell to keep children off the streets at night; raising the age of consent for girls; improving the reformatories and prisons of the State; improving the hospital service of the State; improving the sanitary laws, affecting the health of the homes of the State. Their [women's] interest in the public health is a matter of great importance. Above all, there resulted laws for improving the school system. . . .

Source: Senator Robert L. Owen, Introductory Remarks of Presiding Officer, *Significance of the Woman Suffrage Movement*, Session of the American Academy of Political and Social Science, February 9, 1910

2 According to Senator Robert L. Owen, what were **two** effects of the women's rights movement in Colorado? [2]

(1) _____

_____

(2) _____

_____

Document 3

> ... The winning of female suffrage did not mark the end of prejudice and discrimination against women in public life. Women still lacked equal access with men to those professions, especially the law, which provide the chief routes to political power. Further, when women ran for office—and many did in the immediate post-suffrage era—they often lacked major party backing, hard to come by for any newcomer but for women almost impossible unless she belonged to a prominent political family. Even if successful in winning backing, when women ran for office they usually had to oppose incumbents [those in office]. When, as was often the case, they lost their first attempts, their reputation as "losers" made re-endorsement impossible. ...

Source: Elisabeth Perry, "Why Suffrage for American Women Was Not Enough," *History Today*, September 1993

3 According to Elisabeth Perry, what was ***one*** way in which women's participation in public life continued to be limited after winning suffrage? [1]

_____

_____

Document 4a

Building Up His Business

Source: Frank Beard, *The Ram's Horn*, September 12, 1896
(adapted)

Document 4b

This excerpt from the *National Temperance Almanac* of 1876 attacks "King Alcohol."

He has occasioned [caused] more than three-fourths of the pauperism [extreme poverty], three-fourths of the crime, and more than one-half of the insanity in the community, and thereby filled our prisons, our alms-houses [houses for the poor] and lunatic asylums, and erected the gibbet [gallows to hang people] before our eyes.

Source: Andrew Sinclair, *Prohibition: The Era of Excess*, Little, Brown

4 Based on this 19th-century cartoon and this quotation, state *two* effects that alcohol had on American society. [2]

(1) _____

_____

(2) _____

_____

Document 5

"... When four-fifths of the most representative men in America are pronounced unfit for war, what shall we say of their fitness to father the next generation? The time was when alcohol was received as a benefit to the race, but we no longer look upon alcohol as a food but as a poison. Boards of health, armed with the police power of the state eradicate [erase] the causes of typhoid and quarantine the victims, but alcohol, a thousand times more destructive to public health, continues to destroy. Alcoholic degeneracy [deterioration] is the most important sanitary [health] question before the country, and yet the health authorities do not take action, as alcohol is entrenched [well established] in politics. Leaders in politics dare not act, as their political destiny lies in the hands of the agents of the liquor traffic. We are face to face with the greatest crisis in our country's history. The alcohol question must be settled within the next ten years or some more virile race will write the epitaph of this country. ..."

Source: Dr. T. Alexander MacNicholl, quoted in President's Annual Address
to the Women's Christian Temperance Union of Minnesota, 1912

5 According to this 1912 document, why does this speaker think the use of alcohol is "the greatest crisis in our country's history"? [1]

_____

_____

Document 6a

Too big for them

Source: P.W. Cromwell, Bentley Historical Library,
University of Michigan (adapted)

Document 6b

> . . . While in reality national prohibition sharply reduced the consumption of alcohol in the United States, the law fell considerably short of expectations. It neither eliminated drinking nor produced a sense that such a goal was within reach. So long as the purchaser of liquor, the supposed victim of a prohibition violation, participated in the illegal act rather than complained about it, the normal law enforcement process simply did not function. As a result, policing agencies bore a much heavier burden. The various images of law-breaking, from contacts with the local bootlegger to Hollywood films to overloaded court dockets, generated a widespread belief that violations were taking place with unacceptable frequency. Furthermore, attempts at enforcing the law created an impression that government, unable to cope with lawbreakers by using traditional policing methods, was assuming new powers in order to accomplish its task. The picture of national prohibition which emerged over the course of the 1920s disenchanted many Americans and moved some to an active effort to bring an end to the dry law [Volstead Act].

Source: David E. Kyvig, *Repealing National Prohibition*,
Kent State University Press, 2000

6 Based on these documents, what were ***two*** problems that resulted from national Prohibition? [2]

(1) _____

_____

(2) _____

_____

Document 7

> . . . Little girls and boys, barefooted, walked up and down between the endless rows of spindles, reaching thin little hands into the machinery to repair snapped threads. They crawled under machinery to oil it. They replaced spindles all day long, all day long; night through, night through. Tiny babies of six years old with faces of sixty did an eight-hour shift for ten cents a day. If they fell asleep, cold water was dashed in their faces, and the voice of the manager yelled above the ceaseless racket and whir of the machines.
>
> Toddling chaps of four years old were brought to the mills to "help" the older sister or brother of ten years but their labor was not paid.
>
> The machines, built in the north, were built low for the hands of little children.
>
> At five-thirty in the morning, long lines of little grey children came out of the early dawn into the factory, into the maddening noise, into the lint filled rooms. Outside the birds sang and the blue sky shone. At the lunch half-hour, the children would fall to sleep over their lunch of cornbread and fat pork. They would lie on the bare floor and sleep. Sleep was their recreation, their release, as play is to the free child. The boss would come along and shake them awake. After the lunch period, the hour-in grind, the ceaseless running up and down between the whirring spindles. Babies, tiny children! . . .

Source: Mother Jones, *Autobiography of Mother Jones*, Arno Press

7 According to Mother Jones, what was *one* situation faced by children in the workplace in the late 1800s? [1]

_____

_____

Document 8

> . . . While states began to pass laws that worked, Mother Jones's dream of a national child labor law remained just a dream. Even if the children [after their labor march in 1903] had managed to see President [Theodore] Roosevelt, it is doubtful that any federal laws would have been passed. In 1906, a federal child labor bill was defeated in Congress. Echoing Roosevelt, many of the bill's opponents said they disliked child labor, but that they believed only states had the authority to make laws against it. In 1916, a bill was passed, but the Supreme Court ruled that the law was unconstitutional. The first successful national law was not passed until 1938, about 35 years after the march of the mill children. . . .

Source: Stephen Currie, *We Have Marched Together: The Working Children's Crusade*, Lerner Publications, 1997

8 According to Stephen Currie, what was *one* reason that ending child labor was difficult to achieve nationally? [1]

_____

_____

Document 9

This is an excerpt from a radio interview given by Elmer F. Andrews, Administrator of the Fair Labor Standards Act. He is discussing the Wage and Hour Law, also known as the Fair Labor Standards Act.

Protection for Children

Announcer—Well, can't you tell us something about this—I know we are all interested in the protection of children from oppressive labor in industrial plants and mines.

Mr. Andrews—The child labor sections are specific. No producer, manufacturer or dealer may ship, or deliver for shipment in interstate commerce, any goods produced in an establishment which has employed oppressive child labor within thirty days of the removal of the goods. The thirty days will be counted after today, so this means that employers of children before today do not come under the act.

Announcer—And oppressive child labor is—what?

Mr. Andrews—Oppressive child labor is defined as, first, the employment of children under 16 in any occupation, except that children of 14 or 15 may do work which the Children's Bureau has determined will not interfere with their schooling, health or well-being, but this work under the law must not be either manufacturing or mining employment.

In addition oppressive child labor means the employment of children 16 or 17 years in any occupation found by the Children's Bureau to be particularly hazardous or detrimental to health or well-being.

Of course, there are exceptions for child-actors and others, but in general those are the child-labor provisions of the Fair Labor Standards Act, which is now the law of the land.

Source: "Andrews Explains Wage-Hour Law,"
New York Times, October 25, 1938 (adapted)

9 According to Elmer F. Andrews, what were *two* ways the Fair Labor Standards Act protected children? [2]

(1) _____

_____

(2) _____

_____

Part B: Essay

Directions: Write a well-organized essay that includes an introduction, several paragraphs, and a conclusion. Use evidence from *at least **four*** documents in the body of your essay. Support your response with relevant facts, examples, and details. Include additional outside information.

Historical Context:

> Reform movements developed during the 19th century and early 20th century to address specific problems. These included the ***women's rights movement***, the ***temperance movement***, and the ***movement to end child labor***. These movements met with varying degrees of success.

Task:

> Using information from the documents and your knowledge of United States history, write an essay in which you
>
> Choose ***two*** reform movements mentioned in the historical context and for ***each***
> - Describe the problems that led to the development of the movement
> - Discuss the extent to which the movement was successful in achieving its goals

Guidelines:

In your essay, be sure to:
- Develop all aspects of the task
- Incorporate information from *at least **four*** documents
- Incorporate relevant outside information
- Support the theme with relevant facts, examples, and details
- Use a logical and clear plan of organization, including an introduction and conclusion that are beyond a restatement of the theme

Answers
June 2010
United States History and Government

Answer Key

PART I

1. 2	14. 4	27. 2	40. 3
2. 3	15. 1	28. 3	41. 1
3. 4	16. 3	29. 2	42. 2
4. 4	17. 3	30. 3	43. 1
5. 3	18. 1	31. 2	44. 4
6. 2	19. 3	32. 4	45. 3
7. 4	20. 4	33. 1	46. 2
8. 1	21. 2	34. 4	47. 2
9. 4	22. 1	35. 1	48. 4
10. 1	23. 3	36. 2	49. 1
11. 2	24. 1	37. 2	50. 1
12. 1	25. 4	38. 1	
13. 3	26. 3	39. 4	

PART II: Thematic Essay   See answers explained section.

PART III: Document-Based Essay   See answers explained section.

Answers Explained

PART I (1–50)

1. **2** The map shows the western limit of colonial settlement that resulted from the Proclamation of 1763. The act established the Proclamation Line along the crest of the Appalachian Mountains that the colonists were not supposed to cross. The main reason Great Britain established the Proclamation Line was to avoid conflicts between colonists and Native Americans. The line was established just after the conclusion of the French and Indian War (1754–1763), which was caused, in part, by colonial expansion into the land beyond the Appalachians. Before the war, a few settlers crossed over the Appalachian Mountains and established farms in the Ohio River valley. This expansion led to conflicts with the French, who had earlier established outposts in the area. Eventually this movement of settlers led to the French and Indian War. After the war, the British were determined to prevent skirmishes between the colonists and Native Americans beyond the Appalachian Mountains. This act contributed to colonial resentment of British policies.

WRONG CHOICES EXPLAINED:

(1) The founding of Jamestown (1607) occurred over a century and a half before the drawing of the Proclamation Line. The Appalachians were unexplored by the British at such an early date. There was no need to restrict the movements of the few English settlers present in North America in 1607.

(3) The Monroe Doctrine (1823) was put forth over a half century after the drawing of the Proclamation Line. It was designed to prevent further European colonial claims in the New World, not to restrict movement within the North American continent.

(4) The Compromise of 1850 occurred almost a century after the drawing of the Proclamation Line. It was an attempt to deal with the question of the expansion of slavery in the United States. It allowed for the admission of California as a free state and for the passage of a stronger Fugitive Slave Act.

2. **3** Climatic conditions in the southern colonies most directly influenced the development of the plantation system. The fertile soil, relatively flat land, and long growing season of the coastal regions of the southern colonies made the area ideal for large tobacco and cotton plantations. These large plantations lent themselves to a slave system of labor. In contrast, the hilly, rocky soil and shorter growing season of the northern colonies proved more suitable for smaller-scale agriculture and a more mixed economy. The smaller farms of the northern colonies were generally worked by the owner of the property and his family, perhaps with more people hired for planting and harvesting.

WRONG CHOICES EXPLAINED:

(1) The climatic conditions of the southern colonies did not influence the development of democratic institutions. The plantation system that developed in the South created great inequalities in wealth and status among the residents of these colonies. The plantation-owning grandees of these colonies were far wealthier and more powerful than the indentured servants and enslaved Africans who worked the land. Such stark inequality did not lend itself to the development of democratic political institutions.

(2) Most of the early settlers in the southern colonies built plantations along the coast or adjacent to navigable rivers. There was thus less of a need to develop a network of canals.

(4) Coal was later discovered in the South (notably in West Virginia), but there was not a demand for coal during the colonial period. Such a demand came in the 19th century with the development of steam power.

3. **4** The heading "Influences on United States Constitutional Government" best completes the partial outline. All the elements in the outline were influences on the principles of governance as expressed in the United States Constitution. The Magna Carta was a document written by English barons in 1215 to limit the power of the king. The document puts forth the idea that the will of the monarch can be bound by law and by legal procedures. In other words, the king's power is limited. This idea of a government bound by legal procedures is central to the Constitution. The House of Burgesses is an early example of representative government. It was created by the Virginia Company in 1619. The company had founded the colony of Virginia in 1607 as a profit-generating venture. The company saw the need for some sort of body to govern the inhabitants of the colony and created this representative assembly. Town meetings developed in New England towns during the colonial period. These meetings were face-to-face decision-making assemblies that were open to all free male residents of a town. This form of direct democracy allowed for a high degree of citizen participation in decision making.

WRONG CHOICES EXPLAINED:

(1) The elements of the outline are not ideas of Social Darwinism. Social Darwinism is a school of thought that gained popularity during the industrial revolution of the late 1800s. It was an attempt to apply Charles Darwin's ideas about the natural world to social relations. Social Darwinists argued against any attempt at government intervention into economic and social spheres. Interference, they argued, would hinder the evolution of the human species. The inequalities of wealth that characterized the late 1800s, they argued, were part of the process of survival of the fittest.

(2) The elements of the outline are not the basis of British mercantilism. Mercantilism is essentially an economic theory based on the idea that only a limited amount of wealth exists in the world. Nations increase their power by

increasing their share of the world's wealth. One way of acquiring wealth, measured in the accumulation of precious metals, is to maintain a favorable balance of trade, with the value of exports exceeding the value of imports. Mercantilist theory suggests that governments should advance these goals by maintaining colonies so as to have a steady and inexpensive source for raw materials.

(3) The elements of the outline are not contributions to American literature. None of the elements are literary figures or works of fiction.

4. **4** The main reason the Articles of Confederation were replaced as the basis of the United States government was that they failed to give the central government enough power to govern effectively. Under the Articles of Confederation (1781–1788), most power remained with the state governments. The framers of this first American government created a firm league of friendship among the states, rather than a strong, centralized nation. Before 1776, they had lived under a powerful, distant authority and did not want to repeat that experience. Also, many of these early leaders were fiercely loyal to their states and did not want to see state power superseded. Routine decisions under the articles required the agreement of seven of the 13 states, and major decisions required the approval of nine states. Altering the document required the consent of all 13 states. Funding the government proved to be a major problem. As written, the articles did not give the national government the power to levy taxes.

WRONG CHOICES EXPLAINED:

(1) Under the Articles of Confederation, there was a national congress. It was a unicameral body with limited powers.

(2) The Articles of Confederation did not declare political protests unconstitutional. In fact, the very word unconstitutional does not have meaning in the United States until the promulgation of the U.S. Constitution, which replaced the Articles of Confederation as the governing framework of the United States. Political protests did occur during the Articles of Confederation period. The most serious, which turned violent, was Shays' Rebellion (1786).

(3) The Articles of Confederation did not put excessive restrictions on the activities of state governments. State governments were given a relatively free hand during the Articles of Confederation period. In contrast, the central government was hamstrung.

5. **3** In the excerpted passage, the authors are stating that sovereignty belongs to the people of the nation. They state that the Constitution, and the government that was established by the Constitution, were created by "we the people." Sovereignty, or the power to govern, therefore rests with the people. This was a radical idea in the United States at the time. In the previous governing document, the Articles of Confederation (1781–1788), power

rested with the states. In this respect, the Constitution (ratified in 1788) skirted the states. It exists as a creation of the people themselves.

WRONG CHOICES EXPLAINED:

(1) The passage does not mention voting rights for men and women. Women did not get the right to vote in the United States until the ratification of the 19th Amendment to the Constitution (1920).

(2) The passage states that the people, not the states, created the United States government. The framers of the Constitution were conscious of circumventing the states in creating a new government and appealing directly to the people.

(4) The passage does not state that people obtain their rights from a monarch. The founders of the United States very specifically broke from rule by a monarch.

6. **2** Federalists and Antifederalists debated the ratification of the new Constitution. The Federalists argued that the existing governing structure was inadequate for the United States. Many Federalists were alarmed at the inability of the central government under the Articles of Confederation to raise revenue or to put down rebellions. Leading Federalists included John Jay, Alexander Hamilton, and James Madison. These men wrote a series of articles in defense of the Constitution that were collected and published as *The Federalist*. The opponents of the Constitution were given the label Antifederalists. One of their primary concerns was that individual rights were not adequately protected by the Constitution. The Constitution itself does not devote much attention to individual rights. Antifederalists demanded a list of individual rights that the government would not be allowed to take away. Many Antifederalists in the various states refused to support ratification of the Constitution unless such a list was added. The Federalists promised to add such a list if the Antifederalists agreed to support ratification. This agreement led to the writing and ratification of the first ten amendments to the Constitution, known as the Bill of Rights.

WRONG CHOICES EXPLAINED:

(1) Loyalists and revolutionaries were groups of Americans that formed at the time of the American Revolution (1775–1783). Loyalists advocated remaining loyal to the crown; revolutionaries advocated breaking all ties with the crown and establishing a new, independent nation.

(3) The Democratic Party and the Whig Party were competing political parties in the United States from the time of President Andrew Jackson to the 1850s. Jackson was a Democrat. The Whigs were established in 1833 to oppose his policies. The Whigs argued that Jackson was exercising almost kinglike power. The Whigs took their name from the British political party that opposed absolute power of the monarch. The Whigs broke up in 1856 over the slavery question. The Democratic Party continues to exist.

(4) The executive and the judicial branches are two of the three branches of government in the United States. The legislative branch is the third. The powers of these three branches, as well as checks on their powers, are all outlined in the Constitution. However, the branches are not the subject of the passage.

7. **4** The heading "Unwritten Constitution" best completes the partial outline. The unwritten constitution refers to those traditions and practices that have become part of the American political system but were not mentioned in the Constitution. Many of these practices date back to the administration of George Washington. His administration witnessed the development of political parties, a practice unforeseen by most of the founding fathers and not mentioned in the Constitution. These political parties hold a national nominating convention every four years to decide upon a presidential and a vice presidential candidate. This procedure is not discussed in the Constitution. In addition, congressional committees are not mentioned in the Constitution, yet the committee system has become instrumental to the functioning of Congress. Although individual members initiate and ultimately vote on legislation, a bill can survive only if it wins the approval of one of the congressional committees.

WRONG CHOICES EXPLAINED:
(1) The elements of the outline are not parts of the Articles of Confederation. The Articles of Confederation was the first document that established a framework for the United States government. It was in effect from 1781 to 1788, preceding the Constitution. The Articles of Confederation created a firm league of friendship among the states rather than a strong, centralized nation.

(2) The elements of the outline are not examples of Constitutional compromises. Several key compromises were central to the structure of the Constitution. For example, the Great Compromise created a two-house legislature. The Three-Fifths Compromise settled the issue of how to count slaves in the census.

(3) The elements of the outline are not examples of Jeffersonian democracy. The term Jeffersonian democracy refers to the political ethos of Thomas Jefferson. This approach to politics emphasizes limits on the powers of the central government, a strict interpretation of the Constitution, representative government, and faith in hard-working independent farmers.

8. **1** The amendment process was included in the Constitution to allow for change over time. The Constitution is sometimes described as a living document. The amendment process, which allows for additions to the Constitution, has led to the ending of slavery (13th Amendment, 1865), the federal income tax (16th Amendment, 1913), women's suffrage (19th Amendment, 1920), and a reduction in the voting age to 18 (26th Amendment, 1971).

WRONG CHOICES EXPLAINED:

(2) The amendment process was not designed to expand the powers of the president. In theory, an amendment could have that effect. The 22nd Amendment (1951) did the opposite. It limited presidential power by allowing the president to serve only two terms.

(3) The amendment process was not designed to increase citizen participation in government. However, several amendments have done just that. The 15th Amendment (1870) prohibits denying people the right to vote based on race. The 17th Amendment (1913) allows for the direct election of senators. The 19th Amendment (1920) extends voting rights to women.

(4) The amendment process was not designed to limit the authority of the United States Supreme Court. None of the amendments directly addresses the powers of the Supreme Court.

9. **4** The situation that best illustrates the practice of lobbying is environmental groups trying to persuade members of Congress to vote for the Clean Air Act. Lobbying involves urging elected officials to support or oppose a particular public policy or piece of legislation. The term is derived from the traditional locale of these interactions—the lobby of the Capitol. Lobbying groups are very powerful forces in government. Some lobbying groups work on a particular issue, such as human rights, environmental issues, or abortion. Other lobbying groups work on behalf of a membership, such as unionized workers or senior citizens. Still other groups work on behalf of a particular industry, such as coal mining or plastics production. Some people see lobbying groups as important parts of the democratic system, letting legislators know how constituents feel about an issue and providing valuable information. Others see the money and power of lobbying groups as interfering with the democratic process.

WRONG CHOICES EXPLAINED:

(1) Congress making a particular decision—in this case reducing the number of military bases—does not illustrate lobbying. Lobbyists might have pushed for or against the decision, but the decision itself is not lobbying.

(2) The federal government taking an action—in this case canceling a defense contract—does not illustrate lobbying. Lobbyists might have pushed for or against the action, but taking the action itself is not lobbying.

(3) Senators agreeing to work together does not illustrate lobbying. Lobbyists might have tried to push the senators either to work together or not to work together. However, the agreement itself is not lobbying.

10. **1** A major purpose of the president's cabinet is to offer advice on important issues. The cabinet is a group of advisors to the president. It is comprised of the heads of major government departments as well as some nondepartmental heads. There are currently 15 cabinet level departments, including the Department of Defense, the State Department, and the

Department of the Interior. An additional seven members are cabinet level officers. They include the vice president, White House Chief of Staff, and U.S. trade representatives. Cabinet members are nominated by the president and confirmed by the Senate. The cabinet is an example of the unwritten constitution. The unwritten constitution refers to those traditions and practices that have become part of the American political system but were not mentioned in the Constitution. Many of these practices, including the formation of a cabinet, date back to the administration of George Washington.

WRONG CHOICES EXPLAINED:
(2) The president's cabinet does not nominate ambassadors. This is done by the president.

(3) The president's cabinet does not conduct impeachment trials. This is done by the Senate.

(4) The president's cabinet does not regulate the amount of money in circulation. This is done by the Federal Reserve Board.

11. **2** The Louisiana Purchase (1803) was a foreign policy success for the United States primarily because it ended French control of the Mississippi River. For $15 million, the United States bought this vast expanse of land, which included the port city of New Orleans, and nearly doubled its size. The whole transaction happened quickly. The Louisiana Territory was long held by France until France ceded it to Spain in 1763 following the Seven Years' War. France then regained the territory in 1801. The Mississippi River was, at the time, the western boundary of the United States. Farmers depended on the Mississippi River to transport goods. However, Spain and then France controlled the waterway as well as New Orleans. The purchase gave the United States control of both sides of the river and allowed farmers full use of the river for transporting goods.

WRONG CHOICES EXPLAINED:
(1) The Louisiana Purchase did not involve Spanish control of Florida. The United States did get control of Florida from Spain with the Adams-Onis Treaty (1819).

(3) The Louisiana Purchase did not involve British occupation of forts on American soil. British forces did not immediately abandon forts in the American West after the conclusion of the American Revolution. President Washington sent John Jay to Great Britain in 1794 to address several grievances the United States had with Great Britain, including the continued British presence in the West. These talks led to Jay's Treaty. One element of the treaty was that the British agreed to withdraw from the West but only after 18 months.

(4) The Louisiana Purchase did not affect Russian influence in North America. The issue of Russian influence in North America led, in part, to the Monroe Doctrine (1823). President Monroe was opposed to a decree by the Russian Czar that claimed all the Pacific Northwest above the 51st parallel.

The Monroe Doctrine warned European nations not to establish additional colonies in the Americas.

12. **1** Under Chief Justice John Marshall, the Supreme Court strengthened its authority by applying judicial review to state and national laws. The court's power of judicial review grew out of the case of *Marbury* v. *Madison* (1803). This was perhaps the most important decision in the history of the Supreme Court. The decision strengthened the judiciary by asserting that the Supreme Court has the power to review laws and determine whether they are consistent with the Constitution. The details of the case concern the seating of judges who were appointed during the last days of the John Adams administration. However, the case is important because it established the power of judicial review, which has been the main function of the Supreme Court since then. Chief Justice John Marshall presided over the Supreme Court from 1801 to 1835.

WRONG CHOICES EXPLAINED:
(2) The Supreme Court under Chief Justice John Marshall did not change the operation of the electoral college. The 12th Amendment (1803) to the Constitution did change the operation of the electoral college, allowing for separate electoral votes for president and for vice president. Previously, the runner-up in the electoral vote became vice president.

(3) The Supreme Court under Chief Justice John Marshall did not increase the number of Justices on the Court. President Franklin D. Roosevelt did propose increasing the number of Justices on the Court from 9 to 15 because the Court had declared several key New Deal programs unconstitutional. The proposal was roundly criticized, even by Roosevelt's allies, and was withdrawn. The number of justices has always been 9.

(4) The Supreme Court under Chief Justice John Marshall did not expand the freedoms included in the 1st Amendment. Subsequent courts have expanded and, at times contracted, freedoms included in the 1st Amendment.

13. **3** The action most closely associated with the term *Manifest Destiny* is acquiring territory from Mexico in 1848. The term *Manifest Destiny* was coined in an 1845 newspaper article. It captured the fervor of the westward expansion movement, implying that it was God's plan that the United States take over and settle the entire continent. Americans who did settle out West were probably driven more by economic factors, such as cheap land or precious metals, than by a desire to fulfill God's plan. The history of the settlement of the West includes many noteworthy episodes: Texas independence from Mexico (1836), the opening of the Oregon Trail (1841), the Mormon exodus to Utah (1847), and the California gold rush (1849). The question refers to the Mexican-American War (1846–1848), which grew out of the annexation of Texas (1845). The United States and Mexico disagreed over the southern border of Texas. Mexico said it was at the Nueces River. The United

States insisted it was at the Rio Grande, 150 miles to the south. Skirmishes in the disputed area led to war between the two countries. The United States won the war and acquired the huge territory that comprised the northern provinces of Mexico, known as the Mexican Cession.

WRONG CHOICES EXPLAINED:

(1) The United States declaring independence from Great Britain is not associated with the term *Manifest Destiny*. Manifest Destiny refers to western expansion, not political independence from Great Britain.

(2) The decision to end the War of 1812 is not associated with the term *Manifest Destiny*. Manifest Destiny refers to western expansion, not the decision to enter into or to end war with Great Britain (1812–1815).

(4) The United States annexation of Hawaii and the Philippines is not associated with the term *Manifest Destiny*. Manifest Destiny refers to western expansion within the North American continent, not expansion abroad. The United States annexed Hawaii in 1898 and acquired the Philippines following the Spanish-American War, also in 1898.

14. **4** Most Southern political leaders praised the Supreme Court decision in *Dred Scott* v. *Sanford* (1857) because it protected the property rights of slave owners in the territories. The case revolved around Dred Scott, a slave who sued to obtain his freedom on the grounds that he had lived for a time in territories where slavery was banned. The Court ruled that a slave owner still retained his property rights to his slaves, even if he and his slave were in a state or territory where slavery was banned. The decision went further. The Court ruled that Congress did not even have the power to ban slavery in the territories. This part of the decision struck down the Missouri Compromise of 1820, which had banned slavery from the northern portion of the Louisiana Purchase territory. The decision was a blow to the Republican Party, which sought to use the power of the federal government to prevent the spread of slavery into America's new territories. The *Dred Scott* decision went on to declare that no African Americans, not even free men and women, were entitled to citizenship in the United States because they were, according to the Court, "beings of an inferior order." The case alarmed African Americans and many white northerners. It is seen as one of the factors that led to the Civil War.

WRONG CHOICES EXPLAINED:

(1) The Supreme Court decision in *Dred Scott* v. *Sanford* did not grant citizenship to all enslaved persons. It did the opposite. It declared that African Americans, whether free or enslaved, were not entitled to citizenship rights.

(2) The Supreme Court decision in *Dred Scott* v. *Sanford* did not directly address the principle of popular sovereignty. The principle of popular sovereignty held that the people of a state or territory had the right to vote on whether or not to allow slavery.

(3) The Supreme Court decision in *Dred Scott* v. *Sanford* did not directly address the right of a state to secede from the United States.

15. **1** Before the former Confederate states could be readmitted to the Union, the congressional plan for Reconstruction required them to ratify the 14th Amendment. Reconstruction—the process of reuniting the nation following the Civil War—was a contentious issue. President Andrew Johnson put forth a mild, lenient Reconstruction plan, which was in effect from 1865 to 1867. During this period, Southern white political leaders established economic and political systems in their states that resembled the inequities of the pre-Civil War South. Congressional Republicans took the reins of Reconstruction in 1867 and instituted a more sweeping plan. Congress passed the Military Reconstruction Act and three other acts in 1867 in order to reorganize the South (except for Tennessee) as a conquered territory. The act divided the South into five military zones. In order to be readmitted, the Southern states had to provide basic rights to African Americans and had to ratify the 14th Amendment. The amendment punished states that denied voting rights to its citizens and stated that no person shall be denied equal protection of the laws.

WRONG CHOICES EXPLAINED:
(2) The congressional plan for Reconstruction did not require the Southern states to imprison all former Confederate soldiers. There were moves to punish leading Confederate figures. However, imprisoning the hundreds of thousands of Confederate veterans would have been prohibitively expensive and impractical.

(3) The congressional plan for Reconstruction did not require the Southern states to provide 40 acres of land to all freedmen. Some of the Radical Republicans wanted the federal government to confiscate large plantations and divide them among freedmen. This would give African Americans a sound economic basis from which to begin life as free people. However, moderates were not willing to take such a drastic measure.

(4) The congressional plan for Reconstruction did not require the Southern states to help rebuild Northern industries. Very little fighting occurred in the North. Far from being damaged, Northern industries were in good shape following the war.

16. **3** In the late 1800s, southern state governments used literacy tests, poll taxes, and grandfather clauses to prevent African Americans from voting. After the Civil War, the 15th Amendment (1870) to the Constitution was ratified to extend voting rights to African Americans. In response to the 15th Amendment, southern states adopted a variety of measures to prevent African Americans from voting. Poll taxes required people to pay a tax in order to vote. Literacy tests required people to demonstrate their ability to read before they were allowed to vote. Grandfather clauses allowed poor whites to vote if they could demonstrate that they (or their father or their

grandfather) had the right to vote before the Civil War. These laws effectively prevented the vast majority of African Americans in the South from voting from the 1800s until passage of the Voting Rights Act in 1965.

WRONG CHOICES EXPLAINED:

(1) The actions taken by southern state governments in the late 1800s were not intended to ensure that only educated individuals voted. The actual motivation for literacy tests, poll taxes, and grandfather clauses was to prevent African Americans from voting.

(2) The actions taken by southern state governments in the late 1800s were not intended to require African Americans to attend school. To the extent that African Americans went to school in the South in this era, it was against the wishes of mainstream white society.

(4) The actions taken by southern state governments in the late 1800s were not intended to integrate public facilities. The motivation was not to aid the African American community. Both the moves to prevent African Americans from voting and the enactment of Jim Crow segregation laws were intended to relegate African Americans to a second-class status in the South. In 1954, the Supreme Court ordered schools integrated with the decision in *Brown* v. *Board of Education of Topeka*. In 1964, Congress prohibited segregation in public facilities with passage of the Civil Rights Act.

17. **3** The melting pot theory holds that different cultures will blend to form a uniquely American culture. The theory envisions a United States in which the different races and ethnicities that comprise the country shed their old habits and collectively build a new, distinctively American society. The phrase was popularized by the play "The Melting Pot" by Israel Zangwill (1908). At the time, the play and the theory put forth the progressive notion that immigrants were welcome in the United States and were part of the American culture. The theory was in opposition to nativist notions that held that immigrants were so different, and inferior, that they would never fit in to American society. Since the 1970s, immigrants and their advocates have tended to reject the melting pot idea because it urges immigrants to abandon their heritage. New theories envision American society as more of a salad bowl—one product made of many ingredients with each ingredient retaining identifiable characteristics.

WRONG CHOICES EXPLAINED:

(1) The melting pot theory did not hold that only European immigrants would be allowed into the United States. Advocates of the theory welcomed immigrants from all lands into the country.

(2) The melting pot theory did not hold that all immigrant groups would maintain their separate cultures. More recent approaches, including the salad bowl theory, envision a cohesive American culture in which the cultures of the various immigrant groups survive and are celebrated.

(4) The melting pot theory did not hold that immigrant ghettos would develop in urban areas. Impoverished immigrant neighborhoods, such as the Lower East Side of New York City, did develop. However, this was not part of the melting pot theory.

18. **1** In passing the Sherman Antitrust Act (1890), Congress intended to prevent large corporations from eliminating competition. During the Gilded Age of the late 1800s, corporations and trusts came to dominate entire industries. The men who controlled the major industries in the United States came to be known as robber barons, a scornful title meant to call attention to their cutthroat business activities. These robber barons often created trusts (combinations of companies) in order to eliminate competition and control a particular industry. John D. Rockefeller established the first large trust in the oil-processing industry. The formation of trusts in several industries was seen as harmful to the interests of consumers. Critics of corporate power pushed the government to take steps to limit these trusts. However, the government's efforts often did not always end up having the desired effect. The Sherman Antitrust Act was designed to break up trusts, but only a few trusts were challenged. Ironically, the act was used with equal vigor against unions on the grounds that they were illegal formations that interfered with free trade. In the case of *United States* v. *E. C. Knight Company* (1895), the Supreme Court greatly limited the scope of the act by making a distinction between trade (which would be subject to the act) and manufacturing (which would not).

WRONG CHOICES EXPLAINED:
(2) The Sherman Antitrust Act made no distinction between good and bad trusts. Later, President Theodore Roosevelt made such a distinction. He used the power of the government to take action against bad trusts—ones that interfered with commerce. One of his targets was the Northern Securities Company, a railroad holding company.
(3) The Sherman Antitrust Act did not regulate rates charged by railroads. Critics of powerful corporations in the late 1800s did urge the government to take such an action. The federal government created the Interstate Commerce Commission (ICC) in 1887 to regulate railroads. However, the ICC was chronically underfunded and was, therefore, ineffective.
(4) The Sherman Antitrust Act did not force large trusts to bargain with labor unions. Historically, the government has generally not taken action to aid the goals of labor unions. This changed in the 1930s. President Franklin Roosevelt pushed for the creation of the National Labor Relations Board, which does encourage companies to work with organized labor in resolving workplace conflicts.

19. **3** High protective tariffs are intended to encourage American manufacturing. A high tariff would protect American manufacturing by making foreign goods comparatively more expensive to the consumer. Tariff rates

divided Northerners and Southerners in the first half of the 19th century. Northern manufacturing interests supported the Tariff Act of 1828, called by its critics the Tariff of Abominations, which set extraordinarily high tariffs on imported goods. Southern cotton farmers, who supplied much of Great Britain's cotton, feared that high tariffs would cause a drop in international trade. In the 1920s, isolationist senators attempted to limit United States interactions with Europe by raising tariff rates. These high tariff rates contributed to the Great Depression by cutting off foreign markets to United States goods. President Hoover stayed the course, raising tariff rates even higher with the Hawley-Smoot Tariff (1930). In the last decades of the 20th century, the debate has shifted. Business interests now support lowering or eliminating tariffs, while unions have sought to maintain protective tariffs. The United States approved the North American Free Trade Agreement (NAFTA) in 1993 and joined the new World Trade Organization (WTO) in 1994 with the goal of reducing or eliminating tariffs.

WRONG CHOICES EXPLAINED:

(1) High protective tariffs are not intended to promote free trade. Free trade entails an elimination of tariffs and other trade barriers.

(2) High protective tariffs are not intended to limit industrial jobs. High tariffs are intended to protect American industry from foreign competition and to promote the creation of industrial jobs.

(4) High protective tariffs are not intended to expand global interdependence. Lowering or eliminating tariffs would promote international trade and expand global interdependence.

20. **4** The government action associated with the efforts of muckrakers is the passage of the Meat Inspection Act (1906). The term *muckrakers* refers to the crusading journalists and writers of the Progressive Era who exposed wrongdoing by government officials, showed the negative side of industrialization, and let the world see a variety of social ills. Upton Sinclair wrote a stirring book in 1906 called *The Jungle* that exposed conditions in the meat packing industry at the turn of the 20th century. The book is a novel. However, it was thoroughly researched and well written. *The Jungle* exposes the horrible conditions that existed in this industry. Meat that spoiled was brought back to the plant, doused in bleach, and flavored with spices. Workers were not provided facilities to wash their hands. Rat droppings were swept into the hopper and mixed into the sausage meat. The conditions of the meat packing industry were thoroughly unsanitary and dangerous. The public uproar that followed publication of the book led Congress to pass the Meat Inspection Act and the Pure Food and Drug Act, which established the Food and Drug Administration.

WRONG CHOICES EXPLAINED:

(1) The ratification of the 19th Amendment (1920), extending the vote to women, is not associated with muckraking journalism. The issue was put on

the national agenda by the women's suffrage movement, which had been advocating extending the vote to women as early as the Seneca Falls Convention (1848).

(2) Approval of an income tax, which occurred with the ratification of the 16th Amendment (1913), is not associated with muckraking journalism. Progressive reformers pushed for this measure so that those with higher incomes would pay more than the poor.

(3) The creation of the National Forest Service (1905) is not associated with muckraking journalism. This measure was pushed for by President Theodore Roosevelt (1901–1909) as a way to conserve natural resources.

21. **2** In the early 1900s, Progressive Era reformers sought to increase citizen participation by supporting the direct election of senators. Reformers were successful in this effort when the 17th Amendment to the Constitution was ratified in 1913. From the writing of the Constitution until the ratification of the 17th Amendment, senators for each state were chosen by state legislatures. Framers of the Constitution envisioned the Senate as a wise upper house that would check the rashness and instability of the democratically elected House of Representatives. Progressive reformers challenged this and other aspects of the American political system in order to expand democracy.

WRONG CHOICES EXPLAINED:

(1) Expanding the spoils system would not increase citizen participation. The spoils system, which is often associated with the presidency of Andrew Jackson (1829–1837), involved elected officials rewarding supporters with government jobs. The practice continued after Jackson left office and became a public issue when President Garfield was assassinated in 1881 by a disappointed, and deranged, job seeker. Congress passed the Pendleton Act in 1883 to set up the federal civil service, a professional career service that allots government jobs based on a competitive exam.

(3) The electoral college was not created to increase citizen participation. The electoral college, which was written into the Constitution, was created as a check on the popular will of the people. The electoral college, not the popular vote of the people, ultimately determines who will be president.

(4) The Federal Reserve system was not formed to increase citizen participation. One of the main functions of the Federal Reserve Bank (created in 1913) is to regulate economic activity. If the economy is sluggish, the Fed will attempt to stimulate economic growth. If inflation occurs, the Fed will attempt to slow down economic activity. The most important mechanism for regulating economic growth is raising or lowering the interest rate at which the Fed loans money to other banks.

22. **1** The cartoon illustrates actions taken by President Theodore Roosevelt in securing the land to build the Panama Canal. The canal opened in 1903. By that time, the United States already had many possessions in the

Pacific. To reach those islands from the east coast of the United States took a great deal of time and effort. Merchant and naval ships had to travel around the southern tip of South America to reach the Pacific Ocean. The building of the Panama Canal was a major goal of President Theodore Roosevelt. Before 1903, Panama was a region of Colombia. American investors picked the narrow piece of land as an ideal location for a canal. When Colombia refused the United States's offer of $10 million to build a canal, American investors, with the backing of President Roosevelt and the U.S. military, instigated a rebellion in Panama against Colombia. In the cartoon, Roosevelt dumping "the first spadeful" of dirt on Bogota symbolizes Roosevelt's dismissive attitude toward Colombia. Panama became an independent country and immediately signed the Hay-Bunau Varilla Treaty with the United States (the new treaty in the cartoon), allowing the United States to build and administer a canal. President Roosevelt later boasted that he "took Panama."

WRONG CHOICES EXPLAINED:

(2) The cartoon does not illustrate President Roosevelt leading troops in the Spanish-American War. Before he was president, Roosevelt led a group of troops, nicknamed the Rough Riders, up San Juan Hill in Cuba in one of the battles of the Spanish-American War (1898).

(3) The cartoon does not illustrate President Roosevelt ending the war between Russia and Japan. Roosevelt did negotiate an end to the Russo-Japanese War and was awarded the Nobel Peace Prize (1906) for his efforts. However, these events are not depicted in the cartoon.

(4) The cartoon does not illustrate President Roosevelt improving diplomatic relations with Latin American nations. Roosevelt was not known for improving relations with Latin American nations. He claimed that the United States had the right to intervene militarily in the nations of Latin America. This assertion of U.S. might is known as the Roosevelt Corollary to the Monroe Doctrine. Latin Americans did not take kindly to Roosevelt's ventures into the region.

23. **3** Critics of the actions shown in the cartoon claimed President Theodore Roosevelt was following a policy of imperialism. Roosevelt's bold actions abroad won the approval of most Americans; he was a very popular president. However, a sizable number of Americans came to see American imperialist actions abroad, from the Philippines to Panama, in a negative light. These critics wondered how the United States, a country born in an anti-colonial war, could acquire an empire of its own. The most prominent anti-imperialist was the author Mark Twain, who chaired the American Anti-Imperialist League.

WRONG CHOICES EXPLAINED:

(1) The cartoon does not allude to President Roosevelt causing environmental damage. Roosevelt was the first president to show concern for the damage being done to the environment. Roosevelt, an avid outdoorsman and

conservationist, set aside millions of acres as protected areas. These include six national parks.

(2) The cartoon does not allude to President Roosevelt raising taxes. It does not mention the cost of the canal.

(4) The cartoon does not allude to President Roosevelt producing major trade deficits with China. During the period in question, the United States was a major manufacturer and maintained trade surpluses with most foreign nations. Only in recent history have Americans raised concerns about major trade deficits with China.

24. **1** A major reason the United States entered World War I was to maintain freedom of the seas. The United States initially assumed that it could stay neutral in World War I and maintain commercial ties to nations on both sides of the conflict. However, Great Britain successfully blockaded American ships from reaching Germany. Out of necessity, American trade shifted to Great Britain exclusively. Germany responded by warning that American ships in the waters off Great Britain would be subject to attack by U-boats, or submarines. The sinking of the British ocean liner *Lusitania* infuriated many Americans because 128 Americans were among the dead. Germany, however, wanted to keep the United States out of the war and agreed in the Sussex Pledge (1916) to make no surprise submarine attacks on American ships. The United States took advantage of this pledge and traded extensively with Great Britain. In 1917, Germany rescinded the Sussex Pledge and declared that it would resume unrestricted submarine warfare. Soon after, the United States declared war on Germany. The United States entered World War I for other reasons too. However, maintaining freedom of the seas was a paramount one.

WRONG CHOICES EXPLAINED:

(2) The impressment of United States sailors was not a reason the United States entered World War I. Impressment refers to the practice of seizing sailors and forcing them, or pressing them, into the navy. This was done by the British navy to American sailors in the early 19th century and was one of the causes of the War of 1812.

(3) Protection of United States cities from foreign attack was not a reason the United States entered World War I. The United States, with the Atlantic Ocean separating it from Europe, was not in immediate danger of direct attack at the time.

(4) A possible German invasion of Latin America was not a reason the United States entered World War I. Germany made no signals that it wanted to invade Latin America. In fact, it made overtures to Mexico. The Zimmerman Note revealed that if Mexico joined the German war effort, Germany would in turn help Mexico regain the land that the United States took from it following the Mexican-American War (1848). The Zimmerman Note angered Americans and is considered one of the reasons the United States entered the war.

25. **4** Isolationists in the Senate objected to the United States joining the League of Nations because they opposed involvement in future foreign wars. Membership in the League was part of the Treaty of Versailles, concluding World War I. By approving the Treaty of Versailles, the Senate would have also made the United States a member of the League of Nations. During World War I, President Woodrow Wilson championed the idea of an organization of the world's nations in his Fourteen Points document. Wilson pushed for United States approval of the Treaty of Versailles. However, some senators wanted to isolate the United States from world affairs and feared League membership would drag the United States into future foreign wars. These isolationists announced that they would vote to reject the treaty. Some senators took a middle position. They would agree to vote to approve the treaty if the Senate put certain conditions on American participation in the League of Nations. Wilson refused to compromise with these senators and urged his allies in the Senate to reject any conditions. Without these senators in the middle, the Treaty of Versailles and membership in the League of Nations were rejected by the Senate.

WRONG CHOICES EXPLAINED:

(1) The League of Nations did not have a Security Council. The United Nations (created in 1946) has a Security Council. The Security Council is one of the most important parts of the United Nations. It has 15 members—5 permanent members, each with veto power, and 10 rotating members. The United States is one of the permanent members. The Security Council can authorize peacekeeping operations and military actions.

(2) The League of Nations did not initially take a position on colonialism in Africa and Asia. Therefore, membership in the League would not have been tantamount to supporting colonialism.

(3) Isolationists were not concerned about German membership in the League of Nations. Germany was a member from the founding of the League (1919) until 1933.

26. **3** In the mid-1920s, the immigration policy of the United States was mainly designed to establish quotas to limit immigration from certain nations. The Emergency Quota Act (1921) and the National Origins Act (1924) greatly reduced the number of immigrants allowed into the United States. These acts set quotas for new immigrants based on nationality. The first act set the quota for each nationality at 3 percent of the total number of that nationality that was already present in the United States in 1910. The second act reduced the percentage to 2 percent and moved the year back to 1890. This had the effect of setting very low quotas for many of the new immigrants—people from eastern and southern Europe. The laws were passed in response to a large nativist, or anti-immigrant, movement. These quotas were largely in place until the Immigration and Nationality Act of 1965 ended the quota system.

WRONG CHOICES EXPLAINED:

(1) United States immigration policy in the 1920s was not designed to deport illegal immigrants. During the Red Scare of the late 1910s and early 1920s, several thousand suspected communists, anarchists, and radicals were deported. The phrase "illegal immigrants"—immigrants without proper paperwork—came into use in the late 20th century.

(2) United States immigration policy in the 1920s did not continue the traditional policy of open immigration. It did the opposite. It ended the traditional policy of open immigration by greatly reducing the number of immigrants allowed into the United States.

(4) United States immigration policy in the 1920s did not favor immigrants from southern and eastern Europe. It did the opposite. It set low quotas for the nations of eastern and southern Europe, reducing immigration from those nations to a trickle.

27. **2** A major problem facing American farmers in the 1920s was the overproduction of crops. Overproduction is a problem because it tends to push down the price per unit farmers receive for their produce. If prices per bushel of corn or per gallon of milk go down far enough, farmers could actually lose money, with production costs exceeding commodity prices. Overproduction was a problem in the 1920s for a number of reasons. Farmers had put more acres under cultivation during World War I to meet increased demand for agricultural goods. By the 1920s, Europe was back on its feet, yet American farmers did not cut back on production. Mechanization and expansion left the farmers of the 1920s in a cycle of debt, overproduction, and falling commodity prices. In addition, increased tariff rates and an isolationist foreign policy further reduced the international market for American agricultural goods.

WRONG CHOICES EXPLAINED:

(1) A shortage of fertile land was not a problem farmers faced in the 1920s. The states of the Midwest—Kansas, Iowa, Nebraska, and Missouri—provided farmers with fertile land as far as the eye could see. The problem was that too much land was under cultivation.

(3) Low prices on imported farm products was not a problem farmers faced in the 1920s. The government enacted high tariffs on imported goods. This hurt farmers by reducing global trade and cutting off American farmers from European markets.

(4) Limited labor supply was not a problem farmers faced in the 1920s. Mechanization had reduced the need for farm laborers, leading many rural people to migrate to cities.

28. **3** The contributions of Langston Hughes and Duke Ellington illustrate the importance of the Harlem Renaissance to the creative arts. The Harlem Renaissance was a literary, artistic, and intellectual movement that celebrated African-American life and forged a new cultural identity among

African-American people. The movement was centered in the African-American neighborhood of Harlem in New York City. Contributions included the poetry of Langston Hughes, Claude McKay, and Countee Cullen and the jazz music of Louis Armstrong, Duke Ellington, and Bessie Smith. Some of Hughes's important poems include "Harlem," "The Negro Speaks of Rivers," and "I, Too, Sing America." Duke Ellington was a composer, pianist, and bandleader who was perhaps the most important figure in 20th-century jazz. Some of his most important compositions are "Mood Indigo," "Don't Get Around Much Anymore," and "Take the A Train."

WRONG CHOICES EXPLAINED:
(1), (2), and (4) The Harlem Renaissance was not involved in the fields of economic growth, educational reform, or political leadership. Activists were involved in these fields in the 1920s and have been since then, but the Harlem Renaissance was a cultural and artistic movement.

29. **2** The Civilian Conservation Corps (CCC) and the Works Progress Administration (WPA) were both New Deal programs developed to address the problem of high unemployment. The New Deal was a series of programs and agencies that sought to address the economic problems created by the Great Depression. President Franklin D. Roosevelt took the federal government in a new direction by asserting that it should take some responsibility for the welfare of the people. Previously, churches, settlement houses, and other private charities helped people in times of need. High unemployment was a major problem in the 1930s, hovering between 10 and 20 percent of working-age Americans. The Civilian Conservation Corps (1933) provided outdoor jobs for young men. The vast Works Progress Administration (1935) consisted of a myriad of public projects. The WPA built schools, installed sewer lines, wrote guidebooks, and produced theatrical productions. The New Deal did not solve the economic crisis of the 1930s. However, it offered hope to many people and established a new role for the federal government.

WRONG CHOICES EXPLAINED:
(1) The CCC and the WPA were not designed to address the problem of excessive stock market speculation. The Securities and Exchange Commission (SEC) was developed in 1934 to address that problem. The SEC, also a New Deal agency, oversees stock market operations by monitoring transactions, licensing brokers, limiting buying on margin, and prohibiting insider trading.
(3) The CCC and the WPA were not designed to address the problem of increased use of credit. Excessive purchasing on credit was a problem associated with the 1920s more than with the 1930s. By the 1930s, purchasing in general was down.
(4) The CCC and the WPA were not designed to address the problem of limited income for senior citizens. The Social Security Act (1935), also a New Deal act, was designed to address the welfare of retired people and people

with disabilities by creating the Social Security system. The system provides monthly payments to senior citizens.

30. **3** A major reason that President Franklin D. Roosevelt proposed adding justices to the Supreme Court in 1937 was to influence Court decisions related to New Deal programs. Roosevelt grew increasingly frustrated with the conservative approach of the Supreme Court after it shot down the National Recovery Act in *Schecter* v. *United States* (1935) and the Agricultural Adjustment Act in *Butler* v. *United States* (1936). In 1937, he announced a plan to increase the number of justices on the Supreme Court to as many as 15. The president said that some of the older justices had difficulty keeping up with the heavy workload. It was clear, though, that he was trying to create a Supreme Court friendlier to his New Deal programs. In the American political tradition, each of the three branches of government is able to check the power of the other two. In this way, there would be a rough balance between the three. Roosevelt's court-packing scheme would have upset that balance by making the Supreme Court a rubber stamp for New Deal legislation. Congress opposed the plan. After much criticism, Roosevelt eventually backed away from it. Soon, however, openings on the Court allowed Roosevelt to appoint new justices and influence the direction of the Court.

WRONG CHOICES EXPLAINED:
   (1) Roosevelt's proposal to add additional justices to the Supreme Court was not intended to make the Court more democratic. The Court is not democratically chosen; justices are appointed for life. The Court acts as a check on the democratically elected branches of government.
   (2) Roosevelt's proposal to add additional justices to the Supreme Court was not intended to address corruption and favoritism. There were no accusations of corruption or favoritism on the Court at the time.
   (4) Roosevelt's proposal to add additional justices to the Supreme Court was not intended to ensure the appointment of members of minority groups. Roosevelt was not especially concerned with creating a Supreme Court that reflected the diversity of the United States. He did nominate a Jewish justice—Felix Frankfurter, who replaced another Jewish justice, Benjamin Cardozo (1939). However, the first African-American justice (Thurgood Marshall, 1967), the first female justice (Sandra Day O'Connor, 1981), and the first Latina justice (Sonia Sotomayor, 2009), were all appointed well after Roosevelt's time.

31. **2** The development of Dust Bowl conditions on the Great Plains led to the other events listed in the question. The Dust Bowl was the name given to a huge portion of the Great Plains that was devastated by unsustainable overfarming coupled with a long drought. The natural grass cover of the region had been removed in the years leading up to the Dust Bowl as wheat farmers increased the number of acres under cultivation. With this natural

root system gone, the fertile topsoil simply blew away when drought struck from 1934 to 1937.

WRONG CHOICES EXPLAINED:

(1) One effect of the Dust Bowl was the migration of 300,000 people to California to find work. During that decade, approximately 2.5 million people left the southern plain states of Oklahoma, Texas, Kansas, New Mexico, and Colorado to escape the Dust Bowl.

(3) One effect of the Dust Bowl was passage of New Deal legislation to conserve soil. The Resettlement Administration (1935) and the Farm Securities Administration (1937) both addressed the problem of soil conservation.

(4) One effect of the Dust Bowl was publication of John Steinbeck's novel *The Grapes of Wrath* (1939). Steinbeck was a major novelist who chronicled the lives of working-class people and the downtrodden. *The Grapes of Wrath* chronicled the plight of the Joads, an Okie (from Oklahoma) family of Dust Bowl refugees.

32. **4** In 1939, President Franklin D. Roosevelt responded to the start of World War II in Europe by selling military supplies to the Allied nations. Roosevelt supported the cause of the Allies, but Congress was not ready to enter World War II. Isolationists, citing disenchantment with American involvement in World War I, urged the United States to stay neutral. Roosevelt took a middle course, supplying the Allies with needed weaponry. As soon as the war began in 1939, Roosevelt pushed for legislation allowing the United States to send armaments to Great Britain with the condition that Great Britain pay for the weapons upfront and transport them in their own ships. This cash-and-carry policy allowed the United States to support Great Britain without the risk of American ships being destroyed. As time went on, the situation in Europe seemed dire. By 1941, more Americans were ready to help Great Britain directly, even if it risked getting involved in World War II. With this shift in public opinion and with his victory in the presidential election of 1940, Roosevelt pushed for the Lend-Lease Act, which allowed the United States to ship armaments to Great Britain in American ships. Though officially neutral, the United States was moving steadily toward intervening on the side of Great Britain.

WRONG CHOICES EXPLAINED:

(1) In 1939, President Roosevelt did not ask Congress to enter World War II. Americans were divided about participation in World War II. Not until the Japanese attacked American territory—the naval base at Pearl Harbor, Hawaii (December 1941)—did America declare war.

(2) In 1939, President Roosevelt did not urge continued appeasement of aggressor nations. Appeasement is the policy of not challenging a rival's moves in order to avoid a direct conflict. This policy was pursued by Great Britain and France toward Germany in the 1930s. The United States did not

pursue this discredited policy when World War II began. It aided those nations resisting the aggressor nations.

(3) In 1939, President Roosevelt did not attempt to negotiate a peaceful settlement of the hostilities of World War II. Earlier, Franklin D. Roosevelt's distant cousin, President Theodore Roosevelt, negotiated a peaceful settlement of hostilities between Japan and Russia. For his efforts, Theodore Roosevelt won the Nobel Peace Prize (1906).

33. **1** During World War II, federal economic controls increased. The government wanted to ensure a successful transition from a civilian economy to a war economy. The Roosevelt administration created the War Production Board to organize the production of military supplies. The Office of Price Adjustment set up a rationing system in which people could obtain goods needed by the military only if they had rationing coupons. These goods included butter, meat, shoes, and sugar. The system was designed not only to conserve materials for the military but also to keep down inflation. During times of war, inflation is a constant threat due to the lack of consumer goods and the additional money that people have in their pockets from all the work available in defense-related industries. Government efforts to control inflation were moderately successful. Inflation was about half as much as it was during World War I.

WRONG CHOICES EXPLAINED:
(2) The manufacturing of automobiles did not increase during World War II. The opposite occurred. No automobiles were produced in the United States between 1942 and 1945 as factories were converted to wartime production.

(3) Worker productivity did not decline during World War II. Productivity increased in order to meet the needs of the war.

(4) Prices did not fall rapidly during World War II. Inflation often occurs during times of war due to the scarcity of consumer goods and the high levels of employment. Government efforts kept inflation in check, but prices did not fall.

34. **4** The events on the timeline are most closely associated with a fear of communism. The anticommunist movement of the 1950s is known as McCarthyism, named for Senator Joseph McCarthy, who became the central figure in this movement. McCarthy gained prominence when he announced that he had a list of names of State Department employees who were members of the Communist Party (1950). Earlier, Alger Hiss, a State Department official, had been accused of spying for the Soviet Union (1948). Fears of communist spying on the United States intensified when the Soviet Union first tested an atomic bomb (1949). The government accused two members of the Communist Party, Ethel and Julius Rosenberg, of passing secrets of the nuclear bomb to the Soviet Union. The Rosenbergs insisted on their

innocence but were found guilty and sent to the electric chair (1953). The government investigated Communist Party infiltration in different sectors of society. Most notably, the entertainment industry was targeted because of its ability to reach so many people. The Hollywood 10 was a group of 10 prominent figures who refused to cooperate with the House Un-American Activities Committee (1947); they were jailed for contempt and subsequently blacklisted. The most intense period of the movement ended by 1954. The Korean War had ended, and McCarthy himself was discredited for making baseless accusations against members of the military. The hearings on these accusations, known as the Army-McCarthy hearings, were widely seen on the new medium of television (1954), demonstrating to the American public the reckless nature of McCarthy's accusations.

WRONG CHOICES EXPLAINED:

(1) The events on the timeline are not associated with the bombing of Pearl Harbor. The Japanese attack on Pearl Harbor, which brought the United States into World War II, occurred in 1941, before the events on the timeline.

(2) The events on the timeline are not associated with the launching of *Sputnik*. The Soviet Union launched the satellite *Sputnik* in 1957, after the events on the timeline. The launching of *Sputnik*, the first object sent into orbit, surprised the United States.

(3) The events on the timeline are not associated with the need for collective security. The United States did engage in collective security when it formed the North Atlantic Treaty Organization (NATO) in 1949 to challenge Soviet moves, but the actions on the timeline are associated with domestic fears.

35. **1** During the period of intense anticommunism, shown by the events on the timeline, the civil liberty most seriously threatened was freedom of speech. Holding particular views that were deemed subversive could result in loss of job or even prosecution. Many communists were arrested under the Smith Act during this period simply for advocating the agenda of the Communist Party.

WRONG CHOICES EXPLAINED:

(2) Freedom of religion was not seriously threatened during the period of intense anticommunism in the 1950s. Government and civic leaders encouraged public religiosity, in part to differentiate the United States from the atheistic Soviet Union.

(3) The right to bear arms was not seriously threatened during the period of intense anticommunism of the 1950s. Proponents of anticommunism also tended to be supporters of gun rights.

(4) The right to petition the government—the right to complain to the government and to ask for assistance or change—was not seriously threatened during the period of intense anticommunism of the 1950s. Americans

might have feared taking public stands in the 1950s, but they were still permitted to petition the government. The civil rights movement of the 1950s, for example, consistently petitioned the government.

36. **2** The presidential actions listed best support the conclusion that domestic programs are often undermined by the outbreak of war. When World War II began, President Franklin D. Roosevelt shifted his focus from the New Deal to the war. The New Deal became less of a priority because war production had largely ended the Great Depression. New Deal programs were simply not needed anymore. The Korean War had a similar effect on President Truman. His Fair Deal agenda took a back seat to the Korean War. Finally, President Johnson suffered a major political setback as money for his Great Society programs was siphoned off to fund the war in Vietnam. Many of the goals of his war on poverty were left unfulfilled.

WRONG CHOICES EXPLAINED:
(1) The list of presidential actions does not support the conclusion that presidents prefer their role as commander in chief to that of chief legislator. Each president took a great interest in domestic programs. Yet, for each president, wartime concerns superseded domestic ones.

(3) The list of presidential actions does not support the conclusion that Presidents Roosevelt, Truman, and Johnson were not committed to their domestic agendas. Each president took a great interest in his domestic agenda. Yet for each president, wartime concerns superseded domestic ones.

(4) The list of presidential actions does not support the conclusion that large domestic reform programs tend to lead nations toward involvement in foreign wars. The wars came in the aftermath of the domestic reform programs. However, a cause and effect relationship does not exist between the two.

37. **2** The United Nations was created mainly to work for international peace. Following the carnage of World War II, many world leaders as well as ordinary citizens pushed for an international organization that could resolve conflicts and maintain peace. Previously, the League of Nations (1919–1946), promoted by President Wilson and created after World War I, failed as an experiment in maintaining peace through international cooperation. The founders of the United Nations tried to learn from the mistakes of the League. The United Nations formed in 1945, complete with a Security Council and peacekeeping troops. It continues to function as an international organization.

WRONG CHOICES EXPLAINED:
(1) The United Nations was not created to prevent globalization. Globalization is a multifaceted term that refers to the growing interconnectedness of nations and regions. The term is usually used in regard to economic links but can also be used in discussing cultural phenomena that transcend particular nations or regions. (Examples include the Japanese video game

Super Mario Brothers and the American television series *Baywatch*.) Some activists have challenged the push to globalization. They claim that a globalized economy would be dominated by a few powerful nations and corporations, but the United Nations is not part of this movement.

(3) The United Nations was not created to stop the spread of disease. The United Nations has agencies that try to stop the spread of disease, such as the World Health Organization (1948) and the United Nations Children's Fund (UNICEF), created in 1946. However, the original purpose of the United Nations was to work for international peace.

(4) The United Nations was not created to establish democratic governments. It does not generally interfere in the internal politics of a nation unless there is clear evidence of human rights abuses.

38. **1** The United States policy of détente can best be described as an effort to reduce tensions with the Soviet Union. Détente is the French word for "loosening" and refers to an easing of tensions in the Cold War and a warming of relations between the United States and the Soviet Union. The policy was carried out by President Nixon. It may seem ironic that a man who made a name for himself as a strong anticommunist—as a congressman, he pursued suspected Soviet spy Alger Hiss (1950)—would be responsible for the détente policy. However, Nixon's anticommunist credentials enabled him to open relations with communist nations without being accused of being soft on communism. In 1972, Nixon became the first American president to visit communist China. Later in 1972, he held meetings with Soviet leaders in Moscow. The meetings produced several agreements, including an agreement to limit antiballistic missile systems (ABMs).

WRONG CHOICES EXPLAINED:

(2) The policy of détente is not associated with peace agreements with North Korea. No peace agreements have been signed by North Korea and the United States. The United Nations command (with United States support) and North Korea signed an armistice agreement, ending fighting in the Korean War (1953). The two nations currently have no formal diplomatic relations.

(3) The policy of détente is not associated with halting an arms race with China. The United States is currently concerned with increased military spending by China. However, the two nations did not initiate, let alone halt, an arms race.

(4) The policy of détente is not associated with an end to the embargo against Cuba. The United States began its trade embargo against Cuba in the 1960s to encourage political change in Cuba. The United States has had a tense relationship with Cuba since Fidel Castro led a successful revolution in 1959. Although Cuba is not a threat to the United States, neither major political party wants to end the embargo because neither wants to upset the Cuban-American community in Florida and risk losing Florida in the general election.

39. **4** The approach to reform illustrated in the photograph, which shows a nonviolent protest, is most closely associated with Martin Luther King, Jr. of the Southern Christian Leadership Conference. The marchers are demonstrating for an end to school segregation. The Supreme Court declared school segregation to be unconstitutional in its decision in *Brown* v. *Board of Education of Topeka* (1954). Unfortunately, many communities were slow to comply with the decision. Segregation was a focus of the civil rights movement of the 1950s and 1960s, and King was a central figure in the movement. King, a reverend from Atlanta, Georgia, gained prominence in 1956 by being the leader of the Montgomery, Alabama bus boycott. King supported directly challenging unjust practices through civil disobedience.

WRONG CHOICES EXPLAINED:

(1) Malcolm X of the Black Muslims is not closely associated with nonviolent protest. Malcolm X was an important advocate for justice for African Americans in the 1950s and 1960s. Between 1952 and 1964, he was a member and then a leader of the Nation of Islam. The organization advocates that African Americans organize among themselves, separate from whites. After making a pilgrimage to Mecca in 1964 and seeing Muslims of different races interacting as equals, Malcolm X revised his views about black separatism. He was killed by assassins from the Nation of Islam in 1965.

(2) Huey Newton of the Black Panthers is not closely associated with nonviolent protest. The Black Panther Party, which formed in 1966, grew out of the Black Power movement. It embraces self-defense and militant rhetoric. Initially, the Back Panthers focused on community organizing, but their activities grew increasingly confrontational.

(3) Booker T. Washington of the Tuskegee Institute is not closely associated with nonviolent protest. Booker T. Washington founded the Tuskegee Institute in 1881 to teach vocational skills to African Americans. Washington emphasized educational and economic progress for African Americans rather than political equality and civil rights.

40. **3** The activity shown in the photograph can best be described as an example of nonviolent protest. The tactic of nonviolent protest was central to the civil rights movement. Martin Luther King, Jr. stressed the importance of nonviolence. Nonviolence and pacifism have deep roots. Many Christians cite the biblical injunction to turn the other cheek if struck. Pacifism is especially strong in the Quaker tradition. The civil rights movement also got inspiration from Mohandas Gandhi's campaign to resist British authority in India in the first half of the 20th century. Gandhi taught that to resort to violence was to stoop to the moral level of the oppressor.

WRONG CHOICES EXPLAINED:

(1) The activity in the photo is not an example of labor unrest. Labor unrest has occurred periodically at work sites in American history. Labor unrest includes picket lines by striking workers.

(2) The activity in the photo is not an example of judicial activism. Judicial activism describes decisions by courts that, in the eyes of some, go beyond legal precedent. Those who charge judges with judicial activism assert that a decision might be based on personal bias or a political agenda. The term is often contrasted with judicial restraint.

(4) The activity in the photo is not an example of affirmative action. Affirmative action is the practice of employers and colleges taking race into consideration when looking at applicants in an attempt to rectify past discrimination.

41. **1** President Richard Nixon's decision to resign from the presidency in 1974 was based primarily on developments in the Watergate investigation. The Watergate scandal began in June 1972, when five men were caught breaking in to the headquarters of the Democratic Party at the Watergate office complex in Washington, D.C. Persistent reporting by Carl Bernstein and Bob Woodward of the *Washington Post* drew connections between the burglars and Nixon's reelection committee and ultimately the White House. Congressional investigators eventually learned that Nixon had been taping conversations in the White House. These investigators, hoping to find additional evidence, demanded that the tapes be turned over. Nixon argued that executive privilege allowed him to keep the tapes. In *Unites States* v. *Nixon* (1974), the Supreme Court ordered Nixon to turn over the tapes. Less than a month later, Nixon resigned.

WRONG CHOICES EXPLAINED:
(2) Nixon's decision to resign was not based on a backlash from his policies toward China and the Soviet Union. Some conservatives were angry with Nixon for pursuing a policy of détente and improving relations with China and the Soviet Union. However, this type of political disagreement did not lead to a presidential resignation.

(3) Nixon's decision to resign was not based on protests against his secret military actions during the Vietnam War. Protestors challenged the Vietnam War throughout Nixon's years in office, but these protests did not force him to resign.

(4) Nixon's decision to resign was not based on accusations of trading arms for hostages. Later, during the presidency of Ronald Reagan (1981–1989), a plan was devised to sell arms to Iran in violation of an arms embargo. In exchange, Iran would help secure the release of six hostages held by the Lebanese Hezbollah group. This transaction is part of the Iran-Contra scandal. Whether the president was aware of the transaction is still a matter of debate.

42. **2** The main topic of the cartoon is the imbalance in Japanese-United States trade. In the cartoon, Japan is portrayed as a castle. A steady flow of goods is leaving the castle through the large opening, while nothing is coming

into the castle through the much smaller opening. In the 1980s, Americans were concerned about the amount of products coming into the United States from Japan. American consumers were buying more Japanese products for several reasons. By the 1980s, many manufacturing plants in the United States were closing or were moving to countries where they could pay workers less. In addition, American automobile manufacturers were still making large, gas-guzzling cars, in contrast to smaller, fuel-efficient Japanese models.

WRONG CHOICES EXPLAINED:

(1) The cartoon is not commenting on the quality of Japanese goods. Japanese goods had a reputation for high quality.

(3) The cartoon is not commenting on the outsourcing of American jobs to Japan. Outsourcing involves an American company opening up operations in a foreign country. Jobs were not outsourced to Japan in the 1980s. The products made in Japan were made by Japanese, not American, corporations. Today, some Americans are concerned about the outsourcing of jobs to countries such as India.

(4) The cartoon is not concerned about the relocation of American companies to Japan. American companies were not relocating to Japan in the 1980s nor are they today. Today, many American companies are relocating to countries where they can pay workers less, such as Mexico, China, and Indonesia.

43. **1** If the cartoon were redrawn today, China would most likely replace Japan as the subject of the cartoon. Concerns about the imbalance of trade between the United States and China have emerged in the 2000s as China has become the leading manufacturer of consumer goods in the world. The United States has a large and growing trade deficit with China.

WRONG CHOICES EXPLAINED:

(2), (3), and (4) The United States trades with Brazil, Germany, and Russia but does not have a marked imbalance of trade with these countries. These countries do not produce the inexpensive consumer goods that China does.

44. **4** The event in Bill Clinton's presidency that best illustrates the system of checks and balances is his impeachment for alleged perjury and obstruction of justice. The impeachment episode began when accusations were made that he had a sexual affair with a 21-year-old intern named Monica Lewinsky. Clinton denied the accusations publicly and also before a federal grand jury. When Clinton later admitted the affair, congressional Republicans felt they had evidence of an impeachable crime—lying to a grand jury. Clinton emerged from the affair largely unscathed. Many Americans disapproved of his personal misconduct but resented the attempt by Republicans to remove him from office. In the system of checks and balances, each of the three branches of government—the executive, the legislative, and the judicial—has the ability to limit, or check, the powers of the

other two. The goal is to create balance among the three branches with no branch able to dominate the other two.

WRONG CHOICES EXPLAINED:

(1) Hosting peace talks between Israelis and Palestinians does not illustrate the system of checks and balances. The system of checks and balances involves one branch intervening in the activities of another. Clinton did host peace talks in his last weeks in office (2000–2001), but they did not result in an agreement.

(2) Being reelected does not illustrate the system of checks and balances. The system of checks and balances involves one branch intervening in the activities of another.

(3) Selecting a vice presidential candidate does not illustrate the system of checks and balances. The system of checks and balances involves one branch intervening in the activities of another. The president does not need congressional approval for his vice presidential choice, although he does for cabinet members.

45. **3** The letter is referring to the internment of Japanese Americans during World War II. In 1942, President Roosevelt issued Executive Order 9066, authorizing the government to remove 120,000 people, two-thirds of them citizens, from west coast states and relocate them to camps throughout the West. Most of their property was confiscated by the government. In the case of *Korematsu* v. *United States* (1944), the Supreme Court ruled that the relocation was acceptable on the grounds of national security. In 1990, as the letter indicates, the United States government publicly apologized to the surviving victims and extended $20,000 in reparations to each one.

WRONG CHOICES EXPLAINED:

(1) The letter does not refer to the bombing of Pearl Harbor. Japan did bomb the United States navy base at Pearl Harbor, Hawaii, in 1941. This act brought the United States into World War II. President Bush would not have issued an apology to Japan over that incident.

(2) The letter does not refer to the military service of Japanese Americans during World War II. Many Japanese Americans did serve in the United States military during the war and were commended for exemplary service. If anything, the government might issue a thank you letter, not a letter of apology.

(4) There was no specific ban on Japanese immigration after World War II. Earlier, in 1907, President Theodore Roosevelt and Japanese leaders negotiated a gentlemen's agreement in which Roosevelt agreed to reverse discriminatory legislation and Japan agreed to limit the number of emigrants coming into the United States.

46. **2** The terrorist attacks of September 11, 2001 led the federal government to create the Department of Homeland Security. The attacks have had a profound impact on domestic politics and foreign policy. On the morning of

September 11, 2001, 19 terrorists working with the al-Qaeda organization hijacked four domestic airplanes. The idea was to turn the airplanes into missiles that would destroy symbols of American power. One plane was flown into the Pentagon, inflicting heavy damage. Another plane crashed in a field after the hijackers were overtaken by passengers. The other two airplanes did the most damage, crashing into the two towers of the World Trade Center in New York City. The damage inflicted on each building weakened the structure of each so that both buildings collapsed within two hours. Approximately 3,000 people died from the four incidents, with the vast majority of the deaths occurring at the World Trade Center. The Department of Homeland Security was created in 2003, absorbing the Immigration and Naturalization Service. It is a cabinet level department with the responsibility of protecting the United States from terrorist attacks and natural disasters.

WRONG CHOICES EXPLAINED:

(1) The Environmental Protection Agency was created earlier, in 1970. President Nixon created it in response to concerns about damage done to the environment.

(3) The Central Intelligence Agency (CIA) was created earlier, in 1947. It replaced the Office of Strategic Services, created during World War II. The function of the CIA is to provide national security intelligence to senior members of the government and to carry out covert operations.

(4) The Federal Bureau of Investigation (FBI) was created earlier, in 1908. The FBI is a federal criminal investigative body. It also carries out domestic intelligence gathering.

47. **2** The Supreme Court ruled that segregated public facilities were constitutional in the case of *Plessy* v. *Ferguson* (1896). The decision stated that segregation was acceptable as long as the facilities for both races were of equal quality. In the case, the Supreme Court decided that racial segregation did not violate the equal protection provision of the 14th Amendment. The decision was a setback for those who sought an end to the Jim Crow system of racial segregation in the South. Jim Crow laws were state and local ordinances that first appeared after Reconstruction ended (1877). Typical laws called for separate schools or separate train cars for African Americans. Opponents of racial segregation argued that Jim Crow laws violated the 14th Amendment (1868). This amendment, ratified during Reconstruction, stated that no person shall be denied equal protection of the laws. Jim Crow laws, opponents argued, violated the 14th Amendment because the laws relegated African Americans to inferior public accommodations and had the effect of making African Americans second-class citizens. The Court disagreed. The separate but equal doctrine allowed for the continuation of the Jim Crow system until the 1950s and 1960s. The beginning of the end of the system came with the *Brown* v. *Board of Education of Topeka* decision of 1954.

WRONG CHOICES EXPLAINED:

(1) The case of *Worcester* v. *Georgia* (1832) did not deal with school segregation. This case arose in response to the Indian Removal Act (1830). The Supreme Court recognized the Cherokee people as a nation within the state of Georgia and ruled that they would not be subject to the act. The state of Georgia, with the support of President Andrew Jackson, began moving the Cherokee to the West anyway.

(3) The case of *Brown* v. *Board of Education of Topeka* (1954) did deal with segregation. However, it led to a decision opposite that of the *Plessy* case. In the *Brown* case, the court ruled that the separate but equal doctrine was inherently unfair to African Americans and unconstitutional. The Court heard a variety of types of evidence in the case, including studies on the psychological impact of segregation on young people.

(4) The case of *Miranda* v. *Arizona* (1966) did not deal with school segregation. This case revolved around the issue of self-incrimination. The 5th Amendment guarantees that people do not have to testify against themselves. That right is meaningless if arrested people are not aware of it. In this decision, the Court ruled that arrested people must be read basic rights, now known as Miranda rights, including the right to remain silent and the right to have a lawyer.

48. **4** The *Schenck* decision (1919) and the Patriot Act (2001) both deal with the power of the federal government to limit civil liberties for reasons of national security. The decision in *Schenck* v. *United States* upheld the Espionage and Sedition Acts, passed during World War I to put limits on public expressions of antiwar sentiment. Charles Schenck and other members of the Socialist Party had been arrested for printing and distributing flyers opposing the war and urging young men to resist the draft. The Supreme Court argued that freedom of speech is not absolute and that the government is justified in limiting certain forms of speech during wartime. The court argued that certain utterances pose a clear and present danger. By analogy, the court reasoned that one is not allowed to shout "Fire!" falsely in a crowded theater. The Patriot Act was passed by Congress less than two months after the September 2001 terrorist attacks. It greatly expanded the government's authority in the fight against terrorism. Some critics have argued that it gives the government too much power to pry into the affairs of individuals.

WRONG CHOICES EXPLAINED:

(1) Neither the *Schenck* decision nor the Patriot Act suspended the writ of habeas corpus. The writ of habeas corpus was suspended by President Abraham Lincoln during the Civil War. In 1863, he authorized the arrest without due process of people he thought were aiding the Southern cause. By the end of the war, over 14,000 people had been arrested under Lincoln's wartime provisions. Most of those arrested, however, were people actively aiding the Southern side in the Civil War.

(2) Neither the *Schenck* decision nor the Patriot Act deals with freedom of religion. Freedom of religion is enshrined in the 1st Amendment of the Constitution. Numerous Supreme Court cases have dealt with the issue. In *West Virginia State Board of Education* v. *Barnette* (1943), the Supreme Court ruled that it was unconstitutional to compel students to recite the Pledge of Allegiance because reciting it violated the religious freedom of Jehovah's Witnesses, who are not allowed to pledge allegiance to anyone or anything other than God.

(3) Neither the *Schenck* decision nor the Patriot Act deals with the limitation of civil rights of citizens.

49. **1** President Carter's decision to criticize South Africa's apartheid policy and President Clinton's decision to send troops to Bosnia were both responses to human rights abuses. South Africa practiced a system of segregation called apartheid. The system created classes of races, assigning rights and restrictions to each. The white minority rule effectively controlled and subjugated the large black majority. This unjust system was the object of protest throughout the world. Finally, in the 1970s, an American president, Jimmy Carter, strongly criticized the apartheid regime. In the early 1990s, the apartheid system in South Africa ended. In Bosnia, ethnic violence developed after the breakup of Yugoslavia. In 1990, the country divided into several smaller nations and a brutal war ensued. Serbian forces clashed with Bosnian Muslims. The United States and other countries decided to take action as reports of Serbian brutality became known. President Clinton brought leaders from Bosnia, Serbia, and Croatia together in 1995 in Ohio. A peace treaty was signed, and 20,000 NATO troops were dispatched to enforce it.

WRONG CHOICES EXPLAINED:

(2) Carter and Clinton were not responding to civil wars. In the case of South Africa, it was an internal situation but not war. In the case of Bosnia, it was a situation of a foreign country (Serbia) attacking the people of Bosnia.

(3) Carter and Clinton were not responding to immigration policies. Often countries prevent their residents from leaving. For the most part, the United States would not intervene in such a situation.

(4) Carter and Clinton were not responding to trade agreement violations. The United States has taken actions against countries that violate trade agreements. It might take a country to a World Trade Organization hearing, or it might implement some sort of embargo.

50. **1** The Supreme Court rulings in *Roe* v. *Wade* (1973) and *Planned Parenthood of Southeastern Pennsylvania, et al.* v. *Casey* (1992) are similar in that both cases dealt with a women's right to privacy. Both cases revolved around the issue of abortion. In the *Roe* v. *Wade* decision, the Court declared that states shall not prohibit women from having an abortion during the first two trimesters of pregnancy. Previously, the decision had been left to the

states, and many states forbade abortions. The Supreme Court reasoned that the Constitution guaranteed people the right to privacy. Abortion, they argued, was a decision that should be left to the woman with the advice of her physician. This decision echoed the reasoning of an earlier decision, *Griswold* v. *Connecticut* (1965), in which the Court ruled that laws forbidding the use of birth control devices were unconstitutional.

In the *Planned Parenthood* case, the Court upheld *Roe* v. *Wade* but allowed states to put certain restrictions on the right to an abortion. The issue of abortion has proved to be one of the most contentious issues in America in the late-20th and early-21st centuries.

WRONG CHOICES EXPLAINED:

(2) The two cases do not deal with a woman's right to medical insurance. The Court has not ruled that people have a constitutional right to medical insurance.

(3) The two cases do not deal with a woman's right to equal pay for equal work. The Civil Rights Act of 1964 guarantees equal pay for equal work.

(4) The two cases do not deal with a woman's right to participate in school sports. Title IX of the Education Amendments of 1972 banned gender discrimination in educational activities that receive federal assistance. Title IX mandated that schools provide athletic opportunities for female students.

PART II: THEMATIC ESSAY

Technology

Technological developments have had a major impact on American society and on the American economy. Sometimes the impact has been positive, and sometimes the impact has been negative. The cotton gin and the automobile are two technological developments that have dramatically reshaped the economy and the society.

The impacts of the cotton gin—both positive and negative—on American history cannot be underestimated. The cotton gin, invented by Eli Whitney in the late 1700s, was a device to separate the seeds from the strands of cotton. Previously, this tedious work was done by hand. With Whitney's gin, the process became easy and cotton quickly became an important crop throughout the South. Increased cotton production met the demands of a growing market for cotton. First in Great Britain and then in the New England states, manufacturers mechanized the processing of raw cotton into textiles. The cotton gin helped solve the supply problem of cotton production. Mechanized factories, another technological develop-ment, helped solve the demand problem. Soon cotton became so important to the southern states that it was nicknamed King Cotton.

However, the cotton gin also had a negative impact on American society. The work of growing and harvesting the cotton was carried out by slave labor. By the late 1700s, slavery seemed to be on the decline in the United States. Some prominent southern slaveholders were actually freeing their slaves. This occurred partly for political reasons because having slavery in a new, democratic nation looked bad. This also occurred partly for economic reasons. With increased cotton production, though, slavery got a huge boost. Slavery became an extremely profitable institution. Even slave owners changed their tune when talking about slavery. Earlier, they talked about slavery as a necessary evil. Once cotton and slavery became extremely profitable, they were no longer willing to concede that slavery was an evil. They now talked about slavery as a positive good. It was certainly good for the slaveholders. The claim that it was good for the slaves as well was met with a bit of skepticism. It became apparent that slaveholders would defend their profitable institution, come hell or high water. When African Americans (free and enslaved), abolitionists, and Free-Soilers all began to challenge slavery, southern slaveholders dug in their heels. When Abraham Lincoln took office, many of these slaveholders were ready to pull their states out of the United States. A bloody Civil War was needed to bring the country back together and to eradicate slavery.

Another important technological development in American history has been the automobile. Perhaps the automobile has been as important to America in the 20th century as the cotton gin was in the 19th century. The automobile offered freedom of mobility, sometimes called automobility, to Americans. The restless impulse that brought immigrants to this country and that impelled Americans to push farther and farther westward caused Americans to embrace the automobile with enthusiasm. The automobile freed people from living in compact cities. People no longer had to rely on living near a transit line. People could now live in leafy suburbs and vacation in remote places. After Henry Ford developed the assembly line and reduced the price of automobiles, the majority of Americans could afford one. The automobile industry provided a great boost to the American economy. The big three automakers—Ford, General Motors, and Chrysler—hired thousands of workers at decent wages. By the 1950s, many Americans were able to afford two cars, allowing stay-at-home wives a degree of freedom unheard of a generation earlier.

Americans may have gained increased freedom of mobility, but they have sacrificed a great deal for it. The uses of streets completely changed. Previously, urban streets—a precious public commodity in crowded gilded age cities—were used by children to play games and used by adults to carry out commerce. With the advent of the automobile, streets were given over to cars—both for driving and for storage. Children and pushcarts were removed from the streets in the name of automobility. That was only the beginning. To get into and out of cities, highways were built. Sometimes entire neighborhoods were demolished in order to create a path for a new highway. Highways often became barriers in cities, separating one neighborhood from another.

We also have to take into consideration the health and environmental impact of the automobile. Asthma rates have skyrocketed because of automobile exhaust. Also, emissions from automobiles continue to contribute to smog and to greenhouse gases. Americans have given up fresh air in the name of automobility. Finally, the process of acquiring petroleum has proven to be problematic. The United States has had to rely on repressive and unstable regimes in the Middle East to have a steady supply of oil. Recently, as known reserves of petroleum have become diminished, we have taken greater risks in finding the last remnants of petroleum. We have begun deep-sea drilling to extract petroleum. The devastating oil spill in the Gulf of Mexico in 2010 highlights the negative impact of our reliance on the automobile.

Both the cotton gin and the automobile have had major impacts on society. In both cases, the impacts have been both positive and negative.

PART III: DOCUMENT-BASED QUESTION

Part A: Short Answer

DOCUMENT 1

1 (1). According to the document, one right that was denied to women in 1855 was the right to have control or guardianship of their children.

1 (2). According to the document, another right that was denied to women in 1855 was the right to the product of their industry.

These answers receive full credit because they state two rights that were denied to women in 1855.

DOCUMENT 2

2 (1). According to Senator Robert L. Owen, one effect of the women's rights movement in Colorado was an increase in wages for women for doing equal work.

2 (2). According to Senator Robert L. Owen, another effect of the women's rights movement in Colorado was the passage of laws for the protection of children.

These answers receive full credit because they state two effects of the women's rights movement in Colorado.

DOCUMENT 3

3. According to Elisabeth Perry, one way in which women's participation in public life continued to be limited after winning suffrage was that women could not get the backing of the major parties when running for office.

This answer receives full credit because it states one way in which women's participation in public life continued to be limited after winning suffrage.

DOCUMENT 4A AND DOCUMENT 4B

4 (1). According to the 19th-century cartoon and the quotation, one effect that alcohol had on American society was to ruin people's fortunes.

4 (2). According to the 19th-century cartoon and the quotation, another effect that alcohol had on American society was to increase the number of cases of insanity.

These answers receive full credit because they state two effects that alcohol had on American society.

DOCUMENT 5

5. According to the 1912 document, the speaker thinks that the use of alcohol is "the greatest crisis in our country's history" because it weakens the health and virility of the American people.

This answer receives full credit because it states one reason the speaker thinks that the use of alcohol is "the greatest crisis in our country's history."

DOCUMENT 6A AND DOCUMENT 6B

6 (1). According to the two documents, one problem that resulted from national Prohibition was that bootleggers—sellers of illegally made alcohol—became so powerful that they were beyond the reach of the law.

6 (2). According to the two documents, another problem that resulted from national Prohibition was that it generated the perception that the government was not able to enforce the laws adequately.

These answers receive full credit because they state two problems that resulted from national Prohibition.

DOCUMENT 7

7. According to Mother Jones, one situation faced by children in the workplace in the late 1800s was that they did not get enough sleep and were constantly falling asleep at the workplace.

This answer receives full credit because it states one situation faced by children in the workplace in the late 1800s.

DOCUMENT 8

According to Stephen Currie, one reason that ending child labor was difficult to achieve nationally was that many members of Congress believed that only the states could take action against child labor, not the federal government.

This answer receives full credit because it states one reason that ending child labor was difficult to achieve nationally.

DOCUMENT 9

9 (1). According to Elmer F. Andrews, one way the Fair Labor Standards Act protected children was to prevent 14 or 15 year olds from working in hazardous manufacturing or mining operations.

9 (2). According to Elmer F. Andrews, another way the Fair Labor Standards Act protected children was to prevent the transporting of goods produced with oppressive child labor.

These answers receive full credit because they state two ways the Fair Labor Standards Act protected children.

Part B: Document-Based Essay

Reform movements have pushed American society in a variety of directions during the past two hundred years. The democratic spirit that inspired the birth of the nation has also inspired individuals to get involved, to work together, and to take action to improve things. Sometimes people have disagreed over what constitutes an improvement. However, the spirit of reform has been part of American society fairly consistently. Two reform movements that had major impacts on American history have been the women's rights movement and the temperance movement. Both movements had mixed results in terms of their success.

The women's rights movement of the 19th century developed in response to women being treated like second-class citizens. In the eyes of the law, women were practically nonexistent. Men had sole control over a couple's children. Men were legally entitled to their wives' property and even to the products of their wives' work. Women could not sue or inherit property. Women could not even fill out a will. (Document 1) In addition, women had difficulty changing this situation because they were excluded from the political process. Women could not run for office or even vote.

Starting in 1848, women began to challenge this unfair situation. In that year, women met in Seneca Falls, New York, to begin organizing. That meeting, the Seneca Falls Convention, was the beginning of the women's rights movement. Throughout the rest of the century, women like Lucy Stone, Lucretia Mott, and Susan B. Anthony pushed for change. The central focus of their movement was women's suffrage—extending the right to vote to women.

By the late 1800s, the movement was beginning to have victories. Before the United States granted women the right to vote, several states took that step. Most of the states that granted women the right to vote before ratification of the 19th Amendment were out West. Colorado, for instance, allowed women to vote in 1893. It was the second state, after Wyoming, to grant women the right to vote. (Document 2) Other western states followed suit.

The results of women winning the right to vote were, for the most part, positive. For example in Colorado, women successfully pushed for laws on a whole host of reforms. Colorado passed child protection laws, such as making it a crime to contribute to the delinquency of a child. Legislation was passed to provide better treatment for mentally ill people and to reform the prison system. Finally, several public health measures were passed, including one to improve public sanitation. (Document 2)

However, the ability of newly enfranchised women to effect change had limits. Male-dominated institutions often blocked women from exercising real power. For instance, the leadership of the major parties did whatever they could to block women from running for office. On the rare occasion when they could get on the ballot, women often found themselves running against male incumbents. Unseating an incumbent was (and still is) very difficult. (Document 3) Furthermore, other forms of prejudice and discrimination continued even though women earned the right to vote. Women achieved a tremendous victory with gaining the right to vote, but barriers still existed in society to true equality.

Another reform movement that had mixed results was the temperance movement. The movement to curb the consumption of alcohol has deep roots in American history. The movement predated the Civil War and continued through the rest of the 19th century. The movement finally accomplished its goal with Prohibition in 1919. However, the results of Prohibition were decidedly mixed.

The temperance movement advanced a variety of reasons why alcohol consumption was problematic. For one, excessive alcohol consumption ruined lives. People drank their fortunes away. A protemperance cartoon from the 1890s cited dishonored names and ruined characters as reasons to outlaw drinking. (Document 4a) A temperance publication from the 1870s echoes those charges. It asserts that drunkenness leads to poverty, crime, and insanity. (Document 4b) Dr. T. Alexander MacNicholl, quoted by the president of the Women's Christian Temperance Union (WCTU), a major temperance group, expressed concerns in a speech about the future of the United States. He was dismayed about the decline of men in America. He wondered if men would be strong enough to fight in the next war if they are overcome by alcohol. He labeled alcohol a poison that is a "thousand times more destructive" than diseases such as typhoid. He urged political leaders to take a stand, but he feared they were in the hip pocket of the alcohol industry. (Document 5)

All the agitating by the WCTU and other organizations finally paid off. The 18th Amendment to the Constitution was finally ratified in 1919. The movement had reason to celebrate, but it also had reason to worry. Passing Prohibition was one thing; enforcing it was another. Observers in the 1920s noted the difficulty in stopping bootlegging (illegal selling of alcohol). The police and the F.B.I. seemed weak in comparison to the boot-leggers. (Document 6a). The widespread practice of drinking illegal alcohol made the public question the ability of the authorities to enforce the laws of the land. The public became disenchanted, according to one historian, with the high degree of lawlessness in America. (Document 6b) Finally, the contradiction between policy and reality became too much for the public. The 18th Amendment was overturned by the 21st Amendment in 1933. Though drinking levels decreased during Prohibition, lawlessness increased. The experiment in Prohibition came to a quick end.

Both the women's rights movement and the temperance movement had mixed results. Both accomplished important goals—gaining the right to vote for women and prohibiting the sale, consumption, and production of alcohol. Once the goals were achieved, the results were not exactly what the activists had hoped for. Of the two, the women's rights movement has had a more positive and successful impact in the long term. The movement continues to push for change and continues to win victories. That is something the activists can drink to.

Topic	Question Numbers	°Number of Points
American political history	6, 15, 16, 20, 21, 26, 29, 30, 34, 35, 36, 41, 46	16
Political theory	3, 4, 7, 9, 10	6
Economic theory/policy	2, 18, 19, 33, 42, 43, 49	8
Constitutional principles	5, 8, 12, 14, 44, 47, 48, 50	10
American foreign policy	11, 13, 22, 23, 24, 25, 32, 37, 38	11
American studies—the American people	17, 27, 31, 39, 40, 45	7
Social/cultural developments	28	1
Geography	1	1
Skills questions included in the above content area		
Reading comprehension	5, 6, 36, 45	
Graph /table/timeline interpretation	34, 35	
Cartoon/photo interpretation	22, 23, 39, 40, 42, 43	
Map interpretation	1	
Cause-effect relationship	31	
Outlining skills	3, 7	

°Note: The 50 questions in Part I are worth a total of 60 percent of the exam. Since each correct answer is worth 60/50 or 1.2 points, totals are shown to the nearest full point in each content category.

Part I
Multiple-Choice Questions by Standard

Standard	Question Numbers
1—US and NY History	6, 11, 12, 13, 14, 15, 16, 17, 20, 24, 25, 26, 28, 30, 32, 34, 35, 36, 39, 40, 41, 45, 46, 49
2—World History	23, 37, 38
3—Geography	1, 2, 22, 31
4—Economics	18, 19, 27, 29, 33, 42, 43
5—Civics, Citizenship, and Government	3, 4, 5, 7, 8, 9, 10, 21, 44, 47, 48, 50

Parts II and III by Theme and Standard

	Theme	Standards
Thematic Essay	Science and Technology; Factors of Production; Physical Systems; Places and Regions	Standards 1, 3, and 4: US and NY History; Geography; Economics
Document-based Essay	Reform Movements; Civil Life; Change; Factors of Production: Individuals, Groups, and Institutions	Standards 1, 4, and 5: US and NY History; Economics; Civics, Citizenship, and Government

Examination August 2010

United States History and Government

PART I: MULTIPLE CHOICE

Directions (1–50): For each statement or question, write in the space provided the *number* of the word or expression that, of those given, best completes the statement or answers the question.

1 The presence of which pair of geographic conditions discouraged the development of a plantation economy in the New England colonies?

1 wide coastal plain and absence of good harbors
2 rocky soil and short growing season
3 numerous rivers and humid climate
4 flatlands and lack of forests   1 ____

2 What was the main cause of the French and Indian War (1754–1763)?

1 disputed land claims in the Ohio River valley between the French and the British
2 conflicts between American colonists and the French over control of the Great Plains
3 taxation of American colonists without representation in Parliament
4 violation of trade agreements between European nations and Native American Indians   2 ____

3 The British government's use of writs of assistance against American merchants is one reason the Bill of Rights includes protection against

  1 cruel and unusual punishment
  2 self-incrimination
  3 excessive bail
  4 unreasonable search and seizure   3____

4 ". . . Every thing that is right or reasonable pleads for separation. The blood of the slain, the weeping voice of nature cries, 'TIS TIME TO PART. . . ."

—Thomas Paine, *Common Sense*

In this quotation, Thomas Paine is trying to convince the colonists to

  1 accept the Proclamation of 1763
  2 break a treaty with Spain
  3 declare their independence from England
  4 dissolve their alliance with France   4____

5 Shays' Rebellion of 1786 was significant because it

  1 showed that the English still had influence after the American Revolution
  2 convinced many Americans of the need for a stronger national government
  3 revealed the increased threat from rebellious Native American Indians
  4 endangered the lives of many recent immigrants   5____

6 The Great Compromise reached at the Constitutional Convention resulted in the

1 formation of the Supreme Court
2 creation of a bicameral legislature
3 development of a two-party system
4 ban on the importation of enslaved Africans   6____

7 Building support for the ratification of the United States Constitution was the purpose of the

1 *Farewell Address* of George Washington
2 Albany Plan of Union
3 Mayflower Compact
4 *Federalist Papers*   7____

8 *Federalism* is best defined as a principle of government that

1 divides power between the central government and state governments
2 includes a system of checks and balances
3 allows the states to nullify national laws
4 places the most power in the hands of the legislative branch   8____

9 "All bills for raising revenue shall originate in the House of Representatives; . . ."

　　　—Article 1, Section 7, United States Constitution

The main reason the writers of the Constitution included this provision was to

  1 give citizens more influence over taxation issues
  2 assure that all citizens would pay taxes
✗3 deny presidents the power to veto revenue bills
  4 provide the government with a balanced budget　　　9＿＿＿

10 The United States Constitution grants the Senate the power to

  1 impeach governors
  2 issue pardons
  3 appoint ambassadors
  4 approve treaties　　　10＿＿＿

11 Which statement about the electoral college system is accurate?

  1 The number of electoral votes a state receives is based on its geographic size.
  2 A candidate can be elected president without the majority of the popular vote.
  3 Presidential candidates are forced to campaign equally in every state.
  4 The total number of electoral votes has increased with each census.　　　11＿＿＿

12 President George Washington set a precedent for all future presidents by

  1 appointing a career soldier to be Secretary of War
  2 choosing a friend to be Chief Justice of the Supreme Court
  3 campaigning actively for the office
  4 creating a cabinet of advisors   12____

13 A major reason President Thomas Jefferson authorized the Lewis and Clark expedition was to

  1 claim California for the United States
  2 explore a route to the Pacific Ocean
  3 remove British outposts from United States land
  4 establish settlements in the Southwest   13____

14 Starting with the election of President Andrew Jackson (1828), voter participation increased due to the

  1 passage of an amendment ending religious qualifications for voting
  2 extension of suffrage to Native American Indians
  3 end of property requirements for voting by many states
  4 arrival of more immigrants from nations with democratic governments   14____

15 **"Compromise Enables Maine and Missouri to Enter the Union"**

   "California Joins the Union As Part of Compromise of 1850"

   "Kansas-Nebraska Act Establishes Popular Sovereignty in the Territories"

   Which issue is most closely associated with these headlines?

   1 status of slavery in new states
   2 negotiation of the Oregon Treaty
   3 expansion of land for reservations
   4 influence of political parties on economic development   15____

16 During the 1850s, Irish immigrants were often discriminated against because they

   1 refused to participate in local politics
   2 displaced slave labor in the South
   3 arrived in the United States with great wealth
   4 practiced the Roman Catholic religion   16____

17 In his first inaugural address, President Abraham Lincoln stated his main goal for the nation was to

   1 use the vote to resolve the conflict over slavery
   2 free all slaves in the United States
   3 uphold the *Dred Scott* decision
   4 preserve the Union   17____

18 Poll taxes, literacy tests, and grandfather clauses were adopted in southern states primarily to

   1   enforce the terms of the 15th amendment
   2   keep African Americans from exercising their right to vote
   3   stop criminals and immigrants from voting
   4   eliminate bribery and corruption at polling places   18_____

19 During the late 1800s, major improvements to a nationwide system of trade were made with the

   1   construction of a network of canals
   2   use of steamboats on rivers
   3   completion of transcontinental railroads
   4   construction of toll roads   19_____

Base your answer to question 20 on the cartoon below and on your knowledge of social studies.

Next!

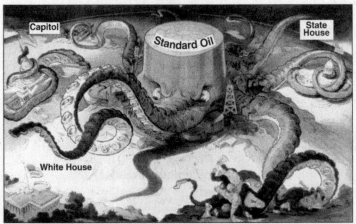

Source: Udo J. Keppler, *Puck*, September 7, 1904 (adapted)

20 The principal message of the cartoon is that the Standard Oil Company

1 used its size to lower the prices of its products
2 protected the nation from foreign competition
3 used its economic power to influence government decisions
✗4 employed violence to gain an unfair advantage for its workers

20 _____

21 Jacob Riis, Ida Tarbell, and Margaret Sanger are best known for their efforts to

  1 create awareness about social problems
  2 gain support for the women's movement
  3 expand the rights of Native American Indians
  4 win equal treatment for African Americans   21 _____

22 The Progressive movement supported the idea that the federal government should

  1 regulate big business
  2 reduce immigration
  3 build an overseas empire
  4 reduce the number of farms   22 _____

23 Which event most influenced President Woodrow Wilson's decision to enter World War I?

  1 defeat of Russia by Germany
  2 assassination of Archduke Franz Ferdinand
  3 raids by Mexico on the southwestern United States
  4 renewal of unrestricted submarine warfare by Germany   23 _____

24 In the early 20th century, what was the primary cause of the large-scale migration of African Americans out of the rural South?

  1 supply of new housing in the suburbs
  2 opportunities for jobs in northern factories
  3 availability of cheap land on the frontier
  4 absence of racial discrimination in northern states   24 _____

25 The conflict between science and religion in the 1920s was most clearly shown in the

1 trial of John Scopes
2 arrest of Sacco and Vanzetti
3 nativist reactions to immigration
4 poetry of the Harlem Renaissance   25 _____

26 One of the major causes of the stock market crash of 1929 was

1 excessive buying of stocks on margin
2 overconsumption of goods and services
3 failure of international banking systems
4 low prices of stocks and bonds   26 _____

27 Which action did President Franklin D. Roosevelt take that helped organized labor gain strength during the New Deal?

1 requiring the American Federation of Labor to admit skilled workers
2 allowing women to work in government agencies
3 signing the National Labor Relations Act (Wagner Act)
4 selecting John L. Lewis as his Secretary of Labor   27 _____

Base your answers to questions 28 and 29 on the cartoon below and on your knowledge of social studies.

"Ho hum! When he's finished pecking down that last tree he'll quite likely be tired."

Source: Dr. Seuss, *PM*, May 22, 1941

28 Which nations are represented by the two birds in this cartoon?

  1 Soviet Union and Great Britain
  2 United States and Soviet Union
  3 Germany and Great Britain
  4 United States and Germany   28 ____

29 Which statement most accurately expresses the point of view of the cartoonist?

1 Isolationism is the safest policy for these countries to follow.
2 The United States is ignoring the threat caused by foreign aggression.
3 Trade restrictions are more of a threat than leaders recognize.
4 England can defend itself against Axis aggression.   29 ____

30 Many of the songs, movies, and books of the 1930s are similar in that they

1 romanticized urban life
2 relived the bad times of the past
3 helped people escape from the realities of everyday life
4 pointed out the mistakes that led to the Great Depression   30 ____

31 What was a major result of the Servicemen's Readjustment Act of 1944 (GI Bill)?

1 Millions of veterans received a college education.
2 Women kept their factory jobs after World War II.
3 Jobs were created by the Manhattan Project.
4 Veterans were exempted from gasoline rationing.   31 ____

32 President Harry Truman changed the United States military after World War II by

  1 allowing women to serve in combat roles
  2 establishing an all-volunteer army
  3 banning racial segregation in the military
  4 withdrawing all military forces from Europe   32 ____

33 The United States committed to a Cold War policy of mutual defense when it

  1 aided the Nationalists in China
  2 established the Eisenhower Doctrine
  3 joined the North Atlantic Treaty Organization (NATO)
  4 rejected United Nations efforts to halt the development of atomic weapons   33 ____

34 Controversies involving Alger Hiss and Julius and Ethel Rosenberg reflected the post–World War II concern over

  1 testing nuclear missiles
  2 joining the United Nations
  3 placing weapons in outer space
  4 spying by communists in the United States   34 ____

35 Which development resulted from the construction of the interstate highway system?

  1 increased suburbanization
  2 reduced air pollution
  3 decreased fuel consumption
  4 growth of long-distance passenger train service   35 ____

Base your answers to questions 36 and 37 on the photograph below and on your knowledge of social studies.

Source: National Archives

36 What is a valid generalization that can be drawn from this photograph?

1 Activists often advocate taking over the government.
2 Demonstrators use nonviolent means to demand equal rights.
3 Civil rights leaders supported "separate but equal" education.
4 Protesters encouraged a nationwide strike by teachers.

36 _____

37 The delay in implementing which Supreme Court decision helped lead to the protest shown in this photograph?

1 *Plessy* v. *Ferguson*
2 *Brown* v. *Board of Education of Topeka*
3 . *Tinker* v. *Des Moines*
4 *New Jersey* v. *T. L. O.*   37____

38 The Supreme Court decisions in *Mapp* v. *Ohio* (1961) and *Miranda* v. *Arizona* (1966) directly expanded the rights of which group?

1 students with disabilities
2 women in the military
3 homeless Americans
4 persons accused of crimes   38____

39 Which development led to the other three?

1 growth of new home construction
2 increase in school populations
3 start of the baby boom
4 pressure on the Social Security system   39____

Base your answer to question 40 on the excerpt below and on your knowledge of social studies.

". . . With America's sons in the fields far away, with America's future under challenge right here at home, with our hopes and the world's hopes for peace in the balance every day, I do not believe that I should devote an hour or a day of my time to any personal partisan causes or to any duties other than the awesome duties of this office—the Presidency of your country.

Accordingly, I shall not seek, and I will not accept, the nomination of my party for another term as your President. . . ."

— President Lyndon B. Johnson, March 31, 1968

40 The decision announced in this speech was based primarily on the

1 assassination of Martin Luther King Jr.
2 growing violence in urban America
3 outbreak of terrorist attacks around the world
4 involvement of the United States in the Vietnam War   40 _____

41 The policy of détente pursued by President Richard Nixon was an effort to

1 increase foreign aid to African nations
2 maintain access to East Asian markets
3 reduce conflict with the Soviet Union
4 end trade barriers among Western Hemisphere nations   41 _____

Base your answer to question 42 on the cartoon below and on your knowledge of social studies.

PRESIDENT BUSH KICKED OFF THE LABOR DAY WEEKEND WITH A SURPRISE VISIT TO WORKERS IN BANGALORE, INDIA.

HELP WANTED

Source: Ed Stein, *Rocky Mountain News*,
September 2, 2004 (adapted)

42 Which statement best describes the point of view of the cartoonist?

1 Outsourcing of jobs has hurt American workers.

✗2 Americans receive most of their news from television.

✱3 United States presidents now seek support throughout the world.

✗4 Low unemployment rates have forced United States companies to expand overseas.

42 ____

Base your answer to question 43 on the cartoon below and on your knowledge of social studies.

Source: Walt Handelsman, *Newsday,* April 5, 2005

43 What is the main issue identified in this cartoon?

  1 the high cost of computer services
  2 conflicts between Congress and the Supreme Court
  3 the increasing lack of privacy
  4 limits placed on the powers of Congress   43 _____

44 A belief in Manifest Destiny is most closely associated with the decision to

  1 create the Bank of the United States
  2 suppress the Whiskey Rebellion
  3 declare war on Mexico
  4 build the Panama Canal   44 _____

45 Which policy of the United States was designed to prevent new colonization of the Western Hemisphere?

1 Monroe Doctrine
2 Open Door
3 Good Neighbor
4 Carter Doctrine 45 _____

46 The United States government is creating memorials along the Trail of Tears because it was

✗1 an important road used by settlers going to the frontier
2 the location of injustices against many Native American Indians
✓3 the site of victories by General Andrew Jackson during the War of 1812
4 the route followed by the first transcontinental railroad 46 _____

47 A goal that was established at the Seneca Falls Convention of 1848 was achieved in 1920 by the

1 creation of a free public education system
2 passage of legislation to end child labor
3 adoption of national woman's suffrage
4 ratification of an amendment requiring national Prohibition 47 _____

48 The emergence of third political parties such as the Know-Nothing Party, the Greenback Party, and the Prohibition Party indicates that

1 basic democratic values are often rejected by many United States citizens
2 a single powerful issue can mobilize political activity
3 third parties have failed to influence governmental policies
4 minor political parties are usually formed by strong leaders 48____

49 One common theme in many of the writings of Ernest Hemingway, F. Scott Fitzgerald, and Langston Hughes was

1 the need to regulate business
2 the benefits of mass production
3 optimism for reforms promised by the Great Society
4 dissatisfaction with the American culture of the 1920s 49____

50 **"Security Council Approves Use of Force Against Communist Invaders"**

"President Truman Fires General MacArthur"

"Armistice Divides Nation at 38th Parallel"

These headlines refer to which international conflict?

1 World War I
2 World War II
3 Korean War
4 Persian Gulf War 50____

In developing your answer to Part II, be sure to keep these general definitions in mind:

(a) <u>describe</u> means "to illustrate something in words or tell about it"

(b) <u>discuss</u> means "to make observations about something using facts, reasoning, and argument; to present in some detail"

PART II: THEMATIC ESSAY

Directions: Write a well-organized essay that includes an introduction, several paragraphs addressing the task below, and a conclusion.

Theme: Presidential Actions

> United States presidents have taken actions that have had a significant effect on United States foreign or domestic policies.

Task:

> Identify *two* presidential actions that have had significant effects on United States history and for *each*
> - Describe the historical circumstances surrounding the action
> - Discuss the impact of the presidential action on United States foreign policy or on American society

You may use any presidential action that has had a significant effect on United States history. Some suggestions you might wish to consider include George Washington issuing the Proclamation of Neutrality, Abraham Lincoln issuing the Emancipation Proclamation, William McKinley calling for war against Spain, Theodore Roosevelt supporting the Meat Inspection Act, Woodrow Wilson proposing the Fourteen Points, Franklin D. Roosevelt proposing the New Deal, Harry Truman making the decision to drop the atomic bomb, and Lyndon B. Johnson signing the Civil Rights Act of 1964.

You are *not* limited to these suggestions.

Do *not* use Thomas Jefferson purchasing the Louisiana Territory as your example of a presidential action.

Guidelines:

In your essay, be sure to:
* Develop all aspects of the task
* Support the theme with relevant facts, examples, and details
* Use a logical and clear plan of organization, including an introduction and a conclusion that are beyond a simple restatement of the theme

In developing your answers to Part III, be sure to keep this general definition in mind:

> <u>discuss</u> means "to make observations about something using facts, reasoning, and argument; to present in some detail"

PART III: DOCUMENT-BASED ESSAY

This question is based on the accompanying documents. The question is designed to test your ability to work with historical documents. Some of the documents have been edited for the purposes of the question. As you analyze the documents, take into account the source of each document and any point of view that may be presented in the document.

Historical Context:

> Geographic factors such as size, location, climate, and natural resources have played a critical role in the development of the United States. They have had both positive and negative effects on the United States throughout its history.

Task:

> Using the information from the documents and your knowledge of United States history, answer the questions that follow each document in Part A. Your answers to the questions will help you write the Part B essay in which you will be asked to
>
> • Discuss the positive **and/or** negative effects of geography on the development of the United States

Part A: Short-Answer Questions

Directions: Analyze the documents and answer the short-answer questions that follow each document in the space provided.

Document 1

> . . . Geography contributed powerfully to a policy of noninvolvement. A billowing ocean moat three thousand miles wide separated but did not completely isolate the American people from Europe. The brilliant young Alexander Hamilton pointed out in 1787, in Number 8 of the *Federalist Papers*, that England did not have to maintain a large standing army because the English Channel separated her from Europe. How much better situated, he noted, was the United States. His point was well taken, for geographical separation—not isolation—made possible the partial success of a policy of nonentanglement during most of the 19th Century. . . .

Source: Thomas A. Bailey, *A Diplomatic History of the American People*, Prentice Hall, 1980

1 According to Thomas A. Bailey, how did geography contribute to the United States policy of noninvolvement? [1]

_____

_____

Document 2

> . . . The President [Thomas Jefferson] was playing for large stakes. Louisiana [Territory] stretched from the Mississippi westward to the Rocky Mountains, and from Canada's Lake of the Woods southward to the Gulf of Mexico. If annexed, these 825,000 square miles would give the new nation access to one of the world's potentially richest trading areas. The Missouri, Kansas, Arkansas and Red rivers and their tributaries could act as giant funnels carrying goods into the Mississippi and then down to New Orleans. Even in the 1790s, with access to the Mississippi only from the east, the hundreds of thousands of Americans settled along the river depended on it and on the port of New Orleans for access to both world markets and imported staples for everyday living. "The Mississippi is to them everything," Secretary of State James Madison observed privately in November 1802. "It is the Hudson, the Delaware, the Potomac, and all the navigable rivers of the Atlantic formed into one stream.". . .

Source: Walter LaFeber, "An Expansionist's Dilemma,"
Constitution, Fall 1993

2 According to Walter LaFeber, what were *two* benefits to the United States from acquiring the Louisiana Territory? [2]

(1) _____

_____

(2) _____

_____

Document 3

. . . Other problems faced by wagoners [settlers] included howling wind, battering hail and electrical storms, lack of sufficient grass for the oxen, and wagon breakdowns. The forty waterless miles across the hot, shimmering desert between the Humboldt Sink and the Truckee River in Nevada exacted its toll of thirst on men and oxen. Rugged mountains of Idaho, Oregon, and Washington debilitated [weakened] men and animals. On the California branch loomed the Sierra Nevada, a formidable barrier of sheer granite. So high and perpendicular towered these granite walls, that wagons had to be dismantled and hoisted by rope, piece by piece, over precipices seven thousand feet above sea level. On some wagon trains, supplies ran low or became exhausted. Aid from California saved hundreds of destitute and emaciated pioneers. The story of the ill-fated Donner party that lost half its roster to starvation, freezing cold, and deep snows just east of Donner Pass in the Sierra Nevada is well-known. The great westward adventure was not for the weak, the timid, the infirm. One emigrant graphically recorded a small incident along the trail:

> On the stormy, rainy nights in the vast open prairies without shelter or cover, the deep rolling or loud crashing thunder, the vivid and almost continuous flashes of lightning, and howling winds, the pelting rain, and the barking of coyotes, all combined to produce a feeling of loneliness and littleness impossible to describe. . . .

Source: H. Wilbur Hoffman, *Sagas of Old Western Travel and Transport*, Howell North Publishers, 1980

3 According to H. Wilbur Hoffman, what are *two* examples of how geography *negatively* affected the westward movement of settlers? [2]

(1) _____

_____

(2) _____

_____

Document 4a

. . . Americans whose lives spanned the era from 1800 to 1850 must have been amazed at the changes in transportation that took place before their eyes. They saw the oxcart, the stage coach, the clumsy flatboat, ark, and scow, give way to the steamboat and to railroads run by steam power. They saw the channels of many rivers widened and deepened, thousands of miles of canals built in the North and West,* and thousands of miles of railroad lines threading their way across the country from the Atlantic coast toward the Mississippi River. They witnessed a transportation revolution. . . .

*In this passage, West refers to the area now known as the Midwest.

Document 4b

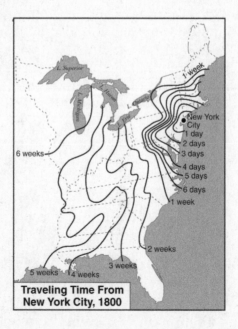

Traveling Time From New York City, 1800

Document 4c

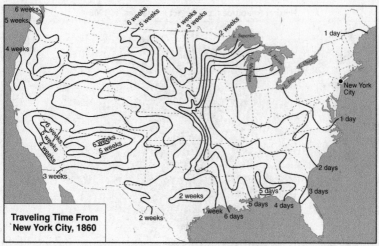

Source: Glyndon G. Van Deusen, *The Jacksonian Era*, Harper & Row, 1959 (adapted)

4 Based on these documents, what are *two* ways the size of the United States has affected its development? [2]

(1) _____

_____

(2) _____

_____

Document 5

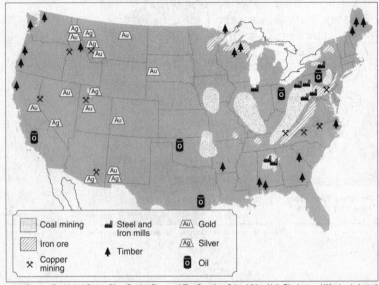

Natural Resources and Select Industries, c. 1900

Coal mining	Steel and Iron mills	Au Gold
Iron ore	Timber	Ag Silver
Copper mining		Oil

Source: *Our United States*, Silver Burdett Ginn, and *The Complete School Atlas*, Holt, Rinehart and Winston (adapted)

5 Based on this map, state *one* way natural resources have affected the economic development of the United States.   [1]

_____

_____

Document 6

... For years conservationists had warned that ecological catastrophe hovered over the Great Plains. The so-called short-grass country west of the hundredth meridian was favored by fewer than twenty inches of rain a year. Early explorers had labeled the frontier beyond the Missouri "the great American desert," and then it was relatively stable, hammered flat by millions of bison and untilled by the Indians. Then the settlers arrived with their John Deere plows. Before the Depression they were blessed by extraordinarily heavy rains, but as they pushed their luck by overgrazing and overplowing, the ineludible [unavoidable] drew nearer. Even in the 1920s a hundred counties in Colorado, Kansas, New Mexico, Texas, and Oklahoma had been called the "dust bowl." Now in 1934 the National Resources Board estimated that 35 million acres of arable [productive] land had been completely destroyed, the soil of another 125 million acres had been nearly or entirely removed, and another 100 million acres were doomed. Abruptly the bowl grew to 756 counties in nineteen states. Like Ireland and the Ukraine in the nineteenth century, the Plains were threatened with famine. ...

Source: William Manchester, *The Glory and the Dream*,
Little Brown, 1974

6 According to William Manchester, what is **one** way climate affected farming on the Great Plains? [1]

_____

_____

Document 7a

European War Narrows the Atlantic

Source: Bailey and Kennedy, *The American Pageant*, D.C. Heath and Co.

Document 7b

> . . . There are many among us who closed their eyes, from lack
> of interest or lack of knowledge; honestly and sincerely thinking
> that the many hundreds of miles of salt water made the
> American Hemisphere so remote that the people of North and
> Central and South America could go on living in the midst of
> their vast resources without reference to, or danger from, other
> Continents of the world.
>
> There are some among us who were persuaded by minority
> groups that we could maintain our physical safety by retiring
> within our continental boundaries—the Atlantic on the east, the
> Pacific on the west, Canada on the north and Mexico on the
> south. I illustrated the futility—the impossibility—of that idea in
> my Message to the Congress last week. Obviously, a defense pol-
> icy based on that is merely to invite future attack. . . .

Source: Franklin D. Roosevelt, Fireside Chat,
"On National Defense," May 26, 1940, FDR Library

7 Based on these documents, what is *one* way that the geographic location of the United States affected its foreign policy
before World War II? [1]

_____

_____

Document 8

Ranges of Offensive Missiles in Cuba

Source: James H. Hansen, "Soviet Deception in the Cuban Missile Crisis,"
Studies in Intelligence: Journal of the American Intelligence Professional,
2002 (adapted)

8 Based on this map, how did the location of Cuba influence the Cuban missile crisis? [1]

_____

_____

Document 9

We're getting a painful lesson in economic geography. What Wall Street is to money, or Hollywood is to entertainment, the Gulf Coast is to energy. It's a vast assemblage of refineries, production platforms, storage tanks and pipelines—and the petroleum engineers, energy consultants and roustabouts [oil field workers] who make them run. Consider the concentration of energy activity. Oil production in the Gulf of Mexico accounts for nearly 30 percent of the U.S. total. Natural-gas production is roughly 20 percent. About 60 percent of the nation's oil imports arrive at Gulf ports. Nearly half of all U.S. oil refineries are there. [Hurricane] Katrina hit this immense system hard. The shock wave to the U.S. and world economies—which could vary from a temporary run-up in prices to a full-blown global recession—depends on how quickly America's energy-industrial complex repairs itself. . . .

Source: Robert J. Samuelson, "Hitting the Economy," *Newsweek*, September 12, 2005

9 According to Robert J. Samuelson, what is *one* reason the Gulf Coast is important to the *economy* of the United States? [1]

_____

_____

Part B: Essay

Directions: Write a well-organized essay that includes an introduction, several paragraphs, and a conclusion. Use evidence from *at least five* documents in your essay. Support your response with relevant facts, examples, and details. Include additional outside information.

Historical Context:

> Geographic factors such as size, location, climate, and natural resources have played a critical role in the development of the United States. They have had both positive and negative effects on the United States throughout its history.

Task:

> Using the information from the documents and your knowledge of United States history, write an essay in which you
> - Discuss the positive *and/or* negative effects of geography on the development of the United States

Guidelines:

In your essay, be sure to:
- Develop all aspects of the task
- Incorporate information from *at least five* documents
- Incorporate relevant outside information
- Support the theme with relevant facts, examples, and details
- Use a logical and clear plan of organization, including an introduction and conclusion that are beyond a restatement of the theme

Answers
August 2010
United States History and Government

Answer Key

PART I

1. 2	14. 3	27. 3	40. 4
2. 1	15. 1	28. 4	41. 3
3. 4	16. 4	29. 2	42. 1
4. 3	17. 4	30. 3	43. 3
5. 2	18. 2	31. 1	44. 3
6. 2	19. 3	32. 3	45. 1
7. 4	20. 3	33. 3	46. 2
8. 1	21. 1	34. 4	47. 3
9. 1	22. 1	35. 1	48. 2
10. 4	23. 4	36. 2	49. 4
11. 2	24. 2	37. 2	50. 3
12. 4	25. 1	38. 4	
13. 2	26. 1	39. 3	

PART II: Thematic Essay See answers explained section.

PART III: Document-Based Essay See answers explained section.

Answers Explained

PART I (1–50)

1. **2** The presence of rocky soil and a short growing season in the New England colonies discouraged the development of a plantation economy. In contrast, the southern colonies, with a longer growing season, had large plantations specializing in crops such as tobacco, rice, indigo, and cotton. These southern plantations lent themselves to a slave system of labor much more so than the small farms of the North. The smaller farms of New England were generally worked by the owner of the property and his family, with more people hired for planting and harvesting. These smaller New England farms grew crops for local consumption rather than for national or international markets.

WRONG CHOICES EXPLAINED:
(1) New England did have an abundance of good harbors, such as Boston, Newport, and New Haven, but it did not have a wide coastal plain. A wide coastal plain is more characteristic of the geography of the South; its presence in New England would have encouraged, rather than discouraged, the development of a plantation economy.

(3) New England did have numerous rivers. Also, New England summers can be quite humid. However, the presence of these factors would not discourage the development of a plantation economy.

(4) New England is not known for extensive flatlands; its terrain tends to be hilly and mountainous. The presence of extensive flatlands would encourage, rather than discourage, the development of a plantation economy. New England was thickly forested; this geographic feature did discourage the development of a plantation economy, as farmers needed to clear these forested areas before they engaged in agricultural practices.

2. **1** A main cause of the French and Indian War (1754–1763) was disputed land claims in the Ohio River valley between the French and the British. In the 17th and early 18th centuries, these competing claims did not cause controversy because few colonists ventured into this territory. The few French colonists in North America remained, for the most part, in established French settlements—Quebec City, Montreal, Detroit, St. Louis, and New Orleans—far away from British claims. Likewise, British colonists stayed put in settlements hugging the eastern seaboard of North America. However, after 1750, as land in the original British colonies became more expensive, a few settlers crossed over the Appalachian Mountains and established farms in the Ohio River valley. These forays to the West led to conflicts with the French who had also established outposts in the Ohio River valley.

The war proved to be a devastating loss for France. It lost virtually all of its territorial claims in North America to the British.

WRONG CHOICES EXPLAINED:

(2) The French and Indian War was not caused by conflicts over control of the Great Plains. The Great Plains refers to the vast expanse of relatively flat land between the Mississippi River and the Rocky Mountains. The United States did not acquire this land until the 19th century, with the Louisiana Purchase (1803), Texas annexation (1845), and the Mexican Cession (1848). After the Civil War, bitter wars took place between the United States and various Native American nations over control of this area.

(3) The French and Indian War was not caused by taxation policies. Taxation policies were an important cause of the American Revolution (1775–1783). Many American colonists insisted that the British government should not be permitted to tax them unless the colonists were represented in Parliament. "No taxation without representation" was a rallying call for rebellious colonists.

(4) The French and Indian War was not caused by violations of trade agreements between European nations and Native American Indians. Such violations did not lead to warfare.

3. **4** The British government's use of writs of assistance against American merchants is one of the reasons the Bill of Rights includes protection against unreasonable search and seizure. The Bill of Rights is the first ten amendments to the Constitution. The protection against unreasonable search and seizure is contained in the Fourth Amendment. Writs of assistance are court orders instructing law enforcement officials to perform particular tasks. During the period leading up to the American Revolution, British courts routinely issued open-ended writs of assistance to customs officials, allowing them to search for smuggled goods. These writs were seen as abusive because they did not expire, nor did they refer to specific goods or specific merchants. The Fourth Amendment to the Constitution stipulates that a specific warrant— based on specific evidence—be issued before officials can engage in a search.

WRONG CHOICES EXPLAINED:

(1) The Bill of Rights does include protection against cruel and unusual punishment, but this protection was not inspired by the British use of writs of assistance. The protection is included in the Eighth Amendment to the Constitution.

(2) The Bill of Rights does include protection against self-incrimination, but this protection was not inspired by the British use of writs of assistance. The protection is included in the Fifth Amendment to the Constitution.

(3) The Bill of Rights does include protection against the imposition of excessive bail, but this protection was not inspired by the British use of writs of assistance. The protection is included in the Eighth Amendment to the Constitution.

4. **3** In the quotation, Thomas Paine is trying to convince the colonists to declare their independence from England. Paine's pamphlet *Common Sense*, written in January 1776, was an important factor in shifting public opinion in the thirteen colonies toward independence. Relations between England and the colonies were strained at the time Paine wrote his pamphlet. In April 1775, fighting began between patriots and British troops in the Massachusetts towns of Lexington and Concord. During the rest of 1775, tensions between the colonies and Great Britain worsened. The Second Continental Congress, a body of representatives from the thirteen colonies, created an army, declared war against Great Britain, and began issuing its own currency. Despite all this, many colonists were still hoping for reconciliation. Congress sent an "Olive Branch Petition" to the king of England in July 1775, affirming loyalty to the monarch and blaming the current problems on Parliament (King George III rejected the petition). Paine refuted the logic of the petition, plainly and forcefully putting the blame on the king. He argued that the thirteen colonies would thrive if they were free of their ties to England. "Tis time to part," he argued. Paine's arguments carried the day. In July 1776, the delegates to the Second Continental Congress formally ratified the Declaration of Independence.

WRONG CHOICES EXPLAINED:

(1) In the quotation, Paine was not trying to convince the colonists to accept the Proclamation of 1763. The Proclamation of 1763 was opposed by many colonists. It forbade colonists from settling in the area beyond the Appalachian Mountains. The quotation calls for "separation" from Great Britain. Further, Paine was still in Great Britain in 1763; he did not come to the thirteen colonies until 1774.

(2) In the quotation, Paine was not trying to convince the colonists to break a treaty with Spain. *Common Sense* addresses the broad issue of the relationship between the thirteen colonies and Great Britain. The quotation does not refer to a specific treaty.

(4) In the quotation, Paine was not trying to convince the colonists to dissolve their alliance with France. Paine was an outspoken supporter of the French Revolution (1789). He even went to France in 1790 and was elected to the National Convention. His enthusiasm waned after he was sentenced to death by the President of the National Convention, Maximilien Robespierre. He narrowly escaped death and ended up back in the United States.

5. **2** Shays' Rebellion of 1786 was significant because it convinced many Americans of the need for a stronger national government. The rebellion grew out of the frustrations of farmers in western Massachusetts. Taxes in Massachusetts were high and had to be paid in hard currency (backed by gold or silver), not cheap paper currency. Unable to pay these taxes, many farmers were losing their farms to banks. The farmers petitioned the legislature to pass stay laws, which would have suspended creditors' right to fore-

close on farms, but the Massachusetts legislature rejected the farmers' petitions. Hundreds of farmers, led by Daniel Shays, protested and finally took up arms. They were responding to a perceived injustice, as they had a decade earlier when under British rule. They closed down several courts and freed farmers from debtors' prison. Local militias did not try to stop the actions, which spread to more towns in Massachusetts. After several weeks, the governor and legislature took action, calling up nearly 4,000 armed men to suppress the rebellion. Concerns about the ability of the authorities to put down future uprisings were on the minds of the delegates to the Constitutional Convention, which convened just three months after Shays' Rebellion ended.

WRONG CHOICES EXPLAINED:

(1) Shays' Rebellion did not show that the British still had influence after the American Revolution. The rebellion was against Massachusetts state policies, not British policies.

(3) Shays' Rebellion did not reveal an increased threat from Native American Indians. Native Americans continued to challenge encroachments by white settlers in different parts of the United States, but the rebellion was against Massachusetts state policies.

(4) Shays' Rebellion did not endanger the lives of recent Americans. The rebellion was against Massachusetts state policies, not against immigrant groups.

6. **2** The Great Compromise reached at the Constitutional Convention resulted in the creation of a bicameral legislature. One of the main disagreements at the convention (1787) was how to create a representative system that met the desires of both the small states and the large states. The states with larger populations thought that they should have a larger voice in Congress. They rallied around the Virginia Plan, which would have created a bicameral legislature that pegged the number of representatives from each state to the population of the state. The small states feared that their voices would be drowned out in such a legislature. They countered with the New Jersey Plan, which called for a one-house legislature with each state getting one vote (similar to the existing Congress under the Articles of Confederation). After much wrangling, the delegates agreed on the Great Compromise, which created the basic structure of Congress as it now exists. The plan called for a House of Representatives, in which representation would be determined by the population of each state, and a Senate, in which each state would get two members.

WRONG CHOICES EXPLAINED:

(1) The Great Compromise did not result in the formation of the Supreme Court. The Supreme Court was called for in the Constitution itself; it is the only court specifically mentioned in the document. Its inclusion did not generate controversy.

(3) The Great Compromise did not result in the development of the two-party system. Political parties developed on their own in the decade after the ratification of the Constitution (1789).

(4) The Great Compromise did not result in the ban on the importation of enslaved Africans. Though the words *slave* or *slavery* do not appear in the Constitution, a compromise was reached between northern and southern states over the importation of enslaved Africans into the United States. The convention decided that the international slave trade could exist in the United States for twenty years, after which time it could be banned. Congress did pass such a ban, which went into effect in 1808.

7. **4** Building support for the ratification of the United States Constitution was the purpose of *The Federalist Papers*. After the Constitution was written in 1787, it needed to be ratified by the states. The framers stipulated that nine of thirteen states needed to ratify the document, despite the requirement in the Articles of Confederation that all the states had to agree to fundamental changes in governance. Delegates at the thirteen ratifying conventions debated the merits of the Constitution. Supporters of ratification called themselves "federalists" and called opponents of ratification "antifederalists." In many states, antifederalist sentiment ran strong. Antifederalists feared the Constitution would create an omnipotent and unaccountable government. They had vivid memories of the intrusions of the royal British government into their lives, and they wanted assurances that the people would have basic protections from government abuses. Three important proponents of ratification—Alexander Hamilton, James Madison (who wrote much of the Constitution), and John Jay—wrote a series of essays that were collected as *The Federalist* (renamed in the 20th century as *The Federalist Papers*). These essays challenged conventional wisdom of the time, arguing for an enlarged republic to prevent tyrannical rule by the majority and for a powerful chief executive. *The Federalist Papers* remain an important primary source, setting forth the philosophical underpinnings of American government.

WRONG CHOICES EXPLAINED:
(1) The *Farewell Address* of George Washington (1796) was not intended to build support for the ratification of the Constitution. It was written eight years after ratification. One of the highlights of the document is Washington's warning to avoid permanent alliances with foreign powers.

(2) The Albany Plan of Union (1754) was not intended to build support for the ratification of the Constitution. It was proposed 33 years before the Constitution was written. The plan, put forth by Benjamin Franklin, proposed cooperation among the thirteen colonies in response to the French and Indian War.

(3) The Mayflower Compact (1620) was not intended to build support for the ratification of the Constitution. It was written more than a century and a half before the Constitution was written. The Mayflower Compact was written and signed by the Pilgrims on board the Mayflower before it touched

land at Plymouth, Massachusetts. The Pilgrims agreed in this document to set up a government and obey its laws.

8. **1** Federalism is best defined as a principle of government that divides power between the central government and state governments. The Constitution created a federal system, granting powers to both the national, or federal, government and the state governments. This system of divided power is different from the government established by the Articles of Confederation (1781–1788). The Articles left most power at the state level and created merely a "firm league of friendship" among the sovereign states. The system is also different from the unitary system of countries such as France. In France the central government sets policies for the entire country with very little decision-making power at the local level.

WRONG CHOICES EXPLAINED:
(2) A definition of *federalism* does not include the system of checks and balances. The concept of checks and balances describes the separation of powers among the three branches of government; federalism describes the division of power between the national government and the state governments. The three branches—the legislative, the executive, and the judicial—each have specific powers spelled out in the Constitution. In order to prevent any branch from acquiring too much power, the framers created a system in which each branch has the ability to check the powers of the other two. The goal was to keep the three branches in balance.

(3) A definition of *federalism* does not include the power of states to nullify national laws. Only the Supreme Court has the power to nullify, or strike down, laws that it deems unconstitutional. This power is called judicial review. The theory that states could declare objectionable laws invalid within their borders was put forth by Thomas Jefferson and James Madison in 1796 in the Virginia and Kentucky resolutions, which were written in response to the Alien and Sedition Acts. The theory was again put forward by John C. Calhoun and other opponents of the Tariff Act of 1828, labeled the Tariff of Abominations.

(4) A definition of *federalism* does not include placing the most power in the hands of the legislative branch. Under the Articles of Confederation (1781–1789), the legislative branch dominated the national government, but under the Constitution, power is separated among the three branches of government—the legislative, the executive, and the judicial.

9. **1** The main reason the writers of the Constitution included the provision quoted in the question was to give citizens more influence over taxation issues. The House of Representatives was the only body within the national government that was directly elected by the people. The electoral college chooses the president. Initially, the electoral college was not constrained by popular votes in the various states; its members voted as they saw fit. Senators were chosen by state legislatures until ratification of the

Seventeenth Amendment (1913). As the only democratically elected body within the national government, the House was granted the important task of initiating taxation legislation. This was consistent with the cry made in the years leading up to independence—"No taxation without representation."

WRONG CHOICES EXPLAINED:

(2) The provision does not assure that all citizens would pay taxes. Taxes, in one form or another, are a reality of life in virtually any society.

(3) The provision does not deny presidents the power to veto revenue bills. The Constitution grants the president the power to veto any bill, including revenue bills.

(4) The provision does not provide the government with a balanced budget. Deficits have often occurred in American history, especially during times of war and economic downturns.

10. **4** The United States Constitution grants the Senate the power to approve treaties.

The president has the power to negotiate treaties with other nations, but those treaties only become binding after a two-thirds vote of approval by the Senate. The Senate does not always follow the president's wishes in regard to approving treaties. The most significant rejection of a treaty occurred in the aftermath of World War I. The Senate rejected the Treaty of Versailles and blocked United States participation in the League of Nations (1919).

WRONG CHOICES EXPLAINED:

(1) The Senate does not have the power to impeach governors. That power is granted to state legislatures by the various state constitutions. Generally, the lower house votes on impeachment and the upper house tries the impeached official, but exact rules vary from state to state.

(2) The Senate does not issue pardons. That power is granted to the president.

(3) The Senate does not appoint ambassadors. That power is granted to the president. The Senate has the power to confirm these appointments.

11. **2** Under the electoral college system, a candidate can be elected president without a majority of the popular vote. After the popular vote for president on Election Day, election boards determine which candidate won in each of the states. Whichever candidate wins in a particular state gets all the electoral votes for that state. The number of electors for each state is equal to the number of members of Congress from that state. States with larger populations, therefore, get more electors. The electors cast their votes 41 days after the popular vote. Presently, there are 538 electoral votes. A candidate must win the majority, or 270 votes, to be declared the president-elect.

A situation could arise in which a candidate loses the popular vote while winning in the electoral college. If candidate A won the popular vote overwhelmingly in several states whose electoral votes totaled 268, while candidate B just squeaked by in the remainder of the states, whose electoral votes totaled 270, candidate B would be declared president-elect even though he or she probably had less of the overall popular vote than candidate A. This scenario is not so farfetched. In 1824, 1876, 1888, and 2000, the candidate who became president had less of the overall popular vote than his challenger. In addition, victorious candidates have often won a plurality of the popular vote without achieving a majority of the popular vote. This occurred in 14 elections between 1844 and 1996.

WRONG CHOICES EXPLAINED:

(1) The number of electoral votes a state receives is not based on its geographic size. The number of electoral votes is based on the size of the state's population.

(3) The electoral college does not force, or even encourage, presidential candidates to campaign equally in every state. Because the electoral vote is determined by the outcome of the popular votes in each of the 50 states (as opposed to the overall popular vote), candidates routinely bypass states in which the outcome is fairly certain. They spend their time in the so-called swing states, which could go either way.

(4) The total number of electoral votes does not increase with each census. For many years, increases in population, as determined by the census, resulted in additional members in the House of Representatives, which resulted in additional electoral votes. However, the number of representatives was capped at 435 in 1911. An increase in the number of representatives from one state would necessarily involve a decrease from another state—keeping the total number of representatives and electoral votes fixed.

12. **4** President George Washington set a precedent for all future presidents by creating a cabinet of advisors. The cabinet is comprised of the heads of key government departments, known as cabinet-level departments. The first cabinet positions were secretary of state, secretary of war, secretary of the treasury, and attorney general. There are currently 15 cabinet-level departments and 7 additional cabinet officers. Cabinet members are nominated by the president and confirmed by the Senate. The precedents set in early American political history, notably by President Washington, have come to be known as the "unwritten constitution." The unwritten constitution refers to those traditions and practices that have become part of the American political system but were not mentioned in the Constitution.

WRONG CHOICES EXPLAINED:

(1) Washington's appointee for the secretary of war, Henry Knox, did have a history in the military, but not all subsequent secretaries of war have been "career soldiers."

(2) Washington appointed John Jay to be the first Chief Justice of the Supreme Court. This appointment was based on Jay's record of public service rather than on personal ties between Jay and Washington.

(3) Washington did not campaign actively for office. Washington was widely popular in the United States and did not have to campaign for office. Further, it was seen as undignified for a figure of such stature to publicly campaign. It was not until the age of Andrew Jackson that candidates actively campaigned for the presidency.

13. **2** A major reason President Thomas Jefferson authorized the Lewis and Clark expedition was to explore a route to the Pacific. The purchase of the Louisiana Territory spurred interest in exploration of the West. The Louisiana Territory was long held by France, until France ceded it to Spain (1763) following the French and Indian War. France then regained the territory in 1801. In need of cash to fund war with Great Britain, the French dictator, Napoleon Bonaparte, was ready to sell the Louisiana Territory at a reasonable price. American negotiators quickly agreed to a price of $15 million. With this purchase, the United States nearly doubled in size, with its territory extending as far west as present-day Montana and Wyoming. President Jefferson was interested in exploring this new territory as well as finding a route beyond it to the Pacific Ocean. Jefferson selected U.S. Army Captain Meriwether Lewis, an aide and friend, to lead the expedition. Lewis asked William Clark, also a member of the military, to co-lead the expedition. They recruited a Shoshone woman, Sacagawea, to act as a guide and interpreter. The expedition lasted from 1804 to 1806. Lewis and Clark reached the Pacific in 1805.

WRONG CHOICES EXPLAINED:
(1) Lewis and Clark were not authorized to claim California for the United States. California was clearly part of Mexico at the time. California, and much of the southwestern United States, did not become part of the country until 1848, following the Mexican-American War.

(3) Lewis and Clark were not authorized to remove British outposts from United States land. By the time of their expedition (1804–1806), the British had evacuated outposts on United States soil. This had been an issue in the decade following the American Revolution.

(4) Lewis and Clark were not authorized to establish settlements in the Southwest. The Southwest of the current United States was part of Mexico at the time. The Southwest did not become part of the country until 1848, following the Mexican-American War.

14. **3** Starting with the election of President Andrew Jackson (1828), voter participation increased due to the end of property requirements for voting in many states. Many states eliminated the requirement that voters had to own property in order to be allowed to vote. In 1824, approximately 27 percent of white men voted. That figure rose to more than 57 percent by 1828 and 78 percent by 1840. White male voter participation increased so significantly that the era following Jackson's election is known as the era of

Jacksonian democracy. The election of 1828 is considered by many historians to be the first modern election. Since the electorate was much broader than in previous elections, candidates had to campaign more aggressively and tailor their appeal to reach a broader audience. Related to the democratization of the voting process was an increased focus on character and personality.

WRONG CHOICES EXPLAINED:

(1) There is not a constitutional amendment ending religious qualifications for voting. In several of the colonies and in several of the states after independence, various religious groups were excluded from voting. Often, voting was limited to Protestants. This ended with the ratification of the Constitution. Article VI of the Constitution forbade such "religious tests" for voting.

(2) Native American Indians were not extended suffrage rights during the period of Jacksonian democracy. In 1924, the Indian Citizenship Act extended citizenship and voting rights to Native American Indians. Several states did not immediately comply. It was not until 1948 that Native American Indians had suffrage rights in all the states.

(4) Immigration patterns did not significantly increase voter participation during the period of Jacksonian democracy.

15. **1** The headlines in the question are associated with the issue of the status of slavery in new states. At the time of the birth of the United States, most politicians, even those critical of slavery, were not prepared to challenge the legitimacy of slavery where it already existed. Even as new states entered the Union in the first decades of the United States, northern politicians were ready to accept new slave states as long as the balance between slave and free states was maintained. The issue became contentious in 1820, when Missouri applied for statehood as a slave state. A compromise was reached (referred to in the first headline), allowing Maine to enter the Union as a free state (1820) and Missouri to enter as a slave state (1821). In addition, the compromise created a line through the territory acquired in the Louisiana Purchase. Above this line slavery would be forbidden (except for in Missouri itself); below this line, slavery would be allowed. Controversy erupted again when California applied for statehood as a free state in 1850. A set of bills was passed, known as the Compromise of 1850 (referred to in the second headline), allowing California to enter the Union as a free state and creating a strong federal fugitive slave law. The most rancorous controversy grew out of the 1854 Kansas-Nebraska Act (referred to in the third headline). The act allowed for the possibility of slavery north of the Missouri Compromise line based on the principle of "popular sovereignty." Anti-slavery Americans were outraged that residents of the Kansas and Nebraska territories could vote to allow slavery in these territories. The rancor resulted in violence in "bleeding Kansas" and set the stage for the Civil War.

WRONG CHOICES EXPLAINED:

(2) The headlines are not associated with the issue of negotiations over the Oregon Territory. Between 1818 and 1846, the United States and Great Britain agreed to "joint occupancy" of the Oregon Country. In 1846, a boundary line was established in the Oregon Country between American and British territory.

(3) The headlines are not associated with the issue of the expansion of land for reservations. Reservations are lands set aside for Native American Indians. The term was used in the Constitution, but the policy of creating reservations in the West was begun with the Indian Appropriations Act (1851).

(4) The headlines are not associated with the issue of the influence of political parties on economic development. Throughout American history, the two major political parties have often differed on economic policies. These differing approaches have influenced economic development in a variety of ways.

16. **4** During the 1850s, Irish immigrants were often discriminated against because they practiced the Roman Catholic religion. Nativism, or anti-immigrant sentiment, became especially widespread at the time of the large wave of Irish immigrants who started arriving in America in the 1840s and 1850s. A potato blight in Ireland caused approximately a million Irish to starve to death between 1845 and 1850, while another million left for America. Most Irish settled in port cities such as New York and Boston. Nativist sentiment manifested itself in the political realm—the anti-Irish "Know Nothing" Party won 25 percent of the vote in New York State elections (1854). Much of the anti-Irish sentiment was based on a prejudice against Catholicism. Nativists thought that the new Irish Catholic immigrants lacked the self-control of "proper" middle-class Protestant Americans. Also, many Protestants came to believe that Catholic immigrants would undermine democracy by following the dictates of the Pope.

WRONG CHOICES EXPLAINED:

(1) Irish immigrants did not refuse to participate in local politics. Irish immigrants were active in local politics, often supporting Democratic "machine" politicians.

(2) Irish immigrants did not displace slave labor in the South. The vast majority of Irish immigrants settled in northern cities. Many Irish immigrants feared that if slavery ended, freed African Americans would displace them at worksites.

(3) Irish immigrants did not arrive in the United States with great wealth. The vast majority were impoverished, and even starving.

17. **4** In his first inaugural address, President Abraham Lincoln stated that his main goal for the nation was to preserve the Union. By the time of Lincoln's inauguration, in March 1861, seven southern states had seceded.

Four more seceded after his inauguration. Lincoln repeatedly stated during the campaign that he would not interfere with slavery in the states where it already existed. Despite his lifelong moral opposition to slavery, he stuck by this position upon assuming the presidency. Gradually Lincoln moved toward policies that led to the abolition of slavery. Abolitionist activists argued that Lincoln should make the Civil War a war for emancipation. In addition, the progress of the war itself pushed Lincoln to see emancipation as a desirable move.

WRONG CHOICES EXPLAINED:

(1) Lincoln did not advocate using the vote to resolve the conflict over slavery. This position, known as "popular sovereignty," was advocated by Lincoln's opponent for the Senate in 1858, Democrat Stephen Douglas.

(2) Lincoln did not initially advocate freeing all the slaves in the United States. At first, as indicated in his 1861 inaugural address, Lincoln's goal was to preserve the Union and not touch the institution of slavery. With the issuance of the Emancipation Proclamation, Lincoln's position changed. The act called for ending slavery in rebel-held Confederate territory. By the end of the war, it was clear that a Union victory meant the end of slavery.

(3) Lincoln did not advocate upholding the *Dred Scott* decision. He was opposed to the decision. The decision revolved around Dred Scott, a slave, who sued to obtain his freedom on the grounds that he had lived for a time in territories where slavery was banned. The Supreme Court ruled that a slave owner still retained his property rights to his slaves even if he was in a state or territory where slavery was banned. The Court also ruled that Congress did not even have the power to ban slavery in the territories. The decision went on to declare that no African Americans, not even free men and women, were entitled to citizenship in the United States.

18. **2** Poll taxes, literacy tests, and grandfather clauses were adopted in Southern states primarily to keep African Americans from exercising their right to vote. After the Civil War, the Fifteenth Amendment (1870) to the Constitution was ratified to extend voting rights to African Americans. In response to the Fifteenth Amendment, Southern states adopted a variety of measures to prevent African Americans from voting. Poll taxes required people to pay a tax in order to vote. Literacy tests required people to demonstrate their ability to read before they were allowed to vote. Grandfather clauses allowed poor whites to vote if they could demonstrate that they (or their father or their grandfather) had the right to vote before the Civil War. These laws effectively prevented the vast majority of African Americans in the South from voting from the 1800s until passage of the Voting Rights Act in 1965.

WRONG CHOICES EXPLAINED:

(1) The three measures were not adopted to enforce the terms of the Fifteenth Amendment. The Fifteenth Amendment extended voting rights to

African Americans; the three measures sought to undermine the Fifteenth Amendment by preventing African Americans from voting.

(3) The three measures were not adopted to stop criminals and immigrants from voting. Immigrants gain the right to vote if they attain citizenship. Many states do not allow convicted criminals to vote, even after they serve their time.

(4) The three measures were not adopted to eliminate bribery and corruption at polling places. Later, during the Progressive Era (1900–1920), reformers pushed for measures to eliminate corruption in voting procedures and to make the process more transparent.

19. **3** During the late 1800s, major improvements to a nationwide system of trade were made with the completion of transcontinental railroads. The completion of the first transcontinental railroad at Promontory Summit, Utah, in 1869 was a milestone in the development of a network of railroad lines that connected the far reaches of the country. Railroads sped up the movement of goods and expanded markets. Production for local and regional markets was replaced by production for national and international markets. The government encouraged this expansion of the railroad network by giving railroad companies wide swaths of land. These generous land grants totaled more than 180 million acres, an area equal to the size of Texas. The railroad companies built rail lines on this land and also sold land adjacent to the tracks. The expansion of railroads into the west also encouraged white settlement in the Great Plains. The railroads provided an economic lifeline for these new settlers. Freight trains brought crops and cattle from the Great Plains states to cities such as Chicago. This increased economic activity led to Native American Indians being pushed off their land.

WRONG CHOICES EXPLAINED:

(1) The construction of a network of canals occurred in the first decades of the 19th century, not the late 1800s. By the 1840s, canals were becoming less important to the economy as railroads became more important.

(2) Steamboats became prevalent in the first half of the 19th century, not the late 1800s. Steam-driven ships continued to be important to economic activity through the first half of the 20th century, but it was railroad networks that created a nationwide system of trade in the late 1800s. During the second half of the 20th century, steamships were gradually replaced by diesel-driven ships.

(4) Rudimentary toll roads were built starting in the first half of the 19th century. The National Road, also known as the Cumberland Road, beginning in Cumberland, Maryland, in 1811, and heading west, facilitated transportation. However, it was the network of railroads that created a nationwide system of trade in the late 1800s. An extensive network of toll highways, built in the decades after World War II, transformed the American economy by allowing for interstate trucking.

20. **3** The principal message of the cartoon is that Standard Oil Company used its economic power to influence government decisions. The cartoon is criticizing monopolies. The specific monopoly being criticized is the Standard Oil Company, created by John D. Rockefeller. The cartoonist is depicting the extent of the power Standard Oil exerted in the United States. Standard Oil is represented as an octopus with its tentacles wrapped around various governmental institutions. The octopus is about to bring the White House under its control. The men who established these giant corporate entities were given the nickname "robber barons," implying that they had the power of a medieval baron and the scruples of a common criminal. In the last three decades of the 19th century, corporations came to play a very large role in society. Several of these corporations were able to exercise near monopoly control of particular industries.

WRONG CHOICES EXPLAINED:

(1) The cartoonist is not asserting that the Standard Oil Company used its size to lower the prices of its products. At times, Standard Oil did reduce the price of its oil, making it impossible for smaller refineries to compete. Once competition was eliminated, Standard Oil often pushed prices back up.

(2) The cartoonist is not asserting that the Standard Oil Company protected the nation from foreign competition. The cartoon makes no reference to foreign oil. It is not until late in the 20th century that the issues of foreign oil and oil dependency came to the fore.

(4) The cartoonist is not asserting that the Standard Oil Company employed violence to gain an unfair advantage for its workers. Large employers often resorted to violence in some of the epic labor battles of the late 1800s and early 1900s, but this cartoon does not allude to such labor conflicts.

21. **1** Jacob Riis, Ida Tarbell, and Margaret Sanger are best known for their efforts to create awareness of social problems. Riis was a photographer who drew attention to the living conditions of the urban poor. He was born in Denmark and immigrated to the United States in 1870. He worked as a police reporter but became interested in photographing the conditions of the urban poor. Riis turned his photographs of the poor in New York into the book *How the Other Half Lives* (1890). The book became influential in making middle-class people aware of the poverty that existed in the United States. Tarbell was an author whose book *The History of the Standard Oil Company* (1904) exposed the ruthlessness of John D. Rockefeller's oil company. Her book contributed to the government breaking up the Standard Oil Trust in 1911. Both Riis and Tarbell were considered "muckraking" journalists, using the power of the press to expose social problems. Sanger was an activist who raised awareness of the problems associated with impoverished women having too many children. As a nurse, she saw the impact of large families on the working class. Sanger coined the term "birth control." She argued that if women could have

some control over the number of children they had, they could avoid dire poverty. Sanger promoted birth control in a newspaper she published called *The Woman Rebel*. Federal authorities used old purity laws, which made it a crime to publish information on birth control devices, to declare Sanger's newspaper "pornographic." In 1916 she opened the nation's first birth control clinic in the United States, in Brooklyn, New York.

WRONG CHOICES EXPLAINED:

(2) The three individuals in the question were not all known for their efforts to gain support for the women's movement. Only Sanger's efforts contributed to the women's movement.

(3) The three individuals in the question were not known for their efforts to expand the rights of Native American Indians. An important activist who raised awareness of the treatment of Native American Indians was Helen Hunt Jackson. She wrote *A Century of Dishonor* (1882) on this topic and sent it to every member of Congress.

(4) The three individuals in the question were not known for their efforts to win equal treatment for African Americans. An important "muckraking" journalist who raised awareness about the treatment of African Americans was Ida B. Wells.

22. **1** The Progressive movement supported the idea that the federal government should regulate big business. Progressives argued that unbridled industrial capitalism was wreaking havoc on the nation. They cited unsafe conditions and long hours at worksites, child labor, and unfair practices by monopolistic corporations as some of the effects of unregulated big business. The Progressives were not socialistic. They wanted to reform capitalism, not abolish it. Out of the movement came the Clayton Antitrust Act (1914), which was designed to break up monopolistic trusts, and the Federal Trade Commission (1914), which was created to regulate business practices and protect consumers from unfair business practices.

WRONG CHOICES EXPLAINED:

(2) The Progressive movement did not support the idea that the federal government should reduce immigration. For the most part, the movement worked toward better treatment of impoverished immigrants.

(3) The Progressive movement did not support the idea that the federal government should build an overseas empire. The movement was largely focused on domestic, rather than international, issues.

(4) The Progressive movement did not support the idea that the federal government should reduce the number of farms. The movement was primarily an urban, rather than a rural, movement.

23. **4** The renewal of unrestricted submarine warfare by Germany most influenced President Woodrow Wilson's decision to enter World War I. The United States initially assumed that it could stay neutral in World War I and

maintain commercial ties to nations on both sides of the conflict. However, Great Britain successfully blockaded American ships from reaching Germany. Out of necessity, U.S. trade shifted to Great Britain exclusively. Germany responded by warning that American ships in the waters off of England would be subject to attack by U-boats, or submarines. The sinking of the British ocean liner *Lusitania* infuriated many Americans (128 Americans were among the dead). Germany, however, wanted to keep the United States out of the war and agreed in the Sussex Pledge (1916) to make no surprise submarine attacks on American ships. The United States took advantage of this pledge and traded extensively with Great Britain. In 1917, Germany rescinded the Sussex Pledge and declared that it would resume unrestricted submarine warfare; soon after, the United States declared war on Germany. Other reasons for U.S. entrance into World War I included President Wilson's promise to make the world "safe for democracy" and public anger over the Zimmerman telegram. The intercepted note from German foreign secretary Arthur Zimmerman indicated that Germany would help Mexico regain territory it had lost to the United States if Mexico joined the war on Germany's side.

WRONG CHOICES EXPLAINED:

(1) Germany did not defeat Russia. After the Russian Revolution (1917), the Bolshevik government, led by Vladimir Lenin, pulled Russia out of World War I with the treaty of Brest-Litovsk (1918).

(2) The assassination of Archduke Franz Ferdinand (1914) was the spark that began World War I. The United States did not enter the war until 1917.

(3) Mexico did not make raids on the southwestern United States. In the Zimmerman telegram (1917), Germany promised to help Mexico regain territory it had lost to the United States in the Mexican-American War (1846–1848) if Mexico entered World War I on Germany's side. Mexico declined the offer.

24. **2** In the early 20th century, a primary cause of the large-scale migration of African Americans out of the rural South was opportunities for jobs in northern factories. By the turn of the 20th century, the industrial revolution was in full swing in northern cities such as New York and Chicago. Factories, using new mass production techniques, were initially able to fill the jobs with local people and European immigrants. But World War I created a labor crisis for these factories. Factories were producing goods around the clock. However, European immigration to the United States dropped significantly due to the war. In addition, millions of potential factory hands were pressed into military service. This was a prime time for African Americans to leave the Jim Crow South and head to what they hoped would be the "promised land" of the North. This "great migration" was stimulated by word of mouth, letters from friends and relatives, and newspaper accounts. In addition, factory agents from the North frequently made recruiting trips to the South, offering immediate employment and free passage to the North.

WRONG CHOICES EXPLAINED:

(1) New suburban housing was not a cause of Africans Americans leaving the rural South in the early 20th century. The flight from city to suburb did not become a major phenomenon in American history until the 1950s. Even then, most of the new suburbanites were white. In fact, many suburbs had covenants that forbade the selling of homes to African Americans.

(3) The availability of cheap land on the frontier was not a cause of Africans Americans leaving the rural South in the early 20th century. The costs of developing land in the west and building a homestead were beyond most rural African Americans. Further, the term *frontier* is usually used in regard to the West in the 19th century and earlier. In 1890, the census office declared the frontier "closed."

(4) The absence of racial discrimination in northern states was not a cause of African Americans leaving the rural South in the early 20th century. Although northern states did not have the rigid Jim Crow codes that were common in the South, racial discrimination in housing, employment, and other areas of life certainly existed in northern states.

25. **1** The conflict between science and religion in the 1920s was most clearly shown in the trial of John Scopes. The Scopes trial involved the teaching of evolution in public schools. Scopes, a Tennessee biology teacher, was arrested for violating a state law forbidding the teaching of evolution. The case turned into a national spectacle, with the famous lawyers Clarence Darrow representing Scopes and William Jennings Bryan representing the state. The trial pitted rural, traditional, religious values against science. It is one of several important events that highlighted cultural divisions in the 1920s.

WRONG CHOICES EXPLAINED:

(2) The arrest of Sacco and Vanzetti did not involve the conflict between science and religion in the 1920s. Nicola Sacco and Bartolomeo Vanzetti were accused of robbing and killing a payroll clerk in Massachusetts in 1920. The evidence against them was sketchy and the judge was openly hostile to the two men, who were not only Italian immigrants but also anarchists. After they were found guilty, many Americans protested the verdict and wondered if an immigrant, especially one with radical ideas, could get a fair trial in the United States. Despite protests, the two men were executed in 1927.

(3) Nativist reactions to immigration did not involve the conflict between science and religion in the 1920s. Nativism was strong in the 1920s and resulted in the passage of legislation greatly limiting immigration into the United States. The Emergency Quota Act (1921) and the National Origins Act (1924) set quotas for new immigrants based on nationality.

(4) The poetry of the Harlem Renaissance did not involve the conflict between science and religion in the 1920s. The Harlem Renaissance was a literary, artistic, and intellectual movement that celebrated African-American life and forged a new cultural identity among African-American people. The

movement was centered in the African-American neighborhood of Harlem, in New York City. Contributions included the poetry of Langston Hughes, whose important poems include "Harlem," "The Negro Speaks of Rivers," and "I, Too, Sing America."

26. **1** One of the major causes of the stock market crash of 1929 was excessive buying of stocks on margin. Buying stocks on margin involves putting only a fraction of the cost of the stock down and promising to pay the rest on some future date. In the 1920s, stockbrokers provided easy access to credit so people could buy stock on margin. Brokers and potential investors reasoned that buying on margin was a sound move. After all, stock prices consistently rose throughout the 1920s. Because of easy access to credit, people were buying stock without even considering the soundness of the company they were investing in. People figured the market would just go up and up indefinitely. However, by the late 1920s, there were signs that the economy was weakening. The whole system of wild speculation and margin buying completely unraveled in October 1929 when investors lost confidence in the market and a selling frenzy overtook Wall Street, sending stock prices down to a mere fraction of their high prices. This crash of the stock market was an important factor that led to the Great Depression.

WRONG CHOICES EXPLAINED:
(2) Overconsumption of goods and services was not a cause of the stock market crash. In fact, the opposite occurred. By the late 1920s, consumption of goods and services could not keep up with production.

(3) The failure of international banking systems was not a cause of the stock market crash. Bank failures, at home and abroad, were a result of the Great Depression, not a cause of it.

(4) Low prices of stocks and bonds were not a cause of the stock market crash. In fact, the opposite occurred. Prices of stocks skyrocketed in the years and months preceding the crash. Low prices on stocks and bonds occurred as a result of the crash.

27. **3** President Franklin D. Roosevelt's signing of the National Labor Relations Act (Wagner Act) helped organized labor gain strength during the New Deal. President Roosevelt encouraged workers to join unions so that their wages, and purchasing power, would rise. He saw that one of the causes of the Great Depression was that workers in the 1920s were not able to purchase enough consumer goods to keep the economy growing. An important aspect of his New Deal was increasing workers' wages. The Wagner Act (1935) strengthened unions by mandating that employers bargain with their unions. It also established the National Labor Relations Board to conduct elections among workers to see if they wanted to be represented by a union. The act also banned certain unfair labor practices.

WRONG CHOICES EXPLAINED:

(1) The American Federation of Labor was already a union of skilled workers. In the 1930s, the Congress of Industrial Organizations broke away from the AFL with the goal of reaching out to unskilled workers.

(2) Women's participation in the workforce did not, by itself, help or hinder organized labor. Initially, New Deal programs were aimed at men, considered the "breadwinners" of American families. Later New Deal programs, such as the Works Progress Administration (1935), hired substantial numbers of women. The WPA, however, only hired single or widowed women, or women whose husbands were unable to work.

(4) Roosevelt did not select John L. Lewis as his secretary of labor. Lewis was the head of the United Mine Workers of America from 1920 to 1960 and was a moving force behind the creation of the Congress of Industrial Organizations in the 1930s.

28. **4** The two birds in the cartoon represent the United States and Germany. The stars and stripes hat on the bird in the foreground indicates the United States. The Nazi swastika on the bird in the background indicates Germany. The bird representing Germany has toppled most of the trees in the forest. These trees represent the countries that the Nazis had already attacked. The last untouched tree represents the United States. The bird in the tree seems oblivious to the obvious threat at hand. This cartoon was drawn in the period between the beginning of World War II (September 1939) and the United States entrance into the war (December 1941). During this period, Americans debated the wisdom of entering the war. This cartoon was created by Dr. Seuss, the pen name of Theodore Seuss Geisel. Dr. Seuss is well known for his successful children's books, such as *The Cat in the Hat* (1957) and *Green Eggs and Ham* (1960). However, working for the left-wing newspaper *PM* in the 1940s, Dr. Seuss created hundreds of pointed political cartoons mocking Hitler and Mussolini, as well as isolationists who opposed the war effort.

WRONG CHOICES EXPLAINED:

(1), (2), and (3) The birds in the cartoon represent the United States and Germany. The pairs of countries in the other choices are incorrect.

29. **2** The cartoonist is making the point that the United States is ignoring the threat caused by foreign aggression. This cartoon mocks those who were opposed to the United States entering World War II. It presents these opponents of intervention, often called "isolationists," as oblivious to the dangers surrounding them. According to the cartoonist, isolationists believed that Hitler would leave the United States alone after toppling all the major powers in Europe. Interventionists, on the other hand, perceived that Hitler and the Nazis were a threat to democracy and even civilization throughout the world. These debates ended abruptly after Japan attacked American forces at Pearl Harbor, Hawaii, in December 1941.

WRONG CHOICES EXPLAINED:

(1) The cartoonist is not asserting that isolationism is the safest policy to follow. The cartoon is asserting that isolationism is impossible. The bird representing the Nazis has attacked almost every tree in the forest. There is no way to prevent it from next attacking the United States.

(3) The cartoonist is not asserting that trade restrictions are more of a threat than leaders recognize. The determination and aggressiveness of the bird representing Nazi Germany would not be hampered by trade restrictions. Only force, the cartoon implies, would stop that bird.

(4) The cartoonist is not asserting that England can defend itself against Axis aggression. The tree representing England seems defenseless; we can expect it to quickly meet a fate similar to that of the other trees in the forest. The only hope, the cartoon implies, is for the bird in the last tree standing, the United States, to wake from its stupor and take action.

30. **3** Many of the songs, movies, and books of the 1930s are similar in that they helped people escape the realities of everyday life. The most important avenue of escapism was the movies. The movie industry, which had entered the "talkie" era in the late 1920s, thrived during the Great Depression. Between 60 percent and 90 percent of the American public went to the movies every week. Escapist musicals with lavish sets and spectacular numbers, such as *Gold Diggers of 1933* and *42nd Street* (1933), proved popular. In *The Wizard of Oz* (1939), Dorothy, played by Judy Garland, escapes the realities of everyday life on an impoverished Kansas farm and is transported, along with the audience, to the magical Land of Oz, shot in color.

WRONG CHOICES EXPLAINED:

(1) For the most part, popular culture of the 1930s did not romanticize urban life. Urban life was often presented as grim and hopeless. Much of popular culture romanticized the virtues of rural life. In *The Wizard of Oz*, Dorothy escapes Kansas for the Land of Oz, but ultimately she concludes, "There's no place like home."

(2) For the most part, popular culture of the 1930s did not relive the bad times of the past. Some books and movies depicted the bad times of the present. For example, *The Grapes of Wrath* by John Steinbeck (written in 1939 and released as a film in 1940) depicted the lives of displaced Oklahoma farmers.

(4) For the most part, popular culture did not point out the mistakes that led to the Great Depression. Generally speaking, economic policy is not the stuff of popular culture.

31. **1** As a result of the Serviceman's Readjustment Act of 1944 (GI Bill), millions of veterans received a college education. The GI Bill provided funds for veterans to attend college as well as low-interest loans to purchase homes.

The intent of the GI Bill was to help the veterans of World War II adjust to life during peacetime. The program was very successful. It helped millions of veterans advance economically. A college education and home ownership have been seen as key components of entrance into the middle class.

WRONG CHOICES EXPLAINED:

(2) The intent of the GI Bill was not to help women keep their factory jobs after World War II. In fact, the government did the opposite. It encouraged women to leave their factory jobs so that returning veterans could find work.

(3) The intent of the GI Bill was not to create jobs with the Manhattan Project. The Manhattan Project was the secret project to develop the atomic bomb. Launched in 1941 in an office building in New York City, the project involved several sites, but the final assembly of the atomic bomb occurred in Los Alamos, New Mexico. The bomb was ready by July 1945, as the United States was preparing for a final attack on Japan.

(4) The intent of the GI Bill was not to exempt veterans from gasoline rationing. By the time the majority of veterans returned to civilian life, the war was over and the need for gasoline rationing had passed.

32. **3** President Harry Truman changed the United States military after World War II by banning racial segregation in the military. Truman issued Executive Order 9981 in 1948, desegregating the armed forces, but he failed to implement it until the Korean War, when the military needed additional personnel. Truman took several steps in support of civil rights for African Americans. He created the Committee on Civil Rights in 1946 and he pushed Congress to enact the committee's recommendations in 1948. Truman was motivated to take these steps both out of personal conviction and in response to actions by civil rights activists. These activists included African-American veterans of World War II who had taken part in the NAACP's "Double V" campaign—victory against fascism abroad and victory against racism at home. Truman, however, felt he could not be too bold on civil rights because he would lose the support of southern Democrats.

WRONG CHOICES EXPLAINED:

(1) Truman did not move to allow women to serve in combat roles in the military. During the Gulf War in 1991, significant numbers of women served in combat roles for the first time.

(2) Truman did not move to establish an all-volunteer army. An all-volunteer army is an army that derives its troops from volunteers rather than draftees. For most of the history of the United States, the army has been an all-volunteer army. The military has resorted to a draft during the American Revolution, the Civil War, World War I, World War II, the Korean War, and the Vietnam War.

(4) Truman did not withdraw all military forces from Europe. The United States maintained a presence in Europe throughout the Cold War.

33. **3** The United States committed to a Cold War policy of mutual defense when it joined the North Atlantic Treaty Organization (NATO). United States participation in NATO, which formed in 1949, was one of several actions designed to check the power of the Soviet Union. The United States and the Soviet Union emerged at the end of World War II as rival superpowers in the Cold War. The Soviet Union occupied the nations of Eastern Europe after the war. In order to block any further aggression by the Soviet Union, Truman issued the Truman Doctrine, in which he said that the goal of the United States would be to contain communism. Toward this end, the United States extended military aid to Greece and Turkey (1947) and economic aid to the war-ravaged nations of Western Europe in the form of the Marshall Plan (1948). In 1948, the United States challenged the Soviet blockade of West Berlin. These moves, along with participation in NATO, represented a clear break with the pre-World War II position of the United States. The United States made it clear even in peacetime that it would be involved in world affairs.

WRONG CHOICES EXPLAINED:
(1) The United States did provide aid to the Nationalists in China, but it did this on its own, not as part of a policy of mutual defense. The Nationalists eventually lost. The Communist Party in China, led by Mao Zedong, established the People's Republic of China (1949) after a protracted civil war.

(2) The Eisenhower Doctrine (1957) made clear that the United States would provide economic and military aid to any Middle Eastern nation resisting communist aggression. The United States made this commitment on its own, not as part of a policy of mutual defense.

(4) The United States did not initially reject United Nations efforts to halt the development of atomic weapons. In fact, the United States made a proposal to the United Nations called the Baruch Plan (1946). In the plan, the United States, which had a monopoly on nuclear weaponry, offered to turn its nuclear arsenal over to the United Nations if other nations abandoned attempts to construct nuclear weapons. The Soviet Union, distrustful of the West, refused to support the plan, and the United States continued its research and development of nuclear weapons.

34. **4** Controversies involving Alger Hiss and Julius and Ethel Rosenberg reflected the post-World War II concern over spying by communists within the United States. Hiss, a State Department official, was accused of spying for the Soviet Union during World War II and earlier. Hiss's main accuser was Whitaker Chambers, who claimed that the two of them had worked together in the Communist Party. Chambers broke with the party and testified on behalf of the government in hearings before the House Un-American Affairs Committee (HUAC) in 1948. One of the leading questioners on HUAC was a young representative, Richard Nixon. Hiss, asserting his innocence, sued Chambers for libel after Chambers repeated his accusations on

television. After additional evidence emerged, federal authorities indicted Hiss for perjury in connection with his HUAC testimony. He was found guilty in 1950 of perjury, but the statute of limitations had passed for action to be taken on charges of spying. Ethel and Julius Rosenberg were accused of passing secrets about the nuclear bomb to the Soviet Union. The Rosenbergs, who were members of the Communist Party, insisted on their innocence and were sent to the electric chair in 1953. The two cases generated a great deal of publicity and emotion in the context of the anti-communist movement of the post-World War II era.

WRONG CHOICES EXPLAINED:

(1) The two cases did not involve the testing of nuclear weapons. The United States tested the first nuclear weapons in New Mexico in 1945. As more nations acquired nuclear weapons, they tested them—in part to monitor their impact and in part to let the world know that they had acquired nuclear weaponry. In 1963, many states, including all the nuclear states, signed the Limited Test Ban Treaty.

(2) The two cases did not involve joining the United Nations. The United States was one of the initiators of the United Nations and was among the first nations to join.

(3) The two cases did not involve placing weapons in outer space. President Ronald Reagan generated controversy in 1983 when he proposed a ground and space-based weapons system capable of shooting down nuclear ballistic missiles. Reagan called this plan the Strategic Defense Initiative; critics labeled it "Star Wars."

35. **1** The construction of the interstate highway system led to increased suburbanization. The federal government hastened development of highways with the Interstate Highway Act (1956). The act initiated the biggest public works project in United States history, a nationwide network of superhighways. The federal government paid 90 percent of the costs of construction, with the states paying the other 10 percent. Between 1956 and 1966, the federal government spent $25 billion to build 40,000 miles of highways. The government also saw the act, initiated during the Cold War, as a defense measure. The highways would allow for quick movement of troops and heavy military equipment. In addition, one could now drive into cities from the suburbs quickly and easily. After World War II, many people left American cities and moved to growing suburbs. This move was especially pronounced among young families, as men and women left the armed forces, married, and sought a better life for themselves in the suburbs. Government loans through the G.I. Bill and inexpensive homes, perfected by developer William Levitt, also made suburbanization attractive. A massive middle-class "white flight" out of New York, Detroit, Philadelphia, Chicago, and other major cities occurred in the 1950s.

WRONG CHOICES EXPLAINED:

(2) The construction of the interstate highway system did not lead to reduced air pollution. It did the opposite. The building of highways made frequent driving an attractive option for many Americans and has led to dramatically increased air pollution.

(3) The construction of the interstate highway system did not lead to decreased fuel consumption. It did the opposite. The building of highways made frequent driving an attractive option for many Americans and has led to dramatically increased fuel consumption.

(4) The construction of the interstate highway system did not lead to the growth of long-distance passenger train service. It did the opposite. The building of highways made frequent driving an attractive option for many Americans and contributed to the decline of long-distance passenger train service.

36. **2** From the photograph, one can draw the conclusion that demonstrators used nonviolent means to demand equal rights. The photograph depicts a civil rights demonstration. Martin Luther King, Jr., and other African-American and white leaders of the movement are seen leading this march. The signs indicate some of the key demands of the movement: an end to segregated public schools, voting rights, and greater access to jobs. The demonstrators are pictured nonviolently marching. King, a reverend from Atlanta, Georgia, supported directly challenging unjust practices through nonviolent civil disobedience. He gained prominence in 1956 by leading the Montgomery, Alabama, bus boycott. In 1963, the Civil Rights Movement held one of the biggest demonstrations in American history in Washington, D.C. More than 200,000 people gathered to march, sing, and hear speeches, including King's "I Have a Dream" speech.

WRONG CHOICES EXPLAINED:

(1) The picture does not depict activists advocating the take over of the government. We see demonstrators exercising their First Amendment right to peaceably assemble.

(3) The picture does not depict civil rights leaders voicing support for the "separate but equal" doctrine in education. Civil rights opposed this doctrine. The phrase came out of the *Plessy v. Ferguson* (1896) decision. That decision upheld segregation, under the condition that facilities for African Americans be of equal quality to those for whites. In practice, facilities for African Americans were almost always of inferior quality.

(4) The picture does not depict a teachers' strike. Teachers' strikes did occur during the time of the Civil Rights Movement. A contentious strike occurred among New York City teachers in 1968. However, the signs indicate a civil rights march rather than a labor action.

37. **2** One of the reasons for the protest shown in the photograph was the delay in the implementation of the Supreme Court decision in *Brown* v. *Board of Education of Topeka* (1954). In this landmark case, the Supreme Court declared school segregation to be unconstitutional, but many communities were slow to comply with the decision. The *Brown* case was actually several cases looked at simultaneously by the Court. The Brown in the case was the Reverend Oliver Brown, whose eight-year-old daughter had to go to an African-American school more than a mile away from her house rather than attend a white school nearby. The Court heard a variety of types of evidence in the case, including studies on the psychological impact of segregation on young people. The Court ruled unanimously that segregation in public schools was unfair and had to end.

WRONG CHOICES EXPLAINED:
(1) The protest did not grow out of the tardy implementation of the *Plessy* v. *Ferguson* (1896) decision. That decision, allowing for segregation under the principle of "separate but equal," was implemented enthusiastically by white authorities throughout the South. The Civil Rights Movement opposed the system of segregation.

(3) The protest does not involve the issues raised in the case of *Tinker* v. *Des Moines* (1969). In that case, the Supreme Court ruled that a school board prohibition against students wearing black armbands in protest of the war in Vietnam was unconstitutional. The Court ruled that students in school had the right to free speech, including symbolic speech, as long as their actions did not interfere with the educational process.

(4) The protest does not involve the issues raised in the case of *New Jersey* v. *T.L.O.* (1985). That case dealt with the legality of searches of students without search warrants. T.L.O. is the initials of a female student in a New Jersey high school who was caught by a teacher smoking in a bathroom. School officials searched T.L.O.'s bag and found evidence implicating her in both taking and selling marijuana. The Supreme Court ruled that the search was permissible, noting that school officials may balance a student's expectation of privacy with the school's need to maintain discipline and security.

38. **4** The Supreme Court decisions in *Mapp* v. *Ohio* (1961) and *Miranda* v. *Arizona* (1966) expanded the rights of persons accused of crimes. In *Mapp* v. *Ohio*, the Court ruled that evidence obtained in violation of the Fourth Amendment protection against "unreasonable searches and seizures" must be excluded from criminal prosecutions in state courts, as well as in federal courts. The *Miranda* v. *Arizona* decision revolved around the issue of self-incrimination. The Fifth Amendment guarantees that people do not have to testify against themselves. However, that right is meaningless if arrested people are not aware of it. In this decision, the Court ruled that arrested people must be read basic rights, now known as "Miranda rights," including the right to remain silent and the right to have a lawyer. These decisions were issued

by the Supreme Court under the leadership of Earl Warren (chief justice from 1953 to 1969).

WRONG CHOICES EXPLAINED:

(1) The two decisions mentioned in the question do not address the rights of students with disabilities. Several court decisions in the early 1970s mandated that states provide educational services to students with disabilities. The Education for All Handicapped Children Act (1975) and the Individuals With Disabilities Education Act (1990) enforce this mandate and provide guidelines for education for students with disabilities.

(2) The two decisions mentioned in the question do not address the rights of women in the military. Women have contributed to military operations throughout American history. The Women's Army Auxiliary Corps was formed during World War II. Women served in combat roles starting with the Gulf War (1991).

(3) The two decisions mentioned in the question do not address the rights of homeless Americans. Courts have generally ruled that laws that, in effect, make it a crime to be homeless are unconstitutional.

39. **3** The start of the baby boom caused a growth of new home construction, an increase in school population, and, much later, an increase in pressure on the Social Security system. The baby boom occurred in the aftermath of World War II. For several years before 1946, birth rates in the United States remained relatively low. Couples tended to have fewer children during the lean years of the Great Depression, and the dislocation and physical separation caused by World War II kept the birthrate even lower. However, when the war ended, returning veterans quickly got down to the business of starting families. The spike in birthrates from 1946 through the early 1960s produced a baby boom that would have lasting repercussions in American society.

WRONG CHOICES EXPLAINED:

(1) Growth in new home construction was an effect of the baby boom, not a cause of it. Following World War II, there was a severe housing shortage in the United States. As veterans began to marry and have children, there was an acute demand for new houses. Developers met this demand by building vast tracts of new housing in the suburbs around American cities. One of the most prominent developers was William Levitt, who applied mass production techniques to housing construction and significantly lowered housing prices.

(2) An increase in school population was an effect of the baby boom, not a cause of it. New schools were needed in the 1950s and 1960s when baby boom children began entering school.

(4) Increased pressure on the Social Security system is an effect of the baby boom, not a cause of it. With large numbers of baby boomers approaching age 65, there will be a substantial increase in the number of people receiving Social Security. The "graying of America," and its impact on the

Social Security system, has been a concern of politicians recently. When such a large percentage of the American public is retired, many people worry that programs extending benefits to the elderly, notably Medicare and Social Security, will be unable to stay financially solvent.

40. **4** President Lyndon Johnson's decision not to run for reelection in 1968 was based primarily on the United States' involvement in the Vietnam War. The United States became heavily involved in the Vietnam War after Congress gave President Johnson a blank check with the Tonkin Gulf Resolution. Despite the presence of more than half a million United States troops and the firepower of the U.S. military, President Johnson was not able to declare victory over the communist rebels in South Vietnam. As the war dragged on, and as the United States suffered more casualties, many Americans began to question the wisdom of American policies in Vietnam. Some thought the war was more of a civil war that the United States should not be part of. Many young men began to oppose the war because they feared they might be drafted. Finally, many Americans grew to oppose the war after seeing unsettling images on television news programs. Families saw American soldiers burn down Vietnamese villages. They saw body bags coming back to the United States. They saw children burned by napalm. All of these images contributed to the growing antiwar movement in the United States. By 1968, Johnson decided that his war policies imperiled his reelection, so he decided not to run for a second term.

WRONG CHOICES EXPLAINED:
(1) The assassination of Martin Luther King, Jr., (April 4, 1968) occurred just after Johnson made his announcement. Further, his mention of "sons in the fields far away" and "the world's hope for peace" allude to a foreign war.

(2) Johnson was troubled by the rioting that was occurring in American cities, but it was the war in Vietnam and the antiwar movement that led to Johnson's decision. His mention of "sons in the fields far away" is an allusion to the war in Vietnam.

(3) Concerns about the outbreak of terrorist attacks have occurred more recently. Several terrorist attacks in the 1990s and 2000s raised concerns. However, the major attacks of September 11, 2001, have led the United States to implement new policies domestically and internationally.

41. **3** The policy of détente pursued by President Richard Nixon was an effort to reduce conflict with the Soviet Union. *Détente* is the French word for "loosening" and refers to an easing of tensions in the Cold War and a warming of relations between the United States and the Soviet Union. It may seem ironic that Nixon, a man who made a name for himself as a strong anticommunist, was responsible for the détente policy. However, Nixon's anticommunist credentials enabled him to open relations with communist nations without being accused of being "soft on communism." In 1972 Nixon

became the first United States president to visit Communist China, and later in 1972 he held meetings with Soviet leaders in Moscow. The meetings produced several agreements, including an agreement to limit anti-ballistic missile systems (ABMs).

WRONG CHOICES EXPLAINED:

(1) The policy of détente does not refer to increasing foreign aid to African nations. The United States does provide foreign aid to Africa, primarily through the United States Agency for International Development, created by President John Kennedy (1961). The amount of foreign aid to Africa has varied over time, depending on conditions on the ground in Africa as well as on domestic considerations.

(2) The policy of détente does not refer to maintaining access to East Asian markets. This has been a goal of the United States since the 19th century. Commodore Matthew Perry's mission to Japan (1852–1854) and the enactment of the Open Door Policy in regard to China (1899) were both designed to gain access to East Asian markets.

(4) The policy of détente does not refer to ending trade barriers among Western hemisphere nations. The United States has pursued this policy actively since the administration of President Bill Clinton. The North American Free Trade Agreement (1994) and the Central American Free Trade Agreement (2003) were both intended to reduce trade barriers among Western hemisphere nations.

42. **1** The cartoonist is making the point that outsourcing of jobs has hurt American workers. *Outsourcing* refers to American companies hiring workers in foreign countries rather than in the United States. Currently, workers in many developing countries in Asia, Africa, and Latin America earn considerably less money than workers in the United States. Consequently, many American companies have outsourced jobs to foreign countries or have moved abroad altogether. Increasingly, many of the products Americans purchase, from automobiles to blue jeans, are produced abroad. The newscaster in the cartoon refers to Bangalore, India, a destination for many American high-tech companies. This trend has led to a decrease in jobs in many fields in the United States. The man in the cartoon is reading the "help wanted" section of the newspaper. Politicians debate whether the government should attempt to protect American jobs or let the market take its course.

WRONG CHOICES EXPLAINED:

(2) The cartoon is not commenting on news consumption trends for Americans. Televised news is becoming less important in American society, as Internet sources of news are becoming more important.

(3) The cartoon is not commenting on presidential approval abroad. The cartoon shows President Bush addressing workers in Bangalore, India, not to gain their approval, but because that is where he can find a group of workers to address on Labor Day.

(4) The cartoon is not implying that United States companies are forced to open up operations abroad because they cannot find workers in the United States. There are workers available in the United States; American companies choose to open operations abroad to take advantage of lower pay scales.

43. **3** The main issue identified in the cartoon is the increasing lack of privacy. The two government agents depicted in the cartoon are discussing the fate of the Patriot Act. The Patriot Act was passed by Congress less than two months after the September 2001 terrorist attacks. It greatly expanded the government's authority in the fight against terrorism. Some critics argued that it gave the government too much power to pry into the affairs of individuals. Congress debated reauthorization of the act in 2005. In 2006, it voted to reauthorize the act with few changes from the original act. The second agent in the cartoon asserts that it might not even matter if the act is not reauthorized, because so much information about Americans is freely available online. This sentiment is surely an exaggeration, but it highlights the growing amount of information about individuals available online. Some of this information is compiled by credit card companies, online retailers, and other entities that track individuals' online activities. Some of this information is freely given by individuals themselves on various social networking sites, such as Facebook.

WRONG CHOICES EXPLAINED:
(1) The cartoon is not commenting on the cost of computer services.
(2) The cartoon is not commenting on conflicts between Congress and the Supreme Court. It was Congress that initially passed the act in 2001 and debated reauthorization in 2005. The Supreme Court has not challenged provisions of the act.
(4) The cartoon is not commenting on limits placed on the powers of Congress. The government agents are discussing limits that Congress might place on implementation of the Patriot Act, not limits that might be placed on Congress.

44. **3** A belief in Manifest Destiny is most closely associated with the decision to declare war on Mexico. The term *Manifest Destiny* was coined in an 1845 newspaper article. It captured the fervor of the westward expansion movement, implying that it was God's plan that the United States take over and settle the entire continent. Americans who did settle out West were probably driven more by economic factors, such as cheap land or precious metals, than they were by a desire to fulfill God's plan. One important instance of the United States pursuing a policy of Manifest Destiny was the Mexican-American War (1846–1848). The war grew out of the annexation of Texas (1845). The two countries disagreed over the southern border of Texas. Mexico said it was at the Nueces River, while the United States insisted it was at the Rio Grande, 150 miles to the south. Skirmishes in the disputed area

led to war between Mexico and the United States. The United States won the war and acquired the huge territory that comprised the northern provinces of Mexico, known as the Mexican Cession. The region includes the present-day states of California, Nevada, and Utah, as well as portions of present-day Arizona, New Mexico, Wyoming, and Colorado. The purchase of this region was part of the Treaty of Guadalupe Hidalgo.

WRONG CHOICES EXPLAINED:

(1) The creation of the Bank of the United States is not associated with a belief in Manifest Destiny. The purpose of the bank was to regulate and facilitate economic activity; Manifest Destiny is the desire for territorial growth.

(2) The Whiskey Rebellion is not associated with a belief in Manifest Destiny. The Whiskey Rebellion involved taxation policies; Manifest Destiny is the desire for territorial growth.

(4) The building of the Panama Canal is not associated with a belief in Manifest Destiny. The purpose of the canal was to create a more direct shipping route between the Atlantic and Pacific oceans; Manifest Destiny is the desire for territorial growth.

45. **1** The Monroe Doctrine was designed to prevent new colonization of the Western hemisphere. President Monroe was alarmed at threats by the Holy Alliance of Russia, Prussia, and Austria to restore Spain's lost American colonies. He also opposed a decree by the Russian czar that claimed all the Pacific Northwest above the 51st parallel. Though both problems worked themselves out, Monroe issued a statement warning European nations to keep their hands off the Americas. The United States did not have the military might to enforce this pronouncement at the time, but it was an important statement of intent. The Monroe Doctrine, along with Washington's farewell address, became a cornerstone of an isolationist foreign policy.

WRONG CHOICES EXPLAINED:

(2) The Open Door policy was not designed to prevent new colonization of the Americas. The Open Door policy (1899) was put forth by President McKinley's secretary of state, John Hay, in order to open up China to American trade.

(3) The Good Neighbor policy was not designed to prevent new colonization of the Americas. President Franklin D. Roosevelt's Good Neighbor policy (1934) was designed mainly to improve relations with Latin American nations. Roosevelt's policies in Latin America were a marked departure from President Theodore Roosevelt's interventionist policy.

(4) The Carter Doctrine was not designed to prevent new colonization of the Americas. The Carter Doctrine (1980) asserted the United States' intention to use military force, if necessary, to defend its interests in the Persian Gulf. Early in 1979, the Soviet Union had invaded Afghanistan. President Jimmy Carter warned the Soviets not to make advances toward the oil-rich Persian Gulf.

46. **2** The United States is creating memorials along the Trail of Tears because it was the location of injustices against many Native American Indians. The Trail of Tears is the name given to the journey that Native Americans from several southern states were forced to take to land designated as "Indian Territory" in present-day Oklahoma. The removal occurred between 1831 and 1838. The most dramatic episode came in 1838 as the Cherokee were forcibly removed; over 4,000 died along the way. These removals were set in motion by the Indian Removal Act (1830), ordering several Native American nations to move west. Many of the proponents of Indian removal were motivated by a desire to expand cotton production, and slavery, in the South. The Cherokee got a short reprieve from the Supreme Court decision in *Worcester* v. *Georgia* (1832), which recognized the Cherokee people as a nation within the state of Georgia and ruled that they would not be subject to the Indian Removal Act. However, the state of Georgia, with the support of President Andrew Jackson, moved them to the West anyway. In recent years, the government has recognized the wrongs done to Native Americans and has tried to raise public awareness of this history with memorials along the removal routes.

WRONG CHOICES EXPLAINED:

(1) The Trail of Tears does not refer to settlers going to the frontier. The Oregon Trail and the Bozeman Trail were prominent frontier trails.

(3) The Trail of Tears does not refer to victories by General Andrew Jackson during the War of 1812. Prominent American victories led by Jackson occurred at the Battle of Horseshoe Bend in Alabama (1814) and at the Battle of New Orleans (1815).

(4) The Trail of Tears does not refer to the route of the first transcontinental railroad (built between 1863 and 1869). The Union Pacific Railroad began laying track for the first transcontinental railroad at Council Bluffs, Iowa. The Central Pacific Railroad began laying track in Sacramento, California. The two lines met at Promontory Summit, Utah.

47. **3** A goal that was established at the Seneca Falls Convention of 1848 was achieved in 1920 by the adoption of national women's suffrage. Suffrage, the right to vote, was a central demand of the women's rights movement. The Seneca Falls Convention was organized by Lucretia Mott and Elizabeth Cady Stanton. The genesis of the convention was their exclusion from an abolitionist conference in London in 1840. Mott and Stanton began thinking not only about the abolition of slavery but also about the conditions of women in the United States. The laws of the country relegated women to a second-class status. Women could not sit on juries. Women were not entitled to protection against physical abuse by their husbands. When women married, any property they owned became the property of their husbands. Finally, women were denied the right to vote. The movement was initially successful on the state level. Wyoming granted women voting rights in 1869, Utah in 1870, Colorado

in 1893, and Idaho in 1896. Several other western states granted women voting rights in the 20th century before ratification of the Nineteenth Amendment in 1920.

WRONG CHOICES EXPLAINED:

(1) The creation of a free public education system was not a goal of the Seneca Falls Convention. Other reformers in the pre-Civil War period, such as Horace Mann, worked on this issue.

(2) The passage of legislation to end child labor was not a goal of the Seneca Falls Convention. Progressives in the first decades of the 20th century worked on this issue. Child labor was not prohibited in the United States until the New Deal of the 1930s. The Fair Labor Standards Act (1938) largely ended the practice of minors under 16 working in the labor market for wages.

(4) Ratification of an amendment requiring national Prohibition was not a goal of the Seneca Falls Convention. Prohibition became national policy in 1919 with the ratification of the Eighteenth Amendment, which banned the manufacture, sale, and transportation of alcoholic beverages. The push to ban alcohol from American society was one of the largest movements in the 19th century. There was a great deal of overlap between the temperance movement and the women's rights movement.

48. **2** The emergence of political third parties, such as the Know-Nothing Party, the Greenback Party, and the Prohibition Party, indicates that a single powerful issue can mobilize political activity. The Know-Nothing Party, active in the 1840s and 1850s, was opposed to the influx of immigrants into the United States, especially from Ireland. Increased emigration from Ireland to the United States during the 1840s was primarily the result of mass starvation caused by the failure of the potato crop. It is estimated that a million Irish starved to death between 1845 and 1850, while another million left for America. Most Irish settled in port cities such as New York and Boston. Many native-born Americans resented these immigrants. Some feared job competition, some were anti-Catholic, and some perceived that the Irish drank excessively. The Know-Nothing Party won 25 percent of the vote in New York State elections in 1854. The Greenback Party, founded in 1878, sought an expansion of the currency supply. The party advocated issuing paper money that was not backed by gold or silver. This had been done briefly during the Civil War, and farmers received higher prices for their goods. The party received a million votes in the 1878 congressional elections. The party soon disbanded, but the call for an expansion of the money supply was taken up again following the panic of 1893. The Prohibition Party, founded in 1869, was part of the temperance movement against alcohol consumption. It was strongest in the late 19th and early 20th centuries. It achieved its ultimate goal with the ratification of the Eighteenth Amendment in 1918. For the next 15 years, the sale, consumption, and production of alcoholic beverages was illegal in the United States.

WRONG CHOICES EXPLAINED:

(1) The emergence of the three parties does not indicate a rejection of basic democratic values. The ability of these parties to participate in the democratic process points toward a vibrant democracy.

(3) The emergence of the three parties does not indicate a failure of third-party politics. All three parties had influence on government policies; the Prohibition Party was most successful, pushing for the Eighteenth Amendment banning the sale, consumption, and production of alcohol.

(4) The emergence of the three parties does not indicate that minor political parties are usually formed by strong leaders. All three of the political parties grew out of grassroots movements.

49. **4** One common theme in many of the writings of Ernest Hemingway, F. Scott Fitzgerald, and Langston Hughes was dissatisfaction with the American culture of the 1920s. Hemingway and Fitzgerald were part of the Lost Generation literary movement, and Hughes was part of the Harlem Renaissance artistic and literary movement. Lost Generation writers expressed a general disillusionment with American society, commenting on everything from the narrowness of small-town life to the rampant materialism of American society. Several writers were troubled by the destruction and seeming meaninglessness of World War I. *The Great Gatsby* (1925) by Fitzgerald exposed the shallowness of the lives of the wealthy and privileged of the era. Hemingway's *A Farewell to Arms* (1929) critiqued the glorification of war. A key goal of the Harlem Renaissance was to increase pride in African-American culture by celebrating African-American life and forging a new cultural identity among African-American people. Contributions included the poems of Hughes, such as "Harlem," "The Negro Speaks of Rivers," and "I, Too, Sing America." He wrote an essay that became a manifesto for Harlem Renaissance writers and artists entitled "The Negro Artist and the Racial Mountain."

WRONG CHOICES EXPLAINED:

(1) The three writers did not emphasize the need to regulate business. Several muckraker writers, such as Upton Sinclair and Ida B. Wells, asserted the need to regulate business.

(2) The three writers did not emphasize the benefits of mass production. The writer and mechanical engineer Frederick Winslow Taylor extolled the benefits of mass production. He developed the field of scientific management, carefully watching workers, noting the most efficient techniques, and writing down in exacting detail how a particular task was to be done.

(3) The three writers did not express optimism for the reforms of the Great Society. The Great Society was President Lyndon Johnson's set of anti-poverty programs implemented in the 1960s. The three writers published their works from the 1920s to the 1950s. Further, they were not especially optimistic about reform.

50. **3** The three headlines refer to the Korean War. The Korean War occurred from 1950 to 1953. It was part of the Cold War between the United States and its allies and the communist world. Korea had been divided into two occupation zones after World War II, one controlled by the United States and one controlled by the Soviet Union. The two sides were unable to agree on a unification plan, and by 1948 two separate nations were established with a border at the 38th parallel. In June 1950, North Korean troops invaded South Korea. President Truman decided to commit troops to support South Korea and managed to secure United Nations sponsorship (the first headline). United Nations forces, led by U.S. General Douglas MacArthur, pushed the North Korean troops back to the 38th parallel and then marched into North Korea. When the U.N. troops got within 40 miles of the border between North Korea and China, China sent 150,000 troops over the Yalu River to push them back. In 1951, General MacArthur made it clear that he thought the United States could successfully invade China and roll back communism there. Truman was convinced that initiating a wider war, so soon after World War II, would be disastrous. MacArthur made public pronouncements about strategy, arguing, "There is no substitute for victory." Truman fired MacArthur for insubordination and other unauthorized activities (the second headline). After intense fighting, the two sides settled into positions on either side of the 38th parallel. By 1953 an armistice was reached accepting a divided Korea (the third headline).

WRONG CHOICES EXPLAINED:
(1), (2), and (4) The headlines do not refer to World War I, World War II, or the Persian Gulf War. The mentions of "communist invaders," the firing of General MacArthur, and the 38th parallel make it clear that the headlines are referring to the Korean War.

PART II: THEMATIC ESSAY

Presidential Actions

At key moments in American history, presidents have made decisions that profoundly impacted United States foreign and domestic policies. In 1898, President William McKinley's decision to declare war on Spain dramatically affected American foreign policy. That decision led to the United States acquisition of an empire and to the beginning of an imperialist foreign policy. In 1964, President Lyndon B. Johnson's decision to push for and sign the Civil Rights Act transformed an important aspect of domestic policy. Following passage of the act, the government of the United States officially ended the Jim Crow system——a system of racial segregation that defined American life for nearly a century.

Before the Spanish-American War, the United States was reluctant to directly engage the European powers in conflict. Early in American history, President George Washington warned America to avoid permanent alliances with European nations. Later, in an effort to keep America separate, President Monroe warned European nations to stay away from the Americas. The United States was not, strictly speaking, isolated from foreign nations. The United States waged war against Great Britain (1812–1815), against Mexico (1846–1848), and against various Native American nations throughout the 19th century, but the Spanish-American War opened an entirely new chapter of assertiveness on the part of the United States.

McKinley's decision to declare war on Spain was based on a number of factors. The United States had become increasingly concerned about Cuba, a Spanish colony 90 miles off the coast of Florida. Newspapers published reports of Spanish atrocities committed against the Cuban people. An independence movement challenged Spanish control of the island. Further, United States businessmen worried that disturbances in Cuba would disrupt the lucrative sugar trade. Finally, an explosion brought down the American battleship the *U.S.S. Maine*, which was anchored in the Havana harbor. The press immediately assumed Spain had done the deed, though evidence was sketchy. McKinley had heard enough and moved to wage war on Spain.

America defeated Spain rather quickly, with fighting stretching from Cuba to the Philippines. Following the war, the United States acquired several Spanish possessions. In the Treaty of Paris (1898), Spain ceded Puerto Rico, Guam, and the Philippines to the United States. Many Filipino people were not happy to see one imperial power (Spain) replaced by another one (the United States). It took the United States seven years and thousands of casualties to gain control of the Philippines. Cuba became independent; however, the Platt Amendment, placed in the Cuban constitution, allowed the United States to intervene in Cuban affairs when it saw fit. Cuba, in effect, became a United States protectorate. All of a sudden, the United States had joined the imperialist powers of Europe. Some critics resisted the move toward empire. These critics wondered how the

United States, a country born in an anti-colonial war, could acquire an empire of its own. The most prominent anti-imperialist was author Mark Twain. Despite these reservations, the United States continued to pursue an imperialist policy and play a major role on the world stage in the 20th century.

Another important presidential decision that profoundly influenced the United States was President Lyndon Johnson's decision to support and sign the Civil Rights Act in 1964. The act put an end to the legal segregation of African Americans from mainstream society. African Americans had been relegated to the status of second-class citizen in the United States. Since the end of Reconstruction, in 1877, Southern states began to pass Jim Crow laws that prevented African Americans from attending school with whites and that mandated separate public facilities for African Americans. African Americans were forced to sit in separate railroad cars and then in the back part of the city buses. Jim Crow laws were a constant insult to African Americans and a constant reminder that whites had power and that African Americans were thought of as inferior.

This system persisted in the United States well into the 20th century. By midcentury, a movement had developed to challenge the Jim Crow system. The Civil Rights Movement first grabbed national headlines in 1956 with a bus boycott in Montgomery, Alabama. By the early 1960s, the movement was becoming more widespread. In June 1963, the same month that civil rights leader Medgar Evers was murdered in front of his house in

Jackson, Mississippi, President Kennedy made a national address in which he called civil rights a "moral issue" and pledged to support civil rights legislation. After Kennedy's assassination in November 1963, President Johnson took up the cause of civil rights legislation with vigor, pressuring reluctant Democrats to support the cause. This was a bold move for Johnson. The Democratic Party still depended on support from white southerners to maintain power. A generation earlier, it would have been difficult to imagine a southern Democrat like Johnson pushing for civil rights legislation.

The Civil Rights Act guaranteed equal access for all Americans to public accommodations, public education, and voting. Another section banned discrimination in employment based on race or sex. The act did not end racism or discrimination in the United States, but it ended the public, overt, government-sanctioned discrimination that had characterized American society for nearly a century.

Both President McKinley's decision to declare war on Spain and President Johnson's decision to push for the Civil Rights Act show the importance of presidential decisions. These two decisions altered American history, pushing the United States into new directions—one toward imperialism and one toward an egalitarian society.

PART III: DOCUMENT-BASED QUESTION

Part A: Short Answer

DOCUMENT 1

1. According to Thomas A. Bailey, geography contributed to the United

States policy of noninvolvement because the Atlantic Ocean created

3,000 miles of separation from Europe.

This answer receives full credit because it explains how geography contributed to the United States policy of noninvolvement.

DOCUMENT 2

2 (1). According to Walter LeFeber, one benefit to the United States from

acquiring the Louisiana Territory was that it gave the United States access

to vast new trading areas.

2 (2). According to Walter LeFeber, another benefit to the United States

from acquiring the Louisiana Territory was that its many rivers contributed

economic growth.

These answers receive full credit because they state two benefits to the United States from acquiring the Louisiana Territory.

DOCUMENT 3

3 (1). According to H. Wilbur Hoffman, one example of how geography

negatively affected the westward movement of settlers was that the

harsh weather, which included strong wind, hail, and electrical storms,

slowed down settlers.

3 (2). According to H. Wilbur Hoffman, another example of how geography

negatively affected the westward movement of settlers was that the

rugged mountain ranges of the West made it difficult to pass.

These answers receive full credit because they state two examples of how geography negatively affected the westward movement of settlers.

DOCUMENT 4A, DOCUMENT 4B, AND DOCUMENT 4C

4 (1). Based on the documents, one way the size of the United States

affected its development was that movement from the east coast to the

west coast was time-consuming, taking more than three weeks in 1860.

4 (2). Based on the documents, another way the size of the United States

affected its development was that improvements in transportation were

necessary in order to bring the country together.

These answers receive full credit because they state two ways the size of the United States affected its development.

DOCUMENT 5

5. Based on the map, one way natural resources affected the economic

development of the United States was that extensive coal reserves were

used in industrial processes.

This answer receives full credit because it states one way natural resources affected the economic development of the United States.

DOCUMENT 6

6. According to William Manchester, one way climate affected farming

on the Great Plains was that heavy rains in the period before the Great

Depression led farmers to overgraze and overplow the land of the

Great Plains.

This answer receives full credit because it states one way climate affected farming on the Great Plains.

DOCUMENT 7A AND DOCUMENT 7B

7. Based on the documents, one way that the geographic location of the

United States affected its foreign policy before World War I was that the

presence of the Atlantic Ocean allowed the United States to stay out of

European conflicts.

This answer receives full credit because it states one way that the geographic location of the United States affected its foreign policy before World War I.

DOCUMENT 8

8. According to the map, the proximity of Cuba to the United States made

the presence of nuclear missiles in Cuba a real threat to the United States.

This answer receives full credit because it explains how the location of Cuba influenced the Cuban missile crisis.

DOCUMENT 9

9. According to Robert J. Samuelson, the Gulf Coast region is important to

the economy of the United States because it supplies the United States

with nearly 30 percent of its oil.

This answer receives full credit because it states one reason the Gulf Coast is important to the economy of the United States.

Part B: Document-Based Essay

Geography is a key factor in shaping a nation's development. Geographic features—size, location, resources, climate—can help a nation thrive or can hinder its development. Several geographic features have been prominent in shaping the development of the United States. One important factor is its remoteness from other major powers; the Atlantic and Pacific oceans separate the United States from Europe and Asia. Another factor is its sheer size; the United States stretches across the vast North American continent. A final factor is the abundance of natural resources in the United States. These factors have had mainly positive impacts on the United States, but, at times, the nation's geography has also posed problems.

The presence of two major oceans to the east and the west has benefitted the United States for much of its history. Throughout the 19th century, the United States was able to maintain a foreign policy of non-involvement. Between the War of 1812 and the Spanish-American War (1898), the United States was largely removed from the conflicts and alliances of the Old World. This allowed the United States to devote resources to internal development rather than developing a standing army to guard its borders (Document 1). The United States developed a network of canals and roads, followed by a network of railroad lines, that contributed to its economic success. Further, the nation was able to devote resources to industrial development—from the textile mills of Lowell, Massachusetts, in the 1810s to the steel plants of Pittsburgh, Pennsylvania, in the 1870s. The

United States funded military campaigns against the rebel South during the Civil War and against Native American nations in the 19th century, but its remoteness from Europe allowed it to funnel resources into other ventures.

The remoteness that the United States enjoyed in the 19th century became less apparent in the 20th century. Though, of course, the size of the oceans did not change, the world changed. This was apparent to Uncle Sam, depicted in a World War II-era cartoon. He looks wistfully at the Atlantic Ocean, which appears no wider than a river, and says, "It ain't what it used to be." The separation and remoteness of the United States was disappearing. The cartoonist was asserting that the nation could not stay aloof from World War II (Document 7a). President Franklin D. Roosevelt concurred with this assessment. No longer, he stated, could the peoples of the Americas continue with life as they knew it without acknowledging, and preparing for, threats from "other Continents of the world" (Document 7b). Submarines, airplanes, and fast-moving battleships made the world a smaller place. Roosevelt urged the nation to prepare for war by pushing for the Lend-Lease Act and a draft, well before the United States was actually involved in the war.

After World War II, the United States stayed engaged in world affairs. During the Cold War, the development of intercontinental ballistic missiles with nuclear warheads and the reach of the Soviet Union again made the world seem like a smaller place. This was brought home when the United

States discovered in 1962 that the Soviet Union was preparing to install nuclear missiles on the island nation of Cuba. Cuba, which had allied itself with the Soviet Union after the 1959 Cuban Revolution, is only 90 miles from Florida. The proximity of Cuba to the United States led American leaders to see these missiles as a potential threat. President John F. Kennedy demanded that the Soviets remove the missiles. A standoff, known as the Cuban Missile Crisis, ensued, threatening the very existence of the world (Document 8). A compromise was finally reached, but the episode demonstrated that the Atlantic and the Pacific oceans no longer provided separation from the conflicts of the world.

Another important factor in the development of the United States was its size. Territorial acquisitions created a massive country. The Louisiana Purchase (1803), for example, provided the United States with an additional 825,000 square miles. Most importantly, the purchase greatly improved trade opportunities for the United States. The territory contained the mighty Mississippi River and the port city of New Orleans. Together, these provided farmers in the interior of the nation access to the markets of the world (Document 2). The size of the country was also a barrier to its rapid development. A harsh climate and rugged mountains posed problems for the early American settlers of the West. Wagon trains of settlers faced great difficulties. Half of the members of the Donner Party, for example, died of starvation over the winter of 1846–1847 (Document 3). Over time, however, innovations in transportation overcame these difficulties. Americans in the first half of the 19th century saw a "transportation revolution" (Document 4a). In 1800, it took nearly six weeks to travel from New York City to the shores of Lake Michigan. By 1860, with the development of the railroad, that time was reduced to a mere two days (Documents 4b and 4c). In another decade, the completion of the transcontinental railroad made travel from coast to coast an easy and quick venture.

Finally, the United States is blessed with abundant natural resources. Iron ore, coal, oil, and precious metals could all be found beneath the nation's surface. Much of the nation was thickly forested, providing ample timber reserves (Document 5). More recently, petroleum deposits have been accessed in the Gulf of Mexico. Oil from this area accounts for nearly 30 percent of the United States total (Document 9). All of these resources have benefitted the United States and have helped it grow to be the preeminent economic power in the world. However, there have been steep costs to America's use of these resources. Unwise agricultural practices, along with a severe drought, caused massive problems in the 1930s. The Great Plains region was enveloped in a "dust bowl," as the nutrient rich topsoil simply blew away. The land was rendered unusable in parts of 756 counties in 19 states. Millions of people had to relocate or face starvation (Document 6). More recently, a host of environmental problems have shed light on our misuse of natural resources. In the summer of 2010, one of the oil rigs in the Gulf of Mexico exploded and began spewing millions of gallons of petroleum into the gulf before the well was plugged.

Nature has provided the United States with abundant resources. These resources have allowed the country to experience unparalleled economic growth. However, recent history has shown that the United States must learn how to use its resources wisely. Already the repercussions of thoughtlessness and greed are being felt, from climate change to water shortages, to toxic chemicals in the environment, to the oil spill in the Gulf of Mexico. If we hope to enjoy the gifts of nature into the future, we must learn to be wise stewards of our natural resources.

Topic	Question Numbers	°Number of Points
American political history	4, 5, 12, 14, 15, 17, 22, 27, 31, 32, 34, 40, 48	16
Political theory	8	1
Economic theory/policy	19, 20, 26, 42	5
Constitutional principles	3, 6, 7, 9, 10, 11, 37, 38	10
American foreign policy	2, 23, 28, 29, 33, 41, 44, 45, 50	11
American studies—the American people	16, 18, 21, 24, 25, 35, 36, 39, 43, 46, 47	13
Social/cultural developments	30, 49	2
Geography	1, 13	2
Skills questions included in the above content area		
Reading comprehension	4, 9, 15, 40, 50	
Cartoon/photo interpretation	20, 28, 29, 36, 37, 42, 43	
Cause-effect relationship	39	

°Note: The 50 questions in Part I are worth a total of 60 percent of the exam. Since each correct answer is worth 60/50 or 1.2 points, totals are shown to the nearest full point in each content category.

Part I
Multiple-Choice Questions by Standard

Standard	Question Numbers
1—US and NY History	2, 4, 12, 14, 15, 16, 17, 18, 19, 21, 25, 27, 29, 30, 31, 32, 34, 36, 40, 43, 44, 46, 47, 49
2—World History	23, 28, 33, 41, 50
3—Geography	1, 13, 24, 35, 39, 45
4—Economics	20, 22, 26, 42
5—Civics, Citizenship, and Government	3, 4, 5, 6, 7, 8, 9, 10, 11, 37, 38, 48

Parts II and III by Theme and Standard

	Theme	Standards
Thematic Essay	Presidential Decisions and Actions; Foreign Policy	Standards 1, 2, and 5; United States and New York History; World History; Civics, Citizenship, and Government
Document-based Essay	Effects of Geography; Presidential Actions; Migration; Places and Regions; Foreign Policy	Standards 1, 2, and 3; United States and New York History; World History; Geography